PROGRAM VERIFICATION USING ADA

Cambridge Computer Science Texts · 13

Program Verification using Ada

ANDREW D. McGETTRICK

Lecturer in Computer Science
University of Strathclyde
Glasgow, Scotland

CAMBRIDGE UNIVERSITY PRESS

Cambridge

London   New York   New Rochelle

Melbourne   Sydney

Published by the Press Syndicate of the University of Cambridge
The Pitt Building, Trumpington Street, Cambridge CB2 1RP
32 East 57th Street, New York, NY 10022, USA
296 Beaconsfield Parade, Middle Park, Melbourne 3206, Australia

First published 1982

Printed in Great Britain at the University Press, Cambridge

Library of Congress catalogue card number: 81-12276

British Library cataloguing in publication data
McGettrick, Andrew D.
Program verification using Ada. – (Cambridge
computer science texts; 13)

1. Ada (Computer program language)
I. Title
001.64'24   QA76.73.A35

ISBN 0 521 24215 0 hard covers
ISBN 0 521 28531 3 paperback

To my wife Sheila and our family

CONTENTS

PREFACE

Initially I had intended to write a text solely on program verification. It had seemed to me that much of the work on program verification was scattered throughout the various research papers that had been produced during the last ten years; little had been coordinated and brought together into one volume. The lovely book of Manna, the *Mathematical Theory of Computation*, went so far but did not cover such topics as lists, procedures, modules, parallelism, etc., nor did it contain modern ideas about verification using arrays and so on.

In attempting to coordinate the work on program verification and to produce a single work which encompassed most of the ideas, the main initial obstacle was one of notation. Which programming language should be used? At that time no suitable language was available and the temptation to introduce a new set of notation was very evident. The timely arrival of Ada, the American Defense Department's language, solved the problem. In adopting the revised version of Ada as the language for the text it then became a challenge to try to verify any reasonable kind of program that could be expressed in Ada. In particular the problem of verifying programs using tasks loomed large. The outcome was chapter 8.

A large part of the thinking and writing of the text was carried out in Canberra, Australia, in the shadow of Black Mountain. As a result of a kind invitation to visit the Australian National University in the spring of 1980, I had the opportunity to study and write in the glorious tranquillity, peace and warmth of an Australian autumn; it must be a close approximation to paradise. For the invitation, for the marvellous hospitality shown by himself, his wife Kerry and their family, and for many interesting and thought-provoking discusions I am indebted to Dr Brian Molinari. Another friend who merits special mention is Dr Robin Stanton. The memories of the runs in the surf under a clear blue sky and of the fins beside the catamaran in Sydney harbour will last for ever.

Numerous other people deserve special mention for their help and encouragement. Professor Ian Pyle of the University of York provided many valuable comments and criticisms of an earlier draft as did several knowledgeable anonymous referees whose help was enlisted by Cambridge University Press. For their valuable assistance in typing the manuscript I must thank my mother Mrs Marion McGettrick, my sister-in-law Miss Patricia Girot and the secretaries in the Computer Science department at Strathclyde University, Mrs Margaret McDougall and Miss Agnes Wisley. Lastly my wife Sheila and my family deserve very special mention for their sacrifices too numerous to mention and for providing the motivating force behind this book; I hope the final product does them justice.

My thanks go to the Syndics of Cambridge University Press for agreeing to publish this work.

A. D. McG. 1981

1   INTRODUCTION

One of the matters which concerns every serious programmer and every computer scientist is the problem of producing computer systems which are of a high quality. Computers, under program control, can be used to perform many vital functions such as controlling air traffic, controlling the landing of space vehicles, controlling railways, monitoring patients in hospitals, and so on. In other ways they provide services of various kinds and the quality of this service is related to the quality both of its hardware and its software. The wide variety of current and future uses of computers, many of a very important nature, dictates that all involved with the production of computer systems should be deeply concerned about the quality of the product they provide.

1.1   Correct software

For several years now there has been considerable disquiet expressed about the problems of designing and producing large software systems. This concern has even been called a crisis and has resulted in the use of the term 'software engineering'. It is said that there is little software which is reliable and which is based on the best techniques currently available.

A reliable program can be expected to produce a high level of performance in a friendly environment, i.e. when the hardware does not malfunction, when the inputs or data are as expected, and so on. But even in a hostile environment it can be expected to behave reasonably and not cause catastrophes. So, associated with the concept of reliability there are qualities which include robustness, fault-tolerance, stability in some sense, and so on. Reliability should be thought of as a relative term, being related in some way to the application under consideration. In applications such as air traffic control the computer system must never fail; in other cases some level of performance slightly short of this may be acceptable.

The notion of reliability not just impinges on but is a fundamental considera-tion in many aspects of the design of the computing system. Included in these aspects would be methods of program construction, the design of programming languages, security and privacy, hardware design, the hardware/software inter-face, program testing in all its forms, error recovery, and so on. In most, if not

1

all, of these cases consideration must be given to including some form of redundancy to ensure a high level of reliability.

In these pages we take one other aspect of the production of reliable software and look at it in some detail. We look at the task of ensuring the correctness of programs. In fact 'correctness' is a technical term and it will have to be defined properly at a later stage. But for the moment we adopt the intuitive meaning: a correct program does as was intended by the programmer.

There have been various approaches to achieving the very desirable goal of encouraging correctness in programming. The most common of these is program synthesis, i.e. the approach of teaching people to program in a way which encourages good design and correctness. Given a large programming task, the programmer should divide his task into manageable pieces and then program these subtasks separately. But how should this division take place? Advocates of structured programming, or more accurately stepwise refinement, would argue that a task should be divided into separate subtasks, these subtasks should themselves be divided into further subtasks, and so on. Continuing in this way the resulting program is structured in a hierarchical fashion. One consequence of this approach is that programmers should normally be discouraged from using certain constructs in a programming language (e.g. jumps) on the grounds that their use betrays a lack of understanding about the proper structure of their program. Indeed these considerations have led to a certain amount of rethinking about the design of programming languages themselves.

But stepwise refinement does not provide the only set of guidelines for dividing large tasks into smaller subtasks and structuring programs. Some people argue that 'information hiding' should be used to break a program into manageable modules. By 'information hiding' is meant the process of refusing one module to see or use directly the variables or objects of another module unless specifically given permission to do so. Again this mode of programming has implications for the language designer.

Another not unrelated approach to achieving the goal of ensuring the correctness of programs is that of verifying by a mathematical argument that programs are correct. This and related topics will form the subject matter of this book.

1.2 Program verification

The basic idea behind techniques of program verification is that the programmer should make certain statements or assertions about the data for his program – the *initial assertion* – and about the results he expects – the *final assertion*. He is then faced with the task of proving, by a mathematical argument based on these assertions and on the text of the program, that the program does indeed do as was intended; this intention of course is reflected in the final assertion.

To illustrate the idea consider a piece of program intended to accept a nonnegative integer N and produce $N!$ in the integer variable F. The initial assertion might state that $N \geqslant 0$. The final assertion might take the form $F = N!$. The task of verifying correctness then involves combining the initial assertion and the statements of the program to show that the program terminates and at that stage the final assertion is true.

Programs which have no data can be dealt with in the same way provided it is assumed that these have an initial assertion *TRUE*.

A possible program, expressed in terms of the programming language Ada, might take the form

```
R := N; F := 1;
while  R /= 0 loop
    F := F * R; R := R−1;
end loop;
```

The values of the integer variables R and F are suitably initialised. On each circuit of the loop the values of F and R are subsequently altered by assignments

$$F := F * R; \quad \text{and} \quad R := R-1;$$

respectively. It is to be hoped that as the computation progresses $N!$ is accumulated in F. To verify that the program is indeed correct it is necessary to produce a convincing mathematical argument which involves both the text of the program and the initial and final assertions.

The process of program proving can be likened to certain aspects of traditional geometry in mathematics. The idea of a geometric construction can be favourably compared with the idea of a program. Both are intended to achieve a particular effect or result. The geometric construction is usually followed by a mathematical proof that the construction does indeed perform the desired task. In a similar way the program prover proves by a mathematical argument that his program performs the intended task.

The analogy with geometry can be carried somewhat further, in the direction of axiomatics. In geometric terms the axiomatic method can be viewed as the process of showing that a geometric theorem is a logical consequence of certain other theorems whose truth has previously been established. These theorems themselves must be proved in a similar way, and so on. Ultimately, of course, it is necessary to stop at some point and assume the truth of a certain set of *axioms* or *postulates*. In this way it can be seen that all theorems of geometry can be derived by rigorous logical argument from a set of axioms. We say that geometry has been axiomatised.

The geometric proofs derived from axioms and from strict rules of logic can be called *formal proofs*. In comparison, the more usual informal proofs are more intuitive in nature, they do not pay such strict attention to axioms or rules of logic.

Many advantages can be claimed for an axiomatic or formal treatment. The essential structure or skeleton of the subject matter is laid bare. In this way it is often easier to identify generalisations or applications that might not be so apparent in a more intuitive approach. There are no hard and fast rules for selecting axioms but care should be taken to ensure that the axioms are

> simple and few in number;
>
> complete in that every theorem of geometry, for example, can be deduced from them;
>
> consistent in that it is impossible to derive contradictions;
>
> independent – in the interests of economy no axiom should be deducible from the others.

A similar formal approach can be taken to the task of proving the correctness of a program. A set of axioms about programs and the objects they manipulate can be postulated and all proofs of program correctness can be phrased in terms of these axioms and a strict discipline of logic. All the advantages of formality and an axiomatic treatment then ensue.

In this book we look initially at informal proofs of program verification. This will have the advantage of familiarising the reader with the fundamental concepts and intuitive methods of proof. At a later stage (in chapter 4) we look at the axiomatic approach to the subject. In this way we follow the usual mathematical development by looking first at informal and then at formal methods of proof.

1.3 Program verification in perspective

It is important to place the topic of verifying a program in some kind of perspective. As we progress it will become apparent that the task of providing a proof is not always simple or inexpensive. Consequently it requires justification. Even when a proof has been provided this does not imply that the program will produce the desired results when submitted to a particular computer for execution. In this section we look more closely at what program verification techniques can do for the programmer. Other advantages will be mentioned briefly in section 1.4.

When a piece of program text is submitted to a computer for compilation and subsequent execution, errors are liable to be detected at various stages. The computer is likely to catch errors such as wrong stropping conventions (i.e. the method of denoting bold words such as **begin** in Algol-like languages), the wrong representation of symbols, and syntax errors of various kinds including undeclared variables, mismatching of brackets, misuse of types or modes, and so on. These may be caused by certain kinds of transcription or typing errors or genuine mistakes in the formation of constructs in the language. Successful compilation implies that the compiler has managed to make sense of the text, i.e. the text has been parsed and the compiler has been able to interpret it as a syntactically legal program.

4

At execution or run time another set of errors show themselves. Typical of these are:

> overflow often caused by attempted division by zero;
> subscript out of range;
> use of uninitialised variables;
> certain kinds of scope errors caused by misusing pointers;
> store violation caused by limits on available resources, e.g. the size of the available store;
> errors caused by inappropriate data;
> errors caused by the violation of assumptions about timing constraints;

and so on. Most common of all are errors in logic, errors which result in the program failing to perform its intended task.

What role then can program verification play in the process of preparing programs? Assume we have a syntactically legal program and consider what happens if verification of such a program is attempted.

Efforts at verifying correctness must rely on suitable assertions being provided. The input assertion will describe the nature of the data and any assumptions that can be made about it. The output assertion must specify the results or effect of the program. These assertions may be complex. Proofs of correctness will make the (often substantial) assumption that these assertions are accurate and complete. This observation has led certain authors to draw a distinction between the correctness of a program and its consistency with respect to the given assertions. The word 'correct' they argue is all-embracing and conveys the idea that every aspect of the program including its assertions are accurate. Consequently 'program verification', 'proving consistency', etc. are all phrases which are often used in place of 'proving correctness'. However, while acknowledging and being sympathetic to the problem we shall not labour the distinction and often use the terms interchangeably. We shall usually assume that assertions have been properly selected, that the data is consistent with respect to the input assertion, and so on.

In simple situations the task of describing an assertion is usually relatively straightforward. But with programs such as operating systems, compilers, certain real-time control problems and so on, the task of supplying suitable and appropriate assertions is far from simple. One type of error which can arise from this is interface violation, caused by interfaces being imprecisely specified in assertions. In many of these cases, however, it is possible to provide simple assertions for subtasks to be performed and subsequent correctness proofs can contribute significantly to the reliability of the overall system.

When the data supplied to a program violates the input assertion a proof of correctness says nothing at all about how the program will react. Considerations such as this lead into the realms of robustness and reliability as opposed to correctness. Correctness says nothing about the efficiency of a program in terms of time and space nor even about programming effort.

A proof of correctness will normally catch most kinds of programming errors. If a program is inconsistent with respect to its assertions, i.e. if it does not perform the intended task, this should be caught. In the process errors which would result from the use of uninitialised variables, subscripts out of bounds, overflow caused by division by zero, etc. should all be highlighted.

But a proof itself can be in error. Just as a mathematician can err in formulating a proof so a program prover can make a similar kind of blunder. This can arise from carelessness or from a misunderstanding of the meaning or intended effect of some construct in the programming language. At this stage we should also note briefly the possibility of a verifier failing to provide a proof of correctness; we assume that this happens not because of any incompetence. Like many of these criticisms regarding program verification it is important to note the observation, but its significance should not be blown up out of proportion.

At one level it is often a simple matter to establish incorrectness – it is only necessary to provide one set of data for which the wrong results are produced. At a deeper level the problem can be much more complex. Failure to provide a proof alone gives no indication of the correctness or otherwise of a program. Again similar situations arise in mathematics where several examples of famous unproved conjectures can be readily cited, for example, Goldbach's conjecture and Fermat's Last Theorem.

Even if assertions are accurate and it has been demonstrated that the program is correct with respect to these predicates there is no guarantee that the program will be executed successfully. There may be errors in the compiler, linker, operating system, input/output devices or even the hardware itself; the program may be corrupted by some other program within the system or there may be collusion between them; an officious operating system may impose limits on time or space. A proof of correctness based on the source program alone cannot be expected to detect these kinds of occurrences.

The above remarks are then related to the environment in which a program is executed. Other aspects of this environment should also be mentioned. Most program verifications pay little or no attention to the physical limitations of the computer, the size and accuracy of numbers, the maximum size of store and so on: proofs are usually implementation-independent.

Idealised assumptions such as those discussed above should not be dismissed. The fact that real numbers are not normally held accurately interferes with the associative laws of addition and multiplication of real numbers; moreover $1/3 * 3$ will not usually produce 1 but instead a real number very close to 1. On the other hand these assumptions should not be allowed to assume too great a significance, but a sensible and realistic attitude should be taken to them. Thus it would be reasonable to note that certain laws of arithmetic, which normally hold, do not hold when real numbers are being manipulated.

Before proceeding we should remark that many of the criticisms mentioned above should not be allowed to take on an undue importance. While admitting the possibility of their occurring we note that by choosing constructs in programming languages carefully, by programming carefully and by using reasonable computing environments many of these criticisms can be severely weakened. A study of program verification will shed light on this area.

Program verification with all its limitations is by far the most satisfactory means of checking that a program does as was intended. It provides a far higher degree of confidence in a program than any of the alternatives such as testing. Let us look at this alternative in some detail.

Various approaches can be taken. At the most trivial level a program can be regarded as a black box, i.e. the tester is assumed to know nothing whatsoever about the internal structure or workings of the program. Consider then a program intended to add together two integers and let us view this as a black box. An exhaustive set of tests for this program would involve checking all possible combinations. If the range of integers acceptable to the computer was $-2^{31} \leqslant N < 2^{31}$ a total of 2^{64} possible tests would have to be made. Even if it could be arranged that one test was performed each 10^{-9} seconds the complete exhaustive testing would take several hundred years. Clearly the approach is impractical and only a very small set of possibilities can be checked.

A more interesting form of program testing does not treat a program as a black box but pays attention to the internal structure of the program.

When tests are selected in a random fashion they are not usually of any great significance. But if they are chosen with a special purpose in mind they can be significant. One approach is to choose a set of tests in such a way that each statement is executed at least once by some test. Then if a particular statement is in error it can be guaranteed that it will be executed for at least one of the tests and it is likely that the error will be revealed in the subsequent behaviour of the program.

Unfortunately there is one particular type of error which will not be caught in this way – this is typified by the conditional forward jump which branches to the wrong statement. If the condition does not cause the jump it can still be argued that each statement has been exercised and the error will not be detected. A more stringent approach to testing (which actually encompasses the benefits of the previous approach and yet catches errors of the kind mentioned) is to use a set of tests which collectively traverse each possible route through the program. Each path, and so each statement on that path, will be tested at some stage.

There are many other approaches to testing. For instance there is much to be said in favour of programmers enlisting the services of colleagues, telling them what the program is intended to do and how it does it and then trying to persuade them of the accuracy of the program. But we shall not dwell on all the variations on testing.

There are considerable drawbacks to testing of any kind. The fact that a program has passed a set of tests involving sample data will not normally guarantee correctness. Testing will generally only highlight errors, it will not guarantee their absence. Moreover, the matter of selecting tests is not necessarily a straightforward process. Large programs often require enormous numbers of tests. Moreover the possibility of the existence of statements which can never be executed raises all kinds of problems and these may not easily be detected – this leads to the topic of data flow analysis.

In many practical programming projects a great deal of time is spent on testing and on similar activities. It has been estimated that something far in excess of 50% of the time taken to construct a working program can be absorbed in this way. When eventually the tests are satisfied 'testing' becomes 'maintenance'!

Although we have pointed out the various drawbacks and weaknesses of program verification it is important not to lose sight of its considerable advantages. Accompanied by suitable testing it provides one genuine ray of hope in the struggle for correct and reliable software. Another very important observation is that a study of program verification will increase considerably our understanding and awareness of all aspects of the programming process; this is something that testing will just not provide.

Some measure of the scale of the software crisis can be gained by looking at certain financial statistics. In the Department of Defense in America it is currently (1978-9) estimated that about $6 billion is spent each year on software. Some 50% of this is spent on testing and editing. A saving of a mere 1% each year on testing alone would save some $25 million annually.

Software with its associated problem of maintenance usually accounts for the bulk of the computing costs of any large organisation. Hardware costs are generally much lower, sometimes as little as a tenth of the software costs. It is reckoned that the falling cost of hardware will make this comparison even more dramatic.

Financially then program verification has a great deal to offer. Yet its use at present tends to be limited to academic circles; it tends not to be in frequent use in other organisations. Yet these organisations spend vast sums of money on less viable alternatives. Program verification can genuinely replace large amounts of testing and can complement and improve the confidence in remaining forms of testing. Verification alone is inadequate since proofs are usually performed on the assumption that the environment in which the program will be eventually executed is in some sense ideal. Tests will reveal how the program performs in an actual environment. A subtle blend of verification and testing with suitable hardware back-up is likely to produce a very high degree of confidence in a program.

1.4   About this book

In these pages we shall be concerned mainly with program verification. We shall not confine the discussion to proving correctness but more generally we shall be concerned with proving properties of programs. We begin with simple programs and progress gradually to programs involving the use of conditionals, loops, arrays, complex data structures, procedures (possibly recursive), etc. The revised version of the programming language Ada will be used for expressing programs.

There is something slightly unnatural about performing the task of writing programs and then proving their correctness separately. It is to be hoped that a study of program verification will shed light on methods of programming which simplify the verification task. So there are lessons to be learned about program design and program methodology and even about language design; by supplying a careful choice of constructs the language designer can attempt to encourage the writing of easily verified programs. Strong arguments emerge to suggest that program verification and program construction can and should go hand-in-hand to some considerable extent. The proof of correctness can guide the programmer in the writing of programs which are correct.

As we become more familiar with techniques of program verification it will become apparent that aspects of the process are rather mechanical and can be programmed. Some people argue that program proving is on the point of being fully automated and that programs that check and ultimately produce proofs will soon be in everyday use. But the author feels that these days are somewhat remote. Even if there is speedy progress in this direction, it is still important for computer scientists to be aware of what is involved in proving properties of programs and to understand what mechanical checkers or provers must do. This they can learn by verifying programs manually.

In the final chapter we make some brief remarks concerning the provision of automatic aids for program verification. Often these automatic methods are implementations of manual methods but able to deal with more complicated and larger programs.

Throughout we shall limit the major part of the discussion to the consideration of relatively small programs. Most of these will manipulate typical objects such as numbers, character strings and later different kinds of data structures. But the arguments and methods are equally valid for programs which sense thermocouples, control lasers, etc. Some mention will be made of large programs but we shall not consider any real-time programs or programs for which a well-defined mathematical specification cannot readily be obtained, e.g. aspects of operating systems or compilers.

2 CORRECTNESS OF SIMPLE PROGRAMS

In this chapter we shall look at the task of verifying the correctness of very simple programs. These programs will not contain procedures, functions, jumps or even loops of any kind. Essentially they will be composed of just assignments and conditionals.

Before looking at proofs of correctness certain preparatory matters must be discussed. In the first place we must give a more formal definition of the concept of correctness. We must also introduce some notation in which to express both the programs we write and the assertions which will be associated with their proofs of correctness. For the programs themselves we begin by using a kind of flowchart. But by the end of this chapter we shall be using the programming language Ada. Apart from its wide acceptability and applicability it possesses certain features which will be convenient at a later stage. The reader need not have a detailed knowledge of Ada – the various constructs will be described as they are required.

We shall encounter an awkward conflict which occurs in selecting the names of variables. Good programming practice suggests that identifiers should be chosen in a way which reflects the role of the identifier in the program; also programs are written once but read often; these considerations tend to lead to the use of multi-character identifiers. But on the other hand, mathematical manipulation is considerably simplified if identifiers are brief. To reconcile these two opposing needs identifiers will tend to be one or two letters long, chosen as appropriately as possible.

We begin then with a formal definition of the meaning of correctness.

2.1 Definition of correctness

In the earlier part of this chapter we shall avoid difficulties resulting from the use of declarations and read and write or print statements.

As far as input is concerned it is convenient to assume that appropriate variables have been declared and initialised. In the usual way these input variables can be represented by any legitimate identifiers. If there are restrictions of any kind on the data, for example if an integer is positive, then the corresponding variable will appear in an appropriate way within the initial assertion. For convenience the input variables will be collectively denoted by $\bar{i}$ – this vector notation covers the possibility of zero, one or several identifiers.

Correspondingly there will be a set of result variables which can again take any form but which we collectively represent by $\bar{r}$. These effectively receive the output, the results of the calculations performed by the program. Each result variable will appear in the final assertion since this assertion merely describes what values these result variables should possess on completion of the program.

With this notation we can now view a program P as a kind of function p which operates on $\bar{i}$ and produces results in $\bar{r}$. In effect we can write

$$\bar{r} = p(\bar{i}).$$

It should be noted however that faults in the program may cause errors for certain sets of data, i.e. p may be undefined for certain values of $\bar{i}$. As such it is more accurate to refer to p as a partial function. How does this help in defining the notation of correctness?

These conventions have the desirable consequence that input variables replace read statements and result variables replace print or write statements. Usually, and certainly in the earlier chapters, we shall regard input variables as being in a sense constant – they should have read-only access and should not be subject to alteration by assignment.

Most programs will require the use of other temporary or auxiliary variables which can be used during a calculation. We shall, meantime, introduce these into programs as and when they are required. No confusion will result.

In chapter 1 we stated that the programmer must make assertions about his input and about his expected results. The input assertion is a function of $\bar{i}$ and will be denoted by ϕ (the Greek letter 'phi'). Thus $\phi(\bar{i})$ delivers true for any valid set of data and false otherwise. ϕ is referred to by different authors as the precondition or as the initial or input assertion or predicate. It is nothing more than a boolean expression which states precisely the domain of values or data on which the program is to operate. It therefore describes the domain of the function p.

The final assertion will be a function of both the input and result variables $\bar{i}$ and $\bar{r}$. It will be denoted by ψ, the Greek letter 'psi'. Thus $\psi(\bar{i};\bar{r})$ will be a boolean expression which is true if the intended relationship between the input and output variables holds, i.e. it is true if the program does as is intended. ψ is known variously as the postcondition or the final or output assertion or predicate; the semi-colon will separate the input and the output variables.

Often the predicate $\psi(\bar{i};\bar{r})$ can be expressed in the simple form

$$\bar{r} = \theta(\bar{i})$$

(θ is the Greek letter 'theta'). In other words, it is often possible to express the results in terms of simple expressions involving only the input variables $\bar{i}$. We then have the situation that

$$\bar{r} = \theta(\bar{\imath})$$

describes the intended effect of a program whereas

$$\bar{r} = p(\bar{\imath})$$

describes the actual effect. It is now a simple matter to describe correctness. We can stipulate that correctness is achieved if, for suitable input,

$$\bar{r} = p(\bar{\imath}) = \theta(\bar{\imath}).$$

More formally, we can give the following definition.

Definition of correctness

A program P is said to be correct with respect to the initial and final assertions ϕ and ψ if for every $\bar{\imath}$ for which $\phi(\bar{\imath})$ is true then $\psi(\bar{\imath}; p(\bar{\imath}))$ is also true.

Let us look again (see section 1.2) at a program which puts in the integer variable F the value $N!$ where N is a non-negative integer supplied as data. In this case the only input variable is N and it is natural to expect the value of N to remain unaltered throughout the course of the program. The input assertion $\phi(N)$ can then be written as $N >= 0$. The only output variable is F and $\psi(\bar{\imath}; \bar{r})$ or $\psi(N; F)$ can be written in the form $F = N!$ The statement of correctness reduces to

$$p(N) = N!$$

i.e. the value calculated by the program and placed in the output variable must be $N!$

Example 2.1a   Choosing assertions

Consider a program to sort into ascending order the value of three integers supplied as data.

The input predicate in this case is simply *TRUE*, i.e., no relationship involving the three integers is assumed. If the output variables are $R1, R2$ and $R3$ then an assertion such as

$$R1 <= R2 <= R3$$

inadequately expresses the desired effect of the programmer. It does not convey the desire that the set of values in the output variables should be the same as the set of values in the input variables; again the input variables should be regarded as constants and unalterable.

It is worth repeating at this stage the remark that the programs we deal with in this chapter will be of a very simple kind. The programs will involve essentially just assignments and possibly conditionals. One of the major difficulties associated with program verification in general is the problem of showing that a program terminates properly. Non-terminating programs require some form of looping mechanism such as jumps, while statements, recursive procedure calls, etc. In this chapter we exclude the possibility of these constructs and so need not concern ourselves with the difficulty. In later chapters however we shall have to consider such possibilities and a general definition of correctness will have to take careful account of it.

2.2   Verifying simple programs

We are at last in a position to start proving the correctness of simple programs. The simple techniques which we study in this chapter do not depend crucially on the programming language used to express the programs. The proofs we provide apply equally well to programs expressed in Ada, Algol 68, Pascal, Fortran 77, Basic, assembly code of various kinds and even programs expressed in flowchart form. In more complex situations the programming language can play a considerable role in making the verification task somewhat simpler and then the choice of programming language becomes more crucial.

Let us consider then a simple program which claims to simulate interchanging the values of two integer variables $I1$ and $I2$. Let the results be placed in $R1$ and $R2$. Then the input assertion $\phi(\bar{i})$ is just *TRUE*; the output assertion must state that the value of $I2$ has been placed in $R1$ and that the value of $I1$ has been placed in $R2$, i.e.

$$\psi(\bar{i};\bar{r}) = (R2 = I1) \wedge (R1 = I2)$$

A program which performed essentially

$$R2 := I1; \quad R1 := I2;$$

would suffice. But to simulate more closely the usual algorithm and to provide a more interesting proof we look at the programs given in figures 2.1–3 or indeed any other equivalent forms. (A or AUX will denote an auxiliary or temporary location.)

It does not matter which version of the program we select for the ensuing discussion. But let us concentrate on the flowchart version in figure 2.3 complete with its labels! How can we prove the correctness of this? There are two approaches we can take to proving correctness: the back substitution method and the method of symbolic execution. We look at the two methods in turn.

Fig. 2.1. Ada version.
$AUX := I1; R1 := I2; R2 := AUX;$

Fig. 2.2. PDP 11 or VAX 11 assembly code version.

$R1 = \%1$
$R2 = \%2$
$\ A = \%3$

$MOV \quad I1, A$
$MOV \quad I2, R1$
$MOV \quad A, R2$

Lest the reader should feel that these pieces of program are terribly trivial we take the opportunity of stressing the fact that the variables we are using are integer variables. Two integer variables have the property that either they are identical or they are completely distinct – they cannot overlap in some peculiar way.

2.2.1 Back substitution

In back substitution we proceed as follows. We have to verify the truth of the predicate ψ at the point D. We ask:

(i) For $(R2 = I1) \wedge (R1 = I2)$ to be true at D what must be true at C? Answer: $(AUX = I1) \wedge (R1 = I2)$. We can now ask:
(ii) For this new predicate to be true at C what must be true at B? Answer: $(AUX = I1)$.
(iii) For this predicate $AUX = I1$ to be true at B what must be true at A? Answer: $TRUE$.

This is clearly satisfied and the program has been shown to be correct.

It is worth taking a closer look at what was happening as we progressed through the above argument. The predicate at D, for example, was

$$(R2 = I1) \wedge (R1 = I2)$$

Fig. 2.3. Flowchart version.

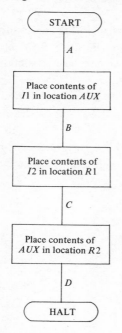

and at C was
$$(AUX = I1) \wedge (R1 = I2).$$
Between D and C there was the instruction:

Place the contents of AUX in location $R2$.

The predicate at C was obtained from the predicate at D by a process of back substitution. To be more precise $R2$ was replaced in the predicate at D by the value assigned to it, namely AUX. This produced the predicate at C. Indeed the successive predicates at C, B and A were all obtained in this way.

The process of proving correctness by back substitution generalises in an obvious way. Starting with the final predicate work backwards through the program making the necessary substitutions. On reaching the start of the program some predicate q will thus be obtained. Now show that, assuming the truth of the input predicate ϕ, the truth of q follows. The correctness of the program then ensues.

To show what happens when the logic of a program is at fault let us consider the flowchart program given in figure 2.4 and suppose we try to prove its correctness with respect to

the input assertion: *TRUE*

the output assertion: $(R2 = I1) \wedge (R1 = I2)$.

Fig. 2.4. Flowchart for simulating interchange.

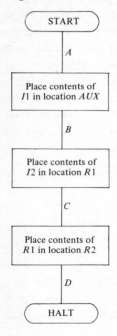

Back substitution produces a set of assertions at the points C, B and A. For

$(R2 = I1) \land (R1 = I2)$ to be true at D

$(R1 = I1) \land (R1 = I2)$ must be true at C

$(I2 = I1) \land (I2 = I2)$ must be true at B

and $(I2 = I1)$ must be true at A.

For the program to be proved correct the input assertion should now imply the truth of this predicate. Clearly it does not. $I2 = I1$ can be satisfied only if the two items of data are equal. The input assertion makes no such claim. We must conclude therefore that the program has not been shown to be correct. Note, however, that the program is correct with respect to

the input assertion: $I1 = I2$

the output assertion: $(R2 = I1) \land (R1 = I2)$.

The reader should note that at no stage have we stated that the failure to prove correctness is itself an indication that the program is incorrect. In this simple case however one has only to choose as data two unequal integers and incorrectness can readily be established. Note that our attempt to prove correctness has indicated the kind of data for which the program fails. This often happens. Indeed a byproduct of such an exercise can also be some indication of the error in the program.

2.2.2 Symbolic execution

In the back substitution process the proof proceeded somewhat unnaturally in the opposite direction to the flow of control of the program. The second technique of symbolic execution is basically a generalisation of the process of tracing a program and overcomes the above deficiency.

Take again the program of figure 2.3. We know that both $I1$ and $I2$ are constants. After the first assignment AUX will take the value $I1$. The two further assignments result in $R1$ receiving the value $I2$ and $R2$ receiving the value lodged in AUX, namely $I1$. The final assertion will be satisfied if it can be shown that

$(R2 = I1) \land (R1 = I2)$.

Substitute for $R2$ and $R1$ their symbolic values expressed in terms of the constant inputs $I1$ and $I2$. This gives

$(I1 = I1) \land (I2 = I2)$

and this is clearly true. The truth of the final assertion follows as does the correctness of the given program.

In the symbolic execution approach then the values of variables are represented by symbols or expressions involving only the input variables. As the various assignments and calculations are performed the programmer performs algebra on these symbols and assigns algebraic expressions to his variables. If, when the end of the program is reached, the truth of the output assertion can be verified then a satisfactory proof of correctness has been given.

2.3   Programs involving conditionals

With our previous techniques we are in a position to verify the correctness of simple programs containing essentially just assignment statements. We now turn our attention to programs which also involve conditional statements. Again we look at the two approaches of back substitution and symbolic execution.

For illustrative purposes take a simple program for finding the maximum value Z of two integer quantities X and Y. See figure 2.5. We wish to prove the correctness of this program with respect to

the input assertion $\phi(X, Y)$:   *TRUE*

the output assertion $\psi(X, Y; Z)$: $Z =$ **if** $X > Y$ **then** X **else** Y **end if**

In the given program there are two routes, namely *ABCD* and *ABD*, from the start to the finish. In more complex programs involving conditionals there may be several such routes. Any proof of correctness must look at each route separately and check the correctness of the program with respect to that route. The program will then be correct only if all routes are correct with respect to the given assertions.

Fig. 2.5. Flowchart for finding maximum of X and Y – boxes are numbered.

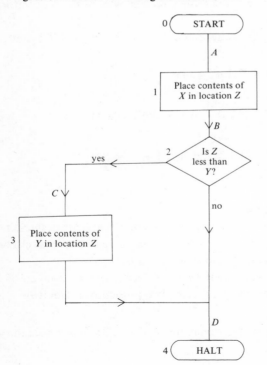

17

Although we will argue in terms of flowchart programs all of the discussion is equally applicable to programs written in programming languages and using assignments and conditionals (which include **if** ... **then** ... **else**, **if** ... **then** ... and even **case** and **switchon** constructions).

2.3.1   Back substitution

In the notation of figure 2.5 let us first consider correctness along route *ABCD* and let us use back substitution. For

$$Z = \textbf{if } X > Y \textbf{ then } X \textbf{ else } Y \textbf{ end if}$$

to be true at *D*

$$Y = \textbf{if } X > Y \textbf{ then } X \textbf{ else } Y \textbf{ end if}$$

must be true at *C*. The next step involves asking: what must be true at *B* for the above predicate to be true at *C*? Now the route which leads to *C* will be followed only if we assume at *B* the truth of $Z < Y$. Therefore we need at *B*

$$(Z < Y) \supset (Y = \textbf{if } X > Y \textbf{ then } X \textbf{ else } Y \textbf{ end if})$$

where $\supset$ denotes the logical operator meaning 'implies'. One more application of back substitution then results in the conclusion that

$$(X < Y) \supset (Y = \textbf{if } X > Y \textbf{ then } X \textbf{ else } Y \textbf{ end if})$$

must be true at *A*. It is. For if $X < Y$ the right hand side of the $\supset$ operator reduces to $Y = Y$.

Correctness along the alternative route *ABD* can be checked in a similar way. For

$$Z = \textbf{if } X > Y \textbf{ then } X \textbf{ else } Y \textbf{ end if}$$

to be true at *D* the assertion

$$(Z >= Y) \supset (Z = \textbf{if } X > Y \textbf{ then } X \textbf{ else } Y \textbf{ end if})$$

must be true at *B* and the assertion

$$(X >= Y) \supset (X = \textbf{if } X > Y \textbf{ then } X \textbf{ else } Y \textbf{ end if})$$

must be true at *A*. It is.

2.3.2   Symbolic execution

As before symbolic execution involves representing the values of variables as algebraic quantities. In the case of the program in figure 2.5 these algebraic expressions will involve only the constant inputs *X* and *Y*.

At *B* we know that *Z* will have the value *X*. Next there is a comparison between the values of *Z* and *Y*. We must look at the two possibilities separately

> case 1: $X < Y$
>
> > The instruction 'Place contents of *Y* in location *Z*' causes the value of *Z* to alter.

At D we have now to verify that indeed

$Z = $ **if** $X > Y$ **then** X **else** Y **end if**.

This is true since this case is characterised by the assumption that $X < Y$.

case 2: $X \geqslant Y$

At D we have to verify that

$Z = $ **if** $X > Y$ **then** X **else** Y **end if**

and again this is easily checked.

With symbolic execution, then, tests generally result in a case analysis of some kind. When there are nested conditionals various cases have to be considered and it becomes convenient to introduce the idea of a 'path condition'. This is often represented by pc and is merely a boolean which specifies the conditions characterising each different path as a function of the constant input quantities. In the previous example (see figure 2.5) the path conditions were

on path AB, $TRUE$; thus all routes pass along AB
on path BCD, $X < Y$
on path BD, $X > = Y$
on the path between D and the HALT box; $TRUE$.

Initially the path condition is set to $TRUE$ but may be altered by the initial assertion or by any test occurring in the program. In general the pc becomes updated whenever a further test is performed. However suppose that a particular boolean b, a (simplified) function of the inputs, is obtained as a result of a test. If, for the current pc, either $pc \supset b$ or $pc \supset \neg b$, there is no need for a further case analysis since only one of the alternative branches can possibly be selected. Otherwise two new subcases with path conditions $pc \wedge b$ and $pc \wedge \neg b$ must be introduced and attributed to the relevant paths through the program.

Symbolic execution can be viewed as a generalised form of testing, for when conditionals are present in a program a case analysis usually results. Each case that is verified represents one route through the program and provides confirmation of correctness for a particular kind of data. A complete proof of correctness is obtained when all possible routes through the program have been checked and verified.

Before ending this discussion of symbolic execution it is convenient to introduce here the idea of a *symbolic execution tree*. The execution of any program can be represented as a tree in which each statement appears as a node. If control passes from one statement to the next this is represented by an arc on the tree. A test instruction will in general cause a branch in the tree; from that node will emanate at least two paths. To each path there will be attached an appropriate path condition which characterises the calculations which take that particular route. The symbolic execution tree corresponding to the program in figure 2.5 is

19

given in figure 2.6. A proof of correctness is obtained provided that at each leaf of the tree correctness can be checked.

2.4   Introduction to Ada

The programs we have written have been expressed until now in flow-chart form. For various reasons it is not satisfactory to continue in this vein:

Flowcharts are bulky and require a lot of paper; for this reason they tend to be intellectually unmanageable and they do not provide a convenient means of expressing programs.

Their use is liable to cause errors since arrows can easily be wrongly directed; moreover their inner syntax (i.e. the contents of boxes) tends to be non-standard and poorly defined.

They are not usually used as a means of presenting programs to a computer.

Fig. 2.6. Symbolic execution tree.

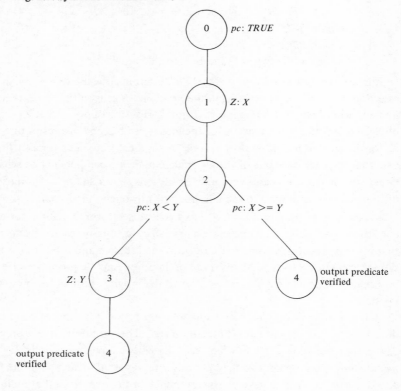

Notes
(a) The nodes in the tree are labelled with statement numbers (see figure 2.5).
(b) The values of pc and Z are given in the form $Z: X$ etc.; these alter as shown as the computation progresses.

20

In their usual form they do not readily provide a means of representing many facilities available in programming languages, e.g. declarations, recursion, assigned GOTO statements and such like, information hiding.

There is another very disturbing aspect of flowcharts which is not made apparent by the simple examples we have so far discussed. Unfortunately, they tend to encourage considerations about flow of control within a program at a time when it is not sensible to do so. Initially a programmer should consider the overall structure of his program and not the flow of control within it. In many ways this is by far the most serious criticism of flowcharts and of the ways in which they tend to be used. From now on we abandon their use.

The verification process that we have been describing is, fortunately, equally valid when applied to programs expressed in any of the usual notations, especially low level or high level languages. From now on we shall tend to express programs in terms of the programming language Ada. In this section we introduce briefly certain aspects of this language. But first we look at some of the background.

In the early 1970s the American Department of Defense was becoming increasingly concerned about the cost of their computing effort, especially the production, testing and development of their software. The Department decided that greater savings could be made if one programming language was adopted as a kind of standard. But this language would have to suit their purposes; it would have to encourage the production of real-time programs using modern programming techniques, it would have to encourage reliability and correctness and it would have to be relatively easy to implement. As none of the languages which existed around 1975 was felt to be satisfactory, the Defense Department decided to encourage the design of a new language which would meet a set of detailed requirements. The outcome was Ada designed by a team from Cii Honeywell Bull and Honeywell Systems and Research Center under the leadership of Jean Ichbiah.

We do not propose to give a complete and comprehensive introduction to Ada in this book. That is not the main aim. But we shall give some brief remarks which will illustrate the flavour of the language.

2.4.1 Types, identifiers and declarations

All the variables introduced by a programmer must be declared.

Example 2.4.1a Declarations

(a) *PI_BY_*4: **constant** *FLOAT* := 3.14159265/4.0;

introduces the identifier *PI_BY_*4 which will thereafter represent the constant value obtained by evaluating 3.14159265/4.0; any attempt to alter *PI_BY_*4 will result in an error

21

(b) *ITEM*1, *ITEM*2 : *INTEGER*;

> introduces two identifiers *ITEM*1 and *ITEM*2 which are not initialised; if the values of *ITEM*1 and *ITEM*2 are constrained to lie in the range 1 to 100 we could write

> *ITEM*1, *ITEM*2 : *INTEGER* **range** 1 .. 100;

(c) *X*, *Y* : *CHARACTER* := '*A*';

> introduces *X* and *Y* and initialises them both to '*A*'.

Declarations serve to introduce identifiers, to associate with these a type and certain characteristics, i.e. certain operations, functions and attributes which can be applied to the associated values. The allowable types include

> the integers which are of type *LONG_INTEGER*, *INTEGER* or *SHORT_INTEGER* – the span of integers decreases as the length decreases

> the floating-point types which include *LONG_FLOAT*, *FLOAT* or *SHORT_FLOAT* – the magnitude and precision decrease with the length; these together with the fixed-point types form the real types

> the numeric types include both the integers and the reals

> the scalars include the numeric types as well as *BOOLEAN*, *CHARACTER* and the enumeration types.

The enumeration types are introduced by type declarations such as

> **type** *UNIVERSITY* **is** (*UNDERGRADUATE*, *POSTGRADUATE*, *LECTURER*, *PROFESSOR*, *PRINCIPAL*, *CHANCELLOR*);

Type declarations like this impose an ordering on the various elements. The first element is less than the second, which is then less than the third and so on.

The types *BOOLEAN* and *CHARACTER* should be regarded as standard enumeration types whose declaration can be assumed by any programmer. In effect

> **type** *BOOLEAN* **is** (*FALSE*, *TRUE*);

and

> **type** *CHARACTER* **is** (..., '0', '1', '2', ..., '9', ...,
> '*A*', '*B*', '*C*', ..., '*Z*', ...);

The operations available on numeric quantities are fairly typical:

> monadic operators + and −

> dyadic operators + and − together with *, / for both integer and ordinary division; **rem** for remainder and **mod** for modulus on division between integers; and ** for exponentiation; for dyadic operators other than exponentiation operands are of the same type

> *ABS* for absolute value.

22

Notes

(*a*) *N*/*M* truncates towards zero.

(*b*) *N* **rem** *M* has the same sign as *N*; *N* **mod** *M* has the same sign as *M*.

(*c*) Integers can be raised only to positive integer powers.

(*d*) Floating-point quantities can be raised to integer powers with the expected results.

The operators available on logical values are the usual **not**, **and**, **or** and **xor** (for exclusive disjunction). For character strings the operator & concatenates two strings.

Apart from these operators there are other relational operators. Both = (equals) and /= (not equals) are defined between any two objects of the same type. The operators <, <=, >, >= are further defined for any two objects of the same scalar type; their meaning is as expected.

For the purposes of understanding the implied bracketing in expressions there are six precedence levels which from lowest to highest are:

logical	**and**, **or** and **xor**
relational	<, <=, >=, >, =, /=
adding	+, −, &
unary	+, −, **not**
multiplying	*, /, **rem**, **mod**
exponentiation	**

Brackets can be used to override these precedence rules. When operators of the same precedence level appear in succession the usual left to right association occurs; however if these happen to be different logical operators, brackets must be used to clarify the meaning.

Another set of attributes allows access to elements of enumeration types. For any scalar type *FIRST* and *LAST* select the minimum and maximum values of a type. For discrete types, i.e. for all scalar types excluding reals, the attributes *PRED*, *SUCC* and *POS* return the predecessor, successor and position of an element in a given range. Moreover **in** and **not in** can be used to ask if some quantity lies in a given range (ranges are of the form *A* .. *B* where *A* and *B* are suitable objects of the same scalar type).

Example 2.4.1b   Enumeration types

Given the definition of the type *UNIVERSITY* given above

UNIVERSITY'FIRST	produces	*UNDERGRADUATE*
UNIVERSITY'SUCC (*PROFESSOR*)	produces	*PRINCIPAL*
UNIVERSITY'POS (*PROFESSOR*)	produces	3 since the numbering of positions starts at zero

PROFESSOR **in** *UNDERGRADUATE* .. *LECTURER* is *FALSE*.

2.4.2 Statements

The statements in Ada can be described in a relatively straightforward manner. Assignment statements have the form one might expect from an Algol-like language. Conditionals are typified by

```
if condition then
    sequence_of_statements
end if;
```

or in more ambitious circumstances

```
if condition then
    sequence_of_statements
elsif another_condition then
    another_sequence_of_statements
elsif ...
    ...
else
    final_sequence_of_statements
end if;
```

The final **else** and its accompanying final_sequence_of_statements may be absent. In all these forms the condition is often just some boolean expression. The operator **and (or)** can be replaced by **and then (or else)** whenever the programmer wishes to evaluate the second operand only if the first is true (or false).

The presence of enumeration types demands the existence of a case statement to allow different actions in different circumstances.

Example 2.4.2a   Case statement

If X has been declared to be of type *UNIVERSITY* the following case statement could be used

```
case X is                    .
    when UNDERGRADUATE|POSTGRADUATE => action_1;
    when LECTURER .. PRINCIPAL => action_2;
    when others => action_3;
end case;
```

If X has value *UNDERGRADUATE* or *POSTGRADUATE*, action_1 would be performed; if it lies in the range *LECTURER .. PRINCIPAL* action_2 would be performed; otherwise action_3 would take place.

The ideas conveyed by the above example generalise in the expected manner. Any suitable expression can appear between **case** and **is**. There may be zero or more **when** parts. Within a **when** part the various choices are separated by the vertical bar. The actions take the form of a sequence of statements. The default part introduced by **when others** may be absent.

24

The simple Ada programs we write will in the meantime take the form of a block, i.e. they will appear as

declare
 sequence_of_declarations
begin
 sequence_of_statements
end;

All variables and so on other than the standard objects supplied by an implementation must be defined in the declarative part. The language is block-structured and so any statement may itself take the form of a block. Blocks with no declarations are permitted and in this case the initial **declare** is omitted.

Ada programs can in general be much more complex than the simple scheme given above suggests. We shall introduce the greater complexity only when it is required – see chapter 7.

Some clarification is needed regarding the distinction between bold words such as **case** and **when** and other words such as *INTEGER* and *LECTURER*. The bold words are Ada reserved words; a complete list of these is given in figure 2.7. Other identifiers must be chosen in such a way that they do not clash with the reserved words. Identifiers such as *INTEGER* have a meaning which is given in the standard environment and which the Ada compiler will understand. Identifiers such as *LECTURER* have a meaning given by the programmer himself.

Finally we mention the commentary facility in Ada. Comments begin with a double hyphen and are terminated by the end-of-line. They have no effect whatsoever on the meaning of the program. It will be convenient to surround assertions by curly brackets and insert these as comments at appropriate places in programs.

Fig. 2.7. Ada reserved words.

abort	declare	generic	of	select
accept	delay	goto	or	separate
access	delta		others	subtype
all	digits	if	out	
and	do	in		task
array		is	package	terminate
at			pragma	then
	else		private	type
	elsif	limited	procedure	
	end	loop		
begin	entry		raise	use
body	exception		range	
	exit	mod	record	when
			rem	while
		new	renames	with
case	for	not	return	
constant	function	null	reverse	xor

2.5   Verification of Ada programs

With these ideas we can now return to our main interest, the task of
verifying programs. The programs we now look at are no longer expressed in
flowchart form but they are Ada programs. Consequently we can no longer
make certain idealised assumptions about the environment in which programs
are to be executed, i.e. we cannot assume that variables and constants have
been properly declared and initialised. Fortunately there is no leap in difficulty
in dealing with this.

Consider again the program designed to simulate the interchange of the
values of two integer variables. This can be written in Ada as

```
declare
        ITEM1, ITEM2, R1, R2: INTEGER;
begin
        GET (ITEM1); GET (ITEM2);
        declare
                I1: constant INTEGER := ITEM1;
                I2: constant INTEGER := ITEM2;
                - - {initial assertion: TRUE}
                R3: constant INTEGER := I1;
        begin
                R1 := I2;
                R2 := R3;
        end;
        - - {final assertion: (R1 = I2) ∧ (R2 = I1)}
        PUT (R1); PUT (R2);
end;
```

Initial declarations introduce the input and output variables. An inner block has
the effect of introducing suitably initialised constants. In general the following
approach is adopted:

```
declare
        declare input and output variables;
begin
        initialise input variables;
        declare
                introduce appropriate constants;
                make initial assertion;
        begin
                perform calculations, introducing temporary variables
                when required and perhaps using other blocks;
```

26

end;

         make final assertion

         perform printing operations (involving only the output and
         perhaps input variables);

  end;

Declarations in general have the effect of introducing variables and associating with these a set of attributes which include the kinds of operations that can be performed on the variables. In the case of integer variables, for example, these operations include the usual addition, subtraction, multiplication, integer division, comparisons such as equality, less than and so on. If declarations have an initialisation part the corresponding variables receive suitable initial values. If there is no initialisation part we say that a variable of type T has been given the value $\bot$, undefined of type T. It is illegal to use this in any calculation whatsoever, even an assignment to another variable or in a comparison with another similarly declared variable. The corresponding variable can therefore be used only in a read or get statement or it can receive some well-defined value.

With these remarks it should now be clear that it is possible to provide a proof of the fact that the required environment for a program has been properly installed. However what we previously referred to as the initial assertion in a sense becomes the final assertion and it must now contain the statement that certain variables have been properly declared and initialised. We illustrate what is involved by referring again to the initial part of the program which simulates the interchange of values of variables

      - - {'initial' assertion: *TRUE*}

    declare

        *ITEM*1, *ITEM*2, *R*1, *R*2: *INTEGER*;

    begin

        GET (*ITEM*1); *GET* (*ITEM*2);

        declare

            *I*1: **constant** *INTEGER* := *ITEM*1;

            *I*2: **constant** *INTEGER* := *ITEM*2;

            - - {'final' assertion: *I*1 and *I*2 are

            - - suitably initialised integer constants;

            - - *R*1 and *R*2 are integer variables whose

            - - values are $\bot$, the undefined value

            - - of type *INTEGER*}

A proof of correctness can be given in the usual way.

In giving correctness proofs in later chapters we shall resort again to our earlier custom of assuming the existence of a suitable environment for our programs. It should now be apparent that proofs of the existence of such environments can be given if and when they are required.

2.6   Concluding remarks

It could be argued that until now the programs we have looked at have been unnaturally simple. This is true. In the next chapter we start discussing programs which contain loops. When considering these more sophisticated programs which will contain possibly nested conditionals or loops, it will be important to remember the basic ideas discussed in this chapter.

We have now looked at two ways of proving the correctness of simple programs – back substitution and symbolic execution. The former was introduced by Floyd around 1967 (see Floyd, 1967). The process of symbolic execution is more recent and was introduced by King (see King, 1976 *a*, *b*). Both approaches can be extended to deal with more complex forms of program.

Both techniques are different ways of viewing the same process, the process of deriving assertions which then have to be verified. Basically assertions, which state the intended relationships between the variables used in the program, are placed at various points in the program – until now these assertions have been placed only at the beginning and end of the program. The assertions convey the hope of the programmer that whenever the program is executed these assertions will be true. To verify the correctness of the program this must be shown mathematically to be so. The basic method, invented by Floyd, is called the method of *inductive assertions* or *invariant assertions*.

Exercises for chapter 2

1. The piece of program

   $Y1 := Y1 - Y2;$
   $Y2 := Y1 + Y2;$
   $Y1 := Y2 - Y1;$

   is intended to interchange the values of the integer variables $Y1$ and $Y2$. Formulate appropriate input and output assertions and prove its correctness.

2. Write and prove correct a program to rotate three given integers cyclically one position to the right. Your program should therefore be proved correct with respect to

   input predicate: *TRUE*
   output predicate: $(Z1 = X2) \land (Z2 = X3) \land (Z3 = X1)$.

3. Design program fragments to evaluate

   (*a*) the absolute value
   (*b*) the sign (-1 for negative, 0 for zero and $+1$ for positive numbers)
   of an integer. Verify the correctness of these.

4. Write programs to calculate the maximum and minimum of three given integers. Prove the correctness of both programs.

5. Two measurements such as

   99 metres 47 cms

and
3 metres 54 cms

are supplied as data. Write a correct program which produces as its result a similar measurement, the sum of the two inputs.

6. Design a program to sort into ascending order three integers which are supplied as data. Prove the correctness of the final program. Draw the symbolic execution tree for your program.

7. Due to differences in accuracy and precision a programmer may find that a program works on one computer but not on another. How did the designers of Ada ensure that such portability problems need not cause undue concern? Consider the problem associated with both types and the operators that act on these.

3   PROGRAMS CONTAINING LOOPS

We now turn to the problem of dealing with programs which contain at least one loop. Immediately we are faced with the possibility of programs which do not terminate. Consequently we must reconsider the meaning of the term *correctness*. We must also look at the looping mechanisms in Ada. We begin with the latter.

3.1   The loop statement in Ada

In Ada there are various forms of loops. The most basic is

loop
> sequence_of_statements

end loop;

This has the effect of repeatedly executing the sequence_of_statements. The execution of this would never stop unless there was some statement which would cause exit from the loop. The statement

exit;

causes termination of the smallest enclosing loop. When

exit when condition;

is executed and the condition found to be true a jump takes place to the statement which follows the smallest enclosing loop statement.

Example 3.1a   A simple loop

The following piece of program reads and prints characters from the standard input file until the first space occurs

declare
> C: *CHARACTER*;

begin
> **loop**
>> *GET* (C);
>> **exit when** C = ' ';

30

```
            PUT (C);
        end loop;
        PUT (NEWLINE & "SPACE NOW OCCURS");
    end;
```

The catenation operator & joins together strings of characters, in Ada *NEWLINE* acts as two characters – carriage return (*CR*) causes the printing position to return to column 1 and line feed (*LF*) causes a new line to be taken.

Loop statements of the above kind tend to take the general form:

```
loop
    sequence_of_statements_needed_to_perform_calculations_
        necessary_for_the_evaluation_of_the_condition;
    exit when condition;
    statement_performing_calculations_of_some_kind;
end loop;
```

Although the exit statement normally causes termination of the current loop statement it can be used to jump out of several nested loops. To achieve this a loop identifier is placed between **exit** and **when**. Thus

```
OUTER_LOOP:
loop
    . . .
    exit OUTER_LOOP when condition;
    . . .
end loop OUTER_LOOP;
```

causes termination of the loop *OUTER_LOOP*.

Though the above is the most basic form of loop it is not the only form. Certain specific kinds of loop frequently occur and it is desirable to have specific forms of loop to deal with these situations. There are two special cases.

The first of these is designed to deal with the situation in which the condition always occurs at the start of the loop. Thus

```
while condition loop
    sequence_of_statements;
end loop;
```

Example 3.1b   Using **while**

Find the smallest positive integer X with the property that $X^3 <= N$, where N is some positive integer supplied as data

```
declare
    X, N: INTEGER;
begin
    GET (N);
```

31

$$X := 1;$$
while $X**3 <= N$ **loop**
$$X := X + 1;$$
end loop;
$$PUT (X - 1);$$
end;

The second special form of loop statement is designed to deal with the situation that occurs when it is known in advance how many times, or at least the maximum number of times, a specific set of instructions has to be performed. If the loop parameter has to run up through some range of values the required form of the loop statement is

for loop_parameter **in** discrete_range **loop**
    sequence_of_statements
end loop;

Alternatively if the loop parameter has to run down through the range the following form is used

for loop_parameter **in reverse** discrete_range **loop**
    sequence_of_statements
end loop;

In both cases the loop parameter must be regarded within the sequence_of_ statements as a constant. Moreover, the very appearance of an identifier after a **for** serves as the declaration of that identifier. The type of the loop parameter is inherited from the types of the objects specifying the discrete range: if the range specifies a range of integers then the loop parameter will be of integer type, if it specifies a range of characters the loop parameter will be of character type, and so on.

Example 3.1c   Using **for**
Print out a table of cubes of all integers from 1 to 100 inclusive.
begin *PUT ("TABLE OF CUBES OF INTEGERS FROM* 1 *TO* 100"
                                        & *NEWLINE*);

for *I* **in** 1 .. 100 **loop**
    PUT (NEWLINE);
    PUT (I);
    PUT (" ");
    *PUT (I**3)*;
end loop;
end;

It should be noted that the **for** form of the loop statement can have as one of its inner statements an exit statement, thus allowing termination of the loop before the entire range has been traversed. Note that as long as a **for** is present this can never lead to non-terminating programs, regardless of whether or not an exit statement is present. This is not true of the earlier versions of the loop statement which can certainly be used to produce programs which can execute indefinitely.

In using the Ada programming language as the vehicle in which to express our programs there is a slight difficulty about including assertions. For uniformity of notation throughout this book we would like to enclose assertions in braces {and}. We shall place these assertions within comments and take advantage of this to exercise considerable freedom in the notation we use for expressing assertions.

We now return to the main theme of this book, namely program verification. In the light of the remarks about the possibility of non-terminating programs we must now reconsider the earlier definition of correctness.

3.2   Correctness revisited

We now introduce two different kinds of correctness distinguished by the fact that

> in one case termination must occur – this is called *total correctness*;
>
> in the other case termination may or may not occur – this is called *partial correctness.*

To be more precise some definitions are required.

Definition of termination

A program P is said to *terminate* with respect to the input predicate ϕ if, for every $\bar{\imath}$ for which $\phi(\bar{\imath})$ is true, the computation of P is finite.

Recall that in chapter 2 we used the function p to describe the actual effect of a program P. The intended or expected effect was described by the output predicate. Correctness was defined by equating these.

Definition of total correctness

A program P is said to be *totally correct* with respect to the input predicate ϕ and the output predicate ψ if, for every $\bar{\imath}$ for which $\phi(\bar{\imath})$ is true, the computation of P terminates and $\psi(\bar{\imath};p(\bar{\imath}))$ is true.

Definition of partial correctness

A program P is said to be *partially correct* with respect to the input predicate ϕ and the output predicate ψ if, for every $\bar{\imath}$ for which $\phi(\bar{\imath})$ is true and the computation of P terminates, then $\psi(\bar{\imath};p(\bar{\imath}))$ is true.

Some of the more extreme possibilities are worth looking at in some detail. If a program never terminates then it is automatically partially correct yet it is certainly not totally correct. In the programs of chapter 2 and even in the programs of this chapter which use only the **for** form of the loop statement there can never be any doubt about termination and so proof of partial correctness implies total correctness.

Total correctness is a stronger concept than partial correctness since it says more about any program to which the term is applied. In general it is correspondingly more difficult to prove total correctness and so we look first at proofs of partial correctness. Having shown that a program is partially correct we can then prove total correctness merely by showing that termination occurs for all possible inputs satisfying the input predicate. The later sections of this chapter deal with this.

3.3   Partial correctness

We now look at ways of extending the idea of inductive assertions to prove the partial correctness of programs involving loops. Again there are the two approaches of back substitution and symbolic execution and we look at these separately.

We again illustrate the technique with an example. Consider the problem of writing a program to place in the integer variable F the value N! where N is some non-negative integer quantity which is supplied as data. Ideally we should use the **for** form of the loop statement for this purpose. But let us first consider the program given in figure 3.1. We hope to prove that this achieves the desired effect, i.e. we require to prove its (partial) correctness with respect to

the input predicate $\phi(N)$: $N >= 0$

the output predicate $\psi(N; F)$: $F = N$!

To extend the inductive assertions technique to this program we proceed as follows. We split the loop at some cutpoint which for convenience we refer to as C; in this example we choose the point immediately following the **while** and before the condition $M /= N$. To this cutpoint we attach an assertion which will be true each time control passes C. This assertion should express the relationship between the various program variables at this point in the program. We then tackle the proof of partial correctness in three stages:

1. We assume the truth of the input assertion; we then prove that when control reaches C the assertion at C is true.

Fig. 3.1. Factorial program.

```
F := 1;
declare
    M: INTEGER := 0;
begin
    while M /= N loop
        M := M + 1;
        F := F * M;
    end loop;
end;
```

2. We assume the truth of the assertion at C together with the fact that the test $M/=N$ is true; then we prove that on returning to C the assertion at C is again true.
3. We assume the truth of the assertion at C together with the fact that the test $M/=N$ is false; then we prove that on reaching the end of the program the output assertion is true.

If all of these can be verified then we have shown that the program is partially correct with respect to the given input and output predicates.

Note the inductive argument in step 2. For obvious reasons the assertion at C is often referred to as the loop predicate or loop invariant. It will be convenient to refer to it as such, even just as the invariant, to distinguish it from the input and output assertions.

Unfortunately there is one substantial difficulty that must be overcome before we can start on a proof of correctness of this example. We do not know what the invariant at C should be. This distinguishes it markedly from the input and output assertions. The choice of invariant is usually non-trivial. To make a sensible choice which is both appropriate and accurate the program prover must understand thoroughly the workings of the program whose correctness he is trying to establish. The invariant must in some way characterise the values of the variables as they pass the cutpoint.

Suppose we trace the above program assuming that the input N is 5, say. The values of M, F are tabulated below

$N = 5$	M	F
	0	1
	1	1
	2	2
	3	6
	4	24
	5	120

From this we can deduce that the loop invariant at C should be

$$(N >= 0) \land (M >= 0) \land (F = M!)$$

We include the fact that $(M >= 0)$ since factorials of negative integers are not mathematically meaningful. The various assertions are shown in the program of figure 3.2.

We can now attempt the proof of correctness of the program in the three stages mentioned above. The proof of each stage can be attempted using either backward substitution or symbolic execution.

3.3.1   Back substitution

We use the notation of figure 3.2 and look at the three different stages in turn.

Stage 1: input assertion to cutpoint C

We require to establish the truth of $(N >= 0) \wedge (M >= 0) \wedge (F = M!)$ at C given the input assertion $N >= 0$. In other words we have to use back substitution to verify

$- - \{N >= 0\}$
$F := 1;$
$M := 0;$
$- - \{(N >= 0) \wedge (M >= 0) \wedge (F = M!)\}$

Thus, to include all the details, we must demonstrate the truth of

$$[N >= 0] \supset [(N >= 0) \wedge (0 >= 0) \wedge (1 = 0!)]$$

This – and we call this the *verification condition* for the path from the start of the program to cutpoint C – is clearly true.

Stage 2: cutpoint C to cutpoint C

To accomplish this stage of the proof we must show that, assuming the truth of the invariant at C and assuming the truth of the condition $M /= N$, then when control next returns to C the invariant is again true. In effect we have to show that the assertion at C is indeed a loop invariant.

The proof involves checking the correctness of

$- - \{(N >= 0) \wedge (M >= 0) \wedge (F = M!) \wedge (M /= N)\}$
$M := M + 1;$
$F := F * M;$
$- - \{(N >= 0) \wedge (M >= 0) \wedge (F = M!)\}$

The appropriate verification condition is

$$[(N >= 0) \wedge (M >= 0) \wedge (F = M!) \wedge (M /= N)]$$
$$\supset [(N >= 0) \wedge (M + 1 >= 0) \wedge (F * (M + 1) = (M + 1)!)]$$

The truth of this is readily checked; this involves assuming that

$$N >= 0, \quad M >= 0, \quad F = M!, \quad M /= N$$

and proving separately that

$$N >= 0, \quad M + 1 >= 0, \quad F * (M + 1) = (M + 1)!$$

Fig. 3.2. Factorial program with assertions added.

```
- - {N >= 0}
F := 1;
declare
    M: INTEGER := 0;
begin
    while - - {(N >= 0) ∧ (M >= 0) ∧ (F = M!)} cutpoint C
                        M /= N loop
            M := M + 1;
            F := F * M;
        end loop;
end;
- - {F = N!}
```

36

Stage 3: cutpoint C to final assertion

For this part of the verification we are entitled to assume the truth of the invariant at C together with the fact that the loop condition is false, i.e. $M = N$. From this information we must show that at the end of the program the final assertion is true. In effect we have therefore to show that the verification condition

$$[(N >= 0) \land (M >= 0) \land (F = M!) \land (M = N)] \supset [F = N!]$$

is indeed true. It is.

All three stages of the proof have now been completed and the partial correctness of the program follows. This then illustrates the back substitution approach to the method of inductive assertion for programs involving loops.

3.3.2   Symbolic execution

We now apply the method of symbolic execution to the factorial program in figure 3.2. The basic ideas are similar to those introduced in chapter 2, i.e. we must consider all possible routes from the start of the program to the end. This we do by again looking separately at the three stages or paths discussed in section 3.3.1. For this purpose imagine symbolic execution starting at the beginning of a path and finishing at the end of that path. There will be assertions associated with the start and finish of each path and consequently the techniques of chapter 2 can be applied to each individual path. Thus the variables can be given symbolic values and the path condition *pc* can be initialised to the assertion at the start of the path under consideration, the variables being replaced by their symbolic values.

We now examine the paths in turn. We represent the values of variables such as M in the form

M: the current value of M

Similarly path conditions appear as

pc: path condition for the current path

We can omit mention of constants.

Stage 1: input assertion to cutpoint

Recall that the uninitialised variables are assumed to possess the undefined value $\perp$. Then at the start of the program

$F: \perp \quad pc: N >= 0$

On reaching the cutpoint symbolic execution ensures that

$F: 1, \quad M: 0, \quad pc: N >= 0$

The invariant at the cutpoint, namely

$(N >= 0) \land (M >= 0) \land (F = M!)$

can be easily checked by substituting the appropriate values for M and F in the expression and using the information given by the path condition pc.

Stage 2: from cutpoint back to cutpoint

At the cutpoint we are entitled to assume the truth of the invariant. Therefore we have

$$pc: (N >= 0) \wedge (M >= 0) \wedge (F = M!)$$

As the computation progresses the path condition alters and the values of the variables M and F change to M' and F'. On reaching the cutpoint again

$$F': F * (M + 1), \quad M': M + 1,$$
$$pc': (N >= 0) \wedge (M >= 0) \wedge (F = M!) \wedge (M \mathrel{/=} N)$$

We have now to establish the truth of the invariant using the new values of the variables. Thus we have to show that

$$(N' >= 0) \wedge (M' >= 0) \wedge (F' = M'!)$$

Given the new values of the variables and the path condition pc' this is easily checked.

Stage 3: from cutpoint to end

At the cutpoint

$$pc: (N >= 0) \wedge (M >= 0) \wedge (F = M!) \wedge (M = N)$$

The truth of the final assertion

$$F = N!$$

is easily obtained.

This then completes the proof of partial correctness of the factorial program, for we have now checked each individual path through the program.

The ground rules which were developed earlier in chapter 2 still apply. But note that some extension of these ideas has occurred:

(i) The paths are no longer paths through entire programs, but paths between particular points within a program.

(ii) The initial and final points on our path may be the same point; this occurred in dealing with stage 2 of the above proof when the cutpoint began and ended the path.

(iii) Instead of assuming that only input variables have symbolic values it may be desirable to associate such values with arbitrary program variables; again this is just what we did in discussing stage 2 of the above proof.

The introduction of these loops into our program implies that the symbolic execution trees corresponding to the programs become potentially infinite. With programs which do not terminate they will certainly be infinite. With programs which do terminate their size may be arbitrarily large though in all cases finite. To cope with this problem of size we essentially look at only a finite section of the symbolic execution tree and appeal to induction to deduce a proof of (partial) correctness of our program.

3.3.3 Other examples

The remarks of the previous section generalise in the expected way. To prove the correctness of any program containing a loop we split the loop at some suitable cutpoint and look for an invariant to associate with that cutpoint. If there are several loops each loop must be split and an appropriate invariant found for each cutpoint. Let us look at another example.

Example 3.3.3a   Square root

The program given in figure 3.3 is intended to calculate the value of the largest integer R less than or equal to the square root of N, where N is given as data. We are required to verify the partial correctness of the program with respect to

the input assertion $\phi(N)$: $N >= 0$

and

the output assertion $\psi(N; R)$: $R^2 <= N < (R + 1)^2 \wedge (R >= 0)$

In designing this program the programmer made use of the fact that

$$1 + 3 + 5 + \ldots + (2 * R + 1) = (R + 1)^2$$

Each time round the loop in the program an extra $2 * R + 1$ is added to the value of S. The values of R, $2 * R + 1$ and $1 + 3 + 5 \ldots + (2 * R + 1)$ are accumulated in R, T and S respectively. Thus R stands for root, T stands for temporary and S stands for square.

The relationships between R, S and T are all clear.

$$T = 2 * R + 1 \quad \text{and} \quad S = (R + 1)^2$$

This suggests that the loop invariant, the assertion which is true each time round the loop, might be of the form

$$(T = 2 * R + 1) \wedge (S = (R + 1)^2)$$

Fig. 3.3. Square root program.

```
R := 0;
declare
      S, T: INTEGER := 1;
begin
      while S <= N loop
            R := R + 1;
            T := T + 2;
            S := S + T;
      end loop;
end;
```

This is not quite sufficient because eventually we want to prove something about the range in which the final value of R lies. To be precise, then, we associate with the loop an invariant

$$(T = 2 * R + 1) \wedge (S = (R + 1)^2) \wedge (R^2 <= N) \wedge (R >= 0)$$

See figure 3.4.

We do not propose to give a complete proof of the partial correctness of the square root program. We look only at part of this. Consider the section of the proof which justifies the choice of loop invariant. We therefore effectively wish to prove the correctness of the following piece of program

$$-- \{(T = 2 * R + 1) \wedge (S = (R + 1)^2) \wedge (R^2 <= N)$$
$$\wedge (R >= 0) \wedge (S <= N)\}$$

$R := R + 1;$
$T := T + 2;$
$S := S + T;$
$$-- [(T = 2 * R + 1) \wedge (S = (R + 1)^2) \wedge (R^2 <= N) \wedge (R >= 0)]$$

To prove the correctness of this by back substitution we require to establish the truth of the verification condition

$$[(T = 2 * R + 1) \wedge (S = (R + 1)^2) \wedge (R^2 <= N)$$
$$\wedge (R >= 0) \wedge (S <= N)]$$

$$\supset$$

$$[(T + 2 = 2 * (R + 1) + 1) \wedge (S + T + 2 = (R + 1 + 1)^2)$$
$$\wedge ((R + 1)^2 <= N) \wedge (R + 1 >= 0)]$$

This is straightforward.

A similar effect could have been obtained using symbolic execution.

The examples we have given so far have been rather mathematical in nature and rather artificial in that little attention has been paid to input and output. Much of computing is concerned with the latter and with text manipulation. In the example that follows we show how the ideas we have developed can be extended to this wider range of problem. Basically some sensible notational conventions have to be introduced.

Fig. 3.4. Square root program with assertions.

```
-- {N >= 0}
R := 0;
declare
    S, T: INTEGER := 1;
begin
    while -- {(T = 2 * R + 1) ∧ (S = (R + 1)²) ∧ (R² <= N) ∧ (R >= 0)}
                S <= N loop
        R := R + 1;
        T := T + 2;
        S := S + T;
    end loop;
end;
-- {R² <= N < (R + 1)² ∧ (R >= 0)}
```

Example 3.3.3b   Text processing

Write and verify a program to replace all occurrences of the underline character by a space. The data will take the form of a sequence of characters (which does not include #) terminated by #.

The required program is of the form

```
declare
      C: CHARACTER;
begin
      loop
          GET (C);
          exit when C = '#';
          if C = '_' then
              C := ' ';
          end if;
          PUT (C);
      end loop;
end;
```

The invariants we introduce must include mention of the current nature of the input, the nature of the output, and so on. Let us consider the input. We are told that this takes the form of a sequence of characters termined by # – it can be represented then as $C_1 C_2 \ldots C\#$. At any stage of the computation some text will have been absorbed and some text will remain (still to be read). The former we denote by A, the latter by R. We note that concatenating A and R produces I, the total input. Thus

$$A \& R = I$$

Initially we know that

$A = \langle \rangle$, the empty sequence of characters

and

$R = I$, the total input.

The effect of an instruction

$GET (C);$

where C is of type *CHARACTER* is as follows:

$A := A \& C;$ - - C is added to the right hand end of what has been
                  - - absorbed

$R := C \backslash R;$ - - C is removed from the left hand end of what remains
                  - - to be read.

It is still the case that

$A \& R = I.$

Essentially this is an invariant.

When the reading process encounters the $'\#'$ character a special situation develops. We have been told that this is the last character of the input. Consequently

$$R := '\#'\backslash R;$$

has the effect of producing the empty sequence in R. Since $A \& R = I$ we can deduce that $A = I$, i.e. all the input has been absorbed.

Now let us consider the output. For the purposes of this example we can again consider this to be a sequence of characters; newlines will merely appear as carriage return followed by line feed. Initially the output O is empty, i.e. in effect

$$O = \langle\,\rangle.$$

The effect of the instruction

$$PUT\,(C);$$

where C is of type $CHARACTER$ is to cause, in effect,

$$O := O \& C;$$

i.e. the character is added to the right hand end of the sequence of characters already printed.

We now return to the problem of verifying the program in example 3.3.3b. We introduce some auxiliary notation: let $ED(S)$ denote the fact that the string or sequence of characters S has been edited – in this context all underline symbols have been replaced by spaces. Then due to the nature of the editing ED has the property that if A and B are two arbitrary sequences of characters then

$$ED(A \& B) = ED(A) \& ED(B).$$

A proof of correctness can now be based on the following

$$- - \{(A = \langle\,\rangle) \wedge (R = I) \wedge (O = \langle\,\rangle)\}$$

declare

      $C: CHARACTER;$

begin

      loop $- - \{O = ED(A)\}$

          $GET\,(C);$

          exit when $C = '\#';$

          if $C = '\,\underline{\ }\,'$ **then**

            $C := '\,\,';$

          end if;

          $PUT\,(C);$

      end loop;

end;

$$- - \{(A = I) \wedge (R = \langle\,\rangle) \wedge (O = ED(I))\}$$

Note that the conditional contained within the loop essentially performs

$$C := ED(C);$$

The usual processes of back substitution and symbolic execution can be applied in the customary way.

In other situations involving text manipulation it may be necessary to introduce a different form of notation. The ideas outlined above should be of assistance.

Other kinds of programs involving input and output may make use, for example, of sequences of integers of a particular size or terminated in some way. Again the ideas outlined above should act as a guide to what is possible.

3.3.4 The problem of finding invariants

It has been remarked that there is often substantial difficulty associated with the problem of finding appropriate invariants to accompany proofs of partial correctness. We have already looked at some simple examples and deduced invariants by tracing programs and looking for the interrelationships between the variables. This is one possible strategy but it is rather naive. Below we look at some alternative strategies.

First we make two important remarks. In what follows the reader should not expect to find any ready-made recipe for finding invariants. Indeed there are sound theoretical reasons why it is in general impossible to provide such a recipe. We shall provide instead a set of possible approaches to the problem of discovering invariants. In a particular case all, some or none of the techniques indicated may be relevant.

The second remark concerns the whole practice of looking for invariants at all. When a program is first written the programmer will be aware of what technique he is using and should be able to give good reasons why his program works. He should be ideally placed to specify the invariants. Indeed modern ideas on programming suggest that program verification and program construction should progress hand-in-hand. If this happens the problem of choosing invariants all but disappears. We look more closely at this in chapter 9. In the meantime we proceed on the assumption that we have to prove the correctness of programs which have somehow been produced, perhaps by others; it is important to develop an understanding of the nature and role of invariants.

How then can we choose invariants? As a loop is executed the values of certain variables change. It often happens that these values can be expressed in a convenient form as a function of the number of times the statements of the loop have been performed. If n denotes the value of the control variable – also called the control constant, the loop parameter, the trip count, etc. – we use $Y(n)$ to denote the value of the variable Y at the start of the $(n+1)$st circuit of the loop. We assume that n is initialised to 0 immediately prior to each execution of the loop. (It is also possible to assume that these control variables are initialised at the start of the program, but this tends to be less convenient.) So $Y(0)$ denotes the initial value of Y prior to the start of the loop.

It is usually a simple matter to express $Y(n)$ in terms of $Y(n-1)$, subject of course to the provision that the loop will be executed for that value of n. Subject, then, to some path condition, $Y(n)$ can often be expressed in terms of $Y(n-1)$. Such an iterative formula together with our initial value of $Y(0)$ is often sufficient to allow the program verifier to deduce a convenient formula for $Y(n)$ as a function of n. If such a formula can be found for all relevant variables then a great deal will have been achieved. Elimination of n from some or all of these formulae and replacing each $Y(n)$ by Y will provide invariants involving just the variables of the program.

Another source of invariants is the placing of bounds on the values of variables. Often it is known that variables do not exceed certain upper or lower bounds and these restrictions can be incorporated into assertions. Alone they do not usually provide a sufficiently complete or powerful invariant but they are often extremely valuable.

Example 3.3.4a   Finding invariants

Consider the piece of program given in figure 3.5. This is intended to find the quotient Q and the remainder R obtained by dividing the integer N (numerator) by the integer D (denominator).

If we use the previous notation and ideas then we can say that, subject to the loop being executed sufficiently often,

$$Q(0) = 0 \text{ and for all } n > 0, \quad Q(n) = Q(n-1) + 1$$
$$R(0) = N \text{ and for all } n > 0, \quad R(n) = R(n-1) - D.$$

These two sets of equations provide, for all $n \geq 0$,

$$Q(n) = n \quad \text{and} \quad R(n) = N - n * D$$

Eliminating n then gives

$$R(n) = N - Q(n) * D$$

i.e.

$$R = N - Q * D$$

This is a loop invariant. Unfortunately it is not sufficiently powerful to provide a proof of correctness. If the reader attempts a proof using this he will fail. The invariant can be strengthened by adding the information that the value of R remains non-negative. Thus a suitable invariant is

$$(R = N - Q * D) \wedge (R >= 0)$$

Fig. 3.5. Quotient and remainder program.

```
--{N >= 0 ∧ D > 0}
Q := 0; R := N;
while R >= D loop
    Q := Q + 1;
    R := R - D;
end loop;
--{(N = Q * D + R) ∧ (0 <= R < D)}
```

We now make some further comments about the problem of finding suitable invariants. These will be of a less formal nature and will tend to provide a set of heuristics by which invariants might be found. We begin by noting that if it is clear that a particular predicate is true at some point on a loop then back substitution will produce an equivalent assertion at a given cutpoint. This may produce a component of the required invariant or even the required invariant itself.

In the kind of programs we have been dealing with in this chapter there is often a strong relationship between the output or final assertion and the invariant associated with a loop. By dragging the final assertion back through the program to the loop (and doing back substitution in the process) some hint might be obtained regarding the nature of the loop invariant.

To illustrate the above idea consider again the program of figure 3.5. We have to deduce some invariant which is true immediately after the **while**. Certainly

$$(R < D) \supset [(N = Q * D + R) \wedge (0 <= R < D)]$$

must be true. Put another way

$$(R \geqslant D) \vee [(N = Q * D + R) \wedge (0 <= R < D)]$$

In some sense this can be regarded as an initial approximation to the choice of invariant. A sensible assertion can be obtained by dropping some of the terms from this. Indeed

$$(N = Q * D + R) \wedge (R >= 0)$$

is an adequate choice.

Let us know look at another example.

Example 3.3.4b   Finding invariants
The piece of program given in figure 3.6 is intended to evaluate N^M and place this result in R. Two temporary variables P and D are employed. P accumulates powers of N and D contains integer division of M by powers of 2.

Fig. 3.6. Exponentiation program.

```
--{M >= 0}
R := 1;
declare
    P: INTEGER := N;
    D: INTEGER := M;
begin
    while D /= 0 loop
        if D mod 2 = 1 then
            R := R * P;
        end if;
        P := P * P; D := D/2;
    end loop;
end;
--{R = N^M}
```

Employing the earlier ideas we obtain

$$P(0) = N \quad \text{and} \quad P(n) = P(n-1)^2$$
$$D(0) = M \quad \text{and}$$
$$D(n-1) = 2 * D(n) + \textbf{if } D(n-1) \textbf{ mod } 2 = 1 \textbf{ then } 1 \textbf{ else } 0 \textbf{ end if}$$
$$R(0) = 1 \quad \text{and}$$
$$R(n) = R(n-1) * \textbf{if } D(n-1) \textbf{ mod } 2 = 1 \textbf{ then } P(n-1) \textbf{ else } 1 \textbf{ end if}$$

Ideally we would like to remove the conditionals involved in the expressions for D and R. The usual mathematical trick required to deal with the situation caused by the 1 and 0 in the first conditional and the $D(n-1)$ and 1 in the second conditional is to use D as an exponent. Thus

$$P(n-1)^{D(n-1)} = P(n-1)^{2D(n)} * \textbf{if } D(n-1) \textbf{ mod } 2 = 1$$
$$\textbf{then } P(n-1) \textbf{ else } 1 \textbf{ end if}$$

Now eliminate the conditional using the iterative formula for $R(n)$. This together with the fact that

$$P(n) = P(n-1)^2$$

produces

$$R(n) * P(n)^{D(n)} = R(n-1) * P(n-1)^{D(n-1)}$$

i.e. $R * P^D$ remains unaltered on each circuit of the loop. By inspecting its initial value we obtain the fact that

$$R * P^D = N^M$$

is a loop invariant. The proof of partial correctness can now be given.

We note that if we consider the variables present in assertions then in all the examples we have examined so far these variables will be in scope. Indeed any variable which is altered within a loop must be present, otherwise the invariant is an incomplete description of what is currently happening within the loop. However there are cases where it is convenient to introduce auxiliary variables. In figure 3.7 we give a program which simulates hardware integer division. In this program the identifiers N (numerator), D (denominator), Q (quotient), R (remainder), P (power of 2) and DS (denominator shifted) are chosen to reflect the roles of the variables. Note the use of n in the loop invariants and the existential quantifier $\exists$ meaning 'there exists'; these are used to indicate that P is some non-negative power of 2. Auxiliary variables such as this n can often be viewed as hidden counters which are incremented by 1 on each circuit of the loop. We shall have more to say about these in section 3.4.3.

In general, various strategies can be outlined assuming either an initial approximation to the predicate obtained by back substitution from the output predicate or approximations obtained by the methods in the earlier part of the section.

(*a*) Convert the approximation to the form

$$a_1 \vee a_2 \vee \ldots \vee a_n$$

Omit some of the terms, typically those that cause exit from the loop, and thereby obtain another approximation. Look initially at the a_i themselves.

(b) Convert the approximation to the form

$$a_1 \wedge a_2 \wedge \ldots \wedge a_n$$

Check whether each a_i in turn remains unaltered after one circuit of the loop. If so, use these a_i in obtaining a better approximation to the required assertion.

Other strategies which can be applied include simplification of logical expressions together with tricks exemplified by the following:

(c) Replace $\{y_1 = 0 \wedge y_2 = y_3 y_4\}$

by $\qquad \{y_2 = y_3 y_4 + k y_1\}$

or by $\quad \{y_2 = y_3 y_4 (k^{y_1})\}$

or by $\quad \{y_2 (k^{y_1}) = y_3 y_4\}$

The quantity k has to be chosen in some suitable way which will depend on the particular problem. Similar tricks can be applied when $y_1 = 1$ appears; multiply both sides of an equality by 1.

To illustrate the applicability of one of these techniques take the program and accompanying input and output assertions of figure 3.6. Dragging the output assertion back to the loop produces

$$R = N^M.$$

Unfortunately this is inadequate; it is not in general true the first time control

Fig. 3.7. Hardware integer division program.

```
-- {N >= 0 ∧ D > 0}
declare
        R: INTEGER := N;
        DS: INTEGER := D;
        P: INTEGER := 1;
        Q: INTEGER := 0;
begin
        while -- {(DS = D * P) ∧ (R >= 0) ∧ (DS > 0) ∧ ∃ n[n >= 0 ∧ P = 2ⁿ]}
            R > DS loop
            DS := DS * 2;
            P := P * 2;
        end loop;
        loop if R >= DS then
                R := R - DS;
                Q := Q + P;
            end if;
            -- {(DS = D * P) ∧ (R >= 0) ∧ (DS > 0) ∧ (R < DS) ∧
            --          (N = Q * D + R) ∧ ∃ n[n >= 0 ∧ P = 2ⁿ]}
            exit when P = 1;
            DS := DS/2;
            P := P/2;
        end loop;
end;
-- {(N = Q * D + R) ∧ (0 <= R < D)}
```

reaches **while**. However if both sides of this equality are multiplied by a suitable quantity the required assertion is obtained, namely

$$(R(P^D) = N^M) \wedge (D >= 0).$$

Somewhat similar to invariants obtained by these techniques are invariants obtained from path conditions. If pc_1, pc_2, etc. represent path conditions associated with the various routes through a piece of program then

$$pc_1 \vee pc_2 \vee \ldots$$

will represent an invariant. These separate path conditions may themselves be augmented with information about the bounds on variables as they take the separate routes.

3.4 Total correctness

We now turn our attention to the problem of proving total correctness. This can be ensured if we show partial correctness and also termination of a program.

The programs of chapter 2 were of such a simple nature that no proof of termination was necessary. The possibility of non-termination is caused by backward jumps and while loops of the kind we have been considering. It is worth remarking that, if a program is written in a high level language using only a carefully chosen set of looping mechanisms, termination can always be guaranteed. This limited set must be restricted in certain ways. There can be no backward jumps, only forward jumps and there can be no recursion. In terms of Ada, loop statements of the kind

> **loop**
>   sequence_of_statements;
> **end loop**;

and

> **while** condition **loop**
>   sequence_of_statements;
> **end loop**;

must be excluded. The **for** version of the loop statement can be used. Note however that there are certain aspects of its design which allow us to be sure that termination will occur: the increment is always in discrete non-zero steps, the range is calculated only once and the loop parameter is regarded as a constant within the loop itself.

Let us begin the discussion of total correctness then by examining correctness proofs of programs which make use of the **for** version of the loop statement.

3.4.1 Using the for

We remarked earlier that it would have been better to write the program for the factorial function using the **for** version of the loop statement. There would have been various advantages: the loop parameter would have been automatically declared, initialised, incremented and kept within the correct range; furthermore, it would have been protected from various kinds of erroneous use such as attempts to alter its value within the loop, or attempts to access it outside the loop; finally we would know that the program would terminate. A better program is therefore given in figure 3.8.

The proof of correctness of this new program is in essence the same as before. However we now know that a proof of partial correctness will guarantee the total correctness of the program since no indefinite looping can occur with this version of the loop statement.

As before we require a loop invariant – which we now know to be

$$(N >= 0) \wedge (M >= 0) \wedge (F = M!)$$

However there is a slight difficulty in deciding which cutpoint to choose. Unfortunately there is no point which corresponds to the point C chosen earlier. To overcome this we introduce two cutpoints, one at the start and the other at the end of the loop. We now introduce assertions as shown in figure 3.9. The two loop invariants are essentially different versions of the very same assertion we used earlier. The first of these is obtained from the second by back substitution. The proof of (partial) correctness can now be given in the usual way. However, the verification process must recognise the fact that it can happen that the loop is not entered. In the factorial example this happens if $N = 0$. Consequently there is a kind of conditional hidden at the start of the loop. The correctness proof more accurately reflects a structure of the form given in figure 3.10.

The general approach to dealing with for loops is similar. The program verifier must be careful to check that the statements of the loop are executed

Fig. 3.8.
```
F := 1;
for M in 1 .. N loop
    F := F * M;
end loop;
```

Fig. 3.9.
```
- - {N >= 0}
F := 1;
for M in 1 .. N loop
    - - {(N >= 0) ∧ (M − 1 >= 0) ∧ (F = (M − 1)!)}
    F := F * M;
    - - {(N >= 0) ∧ (M − 1 >= 0) ∧ (F = M!)}
end loop;
- - {F = N!}
```

Fig. 3.10.
```
F := 1;
if N >= 1 then
    for M in 1 .. N loop
        F := F * M;
    end loop;
end if;
```

at least once. It is often advisable to use two related invariants, one at the start of the loop, the other at the end; in many cases the invariant at the end suffices; when the loop parameter M runs up through a range the first invariant is obtained from the second, essentially by back substitution. On leaving the loop by exhausting the range the value of M will be equal to the upper bound of the range. Analogous situations arise when the loop parameter runs down through a range.

3.4.2 The method of well-founded sets

We now turn our attention to the problem of proving the total correctness of programs which make use of more general forms of loop statement. We already know how to prove partial correctness. We now examine ways of showing that a program also terminates. We begin by looking at the method of well-founded sets.

In employing this method to prove that a program terminates, the program verifier typically looks for a variable whose values are never negative. Yet on each circuit of the loop the values decrease and never become negative. Since this process cannot go on for ever termination is guaranteed.

The method of well-founded sets is more general than the above description might imply. Rather than look at the values of a single variable a more general function can be employed. Rather than assume the values of the function are always non-negative integers, values belonging to a set which has no infinite decreasing sequence can be used; such a set is called a *well-founded set*. To encompass the full generality of the situation we begin with some definitions which define order and this is necessary in talking about decreasing sequences.

Definition

A partially ordered set is defined to be a non-empty set together with a relation $<$; that relation possesses certain properties:

(i) It is transitive, i.e. if $a < b$ and $b < c$ then $a < c$.
(ii) It is asymmetric, i.e. if $a < b$ this implies $\neg (b < a)$.
(iii) It is irreflexive, i.e. $\neg (a < a)$ for all a in a set.

$<$ can be read as 'precedes' and $\not<$ as 'does not precede'. The definition is based on the usual 'less than' ordering.

Example 3.4.2a Partially ordered sets

(i) The set of non-negative integers with the usual 'less than' relation.
(ii) The set of strings of characters of finite length together with a relation $<$ which is defined as follows: $a < b$ provided that both a and b are different but string b starts with string a.

The partially ordered sets themselves are not of most interest in our application to proving program termination. We are interested in a special kind of partially ordered set, a well-founded set.

Definition
A *well-founded set* is a partially ordered set which contains no infinite decreasing sequence. The notion of decreasing is defined in terms of the partial order.

Example 3.4.2b   *Well-founded sets*
(i) The examples of partially ordered sets given above are well-founded.
(ii) The set of integers with the usual 'less than' ordering is not well-founded.

Let us consider then how these ideas should be applied to the problem of proving that a program terminates. Of course, there is a problem only if there are certain kinds of loops in the program. So let us take the program of figure 3.11.

Consider the successive values of Y immediately after **while**. These decrease each time round the loop. So one might hope to be able to show that successive values of Y belong to a well-founded set; in this case the well-founded set is just the set of non-negative integers with the usual ordering. We could then say that there is no infinite decreasing sequence and therefore the loop cannot be executed an infinite number of times. Therefore it must be executed just a finite number of times and so eventually the test must be true and the program then halts.

The successive values of Y are just $X, X-1, X-2, \ldots$ and these certainly decrease. But it would be wrong to stipulate that each $X-n$, for any $n \geqslant 0$, belongs to the set of non-negative integers, our well-founded set. Consequently our original idea has to be modified.

The difficulty encountered above stems from the fact that we tried to show that all $X-n$ are non-negative. Now the program is not going to be executed in such a way that Y spans all possible values of $X-n$. This suggests a solution to our problem. We introduce an assertion which in some sense characterises the computation and yet limits the values of Y to be considered. A suitable such predicate would be

$$Y >= 0.$$

Fig. 3.11.

```
- - {X > 0}
Y := X;
while Y /= 0 loop
        - - some calculation not altering Y;
        Y := Y - 1;
end loop;
```

This would then ensure that all values of Y are non-negative and consequently all its values will belong to a well-founded set.

So far we have looked at just one particular kind of loop but it hints at a general approach to proving the termination of programs containing loops. We take the loop, cut it and associate with the cutpoint both a function and a predicate; both of these may refer to inputs or to the program variables. As the program progresses the successive values of the function should decrease each time round the loop. Moreover the predicate should be true each time the cutpoint is passed and its truth should imply that the value of the function belongs to a well-founded set.

The same general principles apply to programs involving several loops. Each separate loop must be cut and with each cutpoint there should be an associated function and predicate having the properties described above. (In fact, a loop could have several cutpoints each with associated functions and predicates; the above remarks have then to be modified in a straightforward way.)

This method of proving program termination is, for obvious reasons, called the *method of well-founded sets*.

To illustrate a proof that a program terminates we look at the program in figure 3.2 designed to calculate the factorial function. We have already shown that this program is partially correct and this combined with the proof that follows means that the program is totally correct.

We choose as the cutpoint the position immediately following the test $M/=N$ in figure 3.2 and make use of

- (a) the well-founded set consisting of the non-negative integers with the usual 'less than' ordering
- (b) the function u defined by

$$u(N;M,F) = N - M$$

- (c) the predicate q defined by

$$q(N;M,F) = 0 <= M <= N \quad \text{or equivalently } M \text{ in } 0 .. N$$

There are now several points to be checked.

- (i) q delivers *TRUE* each time the cutpoint is passed. Thus we must verify that the input assertion implies the truth of $q(N;M,F)$ for appropriate N, M, F. We must also check that if $q(N;M,F)$ is true and the loop is executed then $q(N;M,F)$ will still be true. Both these facts can be checked in the usual way by using either back substitution or symbolic execution.
- (ii) The truth of $q(N;M,F)$ implies that $u(N;M,F)$ belongs to our well-founded set. This is readily verified.
- (iii) The function decreases in value each time round the loop. This is called the *termination condition* and in verifying this the truth of the predicate

may be assumed. Again, of course, decreasing is defined in terms of the relation associated with the underlying well-founded set. This is also readily checked.

These remarks then show how the method of well-founded sets is applied in practice.

Example 3.4.2c   Method of well-founded sets
In the program of figure 3.3 choose for the cutpoint the well-founded set consisting of the non-negative integers with the usual ordering together with

the predicate: $R^2 <= N$
the function: $N - R^2$.

Termination of the program is then readily checked.

In attempting to prove termination, then, we must associate both a function and a predicate with cutpoints on loops. The methods for choosing invariants – outlined in section 3.3.4 – help with the latter task. In fact much simpler predicates are often adequate for this purpose. To choose suitable functions it often suffices to look at

the individual program variables themselves,
linear combinations of the program and input variables,
more complex functions of these variables (only if the previous methods fail).

3.4.3   The use of counters

We have seen one method of proving termination. Another approach, the *loop approach*, attempts to prove termination by associating with each loop a counter which is incremented by 1 on each circuit of the loop. Note the relationship between these remarks and the remarks made in section 3.3.4 on finding invariants. If these counters can be shown to be bounded from above, termination can be guaranteed.

The method of using counters can be regarded as a special case of the method of well-founded sets. The well-founded set is just the set of non-negative integers; the appropriate function is just

upper_bound − counter

and the predicate is

$0 <= counter <= upper\_bound$.

But on the other hand the loop approach to proving termination does rely on the fact that the loops in the program can easily be established and are nested in such a way that there is only one entrance to the loop.

The use of counters offers advantages other than ease of proving termination. Their use sometimes facilitates proofs of correctness of other properties of programs, e.g. their efficiency. This stems from the fact that the various program variables can often be expressed in a relatively simple way as functions of the counters. We saw this earlier in section 3.3.4.

To demonstrate the use of the loop approach let us consider the program of figure 3.6. In figure 3.12 this program is reproduced but modified to include in comments mention of the counter n.

By tracing the program we can deduce that on successive circuits of the loop we obtain at the **while**:

n	P	D
0	N	M
1	N^2	$M \div 2$
2	N^4	$M \div 4$
3	N^8	$M \div 8$
. . .	. . .	. . .

It can readily be shown by induction on n that

$$P = N^{(2^n)} \quad \text{and} \quad D = M/(2^n)$$

The loop of the program will be executed until such time as $D = 0$, i.e.

$$M/(2^n) = 0$$

and this happens as soon as

$$2^n > M, \text{ that is } n > \log_2 M.$$

Thus n cannot become infinitely large and the program must therefore terminate.

Example 3.4.3a   Using counters

The program of figure 3.3 could be modified so as to insert counters. On the other hand, R acts as a counter. At the start R is initialised to 0 and on

Fig. 3.12.

```
--{M >= 0}
R := 1;
declare
        P: INTEGER := N;
        D: INTEGER := M;
    --n: INTEGER := 0;
begin
     while D /= 0 loop
          if D mod 2 = 1 then
            R := R * P;
          end if;
          P := P * P; D := D/2;
          --n := n + 1;
        end loop;
end;
-- {R = N^M}
```

54

each circuit of the loop is increased by 1. The earlier proof has demonstrated that R is bounded from above.

3.4.4   The exit approach

The main use of this technique is to show that a program is not totally correct basically because it may never terminate. The conditions under which exit from a loop occurs can be specified by means of a suitable predicate using the values of the program and input variables at some cutpoint on the loop. If it can be shown that there is one loop of a program which at some stage will be executed and yet for certain values of the inputs its exit condition can never be satisfied then we will have shown that the program is not totally correct. For termination, though it may usually take place, is not guaranteed.

We can demonstrate the exit approach with a simple example. Take the factorial program of figure 3.1 and suppose the input predicate places no restrictions on the range of values N, i.e. suppose $\phi(N)$: $TRUE$. Then for $N < 0$ it can be shown that

$$M \ /= N$$

is always true at the **while**. Under these circumstances the exit condition, namely $M = N$, is never satisfied and so the program never terminates.

3.5   Some observations

Until now the tasks of proving partial correctness and termination have been regarded as separate. But the reader may have noted certain similarities in the two processes. There are techniques which can be used for proving either total or partial correctness sometimes in just one step.

In section 3.3.4 we made one very important observation which is worth repeating. It is that ideally program verification and program construction should proceed hand-in-hand. Much of what we shall do will be directed towards this end.

Exercises for chapter 3

1. Give a complete proof of the partial correctness of the program discussed in section 3.3.3.
   Show how this can be accomplished using both back substitution and symbolic execution.
   Can termination of this program be simply established?

2. Provide a proof of the total correctness of the program discussed in example 3.3.4*a*.

3. Give a complete proof of the total correctness of the program discussed in example 3.3.4*b*.

4. Complete the proof of partial correctness of the hardware integer division program in figure 3.7.

5. Prove the total correctness of the following program segments with respect to the stated assertions (all identifiers represent integer variables).

(a) -- $\{X2 >= 0\}$

    declare

        $Y1: INTEGER := 0;$

        $Y2: INTEGER := X2;$

    begin

        while $Y2 /= 0$ **loop**

            $Y1 := X1 + Y1;$

            $Y2 := Y2 - 1;$

        end loop;

        $Z := Y1;$

    end;

    -- $\{Z = X1 * X2\}$

(b) -- $\{X2 >= 0\}$

    declare

        $Y1: INTEGER := 1;$

        $Y2: INTEGER := X2;$

    begin

        while $Y2 /= 0$ **loop**

            $Y1 := X1 * Y1;$

            $Y2 := Y2 - 1;$

        end loop;

        $Z := Y1;$

    end;

    -- $\{Z = X1 ** X2\}$

6. Verify that the following program segment places in Z the largest power of 2 which divides the positive integer X.

    declare

        $Y1: INTEGER := X1;$

        $Y2: INTEGER := 0;$

    begin

        while $Y1$ **mod** $2 = 0$ **loop**

            $Y1 := Y1/2;$

            $Y2 := Y2 + 1;$

        end loop;

        $Z := Y2;$

    end;

7. A piece of text is held in a compact form: both commas and full-stops have no spaces following them. Design and verify the correctness of a piece of program to print out the text replacing (i) each comma by a comma followed by a space and (ii) each full-stop by a full-stop followed by two spaces. Assume the existence of some suitable terminator.

8. In the following program all the variables are of type $INTEGER$:

    -- $\{(X1 >= 0) \land (X2 >= 0)\}$

```
declare
    Y1: INTEGER := X1;
    Y2: INTEGER := X2;
    Y: INTEGER;
begin
    if Y2 > Y1 then
        Y := Y1;
        Y1 := Y2;
        Y2 := Y;
    end if;
    while Y2 /= 0 loop
        Y1 := Y1 − 1;
        Y2 := Y2 − 1;
    end loop;
end;
Z := Y1;
-- {Z = ABS(X1 − X2)}
```

Establish the total correctness of this program segment.

9. Write and verify the correctness of a piece of program to remove all commentary from a piece of text which is supplied as data. Comments are enclosed by # and # (these marks are part of the commentary) and some suitable marker terminates the text.

10. Design and verify pieces of program to accomplish the following tasks, all of which have data consisting of a set of positive integers terminated by a negative number:

   (a) find the smallest of the set,
   (b) find the top two elements,
   (c) find the sum of the elements,
   (d) find the largest difference between two consecutive items.

11. The following piece of program is intended to produce in Z the highest common factor of M and N

```
-- {(M > 0) ∧ (N > 0)}
declare
    A: INTEGER := M;
    B: INTEGER := N;
begin
    while A /= B loop
        if A > B then
            A := A − B;
        else
            B := B − A;
        end if;
    end loop;
    Z := A;
end;
--{Z = hcf(M,N)}
```

Establish the total correctness of this program.

12. Write and verify a program which tests if a given positive integer is prime.

13. Design and verify the correctness of a piece of program which accepts text containing capital letters but no small letters and replaces all capitals by smalls except those occurring at the start of sentences. Assume the existence of some suitable terminator for the data.

14. Consider the following piece of program which assumes the existence of four initialised integer variables $X1, X2, X3$ and $X4$ and two other integer variables $Z1$ and $Z2$:

```
-- {(X1 > 0) ∧ (X2 > 0)}
declare
    Y1, Y4: INTEGER := X1;
    Y2, Y3: INTEGER := X2;
begin
    while Y1 /= Y2 loop
        if Y1 > Y2 then
            Y1 := Y1 - Y2;
            Y4 := Y3 + Y4;
        else
            Y2 := Y2 - Y1;
            Y3 := Y3 + Y4;
        end if;
    end loop;
    Z1 := (Y1 + Y2)/2;
    Z2 := (Y3 + Y4)/2;
    -- {(Z1 = hcf(X1, X2)) ∧ (Z2 = lcm(X1, X2))}
```

Here hcf and lcm refer to the highest common factor and the lowest common multiple respectively.

Verify the total correctness of this program.

The next four questions all refer to the program segment outlined in figure 3.13. This calculates what is known as McCarthy's 91-function.

Fig. 3.13.

```
-- {TRUE}
declare
    Y1: INTEGER := X;
    Y2: INTEGER := 1;
begin
    loop
        if Y1 <= 100 then
            Y1 := Y1 + 11;
            Y2 := Y2 + 1;
        elsif Y2 = 1 then
            Z := Y1 - 10;
            exit;
        else
            Y1 := Y1 - 10;
            Y2 := Y2 - 1;
        end if;
    end loop;
end;
-- {Z = if X > 101 then X - 10 else 91 end if}
```

15. Is (this not legal in Ada but the intention should be clear)

$(Y1 = $ **if** $Y1 > 100$ **then** $Y1 - 10$ **else** $Y1 + 11$ **end if**$) \wedge (Y2 >= 1)$

a suitable invariant which is true immediately after the first occurrence of the loop? Give reasons for your answer.

16. Assume an input predicate of $X \leq 101$. By looking at the possible ranges of values of $Y1$ when $Y2 > 1$ and when $Y2 = 1$ deduce a suitable loop invariant. Prove the partial correctness of the program.

17. Prove the termination of the program by the method of well-founded sets. Make use of a function of the form

$\alpha * Y1 + \beta * Y2 + \gamma$.

α, β and γ should be chosen in such a way that on each circuit of the loop the value of the function decreases yet remains non-negative.

18. If the assignment

$Y1 := Y1 = 10;$

is replaced by the assignment

$Y1 := Y1 - 11;$

show that the resulting program need not terminate.

19. See figure 3.14, a modified version of figure 3.13. Express $Y1$ and $Y2$ in terms of the counters I and J. Deduce a lower bound for $Y1$ in terms of N and X. Use this to prove termination of the program.

20. In some programming languages (such as Ada) character strings or string denotations appear within a pair of quote symbols such as $"$ and $"$.

Fig. 3.14.

```
declare
      Y1: INTEGER := X;
      Y2: INTEGER := 1;
   --I, J, N: INTEGER := 0;
begin
   -- I := 0;
   -- J := 0;
   -- N := 0;
      loop
         --N := N + 1;
         if Y1 <= 100 then
            Y1 := Y1 + 11;
            Y2 := Y2 + 1;
         --I := I + 1;
         elsif Y2 = 1 then
               Z := Y1 - 10;
               exit;
         else
               Y1 := Y1 - 10;
               Y2 := Y2 - 1;
         --J := J + 1;
         end if;
      end loop;
end;
```

59

Within these quotes the quote symbol itself can appear as $''$. Write a program which accepts such a string denotation and outputs the string of characters it denotes. For example, given

$$"abc""def""""""$$

the output should be

$$abc"def""$$

Verify the correctness of your program.

21. Prove the total correctness of the following program designed to calculate the product of the two non-negative integers $X1$ and $X2$ by essentially shifting, adding and subtracting

```
--{(X1 >= 0) ∧ (X2 >= 0)}
declare
      Y1: INTEGER := X1;
      Y2: INTEGER := X2;
      Y3: INTEGER := 0;
begin
      while Y2 /= 0 loop
            while Y2 mod 2 = 0 loop
                  Y1 := 2 * Y1;
                  Y2 := Y2/2;
            end loop;
            Y2 := Y2 - 1;
            Y3 := Y3 + X1;
      end loop;
      Z := Y3;
end;
--{Z = X1 * X2}
```

22. Verify the total correctness of the following program given that both B and C are positive integers

```
--{(B > 0) ∧ (C > 0)}
declare
      Y1: INTEGER := X;
      Y2: INTEGER := C;
begin
      loop
            while Y1 <= A loop
                  Y1 := Y1 + B + C;
                  Y2 := Y2 + C;
            end loop;
            exit when Y2 = C;
            Y1 := Y1 - B;
            Y2 := Y2 - C;
      end loop;
      Z := Y1 - B;
end;
--{Z = if X > A then X - B else A - B + C - (A - X) mod C
--                                                    end if}
```

60

23. Prove the total correctness of the program below, intended to evaluate the highest common factor of the two positive integers $X1$ and $X2$:

```
-- {(X1 > 0) ∧ (X2 > 0)}
declare
      Y1: INTEGER := X1;
      Y2: INTEGER := X2;
      K, T: INTEGER;
begin
      K := 0;
      while (Y1 mod 2 = 0) and (Y2 mod 2 = 0) loop
            Y1 := Y1/2;
            Y2 := Y2/2;
            K := K + 1;
      end loop;
      if Y1 mod 2 = 0 then
            T := Y1;
      else
            T := - Y2;
      end if;
      while T /= 0 loop
            while T mod 2 = 0 loop
                  T := T/2;
            end loop;
            if T > 0 then
                  Y1 := T;
            else
                  Y2 := - T;
            end if;
            T := Y1 - Y2;
      end loop;
      Z := Y1 * 2 ** K;
end;
-- {Z = hcf(X1, X2)}
```

4   INTRODUCTION TO AXIOMATICS

In this chapter we look for the first time at the axiomatic approach to the task of proving the correctness of computer programs. In chapter 1 it was pointed out that there is a certain similarity between proving the correctness of a computer program and proving the correctness of a geometric construction in mathematics. Just as the latter could be axiomatised so we shall demonstrate that the former can also be axiomatised.

Many benefits will accrue from this approach. We mention one of these specifically. In the process of designing suitable axioms it will become apparent that we are obtaining a method, albeit a very abstract method, of formally defining the semantics of a programming language, i.e. the meaning of the various constructs in the language.

In looking at the different aspects of axiomatisation there is a substantial danger in becoming deeply involved in strict sets of axioms, in very rigorous mathematical logic, and so on. It might seem that a study of the axioms for integers and reals should lead to a discussion of Peano's axioms and Dedekind cuts respectively. In a sense it should. But this book is not intended to contain a treatise on the foundations of mathematics. Consequently we shall assume that the reader understands the basic properties of the integers and the real numbers. We shall concentrate on the important differences which exist between numbers as they are manipulated within the computer and their mathematical counterparts. We shall reserve the more formal treatment for the discussion of the constructs in programming languages.

In this chapter we look at the axiomatics associated with the basic data types and with the elementary constructs in Ada. The constructs we discuss will be restricted to the set of constructs we have already introduced. In later chapters we look at other more advanced constructs in Ada.

4.1   Axioms for data types

Modern programming languages usually exhibit a wide variety of different data types. Starting from a set of simple or basic types which might include integers, reals, booleans and characters, it is usually possible to con-

62

struct more sophisticated types such as arrays, records or structures, and so on.

In this section we look at a typical selection of data types. We discuss the properties these can be expected to possess, including the basic elementary operations which will typically be defined on them. This has the effect of describing the basic rules of algebra which can be used in manipulating the predicates or assertions which are an essential part of a proof of correctness. The attributes associated with these basic types will later be employed in discussing the attributes of arrays, records, and so on.

The very term 'data type' tends to have different connotations when used in talking about different programming languages. The set of types available also varies from language to language as does the set of operations available for a given type, even a type such as *INTEGER*. Fortunately many modern programming languages provide a facility whereby a programmer can introduce his own types and his own set of operations associated with these types.

We shall look at the kind of axiomatics that might be provided for aspects of Ada and this is typical of many programming languages. The quantities associated with data types are referred to as *characteristics* and this term includes attributes, operators, certain functions, and so on. We shall mention only the basic set of characteristics and in keeping with the usual view of axiomatics as it is presented in mathematical logic this set will be minimal in some sense. In Ada there are mechanisms for defining other characteristics in terms of this basic set and an implementation of Ada can be expected to provide some of these.

We begin with a look at some of the simple data types provided in Ada. We then discuss the attributes these can be expected to possess. We concentrate on the machine- or implementation-independent characteristics and ignore the remainder.

In Ada real numbers of various kinds can be manipulated. There are floating-point numbers which are characterised by so many digits of accuracy; there are fixed-point numbers which are characterised by an absolute accuracy; there are even universal integers and reals which can be introduced by declarations such as

PI_BY_2:   **constant** $:= 3 \cdot 14159\_26536/2 \cdot 0$;
$THOUSAND$: **constant** $:= 1000$;

In the discussion that follows immediately, we shall tend to confine our attention to the floating-point numbers, basically because they are common and appear in such languages as Fortran, Algol 60, Algol 68 and Pascal. At a later stage we shall turn our attention to the fixed-point types.

4.1.1   Scalar types in Ada

In this section we recall and generalise remarks made about types in chapter 2.

The scalar types in Ada are typified by the fact that none of the values of a scalar type has any components or subparts. Moreover all such types possess an ordering. Scalar types include

reals: *SHORT_FLOAT, FLOAT, LONG_FLOAT*
integers: *SHORT_INTEGER, INTEGER, LONG_INTEGER*
characters: *CHARACTER*
booleans: *BOOLEAN*

together with other enumeration types. Certain subsets of the scalars merit special attention:

the reals and integers are collectively referred to as the numeric types, if we ignore the reals the remaining scalars are called the discrete types and these include the integers and the enumeration types.

Note that *SHORT_INTEGER* generally provides a smaller range of values than *INTEGER* and this in turn provides a smaller range of values than *LONG_INTEGER*. In the case of the reals the story is similar but both precision and range are involved.

The discrete types can be used for indexing arrays and for looping. Thus one form of the loop statement can be expressed (possibly with **reverse** included) as

for loop_parameter **in** discrete_range **loop** ...

where the discrete_range takes the form

simple_expression .. simple_expression

Each simple_expression is an ordinary expression which does not involve a comparison of any kind. Thus $M .. N$ describes the set of values which lie between M and N inclusive.

The appearance of an identifier after **for** acts as its declaration and it inherits its type from the nature of the discrete range. As mentioned earlier in chapter 3, the loop parameter is regarded as a constant within the loop body and the discrete range itself is evaluated only once, before the loop is executed.

The enumeration types are introduced in Ada by type declarations and are epitomised by

type *WEEK* **is** (*SUN, MON, TUE, WED, THU, FRI, SAT*);
type *HEX* **is** (*'A', 'B', 'C', 'D', 'E', 'F'*);
type *COMMAND* **is** (*CREATE, EDIT, LISTFILE, DELETE*);
type *OPCODE* **is** (*MOVE, ADD, SUB, INC, JMS, RT*);

The various items enclosed by round brackets are either identifiers or characters, possibly mixed (see type *CHARACTER* below). Both the booleans and the characters can be regarded as special cases of predefined enumeration types (see figure 4.1); type *CHARACTER* makes use of the standard ASCII character set.

Subtypes of the discrete types can be defined by the use of range constraints which are introduced by **range** and which select subsets in some sense. Thus

subtype *LETTER* **is** *CHARACTER* **range** *'A' .. 'Z'*;

i.e. a letter is any character which lies between $'A'$ and $'Z'$ inclusive. Similarly

> **subtype** *WORK_DAY* **is** *WEEK* **range** *MON* .. *FRI*;
> **subtype** *DUO* **is** *HEX* **range** $'A'$ .. $'B'$;

Carrying this idea slightly further yields such possibilities as

> **subtype** *PAGE_NUMBER* **is** *INTEGER* **range** 1 .. 354;

Corresponding subtype definitions for real numbers require an accuracy constraint which specifies in some way the precision of numbers. Thus

> **subtype** *INTERVAL* **is** *FLOAT* **digits** 6;

makes use of real floating-point numbers whose mantissa is correct to six decimal digits of accuracy. The accuracy constraint may be qualified by a range constraint, thus

> **subtype** *SMALL_INTERVAL* **is** *FLOAT* **digits** 6 **range** 0.0 .. 1.0;

The elements of a subtype can be acted upon by the same operations as the elements of the full type. Basically a value belongs to a subtype if it satisfies the range constraint which forms part of the definition of the subtype.

Let us now mention the possibility of derived type declarations. These allow the introduction of types which at the time of declaration inherit all their characteristics from another type. Thus

> **type** *CHAR* **is new** *CHARACTER*;
> **type** *MY_SMALL_INT* **is range** 1 .. 128;
> **type** *MY_SMALL_REAL* **is digits** 4 **range** 0.0 .. 1.0;

Fig. 4.1. The standard types *BOOLEAN* **and** *CHARACTER*.

type *BOOLEAN* **is** (*FALSE*, *TRUE*);

— The following characters comprise the standard ASCII character set.
— Character literals corresponding to control characters are not identifiers;
— They are indicated in lower case italics in this definition:

type *CHARACTER* **is**

(*nul*,	*soh*,	*stx*,	*etx*,	*eot*,	*enq*,	*ack*,	*bel*,
bs,	*ht*,	*lf*,	*vt*,	*ff*,	*cr*,	*so*,	*si*,
dle,	*dc1*,	*dc2*,	*dc3*,	*dc4*,	*nak*,	*syn*,	*etb*,
can,	*em*,	*sub*,	*esc*,	*fs*,	*gs*,	*rs*,	*us*,
$' '$,	$'!'$,	$'"'$,	$'\#'$,	$'\$'$,	$'\%'$,	$'\&'$,	$' \prime '$,
$'('$,	$')'$,	$'*'$,	$'+'$,	$','$,	$'-'$,	$'.'$,	$'/'$,
$'0'$,	$'1'$,	$'2'$,	$'3'$,	$'4'$,	$'5'$,	$'6'$,	$'7'$,
$'8'$,	$'9'$,	$':'$,	$';'$,	$'<'$,	$'='$,	$'>'$,	$'?'$,
$'@'$,	$'A'$,	$'B'$,	$'C'$,	$'D'$,	$'E'$,	$'F'$,	$'G'$,
$'H'$,	$'I'$,	$'J'$,	$'K'$,	$'L'$,	$'M'$,	$'N'$,	$'O'$,
$'P'$,	$'Q'$,	$'R'$,	$'S'$,	$'T'$,	$'U'$,	$'V'$,	$'W'$,
$'X'$,	$'Y'$,	$'Z'$,	$'['$,	$'\backslash'$,	$']'$,	$'\,\hat{}\,'$,	$'\_'$,
$'\,\grave{}\,'$,	$'a'$,	$'b'$,	$'c'$,	$'d'$,	$'e'$,	$'f'$,	$'g'$,
$'h'$,	$'i'$,	$'j'$,	$'k'$,	$'l'$,	$'m'$,	$'n'$,	$'o'$,
$'p'$,	$'q'$,	$'r'$,	$'s'$,	$'t'$,	$'u'$,	$'v'$,	$'w'$,
$'x'$,	$'y'$,	$'z'$,	$'\{'$,	$'|'$,	$'\}'$,	$'\sim'$,	*del*)

In each of these cases the new type inherits at the time of declaration all the properties or attributes from the type from which it is derived. The new derived type can later be given extra properties or attributes which distinguish it from the original type.

Types which are subtypes or derived types of *INTEGER*, *SHORT_INTEGER* or *LONG_INTEGER* we shall henceforth refer to as integer types. Similarly real types include the subtypes or derived types of *FLOAT*, *SHORT_FLOAT* or *LONG_FLOAT*.

In situations where there is likely to be confusion about the type of a quantity a qualifier can be used to make the situation clear. Thus if *HALT* appears in an enumeration of a set of operation codes of type *OPCODE* and also in an enumeration of a set of road signs of type *SIGN* then any situation can be made crystal clear by putting *OPCODE'(HALT)* or *SIGN'(HALT)* as appropriate. Qualifiers such as these can also be used in connection with derived types (where again there may be some ambiguity). Qualification is different from type conversion and the syntax of Ada highlights this.

> *Example 4.1.1a   Type conversion*
>
> (i) *FLOAT* (4) converts the integer 4 into floating-point format.
>
> (ii) *INTEGER* (4.7) produces the integer quantity closest to the stated real, i.e. the result is 5. Note that the inherent inaccuracy of real numbers makes discussion about 4.5, etc. fraught with danger.

Any type or subtype definitions in Ada introduce distinct types, even if the types are apparently identical, e.g. *LETTERA* and *LETTERB* as defined in

> **type** *LETTERA* **is** *CHARACTER* **range** *'A' .. 'B'*;
> **type** *LETTERB* **is** *CHARACTER* **range** *'A' .. 'B'*;

are different types. Also *X* and *Z* as declared in

> *X, Y: CHARACTER* **range** *'A' .. 'B'*;
> *Z: CHARACTER* **range** *'A' .. 'B'*;

are of different types.

All these types and subtypes can be used in declarations. The variety of possibilities is exemplified by the following:

> *Example 4.1.1b   On object declarations*
>
> (*a*) **type** *SWITCH* **is** (*OFF*, *ON*);
> *X, Y: SWITCH* := *OFF*;
> Here *X* and *Y* are two variables of the same common type *SWITCH* and both are initialised to *OFF*.
>
> (*b*) *N: INTEGER* **range** 0 .. 100 := 0;
> *N* is of integer type, initialised to 0 and constrained to be in the range 0 .. 100.

66

(c) X, Y: *FLOAT* **digits** 6;

X and Y are declared as variables capable of holding floating-point reals to six significant decimal figures of accuracy.

(d) *SUMMER_MONTH*: *MONTH* **range** *JUNE .. AUGUST*;

This assumes an obvious previous declaration of the type *MONTH*.

4.1.2 Attributes of scalar types

Let S be any discrete type or subtype. Then it is possible to imagine an (explicit or implicit) declaration of the kind

type S **is** $(s_0, s_1, \ldots, s_n)$;

The following axioms apply

1. $s_0, s_1, \ldots, s_n$ are distinct elements of S
2. these are the only elements of S
3. $\neg (s < s)$ for each $s = s_i$
4. $(s < t) \wedge (t < u) \supset (s < u)$ for each s, t, u in S
5. $s_i < s_{i+1}$ for each $i = 0, 1, \ldots, n - 1$
6. $S'FIRST = s_0$
7. $S'LAST = s_n$
8. s_i **in** S is true only for each $i = 0, 1, \ldots, n$.

These definitions define the first and last elements together with membership and the ordering implied by the enumeration. In the process the meaning of $<$ is supplied.

Given the above axioms it is now possible to define other useful operators in terms of $<$. Thus for any s and t in S

$s > t$ is equivalent to $t < s$

$s <= t$ is equivalent to $\neg (s > t)$

$s >= t$ is equivalent to $\neg (s < t)$

$s = t$ is equivalent to $(s >= t) \wedge (t >= s)$

$s /= t$ is equivalent to $\neg (s = t)$

s **not in** S is equivalent to $\neg (s$ **in** $S)$

An Ada programmer can expect that an implementation will supply all of these.

Further attributes are defined in the following way

$S'SUCC(s_i) = s_{i+1}$ for $i = 0, 1, \ldots, n - 1$

$S'PRED(s_{i+1}) = s_i$ for $i = 0, 1, \ldots, n - 1$

$S'POS(s_i) = i$ for $i = 0, 1, \ldots, n$

$S'VAL(i) = s_i$ for $i = 0, 1, \ldots, n$.

The attributes discussed above do not apply to the real types. Here there are some important differences to be highlighted since real numbers are represented only approximately inside the computer. Consequently a great deal of care is needed in choosing appropriate attributes. In the case of the floating-point real quantities the attributes *FIRST* and *LAST* are again defined but not *SUCC*, *PRED*, *POS* or *VAL*. Instead there are attributes of the following kind:

T'DIGITS gives the number of digits of accuracy for elements of type *T*,

T'SMALL gives the smallest positive value expressible within the representation and precision of type *T*,

T'LARGE gives the largest positive value expressible within the representation and precision of type *T*.

With these types *T*, again it is possible to provide a finite (although usually lengthy) enumeration of the available values $(s_0, s_1, \ldots, s_n)$. We say that

$$s_i < s_j \quad \text{provided } i < j \text{ and the (mathematical) difference}$$
$$s_j - s_i >= T'SMALL$$

Again the other comparison operators can be defined in terms of $<$. Note that this definition says nothing at all about the equality or inequality of two quantities which differ by less than *T'SMALL*. In the case of the reals the operator **in** (and its complement **not in**) test whether or not a specified quantity lies within a range of the reals.

4.1.3 Axioms for discrete types

We now turn to specific sets of scalars and look at other attributes in the form of operators supplied for their manipulation. The operators defined on booleans are **not**, **and**, **or** and **xor** (exclusive or). Conditions give results of type *BOOLEAN*. Axioms could be given for these four operators. Essentially these would just be truth tables giving the results for any possible combination of operands. The usual rules of mathematical logic apply and these are no exceptions.

CHARACTER is also a standard scalar type and its definition was given previously in figure 4.1. There are no special operators which can be used to manipulate them.

There are three basic integer types, namely *SHORT_INTEGER*, *INTEGER* and *LONG_INTEGER*. For each type there are unary operators $+$, $-$ which perform the expected operations; *ABS* is a function which calculates the absolute value of an integer. In these three cases the type of the result is the same as the type of the operand. Binary operators $+$, $-$, $*$, $/$, **rem** and **mod** are all defined in the expected way to operate on integers of the same type to produce a result of that type. Exponentiation is represented by $**$ and the exponent must be a positive integer; the result is of the same type as the type of the left operand.

For real numbers the story is similar. If we concentrate on the type *FLOAT* the reader can assume the existence of similar facilities for the types *SHORT_FLOAT* and *LONG_FLOAT*. Again unary operators $+$ and $-$ are permitted together with the function *ABS*. Binary operators $+$, $-$, $*$, $/$ again operate on operands of the same type to produce a result of that type. Exponentiation is

68

denoted by ∗∗ and can have as a right hand operand any integer quantity.

We mentioned the operations which were available and which could be used to operate on numeric quantities. But we failed to specify the set of axioms these satisfied. There was an underlying assumption that the expected mathematical axioms would hold. It would be very convenient if they did but unfortunately they do not.

In chapter 2 we mentioned the precedence rules for operators and the rules for evaluating operands. These dictate the manner in which expressions must be evaluated.

Now let us turn to the mathematical properties of the various operators and thus to a study of the laws of algebra which can be assumed in manipulating predicates. Take first the integer types.

Computer arithmetic involving some integer type T, say, is similar in many respects to arithmetic performed by mathematicians. Thus there are zero, unity, and so on. Whatever differences exist tend to result from the fact that the magnitude of the integers which a computer can manipulate is limited by a quantity, namely $T'LAST$.

Little would be gained at this stage by giving a complete list of the axioms that hold. Such a list can be shortened by noting such relationships as

A **rem** B is equivalent to $A - (A/B) * B$

and noting the equivalence of $A/(-B)$, $(-A)/B$ and $-(A/B)$. More can be gained by noting the axioms which do not hold and commenting upon the consequences. This is the approach we shall adopt. We look specifically at addition but note that similar relevant observations can be made in connection with binary minus and with multiplication and division (not by zero!).

Let M, N and P denote integers of some integers type T. If we denote computer addition by $+$ and the usual mathematical addition by $\oplus$ (and so be in harmony with the notation in the rest of the book) then we can write

$M + N = M \oplus N$

only if $M \oplus N$ lies within the limits of T. Whenever the latter condition does not hold, the associative law of addition, namely

$(M + N) + P = M + (N + P)$

does not in general hold. Its truth depends on the fact that $M \oplus N, N \oplus P$ and $M \oplus N \oplus P$ all lie within the limits of the type T.

Whenever the limits of a type T are violated by some action of a program then typically execution of the program will halt and some appropriate action will take place – for instance a trace of a program might be given together with the values of certain variables immediately prior to the fault. In Ada the situation is dealt with by exceptions:

> The *CONSTRAINT_ERROR* exception is raised when a value exceeds the declared range of a variable;

The *NUMERIC_ERROR* exception is raised when an arithmetic operation fails in that some value is too large for the particular implementation to handle; division by zero causes this exception to be raised.

The unary minus operator can lead to similar difficulties. It should be apparent that there are circumstances under which its application can lead to the raising of *CONSTRAINT_ERROR*; consider a range such as 1 .. 10. Also, most implementations of integers permit one more negative integer than positive integer (twos complement arithmetic). Consequently the use of unary minus can also give rise to the raising of exceptions.

If we choose to ignore the possibility of the violation of the limits – and the allowable range of integers is usually large enough to make its occurrence unlikely – then one of two alternatives will occur. Either all operations will be performed in accord with the usual laws of mathematics or an exception will be raised and normal program execution will be suspended. For many applications the situation is therefore relatively satisfactory. But for some critical kinds of programs any sort of abnormal termination can lead to disaster. We look in section 4.1.4 at ways of overcoming even these difficulties in Ada.

4.1.4 Axioms for reals

Now let us turn to the real types. Just as the set of integers that can be represented within a computer is limited in magnitude so the set of reals is also limited in this way; consequently the raising of the exceptions *CONSTRAINT_ ERROR* and *NUMERIC_ERROR* are again a possibility. But unlike the integers real numbers are not normally represented exactly. Instead an approximation to each real number is held. This latter observation gives rise to some considerable difficulties since all aspects of arithmetic involving real numbers are therefore liable to be, at best, approximate. To give some feeling for the inaccuracies involved we look briefly at a typical method of representing floating-point real numbers in a computer.

In a simplified but typical scheme a floating-point real number will be represented in the form $f \times 2^e$. Here f is the fractional part or mantissa, a real number between -1 and 1 held to only a limited number of digits of accuracy, and e is the exponent part, an integer whose magnitude is also limited.

Computers typically hold just the values of e and f, both in binary. The electronic circuits take the representation into account when performing addition, multiplication, etc. In this crude scheme a number such as .5 could be represented in several ways. It could be represented by pairs (e, f) such as $(0, .5), (1, .25), (2, .125)$, etc. To obtain as much accuracy as possible fractional parts are usually forced into being as large in magnitude as possible. Since both integers and fractions are usually represented in binary this means that

70

$\frac{1}{2} <= f < 1$ for positive numbers

and

$-1 <= f < -\frac{1}{2}$ for negative numbers.

The range and precision of e and f will usually depend on the constraints stipulated in the type declaration. Such a scheme provides a unique representation for a real number and the representation is then said to be *normalised*. Most computers manipulate normalised floating-point representations.

Let us now relate this to what happens when Ada programs come to be executed. A floating-point type F has a declaration which defines a set of what are called *model numbers M*. For the moment assume no range constraint is present. Let D be the quantity which appears either explicitly or implicitly following **digits** in the type declaration. This determines a certain number of binary digits B, the size of the binary mantissa necessary to hold a real number to at least the accuracy specified in the decimal form. Then B is the smallest positive integer greater than $(\ln(10)/\ln(2)) * D$, i.e. greater than approximately $3.322 * D$. The model numbers associated with the type are 0.0 and all numbers of the form

sign * binary mantissa * 2 ** exponent

where

the sign is $+1$ or -1
the binary mantissa has exactly B binary digits after the point and satisfies

$0.5 <=$ binary mantissa < 1.0

the exponent is an integer in the range $-4 * B$ to $4 * B$.

With this description we can now give a more complete description of the attributes for floating-point types. Let F be such a type. Then

F'DIGITS	is the number of decimal digits of precision
F'MANTISSA	is the length of the binary mantissa of model numbers
F'EMAX	is the number such that the range of exponents for model numbers is $-F'EMAX .. F'EMAX$
F'SMALL	is the smallest positive model number
F'LARGE	is the largest positive model number
F'EPSILON	is the absolute value of the positive difference between 1.0 and the next model number above 1.0.

If there are range constraints associated with a type declaration of F then the same set of model numbers are used. This has the desirable consequence that $F'SMALL$, etc. remain defined though the range constraint may be of the form $-2.0 .. -1.0$. All values of the type must, however, satisfy the constraint.

As far as subtypes are concerned the expected restrictions apply. Ranges must be subranges and the accuracy cannot exceed the accuracy of the base type.

Model intervals and model numbers provide the clue to the understanding of computer arithmetic involving real numbers. Remember that $+, -, /$, etc. are defined on operands of the same real type and they produce a result of that type; exponentiation is different but no more complex. Comparison operators have operands of the same numeric type but produce *TRUE* or *FALSE*.

Within an Ada program a real number may be expressed as a universal real such as 2.0, *PI_BY_*2, etc. Universal reals are converted into a form such that

(*a*) if the universal real is itself a model number there is a guarantee that the conversion is precise,

(*b*) otherwise the real is converted into any value within the range specified by the next model number above and below.

Both cases can be subsumed under the one description by saying that a real number defines a model interval which bounds the real value; in case (*a*) the interval happens to contain a single number.

If an arithmetic operator involving reals has two operands then

(i) a model interval is associated with each operand

(ii) a new interval is formed by applying the exact mathematical operation to all pairs in the respective intervals; a range of results is thus produced

(iii) the smallest model interval which includes all the results obtained in (ii) above is then formed.

Note that step (iii) describes the accuracy of the result. When a unary operator and a single operand is present the matter is simpler.

When comparisons are involved the exact mathematical results apply as long as the model intervals are disjoint. Otherwise

(*a*) if they have a single element in common this element must be a model number and the result is either the exact mathematical result or the result of comparing the first operand with itself,

(*b*) if they have more than one element in common the result is implementation-defined.

We are now in a position to relate the behaviour of these representations under computer arithmetic to the normal behaviour of their mathematical equivalents. These ideas can of course be expressed in a more general form which is independent of the actual representation used for real numbers. Thus it is possible to talk about sets F, M and R and merely state that to each x in F there is a model interval $\tilde{x}$ which has certain desirable properties. But the basic ideas or axioms are motivated by the previous discussion.

Let us now look at the axioms that these operations satisfy and compare them with the mathematical equivalents. Let F denote some floating-point type. An Ada programmer will think of F as a subset of the real numbers R, limited in magnitude. Each real number x from F will be represented by some model interval $\tilde{x}$. The model numbers M are a subset of F.

We use x, y, z, etc., possibly subscripted, to represent real numbers. The corresponding model intervals appear as $\tilde{x}, \tilde{y}, \tilde{z}$, etc. The basic arithmetic operators will be written as $\oplus, \ominus, \circledast$, etc. together with $<, <=, =$, etc. Their counterparts in computer arithmetic we denote by $+, -, *$, etc. together with $<, <=$, etc.

We can then assume the following (using some obvious shortcuts to avoid tedious details):

Model intervals

1. Each x in F and not in M is represented by a model interval $\tilde{x}$ of the form $x_1 .. x_2$ where x_1 and x_2 are in M. Each x in M is represented by the model interval $x .. x$.
2. If $\tilde{x}_1$ and $\tilde{x}_2$ are the same model interval and if x lies between x_1 and x_2 then $\tilde{x}$ is the same model interval.
3. 0.0 and 1.0 are in M.
4. Model intervals are symmetric with respect to 0, i.e.
$$-\tilde{x} = (\widetilde{-x}).$$

Arithmetic operators

Ignore, for the moment, the possibility of a numeric error.

5. The model numbers $\widehat{0.0}$ and $\widehat{1.0}$ satisfy
$$\tilde{x} + \widehat{0.0} = \tilde{x} \quad \tilde{x} * \widehat{1.0} = \tilde{x}$$
$$\tilde{x} * \widehat{0.0} = \widehat{0.0}$$

6. Arithmetic operations involving model intervals produce the smallest possible model interval which contains the set of mathematically exact results previously described.
7. $+$ and $*$ are commutative, i.e.
$$\tilde{x} + \tilde{y} = \tilde{y} + \tilde{x}, \quad \tilde{x} * \tilde{y} = \tilde{y} * \tilde{x}.$$
8. The basic operations are symmetric with respect to 0.0, i.e.
$$\tilde{x} - \tilde{y} = \tilde{x} + (-\tilde{y}) = -(\tilde{y} - \tilde{x}),$$
$$(-\tilde{x}) * \tilde{y} = \tilde{x} * (-\tilde{y}) = -(\tilde{x} * \tilde{y}),$$
$$(-\tilde{x}) / \tilde{y} = \tilde{x} / (-\tilde{y}) = -(\tilde{x} / \tilde{y}).$$

Comparison operators

9. The comparison operators involving model intervals produce results of the form indicated earlier.

10. The basic operations $+, -, *$ and $/$ are monotonic

$$0 <= x <= x_1, \quad 0 <= y <= y_1$$

implies that

$$\bar{x} + \bar{y} <= \bar{x}_1 + \bar{y}_1, \quad \bar{x} - \bar{y}_1 <= \bar{x}_1 - \bar{y},$$
$$\bar{x} * \bar{y} <= \bar{x}_1 * \bar{y}_1, \quad \bar{x} / \bar{y}_1 <= \bar{x}_1 / \bar{y}.$$

Similar properties hold for the other comparison operators.

From the set of rules given here many of the usual laws of arithmetic can be derived. For example

$$x < y \quad \text{implies} \quad \bar{x} <= \bar{y}$$
$$y >= 0 \quad \text{implies} \quad \bar{x} + \bar{y} >= \bar{x}$$

and so on. But many laws cannot be derived.

Noticeably absent from the list of axioms and properties are the associative laws of addition and multiplication. Their absence is not caused by difficulties over numeric errors. Their absence is related to the fact that numbers are held only approximately. For the same reason the distributive law is missing.

To give some feeling for why the laws fail to hold let us look at some examples. To save getting involved in binary arithmetic etc., let us assume that model numbers appear in the form (e, f) where this is now an abbreviation for

$$f * 10^e.$$

It is assumed that e is some integer in the range $-4 .. 4$ and that f is a decimal fraction held to four decimal places of accuracy after the point. Moreover, $0.1 <= ABS(f) < 1.0$.

Now let

$$x = 5.643, \qquad \text{i.e. } (1, +0.5643);$$
$$y = -5.641, \qquad \text{i.e. } (1, -0.5641);$$
$$z = 0.0007311, \quad \text{i.e. } (-3, +0.7311).$$

If we proceed to perform interval arithmetic in the manner described previously and if we use $0.273\frac{1}{2}$ to indicate the interval $0.2731 .. 0.2732$ for instance we obtain

$$(\bar{x} + \bar{y}) + \bar{z} = (-2, +0.2000) + (-3, +0.7311)$$
$$= (-2, +0.273\tfrac{1}{2})$$
$$= 0.002731 .. 0.002732$$
$$\bar{x} + (\bar{y} + \bar{z}) = (+1, 0.5643) + (+1, -0.564\tfrac{0}{1})$$
$$= (-2, +0.\tfrac{2}{3})$$
$$= 0.002 .. 0.003$$

Note the considerable discrepancy. The ranges overlap of course and the correct answer is somewhere within the smaller range.

Now let us look at the distributive law. Assume the same values as above for x and y but let $z = 400.0$. Then

$$\tilde{z} * \tilde{x} + \tilde{z} * \tilde{y} = (+4, +0.225_8^7) + (+4, -0.225_7^6)$$

$$= 0.0 .. 2.0$$

$$\tilde{z} * (\tilde{x} + \tilde{y}) = (+2, 0.4000) * (-2, +0.2000)$$

$$= 0.8$$

Again a discrepancy exists.

These two examples illustrate the kind of error that can be introduced. In the cases that give rise to large model intervals note the addition of two quantities which are close together in magnitude but of opposite sign. This observation is crucial.

As a result of the above discussion it is not possible to prove certain axioms of arithmetic. For instance, even ignoring numeric errors, *none* of the following can be assumed.

Laws involving zero and one:

$$\tilde{x} - \tilde{x} = \tilde{0.0}$$

$$\tilde{x} / \tilde{x} = \tilde{1.0} \quad \text{for } \tilde{x} \mathrel{/=} \tilde{0.0}$$

Cancellation laws:

if $\quad \tilde{x} * \tilde{y} = \tilde{x} * \tilde{z} \quad$ and $\quad \tilde{x} \mathrel{/=} \tilde{0.0} \quad$ then $\quad \tilde{y} = \tilde{z}$

if $\quad \tilde{x} + \tilde{y} = \tilde{x} + \tilde{z} \quad$ then $\quad \tilde{y} = \tilde{z}$

Laws involving comparison:

if $\quad \tilde{x} < \tilde{y} \quad$ then for all $\tilde{z}, \quad \tilde{x} + \tilde{z} < \tilde{y} + \tilde{z}$

if $\quad \tilde{x} < \tilde{y} \quad$ and $\quad \tilde{z} > \tilde{0.0} \quad$ then $\quad \tilde{x} * \tilde{z} < \tilde{y} * \tilde{z}$

if $\quad \tilde{x}_1 < \tilde{y}_1 \quad$ and $\quad \tilde{x}_2 < \tilde{y}_2 \quad$ then $\quad \tilde{x}_1 + \tilde{x}_2 < \tilde{y}_1 + \tilde{y}_2$

if $\quad x \mathrel{/=} y \quad$ then $\quad \tilde{x} \mathrel{/=} \tilde{y}$

Laws involving multiplication and division:

if $\quad \tilde{x} \mathrel{/=} \tilde{0.0} \quad$ then $\quad \tilde{x} * (\tilde{y} / \tilde{x}) = \tilde{y}$

Viewed in the above light the situation seems almost hopeless. Note, however, that many of these results will hold when the operands are model numbers. In section 4.1.6 we discuss what can be done to counter this situation. First we make some remarks about exceptions.

In performing floating-point arithmetic limits of various kinds can be violated and a suitable exception raised:

> *NUMERIC_ERROR* is raised when the result of a numeric operation does not lie within the range of the appropriate type; in particular division by zero causes this exception to be raised.

4.1.5 Fixed-point arithmetic

Besides floating-point reals the designers of Ada also introduced fixed-point real numbers. Whereas **digits** introduces an accuracy constraint for the floating-point numbers **delta** introduces the accuracy constraint for fixed-point types, thus

type A **is delta** 0.25 **range** $-10.0 .. +10.0$;

Following the accuracy constraint there must appear a compulsory range specification.

From the above definition of A the programmer can infer an implementation. Within the computer there must be representatives of each real between -10.0 and $+10.0$. These are separated from each other by a maximum distance of 0.25. Thus one can imagine each real having a representative of the following kind

$$\pm BBBB.BB$$

where each B is either 0 or 1. These representatives then can be thought of as corresponding to $-10.0, -9.75, -9.5, \ldots, 9.75, 10.0$. The difference between a real number and its representative is then less than 0.25/2.0. Whereas the floating-point types have a relative accuracy the fixed-point types have an absolute accuracy, namely the delta value.

Example 4.1.5a   Fixed-point declarations
The following are all permissible

type *SIZE* **is delta** 0.5 **range** 0.0 .. 100.5;
subtype *SMALL_SIZE* **is** *SIZE* **range** 0.0 .. 50.0;
type *COMMON* **is new** *SIZE* **range** 25.0 .. 75.0;

For fixed-point types the attributes are slightly (but not surprisingly) different from those of the floating-point types. Both *SMALL* and *LARGE* have their expected meaning. *DIGITS* is not defined but instead *DELTA* gives the value of the delta in the specification of the type declaration.

In discussing the available operators a certain complication arises. It will transpire that multiplication of two fixed-point types is allowed. The result is said to be of *universal fixed* type and is of arbitrary accuracy. Whenever such types are introduced in a program the result must be qualified so that the accuracy and precision of any computation again become determinate; operations on universal fixed types do not exist.

The following operators are permitted, assuming that the usual range constraints, etc., are not violated:

monadic $+$ and $-$ which when applied to a fixed-point number give the expected result which is of the same type as the operand,

dyadic $+$ and $-$ operate on operands of the same fixed-point type and give the expected results of the same type,

76

multiplication * between an integer and a fixed-point number or vice versa is permitted and the result is of the same fixed-point type as the real operand,

multiplication * between two fixed-point reals possibly of different types is permitted and the result is of type universal fixed,

division / between a fixed-point number and an integer is permitted, the result being of the fixed-point type,

division / between two fixed-point reals possibly of different types is allowed and the result is of universal fixed type,

the relational operators are defined (the usual ambiguity exists about the equality and inequality of numbers that are very close).

Notes
1. Addition and subtraction are performed to within the accuracy of the fixed-point types.
2. Multiplication of a fixed-point number by an integer is effectively repeated addition.
3. Division is approximate, whether the right hand operand is an integer or a real.
4. The *NUMERIC_ERROR* exception is likely to be raised in the usual circumstances.

As might be supposed the axioms and properties of fixed-point types can be described accurately in terms of model numbers.

Assume a fixed-point type F. The model numbers are all integer multiples of a quantity called *actual delta*; the multipliers are all integers in a range of the form

$$-(2 ** N) + 1 .. (2 ** N) - 1$$

for some positive integer N. The quantity actual delta is a positive quantity and is not greater than the delta specified in the type declaration. The quantity N is chosen in such a way that the limits of the compulsory range constraint are within $F'DELTA$ of a model number. Indeed each real in the range can be associated with a real model number within $F'DELTA$ of the real number.

The complete set of attributes of a fixed-point type F can now be explained:

$F'DELTA$	is the delta specified in the type declaration of F;
$F'ACTUAL\_DELTA$	gives the actual delta of F, a universal real number;
$F'BITS$	gives N, the number of bits used to hold the multipliers described above;
$F'LARGE$	is the largest model number of F.

As far as subtypes are concerned any range constraint must be a subrange of the range of the base type. The actual delta of a subtype must be of the form

$2 ** M * F'ACTUAL\_DELTA$ where M is a non-negative integer and F is the base type; this actual delta must not be greater than the specified delta of the subtype.

As before, we can now talk in terms of a model interval being associated with any real number within the particular range. Arithmetic is then basically interval arithmetic of the kind described in section 4.1.4.

4.1.6   Remarks about programming

What can be said about the verification of programs which manipulate real numbers? If all the real numbers that are operands or are the results of expression or subexpression evaluation happen to be model numbers a program verifier can foretell exactly what will happen and produce appropriate proofs. If results are not model numbers difficulties are introduced. Even in this case, however, the program verifier will be able to assess the errors in his program for he can perform the necessary interval arithmetic. The errors will be relative for floating-point reals and absolute for fixed-point numbers. For the moment let us concentrate on fixed-point numbers.

As fixed-point numbers are added together errors can accumulate in the following fashion:

> any one number is accurate to within $T'DELTA$
> the addition of two numbers is accurate to $2 * T'DELTA$
> the addition of three numbers is accurate to $3 * T'DELTA$
> the addition of N numbers is accurate to $N * T'DELTA$.

It is important that errors such as these do not start to dominate any computation. In particular the error should be far less than the sum being accumulated. For this reason a programmer must often choose a delta value much smaller than he might initially anticipate.

Similar kinds of errors result from the use of the other operations such as subtraction, multiplication and division. Depending on the values involved multiplication and division can cause the errors to grow rapidly.

The whole topic of error analysis, both for floating-point and fixed-point numbers, is a very important aspect of a branch of mathematics known as numerical analysis. Anyone hoping to properly understand the workings of programs which manipulate real numbers should be properly acquainted with the foundations of this subject.

In what follows we shall concentrate mainly on programs which use floating-point arithmetic. This judgement is based on the observation that most serious computing is done in this way; the concept is flexible and usually has hardware support in terms of hardware floating-point units. In using fixed-point arithmetic it is all too easy to violate the accuracy constraint – it is often not clear how often a loop body will be performed and the determination of this may be messy or complicated.

The situation as it now stands is somewhat awkward from a verification point of view. A verifier must take note of the errors which occur whenever a calculation is performed. Note, however, that the order in which operations are performed in Ada programs is well-defined. We do not have to consider the possibility of several possible evaluation sequences and take a pessimistic view of the results. This is so only because we currently assume there are no functions present in expressions.

These remarks indicate why, in the earlier chapters of this book, we studiously avoided any mention of real arithmetic within programs. In this section we propose to look closely at the situation and ask what can be done. Let us begin with exceptions and exception handling. The general principles we develop apply to any situation involving exceptions; in particular they apply to both integer and real arithmetic.

When exceptions of any kind are raised the normal execution of a program is terminated. However a programmer has the ability to write a piece of program which will be executed in the event of an exception being raised. Such a piece of program is called an *exception handler* and is introduced by the word **exception**. Let us illustrate the possibilities with an example.

Suppose that at some point in a program two real quantities X and Y have to be multiplied together and the result assigned to the real variable Z. The situation may exist whereby overflow is liable to occur. If the programmer foresees this he can supply at the end of the current (or any enclosing) block a suitable handler:

```
declare
      X, Y: FLOAT;
begin
      . . .
      Z := X * Y;
      . . .
exception
      when NUMERIC_ERROR =>
          Z := FLOAT'LARGE;
end;
```

If overflow does occur as a result of the multiplication the exception is raised and the normal flow of control within the block is terminated. Execution of the exception handler replaces the execution of the remaining statements in the block.

If there is no appropriate exception handler within the current block we say that the exception is propagated, i.e. it is raised in the enclosing block. This causes any suitable handler within that block to be executed or the exception is further propagated.

Within the one block several exceptions can be processed. For instance it is quite possible to have something like

```
declare
    X, Y: FLOAT;
begin
    . . .
    Z := X * Y;
    . . .
exception
    when NUMERIC_ERROR | CONSTRAINT_ERROR =>
        Z := FLOAT'LARGE;
    when others
        PUT ("EXCEPTION RAISED");
end;
```

The vertical bar separates alternatives. The bold word **others** introduces a default part.

Exceptions can be raised while declarations are being evaluated, but in the enclosing block. It is even possible to re-raise the exception which caused the interruption – this is done by inserting the statement

raise;

This causes the exception to be propagated out to enclosing blocks. Further handlers are called into action as appropriate.

In Ada a programmer can introduce his own exceptions by declarations of the following kind

UNDERFLOW: **exception**;

Such an exception might be raised by a statement such as

```
if X < 1.0E − 6 then
    raise UNDERFLOW;
end if;
```

Then exception handlers may have a section which reads

```
when UNDERFLOW =>
    RESULT := 0.0;
```

In this way then the programmer can deal to some extent with error situations caused by overflow and so on. The ability to do so (provided within the framework of the programming language Ada) can help to counter some of the criticisms of program verification. But what can be done about the inherent inaccuracy of real arithmetic?

There are two situations worthy of special mention.

(*a*) The subtraction of almost equal real numbers tends to cause the cancellation of significant digits; the less significant digits then take on an importance which becomes exaggerated. Similar difficulties occur with the addition of quantities which are almost equal in magnitude but are opposite in sign.

(b) Division by zero, of course, causes an exception to be raised. But division between two quantities close to zero can also result in large inaccuracies and this should be avoided whenever possible.

Programmers should take extreme caution to avoid these and similar situations. As a general rule, if such care is exercised and if certain other precautions are taken the usual laws of mathematics are 'almost true'.

We shall consider certain classes of programs which normally make substantial use of real arithmetic. These illustrate the type of precaution that must be taken to avoid certain dangerous pitfalls. But we shall only be touching the tip of a very large iceberg. The topic of numerical analysis is a major branch of mathematics and is concerned with situations of the kind we mention.

One fairly large class of programming problems comes under the heading of iteration. There are various kinds of iterative problems. Let us look at some typical examples and examine the dangers involved in producing programs for them.

Suppose we wish to calculate the square root of some non-negative real number A. If x_n is an approximation to the square root then x_{n+1} as given by

$$x_{n+1} = (x_n + A/x_n)/2$$

is an even better approximation. This suggests a piece of program such as

```
X := initial approximation;
loop
    Y := (X + A/X)/2.0;
    exit when ABS(X − Y) < 1.0E − 5;
    X := Y;
end loop;
```

The above terminates when the difference between successive approximations is less than 10^{-5}. The program raises various matters worthy of discussion.

The assignment to Y involves a calculation which is likely to result in some small error, some deviation from the expected mathematical result. But on repeating the execution of the statements in the loop note that the calculation merely regards the new value of X as essentially a new approximation to the required square root. Although there was probably a small error in the calculation the value obtained would have been a better approximation than the previous first estimate. The process is in a sense self-correcting.

The program given above works properly and gives a result correct to about 5 decimal places. To obtain a result correct to about 8 decimal places a simple change is required – merely replace $1.0E − 5$ by $1.0E − 8$. How can one obtain as accurate an answer as the machine permits? This can be done by replacing the

test
$$ABS(X - Y) < 1.0E - 5$$
by either
$$ABS(X - Y) < FLOAT'SMALL$$
or by the implementation-dependent expression
$$X = Y.$$

Note that mathematically it is just not possible to prove that in general two successive approximations become equal, because they are never mathematically equal. Some simple mathematics shows that

$$x_{n+1}^2 - A = [\tfrac{1}{2}(x_n + (A/x_n))]^2 - A$$
$$= [\tfrac{1}{2}(x_n - (A/x_n))]^2$$
$$> 0 \quad \text{provided } x_n^2 /= A.$$

Consequently if the initial approximation is not exact no subsequent approximation will provide the exact square root.

However to put a test such as $X = Y$ in a program means that X and Y must agree to within the accuracy permitted by the machine (or to within $FLOAT'$-$SMALL$). Thus it merely means that successive approximations must come very close together. The mathematics of the problem can be used to show that indeed this is so. In fact it can be shown that if an approximation x_n is correct to k digits of accuracy then x_{n+1} will be correct to about $2k$ digits of accuracy.

The example given above is representative of a whole class of similar problems. These are concerned essentially with finding the root of an equation $f(x) = 0$; in the above case the equation was $x^2 - A = 0$. Now if x_0 is an initial approximation which is wrong by a quantity ξ we can write

$$0 = f(x_0 + \xi) = f(x_0) + \xi f'(x_0) + \dots$$

using the Taylor series expansion of f. An estimate of ξ can be obtained by ignoring all terms involving powers of ξ beyond ξ^2. Thus

$$.\xi = -f(x_0)/f'(x_0).$$

Then a better approximation x_1 is given by

$$x_1 = x_0 - f(x_0)/f'(x_0).$$

Successive approximations $x_0, x_1, x_2, \dots$ can be obtained by applying the iterative formula

$$x_{n+1} = x_n - f(x_n)/f'(x_n).$$

This is usually referred to as Newton's formula.

Viewed in another way the above formula involves drawing a tangent to $f(x)$ at x_0 and using the point of intersection with the x-axis as a better approximation (see figure 4.2).

The general situation for iterative schemes of the above kind is similar. Often some mathematical manipulation is required to establish termination or the like. But the important observation is that the usual laws of mathematics can be assumed to hold with the reservations outlined above.

For another class of iterative problems the situation is less simple. Consider the following

$$\cos\,[(n+1)\theta] = 2\cos\theta\cos\,(n\theta) - \cos\,[(n-1)\theta].$$

Such a relationship might form the basis of an iterative scheme of the following kind

$$C_{n+1} = 2\cos\theta C_n - C_{n-1}$$

and might suggest that $\cos\,[(n+1)\theta]$ can be calculated iteratively starting with a knowledge of $\cos\theta$. An attempt to base a program on such a scheme is liable to result in very poor results. The process is not self-correcting. Indeed errors are liable to accumulate rapidly and very uncertain results can be obtained. A proper correctness proof should include this error analysis and highlight the fact.

Somewhat similar to the problem of evaluating the terms of a sequence is the problem of evaluating the sum of a series. Typical problems might involve calculating

$$1 - 1/2 + 1/3 - 1/4 \ldots$$

or evaluating the exponential or sine functions using

$$\exp\,(x) = 1 + x + x^2/2! + x^3/3! + \ldots$$

and

$$\sin\,(x) = x - x^3/3! + x^5/5! - \ldots$$

respectively. If programs are produced for series of this kind without giving due thought to the inherent inaccuracy of the arithmetic disaster can result. Let us examine the difficulties.

A first rule is that series which converge quickly for a particular value of x are more likely to produce a good result than series which converge slowly for

Fig. 4.2.

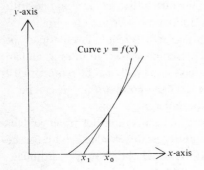

that value of x. For then fewer additions etc. have to be performed and fewer errors are likely to be propagated. It should be pointed out that a program can give the impression that apparently a series converges when in fact it diverges. Mere tests on the magnitude of terms are an inadequate test for convergence.

Series such as the exponential and sine series given above converge rapidly. Yet for values of x such as $x = 10$ many terms have to be evaluated. Moreover the initial terms tend to be large and in the case of the sine series cancel to eventually produce a small quantity with a consequent loss in accuracy. If the rules which state that

$$\sin (x + 2\pi) = \sin (x)$$
$$\sin (\pi - x) = \sin (x)$$

etc. are employed to equate $\sin (x)$ and $\sin (y)$ where y is now small and between 0 and $\pi/2$ (or better $\pi/4$ if the cosine series is introduced) much can be gained.

The evaluation of alternating series has several other potential pitfalls. Since adjacent terms are of differing signs a straightforward calculation can lead to trouble. This can be overcome by adding all the even terms and all the odd terms separately. But if the final subtraction involves almost equal quantities nothing is gained. Often with alternating series it is again possible to resort to mathematical manipulation, e.g.

$$\exp (-x) = 1/\exp (x).$$

Therefore instead of evaluating $\exp (-x)$ merely calculate $\exp (x)$ and invert the result.

In summing series of any kind it sometimes pays to start with smaller terms (if the starting point is known) and accumulate these before adding in the larger terms. If smaller terms have a significant contribution to make they may well be swamped in a straightforward evaluation.

Summing series, then, is not in general straightforward. The difficulties mentioned above and many others are liable to arise. For these reasons numerical analysts often approximate to series over some range by means of polynomials using a process called economisation of power series.

These remarks give some insight into the difficulties involved in real arithmetic. To some extent multi-precision arithmetic can be used to obtain a greater degree of accuracy. If complete accuracy is required sometimes special actions can be taken: rationals can be represented as pairs of integers and arithmetic on these can be performed accurately; some reals can be represented as the roots of equations with integer coefficients; fixed-point arithmetic can be employed if the programming language permits; and so on.

Programs which use real arithmetic should keep within the broad guidelines outlined above. In this way meaningful results can be obtained and it can be assumed that the usual laws of arithmetic 'almost hold'. However, although verification of programs can be carried out this inevitably involves an analysis of the errors involved in calculations. The results obtained can be expected to be accurate only in special cases; in general only a limited degree of accuracy will be obtained. By following the broad guidelines set out above small model intervals will result rather than large model intervals.

4.2   Axioms for constructs

We have now given axioms for integers, reals, characters, booleans, and other scalar types. These axioms essentially provide the operators and other attributes that can be used within programs. The underlying mathematical properties of the operators provide meaning: they describe the effect of performing the evaluation of arithmetic expressions, etc.

We now turn to the other aspects of programming languages, i.e. to declarations, statements, and so on. Again Ada is typical of many programming languages. We shall attempt to axiomatise its constructs. The axioms we deduce will thus describe the constructs that can be used in Ada programs and will describe the meaning to be associated with these. In this section we look only at the constructs we have been using in the programs of the earlier sections.

4.2.1   Notation for proof rules

We begin by introducing some notation which will be useful for expressing the axioms, etc., for constructs in programming languages.

In earlier chapters of this book the importance of the idea of back substitution has been demonstrated. Our first step is therefore to introduce some notation for substitution. Let P denote some predicate. Then $P(y/x)$ means: systematically replace all occurrences of x by y. This piece of notation can easily be extended to deal with several simultaneous substitutions. Thus $P(y_1/x_1, y_2/x_2, \ldots, y_n/x_n)$, where all the x_i are distinct, means: simultaneously replace each x_i by the corresponding y_i. Note the importance of *simultaneous*; this then allows the possibility of some y_i containing some x_k and no ambiguity results.

The effects of statements in programming languages will have to be defined in an axiomatic manner. To accomplish this it is necessary to provide a formal statement, an axiom, which describes precisely the effect of each different kind of statement in the programming language. These axioms are called *proof rules* – formalised correctness proofs can be constructed from them. There will be one proof rule for each kind of construct in the language.

Proof rules are normally expressed using two different pieces of notation, inductive expressions and rules of inference. *Inductive expressions* are of the form

$$\{P\} S \{Q\}$$

where P and Q are predicates and S is a phrase or sequence of phrases of some kind – 'phrase' covers both declarations and statements. The above inductive expression has the following meaning:

> If the predicate P is true before the execution of S commences then when that execution is complete the predicate Q will be true.

Note that this says nothing at all about whether or not the execution of S terminates. Thus inductive expressions are related to partial correctness, not total correctness. As might be supposed P is referred to as the *precondition* and Q is referred to as the *postcondition* of the above inductive expression.

It is too ambitious to hope that we can provide inductive expressions for all the various constructs in a programming language. There is a sense in which the assignment statement is a primitive kind of construct – it is not composed of any other kinds of statements. It will be possible to produce in the form of a single inductive expression a proof rule which captures the essence of the meaning of assignment. As such this is usually referred to as the 'assignment axiom'. Other constructs such as conditionals, loop statements, and so on are different – they are typically composed of simpler statements, e.g. branches of conditionals may contain assignments. In these more complex cases inductive expressions alone are inadequate. It transpires that what is required in these cases is a notation which says: to prove that $\{P\} S \{Q\}$ is true for some 'complex' statement S it is sufficient to prove the truth of some other predicate which typically involves simpler inductive expressions. Accordingly we introduce a notation for inference rules (or rules of inference).

Inference rules are a notation borrowed from mathematical logic. Typically they come in two forms:

Form I

$$\frac{H_1, H_2, \ldots, H_n}{H}$$

means that whenever the hypotheses $H_1, H_2, \ldots, H_n$ are true then the hypothesis H is true.

Form II:

$$\frac{H_1, H_2, \ldots, H_n \vdash H_{n+1}}{H}$$

should be interpreted to mean that, whenever it is possible to prove H_{n+1} given the truth of $H_1, H_2, \ldots, H_n$, then H is true.

Both these inference rules are of the form

$$\frac{\alpha}{\beta}$$

The 'numerator' α is usually referred to as the *antecedent* or *premise* of the inference rule and the 'denominator' β is usually called the *consequent*. In all the cases which shall concern us β will take the form of a single inductive expression concerning some phrase of the programming language. The antecedent on the other hand will often consist of several inductive expressions combined into a more complex boolean expression.

Let us now give proof rules for various constructs in the programming language Ada. These rules will make use of the various pieces of notation we have just introduced.

4.2.2 Declarations

We have seen essentially two different kinds of declarations in Ada. There are the type (and subtype) declarations and there are object declarations.

When type declarations appear within a program they mean that certain attributes and a corresponding set of axioms are introduced. These can all be employed in programs to manipulate objects of that type:

For scalar types there are attributes such as $SUCC, PRED, VAL, POS,$ $FIRST$ and $LAST$.

For subtypes the set of attributes is the same as for the original type but the necessary constraint (as evaluated at the time of declaration) must be satisfied by all values of that type.

For derived types the attributes are inherited at declaration time from the original type.

For new types the attributes available depend on the precise nature of that declaration (is it an enumeration type, integer type, real type or whatever?).

Object declarations in programming languages usually serve several different purposes. These might include the attributing of scopes and the provision of information about storage requirements. But from the point of view of the program verifier the most important purpose is that object declarations of the kind we have so far encountered serve to introduce an identifier and to associate with it a type and thereby a set of attributes for which there are known axioms.

Blocks in Ada are of the general form

declare D **begin** S **end**;

where D represents a set of declarations of possibly different varieties and S represents a sequence of statements. A first attempt at a proof rule for such a block might take the form

$$\frac{H \vdash \{P \wedge R\}\, S\, \{Q\}}{\{P\}\, \textbf{declare}\, D\, \textbf{begin}\, S\, \textbf{end}\, \{Q\}}$$

Here

(a) H represents the information including the set of axioms and attributes derived from the declarations contained in D.

(b) R represents the set of initialisations derived from the declarations of D; uninitialised variables of type T are assumed to be given the undefined value $\perp_T$ a value on which no operation can be performed, not even a test for equality.

As it stands this rule is an inadequate description of the situation. It fails to take account, for instance, of the possibility of D containing a declaration of an object X where X appears in either P or Q. A proper study of the effect of declarations involves looking at the different kinds of declarations.

In what follows it will be assumed that no identifier is declared twice within the one declarative part. This would normally have been checked by a compiler. Basically we are assuming therefore that the pieces of program are syntactically correct. We now give examples of more precise proof rules. In these rules we let $X\#$ denote an identifier which is guaranteed not to clash with any other identifier.

Type declarations

$$\frac{H \vdash \{P\} \text{ declare } D \text{ begin } S \text{ end } \{Q\}}{\{P\} \text{ declare type } T \text{ is } \ldots; D \text{ begin } S \text{ end } \{Q\}}$$

H includes all the attributes and associated axioms, etc. associated with the type T. (Any more global declarations of T are rendered irrelevant.)

Subtype declarations possess a similar proof rule.

Object declarations

We look at three different kinds of object declarations. The first involves an uninitialised variable, the second involves an initialised variable and the third involves a constant.

Uninitialised variable:

$$\frac{H \vdash \{P \wedge X \# = \perp_T\} \text{ declare } D(X\#/X) \text{ begin } S(X\#/X) \text{ end } \{Q\}}{\{P\} \text{ declare } X: T; D \text{ begin } S \text{ end } \{Q\}}$$

Here H contains information about X derived from its declaration; this includes its attributes and the axioms these satisfy.

Initialised variable:

$$\frac{H \vdash \{P \wedge X \# = E\} \text{ declare } D(X\#/X) \text{ begin } S(X\#/X) \text{ end } \{Q\}}{\{P\} \text{ declare } X: T: = E; D \text{ begin } S \text{ end } \{Q\}}$$

Here H has the same meaning as in the rule for uninitialised variables.

Constant:

$$\frac{\{P\} \text{ declare } D(E/X) \text{ begin } S(E/X) \text{ end } \{Q\}}{\{P\} \text{ declare } X: \text{ constant } T := E; D \text{ begin } S \text{ end } \{Q\}}$$

These proof rules describe more accurately the effects of declarations. Note that declarations involving several identifiers, e.g. $X, Y, Z: FLOAT$; can be covered by very similar rules.

4.2.3 Proof rules for statements

In giving proof rules for individual statements of various kinds we use P and Q, possibly decorated with subscripts, to refer to predicates. Similarly S, T and R, possibly subscripted, will refer to single statements or sequences of statements. For the more experienced reader we note that we have no means yet of introducing side-effects into programs, because we have not yet introduced procedures or subprograms. Side-effects tend to play havoc with proof rules. This can be viewed in two ways: either the proof rules are inadequate or side-effects are undesirable. This debate will have to be looked at seriously at a later stage. For the moment we remain content in the knowledge that side-effects are not yet a serious consideration.

We now look at the proof rules for various kinds of statements in Ada. We do not claim to cover all the possible statements in Ada. But the selection of rules we do give covers most of the possibilities. To save tedious discussion about semi-colons, the rules are given without the terminating semi-colons of statements.

Assignment axiom

$$\{P(E/X)\}\ X := E\ \{P\}$$

This rule is merely a formalisation of the back substitution procedure which we had earlier.

Concatenation rule

The following rule describes what is involved in combining two (and therefore by induction any number of) statements.

$$\frac{\{P\}\,S\,\{Q\} \land \{Q\}\,T\,\{R\}}{\{P\}\,S\,T\,\{R\}}$$

This again merely formalises what we have been doing – we must find a predicate Q which has the properties given in the antecedent.

If statements

There are two versions of the if statement caused by the inclusion or exclusion of an else part:

$$\frac{\{P \land B\}\,S\{Q\} \land \{P \land \neg B\}\,T\{Q\}}{\{P\}\ \text{if } B \text{ then } S \text{ else } T \text{ end if}\ \{Q\}}$$

and

$$\frac{\{P \land B\}\,S\{Q\} \land (P \land \neg B) \supset Q}{\{P\}\ \text{if } B \text{ then } S \text{ end if}\ \{Q\}}$$

Case statements

Case statements are similar to if statements in many ways. Below we use the notation $E \equiv C_i$ to imply that the expression E has a value which is selected by choice C_i; this should be taken to cover the **when others** alternative if it is present.

$$\frac{\text{for each } i\, \{P \wedge (E \equiv C_i)\}\, S_i\, \{Q\}}{\{P\}\, \textbf{case } E \textbf{ is when } C_1 => S_1 \textbf{ when } C_2 => S_2 \ldots \textbf{ end case } \{Q\}}$$

The null statement

The Ada null statement

$\{P\}\, \textbf{null}\, \{P\}$

has no effect.

Loop statements

A multitude of different kinds of loop statements is permitted in Ada. We give a selection of the relevant proof rules but note that for completeness others are necessary, e.g. if **reverse** is included in an iteration specification. Below we assume that B, I, etc. have their obvious interpretation and that statement sequences do not contain exit statements.

While version:

$$\frac{\{P \wedge B\}\, S\, \{P\}}{\{P\}\, \textbf{while } B \textbf{ loop } S \textbf{ end loop}\, \{P \wedge \neg B\}}$$

Note that P is essentially the loop invariant.

For version:

The rule below makes use of intervals of any discrete type

$[G .. H]$ is the set $\{I: G <= I <= H\}$

$[G .. H)$ is the set $\{I: G <= I < H\}$

$[\ ]$ is the null interval.

It is also customary to use

$(G .. H]$ to be the set $\{I: G < I <= H\}$

$(G .. H)$ to be the set $\{I: G < I < H\}$

The predicate P is assumed to be a predicate which describes intervals; again it is essentially the loop invariant.

$$\frac{(M <= I <= N) \wedge \{P([M .. I))\}\, S\, \{P([M .. I])\}}{\{P([\ ])\}\, \textbf{for } I \textbf{ in } M .. N \textbf{ loop } S \textbf{ end loop}\, \{P([M .. N])\}}$$

Exit version:

$$\frac{\{P\} S \{Q\} \wedge \{Q \wedge B\}\, T \{P\}}{\{P\}\, \textbf{loop } S \textbf{ exit when } \neg B;\, T \textbf{ end loop}\, \{Q \wedge \neg B\}}$$

This then provides an adequate set of proof rules for constructs in Ada. Others can be readily deduced. But unfortunately these alone are inadequate for proving formally the correctness (partial) of even very simple programs. Consider for instance the following piece of Ada program:

$$--\{X = 3\}$$
$$X := X + 1;$$
$$--\{X > 3\}$$

The assignment axiom is of course applicable but it is the only rule that is applicable. It does not provide the means whereby the above can be shown to be formally correct.

4.2.4 Formal proofs of (partial) correctness

The extra rules needed to provide formal proofs of correctness are called the *consequence rules* and these are as follows:

$$\frac{P \supset Q \land \{Q\} S \{R\}}{\{P\} S \{R\}}$$

and

$$\frac{\{P\} S \{Q\} \land Q \supset R}{\{P\} S \{R\}}$$

Basically these rules allow us to prove results which are slightly weaker in a logical sense than the previous proof rules permit. They complete the rules needed for formal proofs of correctness.

At this stage of the development of the axiomatics of some branch of mathematics the next step would be to develop certain simple but useful results which would obviate the need to continually cite axioms. The analogy in our case is to develop proof rules of a kind which will be more useful than the axioms we already have. It is possible to do this. Of course formal proofs of the correctness of these rules are necessary. Let us look at two examples.

We could provide a modified assignment rule of the form:

$$\frac{P \supset Q(E/X)}{\{P\} X := E \{Q\}}$$

How can we establish the truth of this? From the first version of the consequence rule it follows that the truth of

$$\{P\} X := E \{Q\}$$

can be established if it can be shown that

$$P \supset Q(E/X) \land \{Q(E/X)\} X := E \{Q\}.$$

But the assignment axiom indicates that

$$\{Q(E/X)\} X := E \{Q\}$$

91

is always true. Therefore to prove the truth of

$$\{P\}\, X := E\, \{Q\}$$

it is sufficient to show that

$$P \supset Q(E/X),$$

i.e.

$$\frac{P \supset Q(E/X)}{\{P\}\, X := E\, \{Q\}}$$

as required.

Another useful rule is the modified rule for the **while** version of the loop clause:

$$\frac{\{P \land B\}\, S\, \{P\} \land (P \land \neg B) \supset Q}{\{P\}\ \textbf{while}\ B\ \textbf{loop}\ S\ \textbf{end loop}\ \{Q\}}$$

One application of the second consequent rule and an argument similar to that given above allows the necessary proof to be given.

We give now a formal proof of one of the programs we dealt with earlier. We take the factorial program:

```
- -{N >= 0}
F := 1;
declare
     M: INTEGER := 0;
begin
     while - -{(N >= 0) ∧ (M >= 0) ∧ (F = M!)}
                         M /= N loop
          M := M + 1;
          F := F * M;
     end loop;
end;
- -{F = N!}
```

The proof we give cannot be described as completely formal since we do not justify by citing axioms for the algebraic manipulation involved: a completely formal proof would be monotonous and not sufficiently more informative.

In the proof below the proof works from the inside out. In other words we start within the loop and we gradually work outwards. Note that steps 4 and 5 could be combined. However step 4 alone establishes the loop invariant and so we have kept it separate.

1. - -{(N >= 0) ∧ (M + 1 >= 0) ∧ (F = M!)}
    M := M + 1;   by assignment axiom
    - -{(N >= 0) ∧ (M >= 0) ∧ (F = (M - 1)!)}
2. - -{(N >= 0) ∧ (M >= 0) ∧ (F = (M - 1)!)}

92

$$F := F * M;$$ by assignment axiom

    `--` $\{(N >= 0) \land (M >= 0) \land (F = M!)\}$

3.   `--` $\{(N >= 0) \land (M + 1 >= 0) \land (F = M!)\}$

     $M := M + 1;$ by concatenation rule

     $F := F * M;$ using 1 and 2 above

    `--` $\{(N >= 0) \land (M >= 0) \land (F = M!)\}$

4.   `--` $\{(N >= 0) \land (M >= 0) \land (F = M!)\}$

     $M := M + 1;$ by consequence rule

     $F := F * M;$ from 3 above

    `--` $\{(N >= 0) \land (M >= 0) \land (F = M!)\}$

5.   `--` $\{(N >= 0) \land (M >= 0) \land (F = M!) \land (M \mathrel{/{=}} N)\}$

     $M := M + 1;$ by consequence rule

     $F := F * M;$ using 4 above

    `--` $\{(N >= 0) \land (M >= 0) \land (F = M!)\}$

6.   `--` $\{(N >= 0) \land (M >= 0) \land (F = M!)\}$

     while $M \mathrel{/{=}} N$ **loop**

        $M := M + 1;$ by while rule

        $F := F * M;$ using 5 above

     end loop;

    `--` $\{(N >= 0) \land (M >= 0) \land (F = M!) \land (M = N)\}$

7.   `--` $\{(N >= 0) \land (M >= 0) \land (F = M!)\}$

     while $M \mathrel{/{=}} N$ **loop**

        $M := M + 1;$ by consequence rule

        $F := F * M;$ using 6 above

     end loop;

    `--` $\{F = N!\}$

8.   `--` $\{(N >= 0) \land (M = 0) \land (F = M!)\}$

     while $M \mathrel{/{=}} N$ **loop**

        $M := M + 1;$ by consequence rule

        $F := F * M;$ using 7 above

     end loop;

    `--` $\{F = N!\}$

9.   `--` $\{(N >= 0) \land (F = 1)\}$

     declare

        $M: INTEGER := 0;$

     begin

        while $M \mathrel{/{=}} N$ **loop**

           $M := M + 1;$ by rule for block

           $F := F * M;$ entry and declarations

        end loop;

     end;

    `--` $\{F = N!\}$

10. $--\{N >= 0\}$
    $F := 1;$
    $--\{(N >= 0) \wedge (F = 1)\}$ by assignment axiom

11. $--\{N >= 0\}$
    $F := 1;$
    declare
        $M: INTEGER := 0;$
    begin
        while $M /= N$ **loop**
            $M := M + 1;$ by concatenation rule
            $F := F * M;$ using 9 and 10 above
        end loop;
    end;
  $--\{F = N!\}$

4.2.5   Axiomatics of jumps or goto statements

The goto statement has aroused a great deal of controversy over the years. This has stemmed from claims that its use often betrays a lack of understanding about the proper structure of a program or a lack of appreciation of the constructs available in a programming language or their proper use.

These remarks explain the absence of the use of goto statements, or jumps as they are sometimes called, in the earlier part of this book. We include this section on the goto statement mainly for completeness but also to demonstrate that loops can often be expressed in terms of other, perhaps simpler, constructs. This leads to interesting proofs about equivalences between sets of statements in programming languages.

In Ada goto statements take the form

    goto *LABEL*;

where *LABEL* represents some appropriately defined identifier which identifies a label. The label is defined by the position it occupies. Thus:

    《*LABEL*》
        statement;

The effect of a jump is to discontinue the usual sequential progression through a program. Instead control is transferred to the statement preceded by the appropriate label.

An example illustrates the use of the goto statement:

    Example 4.2.5a   Equivalences between statements
(i) The effect of

    if B **then** S_1 **else** S_2 **end if**;

94

can be achieved in the following way

if B **then** S_1; **goto** LAB; **end if**;
S_2;
$\langle\langle LAB \rangle\rangle$

It is assumed that $\langle\langle LAB \rangle\rangle$ appears nowhere else in the program.

(ii) The effect of

loop S_1; **exit when** B; S_2 **end loop**;

can be achieved without the use of a loop statement in the following way:

$\langle\langle LAB \rangle\rangle$
    S_1;
    if B **then**
        goto $EXIT$;
    end if;
    S_2;
        goto LAB;
$\langle\langle EXIT \rangle\rangle$

The labels $\langle\langle LAB \rangle\rangle$ and $\langle\langle EXIT \rangle\rangle$ do not appear elsewhere in the program.

There are problems in verifying the correctness of programs which use jumps. However, when the jumps are used in a sensible way the difficulties vanish.

That the goto is a source of potential danger shows itself in the proof rules for goto statements. The idea that a goto statement can occur within a sequence of statements means that the sequence may terminate naturally in the usual way. Alternatively there may be jumps to labels which occur elsewhere in the program. Thus there arises the possibility of several forms of exit from a sequence of statements. We require a notation which exhibits possibly several postconditions for a sequence of statements. There will be one for normal termination of the sequence and one for an exit to each distinct label.

Before looking at the consequences of these remarks we introduce some notation.

Definition

A sequence of statements S_L is said to be an *L-statement* if it contains one or more **goto** L statements but does not contain the label $\langle\langle L \rangle\rangle$ itself.

It should be clear that this idea can be extended to include (L_1, L_2)-statements and so on. The remarks which follow also generalise. However we shall conduct the discussion in terms of the conceptually simpler *L*-statement and leave the reader to infer or deduce the obvious analogies.

We write

$$\{P\}\, S_L\, \{Q\} \text{ or at } \langle\langle L\rangle\rangle\, \{R\}$$

to indicate that if the precondition P is true then

    (i) if the execution of the L-statement S_L terminates normally the post-condition Q will be true,

    (ii) if the execution of S_L terminates by jumping to label L then postcondition R will be true on reaching L.

We can now make a simple observation:

        if P is a suitable precondition then

$$\{P\}\, \mathbf{goto}\ L\ \{FALSE\} \quad \text{or at} \quad \langle\langle L\rangle\rangle\, \{P\}$$

It is possible to extend the meaning of this new notation to cover the case where S is not an L-statement. If S is not an L-statement then we can say that the truth of

$$\{P\}\, S\, \{Q\}$$

implies the truth of

$$\{P\}\, S\, \{Q\} \quad \text{or at} \quad \langle\langle L\rangle\rangle\, \{FALSE\}.$$

In other words, it is impossible to jump to a label L external to the sequence of statements S.

Now the new notation allows statements of a general kind, either L-statements or statements without jumps. The proof rules for normal program constructs must now be adjusted to take this new notation into account. The rule for statement sequences can be written as

$$\frac{\{P\}\, S\, \{Q_1\} \text{ or at } \langle\langle L\rangle\rangle\, \{R\} \wedge \{Q_1\}\, T\, \{Q\} \text{ or at } \langle\langle L\rangle\rangle\, \{R\}}{\{P\}\, S\, T\, \{Q\} \text{ or at } \langle\langle L\rangle\rangle\, \{R\}}$$

The rules for conditionals, loops, etc. must all be written in an appropriate manner:

$$\frac{\{P \wedge B\}\, S\, \{Q\} \text{ or at } \langle\langle L\rangle\rangle\, \{R\} \wedge \{P \wedge \neg B\}\, T\, \{Q\} \text{ or at } \langle\langle L\rangle\rangle\, \{R\}}{\{P\}\, \mathbf{if}\ B\ \mathbf{then}\ S\ \mathbf{else}\ T\ \mathbf{end\ if}\ \{Q\} \text{ or at } \langle\langle L\rangle\rangle\, \{R\}}$$

$$\frac{\{P \wedge B\}\, S\, \{Q\} \text{ or at } \langle\langle L\rangle\rangle\, \{R\},\ (P \wedge \neg B) \supset Q}{\{P\}\, \mathbf{if}\ B\ \mathbf{then}\ S\ \mathbf{end\ if}\ \{Q\} \text{ or at } \langle\langle L\rangle\rangle\, \{R\}}$$

and so on.

We illustrate the use of some of these rules by means of a simple example.

Example 4.2.5b   Equivalences involving loop statements

If S_1 and S_2 are statements which do not contain jumps then the proof rule

$$\frac{\{P\}\, S_1\, \{Q\} \wedge \{Q \wedge \neg B\}\, S_2\, \{P\}}{\{P\}\, \mathbf{loop}\ S_1;\ \mathbf{exit\ when}\ B;\ S_2;\ \mathbf{end\ loop}\ \{Q \wedge B\}}$$

is appropriate. Let T denote the sequence of statements mentioned in example 4.2.5a as being equivalent to the above kind of loop. If the equivalence is accurate then on the assumption that

$$\{P\}\,S_1\,\{Q\} \quad \text{and} \quad \{Q \wedge \neg\, B\}\,S_2\,\{P\}$$

are true it should be possible to show that

$$\{P\}\,T\,\{Q \wedge B\}$$

is true.

A formal proof of this can be based on the details of the following:

```
- -{P}
《LAB》
   S₁;
   - -{Q}
   if B then
       goto EXIT;
   end if;
   - -{Q ∧¬ B} or at 《EXIT》 {Q ∧ B}
   S₂;
   - -{P}
   goto LAB;
   - -{FALSE} or at 《LAB》 {P}
《EXIT》
```

4.2.6 Axiomatics of exceptions

The Ada mechanism for exceptions suggests that the axioms associated with these will resemble the axioms associated with jumps. After all, when an exception is raised there is a jump to the corresponding exception handler.

We have already mentioned the existence of the standard exceptions *CONSTRAINT_ERROR* and *NUMERIC_ERROR*. A programmer can also introduce his own exceptions and raise them when appropriate using a raise statement. The mechanisms for dealing with both situations are the same.

From the program verification point of view the situation is relatively straightforward. The effect of a block, or whatever, in which an exception may occur is equivalent to the effect of either

(a) the normal execution of the statements of the block;

or

(b) the normal execution of the statements up to the raising of the exception followed by the effect of executing the appropriate exception handler.

The program verifier can and should construct his proofs accordingly.

If an exception happens to be raised within an exception handler itself, it is propagated out to the enclosing block. Note the desirable consequence – the exception handling mechanism alone cannot cause a program to loop indefinitely.

What now of the axiomatics associated with exceptions? By analogy with the discussion of section 4.2.5 we introduce the following notation:

$$\{P\}\,S\,\{Q\}\ \text{or } \textbf{when } FLAG\,\{R\}$$

to indicate that if the precondition P is true then

(i) if the execution of S terminates normally then postcondition Q will be true:

(ii) if the execution of S causes the exception $FLAG$ to be raised then at the

when $FLAG =>$

part of the program the postcondition R will be true.

Note that the exception handler may not be present in the current block but may exist at an outer level.

It should be clear that the above notation can be extended in an obvious way to accommodate the possible raising of several exceptions and indeed the presence of jumps. Thus it would be possible to have

$$\{P\}\,S\,\{Q\} \quad \text{or} \quad \text{at } \langle\!\langle L \rangle\!\rangle\,\{R_1\}$$
$$\text{or} \quad \textbf{when } NUMERIC\_ERROR\,\{R_2\}$$

and so on.

A simple illustration of this notation is:

$$\{P\}\,\textbf{raise } FLAG\,\{FALSE\} \quad \text{or} \quad \textbf{when } FLAG\,\{P\}$$

For more sophisticated applications we shall wait until chapter 7.

4.2.7 Total correctness

The present discussion on axiomatics and proof rules has concentrated entirely on partial correctness. No mention has yet been made of total correctness. We shall now look at this.

In place of the notation

$$\{P\}\,S\,\{Q\}$$

we introduce a notation for total correctness:

$$\langle P \rangle\,S\,\langle Q \rangle$$

is given the following interpretation:

if the precondition P is true then the computation of S terminates and the postcondition Q is true.

Example 4.2.7a   Illustration

If S is some sequence of statements then the truth of

$$\langle P \rangle\ S\ \langle TRUE \rangle$$

is merely a statement that the execution of S terminates.

All the proof rules for statement sequences, for conditionals, for assignments, etc. continue to hold when each inductive assertion is replaced by this new kind of expression. The only rules which do not hold are the rules which involve possibly non-terminating forms of loop statements.

To show the kind of adjustment that has to be performed on the loop proof rules consider the while version of the loop statement

while B **loop** S **end loop**;

In discussing total correctness in chapter 3 we saw that we could introduce functions and well-founded sets, etc. Alternatively we could use counters. The formal proof rules for total correctness can be phrased in terms of either of these concepts or any equivalent concepts. For simplicity we shall concentrate on the use of counters. In proving total correctness earlier we saw that certain properties of counters had to be established. These should be reflected in the eventual proof rule.

The rule for while loops can be written in the form:

$$\frac{(P(I) \wedge \neg B) \supset Q, \quad P(I) \supset (I <= K), \quad \langle P(I) \wedge B \rangle\ S\ \langle P(I+1) \rangle}{\langle P(0) \rangle\ \textbf{while } B \textbf{ loop } S \textbf{ end loop } \langle Q \rangle}$$

In this rule

I should be interpreted as the counter,

P is the loop invariant which is now a function of I and also of the other program variables,

K is some constant which is independent of I and of the variables altered within S.

The rule

$$\langle P(I) \wedge B \rangle\ S\ \langle P(I+1) \rangle$$

ensures that the computation of S itself must terminate.

Proof rules for other forms of potentially non-terminating loops can be given in an analogous fashion.

4.3   **Remarks**

Formal proofs of correctness are very long and very detailed. To give such a proof for each program is too time-consuming and unnecessary. The usual solution is to give informal proofs of correctness of the kind given in chapters 2 and 3. However, we now note that axioms can be provided for the different aspects of programming languages. If they are required all the details of formal proofs of correctness can be provided.

One very important observation should be made at this stage. The axiom or proof rule for a particular construct captures the essential meaning of that construct. The collection of proof rules therefore provide a very formal method whereby the meaning of the constructs in a programming language can be defined. This approach to describing the semantics of a programming language is for obvious reasons usually referred to as the *axiomatic approach*. It is of course particularly suited to the needs of the program verifier. It provides little in the way of assistance to other users of a language definition such as users, language designers, compiler writers and manufacturers.

Exercises for chapter 4

1. In section 4.1.3 we discussed axioms and properties of floating-point numbers. How relevant was this discussion to fixed-point numbers?

2. Given that the mathematical quantities x and y are represented as reals only approximately in Ada compute the errors involved in calculating (by program) the values of

$$x - y, x * y, x / y, x * n \text{ and } x^n$$

where n is some positive integer. Look at both representations as floating-point and fixed-point numbers.

3. Implement Newton's method for finding the square root of a real number to a high degree of accuracy – see section 4.1.4. Formulate appropriate input and output assertions and prove the total correctness of your program.

4. The reciprocal of a real number A can be found (without having to resort to division) by using the iterative scheme

$$x_{n+1} = 2x - Ax_n^2$$

Design algorithm which will give as accurate an answer as your computer will reasonably permit (i.e. without having to resort to multiple precision arithmetic).
Formulate appropriate input and output assertions and prove the total correctness of your program.

5. The cube root of a positive number A can be calculated using the iterative formula

$$x_{n+1} = (2x_n^3 + A)/3x_n^2$$

and taking as an initial approximation $x_1 = A$.
Write a program to implement this.
Formulate appropriate input and output assertions and verify the total correctness of the program.

6. Derive a proof rule for a **for** version of the loop statement which contains **reverse**.

7. See example 4.2.5a. Using the proof rules for the **if** ... **then** ... **end if** statement, for concatenation and for jumps derive formally the rule for the **if** ... **then** ... **else** ... **end if** statement.

8. Devise a proof rule for the **for** version of the loop statement which contains an exit statement.
   What happens when the exit statement is the

   (*a*) first   (*b*) last   (*c*) only

   element of the loop body?
   When the condition which causes exit is set to *TRUE* does the rule degenerate into the original rule for the **for** version of the loop statement?

9. Devise a set of statements which includes jumps and conditionals and is equivalent to the **for** version of the loop statement.
   Using the proof rules for jumps deduce the proof rule for the for statement.

10. Give a formal proof of the total correctness of a program to evaluate the factorial of a given positive integer N.

11. Give a formal proof rule for the version of the loop statement which contains an exit statement.

12. Give an informal proof and thereby a formal proof of the termination of the following program (both X and Y are integer variables):

    ```
    --{X >= 0}
    Y := 0;
    while X > 0 loop
            while X > 0 loop
                    X := X - 1;
                    Y := Y + 1;
            end loop;
            Y := Y - 1;
            while Y > 0 loop
                    X := X + 1;
                    Y := Y - 1;
            end loop;
    end loop;
    ```

13. Devise separate proof rules for calls of the procedures *GET* and *PUT*. For the procedure *GET*, for example, the precondition should indicate some initial state of the input file and the postcondition should include mention of its state and the state of the variable holding the input on completion of the execution of the *GET* statement.

14. Devise a program to output a multiplication table for any integer N between 2 and 12. The value of N is supplied as data. Give a proof of the total correctness of your program.
    In providing a proof it will be necessary for the verifier to invent some sort of notation for expressing the output file in terms of a sequence of lines of a particular size. Certain assumptions may also have to be made about the number of character positions occupied by a printed integer, a complete line, and so on.

101

5 ARRAYS AND RECORDS

Previous chapters have dealt with programs which make use of integer variables, character variables and so on, or the corresponding constants. Much of computing is concerned with:

(*a*) groups of integers, reals, etc. and might involve the manipulation of vectors, matrices, strings of characters and so on;

(*b*) sets of related pieces of information such as a person's age, height, weight, date of birth, name, address, etc.;

(*c*) lists of items of the same type, tree structures, etc.

In Ada, discussion of (*a*) centres around the use of arrays, discussion of (*b*) involves the use of records and (*c*) involves the use of access types.

In this chapter we look at these three topics of arrays, records and access types. In each case we show how these objects can be introduced into Ada programs. We then look at methods of verifying the correctness of programs which manipulate these objects.

5.1 Arrays

5.1.1 Arrays in Ada

The declaration

A : **array** (1 .. 10) **of** *INTEGER*;

introduces an array A. This makes available a set of subscripted variables $A(J)$ where J is an integer in the range 1 to 10. These variables can be used like integer variables. They can be given values as in

$A(J) := 4$;

or their values can be used in the evaluation of an arithmetic expression as long as it produces an integer in the range 1 .. 10.

An example demonstrates some of the other alternatives.

Example 5.1.1a   Declaration of arrays

(i) The declaration

B, C : **array** (1 .. 10) **of** *INTEGER*;

introduces two arrays B and C of the same type.

(ii) Given the declaration

type *DAY* **is** (*SUN, MON, TUE, WED, THU, FRI, SAT*);

then a declaration such as

HOURS_WORKED : **array** (*MON .. FRI*) **of** *INTEGER* **range** 0 .. 24;

is permissible. The variables made available by this are then written in the form

HOURS_WORKED (*MON*), . . ., *HOURS_WORKED* (*FRI*)

The values these can hold are all integers in the range 0 .. 24.

(iii) Type declarations such as

type *TABLE* **is array** (1 .. 10, 1 .. 20) **of** *FLOAT*;

are possible and can be followed by a declaration such as

STATS : *TABLE*;

This has the effect of introducing a two-dimensional array called *STATS*. By this declaration real variables $STATS(I, J)$ where $1 <= I <= 10$ and $1 <= J <= 20$ are made available. Again these can be initialised and used in expressions just like real variables.

Associated with arrays of all kinds are certain attributes. If X is some arbitrary array possibly containing several dimensions then

$X'FIRST$	will select the lower bound of the first dimension
$X'LAST$	will select the upper bound of the first dimension
$X'RANGE$	produces the subtype defined by $X'FIRST .. X'LAST$
$X'LENGTH$	will select the length of the first dimension.

Corresponding attributes are associated with the other dimensions. Thus for the Jth dimension there are

$X'FIRST(J), X'LAST(J), X'RANGE(J)$ and $X'LENGTH(J)$.

Example 5.1.1b   Predefined attributes for arrays
Using the arrays declared earlier we have

$A'FIRST$	produces 1
$HOURS\_WORKED'RANGE$	produces *MON .. FRI*
$TABLE'LENGTH$ (2)	produces 20.

Having introduced arrays it is convenient to be able to assign values to them in a simple way. It is possible to give values to individual items. This is tedious and can lead to unnecessary complications in programming. We now introduce the idea of aggregates to simplify this task. In the examples given below we again make use of the array declarations given earlier.

To initialise the ten integers in A to be the first ten prime numbers we would write

103

A : **array** $(1 \ldots 10)$ **of** $INTEGER$:= $(2, 3, 5, 7, 11, 13, 17, 19, 23, 29)$;

After such a declaration $A(1)$ would hold the value 2, $A(2)$ would hold the value 3, and so on. The bracketed expression on the right of the becomes symbol (:=) is called an *aggregate*. It holds the initial value adopted by A; if an integer N is held in position J of the aggregate then $A(J)$ is initialised to N.

Alternatively the components of an aggregate can be named in a choice section. Thus the array $HOURS\_WORKED$ could be initialised at declaration time or alternatively in an assignment in the following way

$$HOURS\_WORKED := (MON \ldots WED \mid FRI => 8, \textbf{others} => 0);$$

The MON, TUE, WED and FRI components are given the value 8, the remaining THU component is given the value 0.

A more complex example shows a possible assignment to the array $STATS$:

$$STATS := (1 \ldots 3 \mid 7 \mid 8 => (1 \ldots 20 => 1.0),$$
$$4 \ldots 6 \qquad => (1 \ldots 20 => 2.0),$$
$$\textbf{others} \qquad => (1 \ldots 10 \mid 12 => 3.0, \textbf{others} = 0.0));$$

The first, second, third, seventh and eighth rows of $STATS$ are all given the same set of values namely a row of ones, the fourth, fifth and sixth rows are given a row of twos and remaining rows are again given the expected values.

Having introduced the idea of an aggregate it makes sense to talk about constant arrays:

$$PRIMES: \textbf{constant array} \ (1 \ldots 10) \ \textbf{of} \ INTEGER :=$$
$$(2, 3, 5, 7, 11, 13, 17, 19, 23, 29);$$

Now $PRIMES(J)$ for all J in the range $1 \ldots 10$ are constant and any attempt to alter them will result in error. Other similar declarations can be given.

In the course of introducing aggregates we also introduced assignments involving complete arrays. To be more forthright about this we note that

$$P := Q;$$

is acceptable provided that P and Q are arrays (or subarrays) of the same type and with the same size (Q may be any expression provided it delivers an array of the proper kind).

Example 5.1.1c   Overlapping arrays

Let QQ be declared as

QQ : **array** $(1 \ldots 20)$ **of** $ITEM$;

Then assuming QQ has been initialised in some appropriate way

$$QQ \ (1 \ldots 3) := QQ \ (4 \ldots 6);$$

is acceptable. The effect is the same as

$$QQ(1) := QQ(4); \quad QQ(2) := QQ(5); \quad QQ(3) := QQ(6);$$

In fact the assignments can be performed in any order whatsoever. Even

$QQ(2 .. 4) := QQ(1 .. 3);$

is acceptable though the arrays overlap but the effect is *not* equivalent to the corresponding set of simpler assignments

$QQ(2) := QQ(1); \quad QQ(3) := QQ(2); \quad QQ(4) := QQ(3);$

In assignments involving arrays the right hand side is first evaluated. It should then be imagined that the array so obtained is assigned *en bloc* to the left hand array variable.

The arrays we have so far introduced have all had fixed bounds, bounds known at compile time. Situations arise in which bounds are not known until execution time. In these cases at least one bound inevitably depends on the value of some quantity which has to be calculated. In Ada there are various ways of introducing these *dynamic* arrays.

The declaration

D : **array** $(1 .. N)$ **of** *INTEGER*;

introduces an array D where bounds are 1 and N. More precisely the upper bound is the value held in N at the time the array declaration is elaborated or executed. It is dynamic.

In all the examples given above the bounds of the arrays have been specified in an explicit fashion. Consider now

type *VECTOR* **is array** (*INTEGER* **range** $<>$) **of** *FLOAT*;

or

type *MATRIX* **is array** (*INTEGER* **range** $<>$, *INTEGER* **range** $<>$) **of** *FLOAT*;

In both these type declarations the bounds are unspecified. Basically the type declaration provides a kind of template which describes objects of type *VECTOR* or *MATRIX*. When an actual object of one of these types has to be introduced the bounds must be named explicitly. Thus

V: *VECTOR* $(1 .. 100);$

introduces a vector V, essentially an array of 100 real variables. Likewise the declarations

$M1, M2$: *MATRIX* $(1 .. 10, 1 .. 20);$
$M3$: *MATRIX* $(1 .. 15, 1 .. 15);$

introduce three different matrices, the first two being of identical size.

In the standard environment there is a standard type called *STRING* whose declaration is essentially of the form

type *STRING* **is array** (*NATURAL* **range** $<>$) **of** *CHARACTER*;

With this available it becomes possible to have declarations such as

ALPHA : *STRING* := "*ABCDEF*";

or even

$$BLANKS : \textbf{constant } STRING := \text{"} \qquad \text{"};$$

Now character strings can be regarded as special kinds of aggregates peculiar to characters. These arrays *ALPHA* and *BLANKS* inherit their size from the initial values given to them. Thereafter the sizes remain fixed.

Both the equality and the inequality operators are defined when the operands are arrays; the comparisons test for the equality or inequality of the corresponding elements. The remaining comparison operators are defined between two one-dimensional arrays whose elements are of the same discrete type; then the usual lexicographic ordering is implied.

The special operator &, called catenation, can be used to join together (i.e. lay end to end) the elements of two one-dimensional arrays. Moreover a single element can be joined to the left or right hand end of an array in the expected manner. Since the type *STRING* is effectively an array type we note that

$$\text{"}ABCD\text{"} \text{ \& } \text{"}E\text{"}$$

produces *"ABCDE"*.

The *BOOLEAN* operators **not**, **and**, **or** and **xor** can all be used on one-dimensional arrays of *BOOLEAN* values. **not** inverts individual elements and the binary operators operate on corresponding pairs of elements.

5.1.2 Axiomatics of arrays

In this section we look at various aspects of the semantics of arrays. There are various matters which require explanation. We require to explain precisely what it means to introduce an array of a particular kind. We also require to re-examine the concept of an assignment since subscripted variables introduce certain problems as do assignments involving either complete arrays or subarrays.

We begin with what might appear to be a special case of array types. We restrict ourselves to one-dimensional arrays and we talk only about special kinds of type declarations involving arrays. The latter is not really a serious restriction since ultimately all one-dimensional arrays that are introduced into Ada programs will essentially be of a type like this though the type name may be implicit.

The extension to multi-dimensional arrays is for the most part relatively straightforward. In mathematical terms the indices are then taken from the Cartesian product of several ranges and the definitions below can be extended accordingly. Most of the important ideas will be illustrated by restricting the discussion to arrays of one dimension.

Assume we have a type declaration of the following kind:

type T **is array** (I) **of** T_0;

where I is some discrete range and T_0 is some previously known type. Let

$$M = I'FIRST, \quad N = I'LAST.$$

Then

1. If X is an element of T then for all i in I

   $T(X_M, \ldots, X_i, \ldots, X_N)$

   is an element of type T.
2. The elements described above are the only elements of type T.
3. If we let X denote $T(X_M, \ldots, X_N)$ then

   $X(i) = X_i$ for all $M <= i <= N$.
4. Using the notation of 3 above and assuming i and j are elements in I
   then $X(i .. j)$ is an element of type T. If $M <= i <= j <= N$
   then the indices of $X(i .. j)$ are constrained to lie in the range $i .. j$ and
   $X(i .. j)$ consists of the elements

   $(X_i, \ldots, X_j)$.

   If $j < i$ then $X(i .. j)$ is the empty element.
5. Using the notation of 3 above

   $X'FIRST = M, \quad X'LAST = N, \quad X'RANGE$ is $M .. N$;

   moreover

   $$X'LENGTH = \begin{cases} 0 \text{ if } M > N \\ 1 + Y'LENGTH \text{ if } M <= N \text{ where } Y = X(I'SUCC(M) .. N) \end{cases}$$
6. The assignment axiom.

Note that in 1 and 2 above we mention only the positional form of (qualified) aggregate; we have not mentioned the non-positional version. However, the latter is merely another way of expressing the former.

The above axioms are complete apart from axiom 6, the assignment axiom, which merits some close examination and some discussion. We shall spend the rest of this section considering this.

The axioms 1 to 5 given above are applicable whether or not X, as defined by axiom 3, is a constant or a variable array. Axiom 6 is of interest only when X is a variable. So the ensuing discussion about the assignment axiom will be restricted to this case.

Before going further we shall explain the need for having to be concerned about a new assignment axiom. The assignment axiom of chapter 4 took the form

$\{P(Y/X)\}\ X := Y\{P\}$

i.e. the precondition was obtained from the postcondition by replacing all occurrences of X by Y. Consider the following situation

$--\{A(I) = I \land I = 4\}$
$A(A(I)) := 0;$
$--\{A(4) = 0\}$

Application of the original assignment axiom will not allow the formal verification of the above. So for subscripted variables and arrays in general we have to replace the assignment axiom.

Behind the axiom for assignment that follows there is a kind of philosophy about the view one can take of an array. There are two possible views:

(a) An array can be regarded as a function from subscripts into variables, i.e. A maps the subscript I, for example, into the array variable $A(I)$.

(b) An array of type T is a variable whose value is a function which maps subscripts into elements of type T_0.

(a) is the more traditional but less helpful view. It suffers from the drawback that the idea permits the possibility of sharing – a function may map two subscripts onto the same variable. View (b) has the effect of removing this possibility and so is the approach we adopt.

Taking this view the assignment

$$X(I) := Y;$$

alters the value of the function referred to by X. We can express this by saying that the effect of the above is effectively

$$X := [X | I | Y];$$

where $[X | I | Y]$ is the function which is similar to the original function except at the point I where its value is now Y. In other words if J belongs to the domain of X

$$[X | I | Y](J) = \begin{cases} X(J) & \text{if } J \mathrel{/}= I \\ Y & \text{if } J = I \end{cases}$$

The assignment axiom for subscripted variables is now modified so that it reflects the assignment

$$X := [X | I | Y];$$

Thus

$$\{P([X | I | Y]/X)\}\, X(I) := Y\, \{P\}$$

Example 5.1.2a   Use of the assignment axiom
Consider the little program given earlier, namely

- - $\{A(I) = I \wedge I = 4\}$
$A(A(I)) := 0;$
- - $\{A(4) = 0\}$

The correctness of this can now be established. One application of the assignment rule leaves us with the task of verifying

$$(A(I) = I \wedge I = 4) \supset [A | A(I) | 0]\,(4) = 0$$

The truth of this is readily established.

Example 5.1.2b Swapping elements

The effect of interchanging two elements of an array produces a re-arrangement of the array. In other words

$$[[X \mid I \mid X(J)] \mid J \mid X(I)]$$

is a rearrangement of the array X.

The ideas given above can be extended in a straightforward manner to cover assignments of the form

$$X(I \, . \, . \, J) := Y;$$

where Y is an array of appropriate size and type. We regard this assignment as an abbreviation for

$$X := [X \mid I \, . \, . \, J \mid Y];$$

where

$$[X \mid I \, . \, . \, J \mid Y](K) = \begin{cases} Y(K) & \text{if } I <= K <= J \\ X(K) & \text{otherwise} \end{cases}$$

The assignment axiom is then just

$$\{P([X \mid I \, . \, . \, J \mid Y]/X)\} \, X(I \, . \, . \, J) := Y \, \{P\}$$

This now completes the discussion about the axioms associated with arrays, at least some of them. No mention has been made of the standard operators that can be used with arrays. We shall leave consideration of these as exercises for the willing reader.

5.1.3 Verification of programs which use arrays

In this section we look at last at the problem of verifying the correctness of programs which use or manipulate arrays. We shall begin by considering some simple programs and gradually progress to more complex programs which perform merging, partitioning and sorting.

Perhaps the major problem in this area is, rather curiously, one of notation. We shall not highlight this problem initially but as we progress through the more difficult examples the reader should pay attention to the problem of specifying assertions and invariants at each stage. As we look at these examples it will be necessary to introduce some convenient notation to avoid long, complex and somewhat opaque assertions.

Adding elements of an array

Let us begin by attempting to prove the correctness of the following program intended to find the sum of all the elements in the integer array A.

```
SUM := 0;
for I in A'RANGE loop
    SUM := SUM + A(I);
end loop;
```

We require to establish that at the end of the piece of program

$$SUM = \sum_{N=A'FIRST}^{A'LAST} A(N)$$

using the usual mathematical notation for summation. Appropriate assertions can be incorporated into the program as follows:

```
SUM := 0;
-- {SUM = 0}
for I in A'RANGE loop
    SUM := SUM + A(I);
```

$$-- \left\{ SUM = \sum_{N=A'FIRST}^{I} A(N) \right\}$$

```
end loop;
```

$$-- \left\{ SUM = \sum_{N=A'FIRST}^{A'LAST} A(N) \right\}$$

A proof of correctness can be given in the usual fashion.

This example is relatively straightforward but one point can be mentioned. Note that we initialised SUM to zero, not to $A(A'FIRST)$. Having taken the latter course of action the program would have failed in the event of the array A being empty. As presented above the program and its correctness proof are valid in all cases.

Finding maximum and its position

Let us now turn our attention to the problem of finding the maximum value of all the elements of a non-empty array together with the position of the maximum. The following program is intended to do this:

```
POSN := A'FIRST;
MAX := A(POSN);
for I in A'FIRST + 1 .. A'LAST loop
    if A(I) > MAX then
        POSN := I;
        MAX := A(POSN);
    end if;
end loop;
```

From the notational point of view complications now start to appear. As execution of the program progresses MAX holds the largest value of the array A so far found, i.e.

$$MAX >= A(A'FIRST), MAX >= A(A'FIRST + 1), \ldots$$

and so on.

We shall use the notation $A(I \, . \, . \, J)$ – or just A if I and J are the lower and upper bounds respectively – to represent the subset of the array A consisting of all $A(K)$ where $I \leq K \leq J$. Whenever this notation is used in assertions it will be implicitly assumed that both I and J lie between the bounds of array A, i.e.

$$A'FIRST \leq I \leq J \leq A'LAST.$$

There is one exception to this. To accommodate the null case we also permit $J = I - 1$ and then $A(I \, . \, . \, J)$ contains zero elements. Only in this situation can I or J lie outside the bounds of A.

To express the fact that some element is greater than or equal to all the elements in some array we introduce the following idea. We could write

$$MAX \geq A(I \, . \, . \, J) \quad \text{or} \quad GE(MAX, A(I \, . \, . \, J))$$

to mean that

$$MAX \geq A(K)$$

for each K in $I \, . \, . \, J$. We extend this idea further and write

$$A(IA \, . \, . \, JA) \geq B(IB \, . \, . \, JB) \quad \text{or} \quad GE(A(IA \, . \, . \, JA), B(IB \, . \, . \, JB))$$

to mean that

$$A(KA) \geq B(KB)$$

for all KA in $IA \, . \, . \, JA$ and all KB in $IB \, . \, . \, JB$. If arrays happen to be empty we assume that the relationships are trivially true.

These extensions to the meaning of the operator $\geq$ are sometimes referred to as the *pointwise extensions* of the operator $\geq$. Similar extensions can be introduced for all the relational operators $>, \geq, =, /=, \leq, <$ with the expected meaning.

The reader should note the conflict of notation. Operators such as $\geq$ are already defined for array operands in the standard environment: there they refer to lexicographic ordering. This conflicts with the idea of pointwise extension. Clearly the one symbol should not be used in an ambiguous fashion. Accordingly we shall use LT, LE, EQ, NE, GE and GT as our pointwise extensions corresponding to $<, \leq$, etc. At first glance it might appear as if we can no longer abuse notation in the normal mathematical fashion, e.g. $A \leq B \leq C$. But the **in** operator comes to the rescue and we can write B **in** $A \, . \, . \, C$. Indeed this can be extended to operate in the case where A, B and C are arrays and then to mean $LE(A, B) \wedge LE(B, C)$; such a definition is not permitted within Ada itself.

With this new notation we can now give assertions which point the way to a proof of the correctness of the program to find the maximum element in an array.

```
-- {A'FIRST <= A'LAST}
    POSN := A'FIRST;
    MAX := A(POSN);
```

$- -\{MAX = A(POSN) \wedge MAX >= A(A'FIRST)\}$
for I **in** $A'FIRST + 1 .. A'LAST$ **loop**
    if $A(I) > MAX$ **then**
        $MAX := A(I); POSN := I;$
    end if;
    $- -\{MAX = A(POSN) \wedge GE(MAX, A(A'FIRST .. I))\}$
end loop;
$- -\{MAX = A(POSN) \wedge GE(MAX, A)\}$

Binary search

    The binary search technique is used to find whether or not an element C is present in an initially ordered array A. The usual linear search is rather inefficient and takes the form of a scan through the array from the bottom to the top. In the binary search process we examine the middle of array A and from the relationship between the middle element and C we can determine more accurately where C lies. It will either be the middle element itself, it will lie in the top half of the array or it will lie in the bottom half.

    If we assume initial declarations such as

    A: **array** $(1 .. N)$ **of** $INTEGER$;
    L, U, MID: $INTEGER$;
    $FOUND$: $BOOLEAN$;

and assume that the elements of A are in ascending order, the program can be written as follows (though the final **elsif** could have been replaced by an **else**):

    $L := A'FIRST$;
    $U := A'LAST$;
    $FOUND := FALSE$;
    while not $FOUND$ **and** $L <= U$ **loop**
        $MID := (L + U)/2$;
        if $A(MID) < C$ **then**
            $L := MID + 1$;
        elsif $A(MID) = C$ **then**
            $FOUND := TRUE$;
        elsif $A(MID) > C$ **then**
            $U := MID - 1$;
        end if;
    end loop;

    It is a relatively straightforward matter to express the final assertion. It is just

    $(FOUND \wedge C = A(MID)) \vee (\textbf{not } FOUND \wedge NE(C, A))$

using the pointwise extension of the operator $/=$.

The initial predicate is somewhat more difficult. We introduce some auxiliary notation. Let $ORD_{<=}(X)$ denote the fact that the array X is ordered with respect to the operator $<=$. By this we mean that

$$X(X'FIRST) <= X(X'FIRST + 1) <= \ldots <= X(X'LAST)$$

If the array X happens to be empty we assume that $ORD_{<=}(X)$ is trivially true.

A similar notation can be introduced in an obvious way for the other comparison operators. But in any one piece of program it is likely that only one ordering will be under consideration. In these circumstances it is possible to drop the subscript from $ORD_{<=}$ and use merely ORD, for example.

It is convenient to borrow from mathematics another piece of notation. By

$$P..Q - R..S$$

we shall mean the set of elements in the range $P..Q$ which are not also in the range $R..S$.

We are now in a position to give the assertions which guide the correctness proof of the binary search program. We merely sketch the augmented program:

```
- - {ORD(A)}
L := A'FIRST;
U := A'LAST;
FOUND := FALSE;
while - - {(FOUND ∧ C = A(MID)) ∨
           - - not FOUND ∧ NE(C, A(A'RANGE − L .. U))}
      not FOUND and L <= U loop
    MID := (L + U)/2;
      . . .
end loop;
- - {(FOUND ∧ C = A(MID)) ∨ (not FOUND ∧ NE(C, A))}
```

There is a sense in which the above program and its correctness proof are slightly unsatisfactory. Fortunately the array A is constant throughout and so we were able to omit mention of the fact that A remains unaltered. However, as soon as we start looking at programs which manipulate and alter arrays this is no longer feasible.

Merging

We assume that A and B have been declared in the following fashion:

A: **array** $(1 .. N)$ **of** $INTEGER$;
B: **array** $(1 .. M)$ **of** $INTEGER$;

where N and M are previously declared and previously initialised integer variables. We assume further that the elements of both A and B are in increasing order and the problem is to merge the two arrays to produce a third array C.

On completion of the program C will contain all the elements of A and all the elements of B and will be ordered in the same way as A and B.

Some preliminary declarations are

C: **array** $(1 \ .. \ N + M)$ **of** $INTEGER$;
A_PT: $INTEGER$ **range** $1 \ .. \ N + 1 := 1$;
B_PT: $INTEGER$ **range** $1 \ .. \ M + 1 := 1$;
C_PT: $INTEGER$ **range** $1 \ .. \ N + M + 1 := 1$;

A_PT, B_PT and C_PT will be used as pointers into the arrays A, B and C respectively.

The following program is intended to perform the required task:

```
while C_PT <= N + M loop
    if A_PT > N then
        C(C_PT .. N + M) := B(B_PT .. M);
        C_PT := N + M + 1;
        B_PT := M + 1;
    elsif B_PT > M then
        C(C_PT .. N + M) := A(A_PT .. N);
        C_PT := N + M + 1;
        A_PT := N + 1;
    elsif A(A_PT) <= B(B_PT) then
        C(C_PT) := A(A_PT);
        C_PT := C_PT + 1;
        A_PT := A_PT + 1;
    else
        C(C_PT) := B(B_PT);
        C_PT := C_PT + 1;
        B_PT := B_PT + 1;
    end if;
end loop;
```

The program proceeds basically by inspecting successive elements of A and B and moving the smaller elements into C. At any stage during the execution of the program all the elements of C will be ordered and they will all be smaller than the remaining elements of A and B.

Again we encounter a problem of notation. We know how to express the idea that an array or part of an array is ordered. We also know how to express the fact that the elements in one array are smaller than the elements in another array. But how do we express the remaining ideas?

We introduce a new piece of notation.

Rearrangement

We write $X \sim Y$ to mean that the array X is a rearrangement of the elements in array Y. Thus X and Y contain the same number of elements and each element occurs with the same frequency in both arrays.

We are now in a position to express the assertions for the merge program. In particular

the input assertion is $\quad ORD_{<=}(A) \wedge ORD_{<=}(B)$

and

the output assertion is $\quad ORD_{<=}(C) \wedge (C \sim A \,\&\, B)$.

Note that this succinct notation includes all kinds of information. For instance, it contains the fact that the number of elements in C is the sum of the number of elements in A and the number of elements in B.

We can now rewrite in skeleton form the merge program including all the assertions necessary for a correctness proof. In mentioning the ordering property we write ORD as an abbreviation for $ORD_{<=}$.

```
- - {ORD(A) ∧ ORD(B)}
declare
        A_PT: INTEGER range 1 .. N + 1 := 1;
        B_PT: INTEGER range 1 .. M + 1 := 1;
        C_PT: INTEGER range 1 .. N + M + 1 := 1;          :
begin
        while - - {ORD(C(1 .. C_PT − 1)) ∧
                - - C(1 .. C_PT − 1) ~ A(1 .. A_PT − 1) & B(1 .. B_PT − 1) ∧
                - - LE(C(1 .. C_PT − 1), A(A_PT .. N) & B(B_PT .. M))}
                                        C_PT <= N + M loop
        if A_PT > N then
        . . .
        end loop;
end;
- - {ORD(C) ∧ (C ~ A & B)}
```

Note that the loop invariant contains implicitly the information that

$$C\_PT - 1 = A\_PT - 1 + B\_PT - 1$$

i.e.

$$C\_PT = A\_PT + B\_PT - 1$$

The loop terminates when $C\_PT > N + M$ and from an inspection of the range of C_PT it follows that $C\_PT = N + M + 1$. This implies that $A\_PT = N + 1$ and $B\_PT = M + 1$. The final assertion can now be deduced in a straightforward manner from the loop invariant.

Partitioning an array

Consider the problem of partitioning or splitting a non-empty array A into two smaller arrays B and C with the property that all the elements in B are

115

less than or equal to the elements in C, i.e. using our pointwise extension notation $LE(B, C)$. We provide a program below which claims to accomplish this task.

Assume initial declarations:

A: **array** $(1 .. N)$ **of** $INTEGER$;
I: $INTEGER$ **range** $1 .. N$;
J: $INTEGER$ **range** $0 .. N$:
$VAL, TEMP$: $INTEGER$;

Then assuming the elements of A have been initialised in some appropriate way the partitioning section of program can take the form

```
I := 1;
J := N;
VAL := A (N/2)
while I <= J loop
        while A (I) < VAL loop
            I := I + 1;
        end loop;
        while VAL < A (J) loop
            J := J - 1;
        end loop;
        if I <= J then
          TEMP := A(I);
          A(I) := A(J);
          A (J) := TEMP;
          I := I + 1;
          J := J - 1;
        end if;
    end loop;
```

This is our first encounter with a program which actually makes alterations to an array itself. We could like to be able to include in our assertions some indication of the fact that the final array is a rearrangement of the original array. So we introduce an auxiliary variable, not present in the program, which denotes the original array. We use $A'IN$ to denote the original version of array A. This is the only new piece of notation we require. So we can now rewrite the partitioning program annotated with appropriate assertions. The initial $A = A'IN$ is trivially true. Further, we assume the loop invariant true initially.

```
- -{A'LAST >= A'FIRST ∧ A = A'IN}
I := 1;
J := N;
VAL := A (N/2);
while - - {VAL in A (1 .. I - 1) .. A (J + 1 .. N) ∧ A ~ A'IN}
                    I <= J loop
```

116

```
    while A(I) < VAL loop
        I := I + 1;
    end loop;
    --{VAL in A(1 .. I − 1) .. A(J + 1 .. N) ∧ VAL <= A(I) ∧ A ~ A'IN}
    while VAL < A(J) loop
        J := J − 1;
    end loop;
    --{VAL in A(1 .. I − 1) .. A(J + 1 .. N) ∧ VAL in A(J) .. A(I)}
    if I <= J then
        TEMP := A(I);
        A(I) := A(J);
        A(J) := TEMP;
        I := I + 1;
        J := J − 1;
    end if;
end loop;
--{LE(A(1 .. I − 1), A(J + 1 .. N)) ∧ J < I ∧ A ~ A'IN}
```

Note that as the interchanges occur we effectively replace A by

$$[[A \mid I \mid A(J)] \mid J \mid A(I)]$$

and we know that this is a rearrangement of A (see example 5.2.1*b*).

Sorting an array

Finally we look at a program to sort an array A. The sorting process takes the form of a sequence of scans through the array. On each scan the next smallest item is determined.

We assume declarations

```
A: array (1 .. N) of INTEGER;
TEMP: INTEGER;
```

and the program takes the form

```
for I in 1 .. N − 1 loop
    for J in I + 1 .. N loop
        if A(I) > A(J) then
            TEMP := A(I);
            A(I) := A(J);
            A(J) := TEMP;
        end if;
    end loop;
end loop;
```

We need no new notation to express the assertions required in the proof of correctness of this program.

$$--\{A = A'IN\}$$

```
for I in 1 .. N − 1 loop
    for J in I + 1 .. N loop
        if A(I) > A(J) then
            TEMP := A(I);
            A(I) := A(J);
            A(J) := TEMP;
        end if;
        --{LE(A(1 .. I − 1), A(I .. N)) ∧ LE(A(I), A(I + 1 .. J))
        --ORD(A(1 .. I − 1)) ∧ A ~ A'IN}
    end loop;
    --{LE(A(1 .. I), A(I + 1 .. N))
    --ORD(A(1 .. I)) ∧ A ~ A'IN}
end loop;
--{ORD(A) ∧ A ~ A'IN}
```

This, then, completes our look at the verification of programs which make use of arrays. We have basically restricted our attention to arrays of integers and even then to arrays which were indexed by integers. Extensions to other kinds of arrays and other indexes are relatively straightforward.

5.2 Records

Whereas arrays are used for sets of related items which are all of the same type, records tend to be used for sets of related pieces of information of possibly different types.

5.2.1 Records in Ada

The type associated with an employee might be introduced in the following way:

```
type EMPLOYEE is
    record
        NAME: STRING(1 .. 30);
        EMP_NO: STRING(1 .. 8);
        AGE: INTEGER range 16 .. 65;
        HOURS_WK: INTEGER range 0 .. 168;
    end record;
```

We say that an object of type *EMPLOYEE* has four named components which are denoted by

NAME	a string of 30 characters
EMP_NO	a string of 8 characters
AGE	an integer in the range 16 .. 65
HOURS_WK	an integer in the range 0 .. 168

Objects can be declared in the expected way.

$M: EMPLOYEE$;

introduces a variable M capable of holding a record of the kind described above. The various components of M are accessed by writing $M . NAME, M . EMP\_NO$, and so on.

Arrays can be introduced:

$WORK\_FORCE$: **array** $(1 .. 100)$ **of** $EMPLOYEE$;

Individual variables are selected by writing $WORK\_FORCE(I)$ and the components of such a variable can be accessed by writing $WORK\_FORCE(I) . NAME$, and so on.

Initialisation of records can occur by an appropriate use of aggregates. To initialise M above we could write something of the form

$M := ("\qquad JOHN SMITH", "...", 25, 42)$

In this case the order in which the items are supplied in the aggregate is the same as the order of the components in the record. Alternatively the components could be initialised in the following fashion:

$M := (EMP\_NO => "...",$
$\qquad NAME => "\qquad JOHN SMITH",$
$\qquad HOURS\_WK => 45,$
$\qquad AGE => 25);$

In this case the order of presenting the items in the aggregate is irrelevant.

Constant records can now be introduced. Then we can have

$CHAIRMAN$: **constant** $EMPLOYEE := (..., ..., 60, 168)$;

with appropriate entries for the $NAME$ and EMP_NO components.

Although we have stressed the situation in which the components of a record are of different types there are situations where the components can be of the same type. If we wish to talk about complex numbers, for example, the real and imaginary parts will usually be of the same real type. So we can define

    type $COMPLEX$ **is**
      record
          $RE, IM: FLOAT$;
      end record;

For the manipulation of complex members a record such as the above is more appropriate than an array of two reals. The programmer will normally know whether he wants to access the real or the imaginary part of the record and the selectors allow him to do this in a straightforward fashion. Accessing elements in this way is generally more efficient than accessing the individual elements of an array.

In defining a new record type note that the components are declared in a manner which strongly resembles ordinary object declarations. This similarity can be carried somewhat further since components can receive initial values in the type declaration. For example if in the type declaration of *EMPLOYEE* we had written for the hours worked field

HOURS_WK: *INTEGER* **range** 0 .. 168 := 0;

then this component would automatically be initialised to 0 whenever an object of type *EMPLOYEE* is declared.

It is sometimes convenient to be able to parametrise record types. Consider, for example, the case of a type *BUFFER*, visualised as an array of characters together with a pointer which indicates the section of the array that has been filled so far. Thus

> **type** *BUFFER* (*LENGTH*: *INTEGER* **range** 0 .. *LIMIT* := 100) **is**
> **record**
> > *POSITION*: *INTEGER* **range** 0 .. *LENGTH* := 0;
> > *TEXT*: **array** (1 .. *LENGTH*) **of** *CHARACTER*;
> **end record**;

Note the use of initialisation to give default values. The *LENGTH* component is referred to as a *discriminant* of the record type, a kind of parameter associated with the type. Dynamic arrays in records are permitted only when the dynamic bounds are themselves discriminants.

As might be imagined the discriminants must be given definite values at the appropriate time – not necessarily at declaration time but when initialisation or assignment occurs. As might be supposed assignments are legitimate only under sensible conditions. If we take the above type *BUFFER* as an illustration:

(*a*) the discriminant of a type used in a declaration must always have a value,

(*b*) the discriminant once given a value cannot be altered unless by an assignment of a completely new record,

(*c*) the fields other than the discriminant can be altered only if these remain compatible with the discriminant.

These types can be used in declarations of the form

B: *BUFFER* (40); - - or equivalently *B*: *BUFFER* (*LENGTH* => 40);

In this case the declaration of *B* ensures that the discriminant is constrained to be and to remain 40.

There is another kind of discriminant that can occur in records. Again this is a kind of parameter associated with the record and it brings us to the idea of a *variant record*.

Let us look at the design of a set of records applicable to academic personnel in an educational establishment. There will typically be two disjoint sets of people, the staff and the students. Yet many aspects of the records will be common to both: there might be name, address, age, and so on. On the other hand there will be aspects of records peculiar to the different sets separately: staff may have

120

components for salary, students might have components for fees, etc.

To accommodate these ideas we envisage a kind of parameter (which is of type *STATUS*) that is applicable to records. This is the discriminant. The record then contains a variant part, a case part in which the components peculiar to the different sets of people are itemised. We obtain:

```
type STATUS is (STAFF, STUDENT);
type PERSON (IT: STATUS) is
    record
            NAME: STRING(30);
            AGE: INTEGER range 16 .. 65;
            case IT is
                when STAFF =>
                        SALARY: NATURAL;
                        DEPT: DEPT_NO;
                when STUDENT =>
                        FEES_DUE: NATURAL;
                        COURSE: COURSE_NO;
            end case;
    end record;
```

Note that *IT* is a constant of scalar type: its value is either *STAFF* or *STUDENT*. Staff then have components which are accessed by *SALARY* and *DEPT* whereas students have components which are accessed by *FEES_DUE* and *COURSE*.

It is now possible to make declarations such as

A: *PERSON*;

and to initialise or assign to A in the following fashion

```
A := (STATUS => STUDENT,
      NAME =>"...",
      AGE => 18,
 FEES_DUE => 2500,
    COURSE =>"52.100");
```

The A declared above can be used to hold records about either staff or students. We have shown how a student record might be assigned to A. If we now want to alter it to a staff record this can only be done by assigning a complete staff record to A, i.e.

A := (*STATUS* => *STAFF*,*NAME* =>"...");

It is *not* permissible to merely alter the A . *STATUS* component.

There are two very obvious subtypes of the type *PERSON*:

subtype *LECTURER* **is** *PERSON*(*STATUS* => *STAFF*);

121

and

subtype *UNDERGRAD* **is** *PERSON(STATUS => STUDENT)*;

In these cases we say that the discriminant has been constrained in a particular way. We can now write such declarations as

    BAT_MAN: LECTURER:
      ROBIN: UNDERGRAD;

and these are equivalent to

    BAT_MAN: PERSON(STATUS => STAFF);
      ROBIN: PERSON(STATUS => STUDENT);

Once introduced in either of these ways the *STATUS* may not be altered. It is illegal therefore to write

    BAT_MAN := ROBIN;

though both

    A := BAT_MAN;
and
    A := ROBIN;

are acceptable. On the other hand

    BAT_MAN := A;
and
    ROBIN := A;

may or may not be acceptable. If *A* holds a record of the appropriate kind then the assignment can take place without trouble. If *A* holds a record of the wrong kind then an error, a discriminant error, will be flagged.

To conclude this section, we note that the inequality and equality operators can be used to operate between records of the same type. A comparison is performed on the individual components of the records.

5.2.2   Axioms for records

The axioms associated with records are similar in many ways to the axioms associated with arrays. In various places we appeal to this similarity by citing the corresponding rule for arrays. Let us begin with the straightforward case where the records do not possess discriminants.

Let type T be declared as

    type T **is**
        record
            $s_1: T_1;$
            $s_2: T_2;$
            ...
            $s_m: T_m;$
        end record;

1. If X_i is an element of type T_i for each $i = 1, 2, \ldots, m$ then $T(X_1, X_2, \ldots, X_m)$ is an element of type T.
2. The elements described in 1 above are the only elements of type T, though they can be expressed in equivalent non-positional ways.
3. If X denotes $T(X_1, \ldots, X_m)$ then

    $X . s_i = X_i$

4. If X denotes $T(X_1, \ldots, X_m)$ and

    $X . s_i := Y;$

    is an assignment we regard this as an abbreviation for

    $X := [X \mid s_i \mid Y];$

    Rules analogous to those for arrays now hold.
5. If X denotes $T(X_1, \ldots, X_m)$ and

    $X := Y;$

    is an assignment then the expected assignment rule holds.

Variant records introduce some complications. Let type T be defined as

> **type** T (*disc*: TT) **is**
> > **record**
> > > $s_1: T_1;$
> > >
> > > $\ldots$
> > >
> > > $s_m: T_m;$
> > >
> > > **case** *disc* **is**
> > > > **when** $k'_1 => s'_1 : T'_1;$
> > > > **when** $k'_2 => s'_2 : T'_2;$
> > > >
> > > > $\ldots$
> > > >
> > > > **when** $k'_n => s'_n : T'_n;$
> > >
> > > **end case**;
> >
> > **end record**;

Here *disc* is the discriminant which can take on values $k'_1, k'_2, \ldots, k'_n$. There are two different kinds of situation to consider.

Suppose we look at the type T_0 obtained by specialising the discriminant in such a way that it takes the value k'_j, i.e. T_0 is just $T(disc => k'_j)$.

1. If X_i is an element of type T_i for $1 <= i <= m$ and if Y_j is an element of type T'_j then $T(k'_j, X_1, \ldots, X_m, Y_j)$ is an element of T_0.
2. The elements described in 1 above are the only elements of type T_0 though they can be expressed non-positionally.
3. If X denotes $T(k'_j, X_1, \ldots, X_m, Y_j)$ then

    $X . disc = k'_j$

    $X . s_i = X_i \quad$ for $1 <= i <= m$

    $X . s'_j = Y_j.$

123

4. If X denotes $T(k_j', X_1, \ldots, X_m, Y_j)$ and if

$X . s_i := Z'; \quad (1 <= i <= m)$

and

$X . s_j' := Z;$

are assignments then rules analogous to those for arrays hold.
5. If X denotes $T(k_j', X_1, \ldots, X_m, Y_j)$ and if Y is of type T_0 then

$X := Y;$

is an assignment for which an appropriate proof rule holds.

Let us now consider the second situation where we do not specialise the discriminant. If we use the earlier notation and let Y_j be an element of type T_j':

1. $T(k_j, X_1, \ldots, X_m, Y_j)$ is an element of type T.
2. The elements included in 1 above are the only elements of type T.
3. If X denotes $T(k_j, X_1, \ldots, X_m, Y_j)$ then

$X . s_i = X_i \quad$ for $1 <= i <= m$

and

$X . s_j' = Y_j$

4. If Y is of type T, X_i of type T_i and Y_j of type T_j' then assignments of
the form

$X := Y;$
$X . s_i := X_i; \quad (1 <= i <= m)$
$X . s_j' := Y_j;$

are allowed with the expected effect.

The cases described above do not cover all the possible situations which can occur and so are somewhat special. Yet they cover the majority of situations that are likely to arise in practice. Moreover it is relatively straightforward to infer the axioms for the remaining cases.

We have not mentioned axioms for describing the meaning of the equality and inequality operators when used on records. These are left as exercises for the reader.

At this stage we ought to give examples which demonstrate methods of verifying the correctness of programs which use records. Yet there is little novelty value in this. The techniques tend to be relatively straightforward, bearing in mind the contents of the earlier chapters and our discussion about arrays.

5.3 **Access types**

Large areas of computing are involved with processing lists of elements, queues, tree structures and in general data structures of a bewildering variety. The access types of Ada provide a means of dealing in a sensible fashion with these sorts of structures.

5.3.1 Access types in Ada

We introduce the idea of an access type by looking at an example. Let the types *LIST* and *CELL* be defined in the following way:

> **type** *CELL*;
> **type** *LIST* **is access** *CELL*;
> **type** *CELL* **is**
> > **record**
> > > *ITEM*: *INTEGER*;
> > > *REST*: *LIST*;
> > **end record**;

The initial definition of *CELL*, an incomplete definition, is present because types must be declared before they are used; *CELL* is used in the definition of *LIST*. The complete definition of *CELL* follows later. Incomplete definitions of this kind tend to be a feature of access types.

A declaration such as

> *L*: *LIST*;

or equivalently (thus access type variables are automatically initialised)

> *L*: *LIST* := **null**;

can be given. In this case *L* points to the null object. Alternatively *L* can be made to point to a record consisting of two parts (see the definition of the type *CELL*):

> (*a*) an integer which can be accessed by writing *L . ITEM*,
> (*b*) a pointer to another list and this can be accessed by writing *L . REST*

Records of this kind can be produced only by means of a special procedure **new**.

The effect of

> *L* := **new** *CELL* (*ITEM* => 3, *REST* => **null**);

is then to create a situation which can conveniently be depicted in the following way:

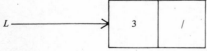

The allocator **new** *CELL* causes the space to be generated. There is placed in *L* a pointer to this space. The aggregate (*ITEM* => 3, *REST* => **null**) causes appropriate initialisation of the various parts of the record. Since the items appear in the order specified in the definition of *CELL* this aggregate can be abbreviated to (3, **null**).

125

Using the above techniques together with loops, chains can be created. For example, a list or chain of non-zero integers can be produced in the following manner:

```
L := null;
loop
      GET(N);
      exit when N = 0;
      L := new CELL(N, L);
end loop;
```

These ideas then convey the basic notions associated with access types. Some further examples will illustrate the range of possibilities.

Example 5.3.1a   Access types

(i) A polynomial in a single variable can be represented by an item of type *POLY* where

```
type TERM;
type POLY is access TERM;
type TERM is
      record
            COEFF: INTEGER;
            EXP: INTEGER range 0 .. INTEGER'LAST;
            REST: POLY;
      end record;
```

In this case a polynomial is regarded as a list of terms each of which is characterised by its integer coefficient and the non-negative integer power of the variable.

(ii) Arithmetic expressions can be represented by tree structures of the kind shown in figure 5.1. These trees can then be depicted as items of type *TREE*

Fig. 5.1.

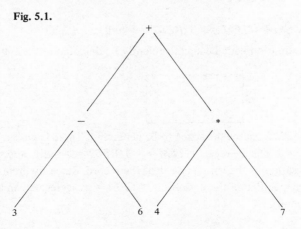

where

```
type KIND is (OPER, INT); type OP is (PLUS, MINUS, TIMES);
type NODE (N: KIND);
type TREE is access NODE;
type NODE (N: KIND) is
    record
        case N is
            when OPER => S: OP;
                            LEFT, RIGHT: TREE;
            when INT => ITEM: INTEGER;
        end case;
    end record;
```

Here *OPER* indicates the presence of an operator such as $+$ or $-$ at a point in the tree whereas *INT* indicates the presence of an integer like 3 or 6.

(iii) A person can be represented as a record which contains information including name, age, date of birth, and so on. This can be made more complex by adding information about parents or the like, thus producing family trees. An appropriate type declaration, stripped down for simplicity would be

```
type RECORD (SIZE: INTEGER range 0 .. INTEGER'LAST);
type PERSON is access RECORD;
type RECORD (SIZE: INTEGER range 0 .. INTEGER'LAST := 0) is
    record
        NAME: STRING(1 .. 30);
        MOTHER, FATHER: PERSON;
        BROTH_AND_SIST: array (1 .. SIZE) of PERSON;
    end record;
```

(iv) A polynomial in several variables can be regarded as a polynomial in a single variable whose coefficients are themselves either polynomials or constants. In many ways the required type declaration resembles that given in (i) above. However, there are difficulties in deciding on the type of coefficient which presumably must include the type of the polynomials themselves.

```
type LISTA;
type POLY_SEV is
    record
        VAR: CHARACTER;
        DETAILS: LISTA;
    end record;
type CELL;
type LISTA is access CELL;
type KIND is (CONST, POLY);
type COEFF (K: KIND);
```

127

```
type CELL is
    record
            C: COEFF;
            EXP: INTEGER range 0 .. INTEGER'LAST;
            REST: LISTA;
    end record;
type COEFF (K: KIND) is
    record
            case K is
                    when CONST => C_COEFF : INTEGER;
                    when POLY => P_COEFF : POLY_SEV;
            end case;
    end record;
```

We shall now give some simple programming examples which further illustrate the use of access types in programming. In the examples that follow we make use of the declarations of access types given above.

Example 5.3.1b   Scanning lists
Count the number of zeros in an item *L* of type *LIST*. Leave *L* unaltered.

```
declare
        H: LIST := L;
        COUNT: INTEGER := 0;
begin
        while H /= null loop
                COUNT := COUNT + 1;
                H := H . REST;
        end loop;
        PUT(COUNT);
end;
```

Example 5.3.1c   Combining lists
Write a piece of program which will take two lists *H* and *K* and produce a third list *L* which contains all the elements in both *H* and *K*.

```
declare
        PT_H: LIST := H;
        PT_K: LIST := K;
            L: LIST := null;    - - or just L: LIST;
begin
        while PT_H /= null loop
                L := new CELL(PT_H . ITEM, L);
```

128

```
            PT_H := PT_H . REST;
        end loop;
        while PT_K /= null loop
            L := new CELL (PT_K . ITEM, L);
            PT_K := PT_K . REST;
        end loop;
        - - {result now resides in L}
    end;
```

Example 5.3.1d   Differentiation

Take a polynomial, represented by an item *P* of type *POLY* (see example 5.3.1a(i)), and differentiate it with respect to the variable. A rather crude solution is given below. The access variable *DERIV* eventually holds the required result.

```
    declare
        Q: POLY := P;
        DERIV: POLY := null;
    begin
        while Q /= null loop
            DERIV := new TERM (Q . COEFF * Q . EXP,
                                Q . EXP - 1,
                                DERIV);
            Q := Q . REST;
        end loop;
        - - final result resides in DERIV
    end;
```

This solution can be criticised on the grounds that

   (i) the list representing the final answer is the reverse of what might be expected,

 (ii) terms with zero coefficients have not been removed.

Both these deficiencies can be easily removed.

Example 5.3.1e   Constructing trees

To construct the tree diagram given in example 5.3.1a(ii) one could write (assuming the obvious declarations for the identifiers used)

   THREE := new *NODE*(*INT*, 3);

together with similar declarations for identifiers *SIX*, *FOUR* AND *SEVEN*. Then we proceed to write

   L := new *NODE*(*OPER*, *MINUS*, *THREE*, *SIX*);
   R := new *NODE*(*OPER*, *TIMES*, *FOUR*, *SEVEN*);

$$RESULT := \mathbf{new}\ NODE\,(OPER, PLUS, L, R);$$

Now *RESULT* points to the required tree structure.

We have now covered the simple and most common uses of access types in Ada. We now look at other more intricate possibilities.

The use of aggregate facilitates assignments and initialisations of access types. Constant access types can now be introduced in an obvious way:

$$CONSTANT\_LIST:\ \mathbf{constant}\ LIST := \mathbf{new}\ CELL\,(2, \mathbf{null});$$

As before the access type must point to space that has been allocated by **new**. Any attempt to alter *CONSTANT_LIST* will result in error. To ensure this, a constant list cannot be assigned to a *LIST* variable which might then be used to alter it.

Previously defined types can be used in the formation of access types. It is permissible to write

type *DATA* **is access** *STRING*;

and to introduce subtypes such as

subtype *LINE* **is** *DATA* (1 .. 80);

with the obvious constraint.

Finally we note that in what follows it will be important to view allocators in a special light. We imagine that allocators for objects of some type *T* generate space from a large pool or reservoir containing space for elements. The space that has been generated to date is referred to as the current *collection* associated with that type. Collections associated with different types are guaranteed to be disjoint and separate. In these circumstances a non-null access type can be regarded as a pointer into a collection. If a collection itself is regarded as a kind of implicit array there is a certain relationship between one's view of an array and an index and one's view of a collection and an access type.

One of the consequences of the above comment is that an access type must either be null or it will index a collection. It is not possible to let an access type point to a static object, i.e. an object declared in an object declaration. This has the very desirable effect of meaning that altering an element pointed to by an access type does not alter the value of static variables and vice versa. It also provides the reason for supplying an initial default value of **null** for elements of an access type – dangling references are not possible.

5.3.2   **Axiomatics associated with access types**

The axiomatics of access types follows the general pattern set forth in the sections on the axiomatics of arrays and records. Explicit mention is made of the idea of a collection – the set of locations so far allocated to the programmer.

Consider the type declaration

type T **is access** T_0;

where T_0 is some other type. The following axioms hold:

1. **null** is the null element of type T.
2. There is potentially available a finite number of access values of type T and we denote these by $\pi_1, \pi_2, \ldots, \pi_{MAX}$.
3. At any moment in time some finite number N (less than or equal to MAX) of distinct access values will have been *created* and thereby made available to a program; initially zero elements are created.
4. If $\pi_1, \pi_2, \ldots, \pi_N$ are the elements of T that have been created and if $\beta_1, \beta_2, \ldots, \beta_N$ are the corresponding values of type T_0 then the set of pairs

   $\{\pi_1 : \beta_1, \pi_2 : \beta_2, \ldots, \pi_N : \beta_N\}$

   is called a collection C_T which is implicitly associated with type T. We say that π_i designates the corresponding β_i ($1 <= i <= N$). Collections for different types are disjoint.
5. If X is a variable of type T the assignment

   $X := \textbf{new } T_0(\beta);$

   either

   (i) creates a new non-null π different from $\pi_1, \pi_2, \ldots, \pi_N$ and this designates β. The allocator **new** is the only means of creating objects.

   or

   (ii) raises the exception *STORAGE_ERROR* if there is no storage left.
6. If C is as above and if X is a variable of type T holding the value π_i then we say that X designates the value β_i.
7. If X holds the value π_i then X . **all** produces β_i.
8. The assignment rule.

The assignment axiom follows the general ideas set out in the section on arrays. Just as subscripted variables have an index and an array name so an access value is an index applied to the collection associated with the type name. The analogy is very strong and the appropriate rule for assignment follows.

As far as operations are concerned, both equality and inequality are defined between objects of the same access type. The expected axioms hold.

5.3.3 Verification of programs using access types

We now examine the problem of proving the correctness of programs which manipulate access types. Just as with arrays, one of the major difficulties in this area is the question of the notation. How do we express assertions about lists, about general data structures, and about access types in general?

Previously we have tried to draw a certain analogy between the idea of an array and the idea of an access type. If this analogy is strong then the notation we introduced for arrays should be some guide in helping us to find suitable notation for access types. Yet the idea of a collection we should keep hidden if at all possible.

We shall proceed by looking at some examples; gradually a notation will emerge.

Adding elements in a linear list

Consider the problem of adding together all the elements in a linear list of integers. Assume the declarations

    type *CELL*;
    type *LIST* **is access** *CELL*;
    type *CELL* **is**
        record
            ITEM: *INTEGER*;
            REST: *LIST*;
        end record;

and suppose *L* has been declared as

    L: *LIST*;

and has been initialised in some fashion. We can present the situation diagrammatically in the following way:

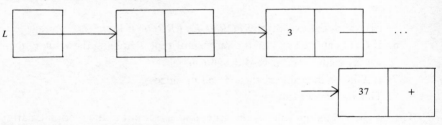

The cross denotes the null value.

A program to accomplish the required task and place the result in the integer variable *SUM* is given below; *H* is declared initially in the following way

    H: *LIST* := *L*;

The program:

    SUM := 0;
    while *H* /= **null loop**
        SUM := *SUM* + *H* . *ITEM*;
        H := *H* . *REST*;
    end loop;

should do as required.

132

We should now introduce some notation in which to communicate about lists. For the moment we assume an absence of loops or circular lists of any kind, i.e. we concentrate on linear lists. We write

$$C(U .. V)$$

to denote that section of a list of the form

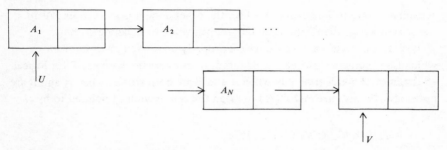

The letter C denotes the collection associated with lists of this type, U and V are access values and $A_1, A_2, \ldots, A_N$ are elements that form that part of the list that lies between U and V. Unlike the analogous situation for arrays it is not convenient to include the element pointed to by V – see exercise 8.

We note the following properties and conventions:

1. If $C(U .. V)$ and $C(V .. M)$ are sections of lists then so also is $C(U .. W)$; in fact it is the concatenation $C(U .. V) \& C(V .. W)$.

Testing if a list is ordered

We now consider the task of taking a non-empty list of elements and testing to see whether or not the elements of that list are in decreasing order. We assume that the list is again called L and we assume that on completion of the piece of program the boolean variable *ORDERED* will hold the required result.

Initial declarations of the form

```
PREVIOUS_VALUE: INTEGER := L . ITEM;
H: LIST := L . REST;
ORDERED: BOOLEAN := TRUE;
```

are required. Then it is intended that the following piece of program accomplishes the required task:

```
while H /= null and ORDERED loop
      ORDERED := PREVIOUS_VALUE > H . ITEM;
      PREVIOUS_VALUE := H . ITEM;
      H := H . REST;
end loop;
```

This example ought to stir memories of our earlier discussion about arrays, in particular ordered arrays. In fact we can adopt an approach similar to that used

133

then and we can write

$$ORD_>(C(U..V))$$

to mean that all the elements in this section of the list are ordered with regard to the relation $>$. Using our earlier notation this means that

$$A_1 > A_2 > \ldots > A_N$$

A similar notation can be employed for the other comparison relations. As in the case of arrays the relation can be dropped when its meaning is clear.

With this introduction we can give a properly annotated program from which a correctness proof can be deduced. In our assertions we use $\equiv$ for logical equivalence: $A \equiv B$ is true only when A and B are both true or when A and B are both false. We also use $PRED(H)$ to mean the cell previously pointed to by H, i.e.

$$PRED(H.REST) = H.ITEM,$$

The required program and its correctness proof can be based on:

```
-- {L /= null}
PREVIOUS_VALUE := L.ITEM;
H := L.REST;
ORDERED := TRUE;
while -- {ORDERED ≡ ORD(C(L..H)) ∧
                               PRED(H) = PREVIOUS_VALUE}
      H /= null and ORDERED loop
      ORDERED := PREVIOUS_VALUE > H.ITEM;
      PREVIOUS_VALUE := H.ITEM;
      H := H.REST;
end loop;
-- {ORDERED ≡ ORD(L)}
```

Counting elements on a circular list

Let *LIST* be defined as above. Now assume that L is a circular list of the kind depicted by

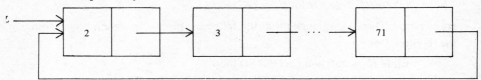

2. Conversely, given that $C(U..V)$ where $U /= V$ is part of a list, we can deduce that

$$C(U..V) = \langle U.ITEM \rangle \& C(U.REST..V)$$

Here $\langle U.ITEM \rangle$ denotes the list containing a single element, namely $U.ITEM$.

134

3. The null object can appear as in $C(U .. \textbf{null})$ and this we abbreviate to U. Thus U is the complete set of values that lies between U and the end of the list.

4. The notation $C(U .. V)$ can be used when $U = V$. There are two possibilities. Either the list is empty or it is non-empty and there is a loop from U back to itself. In any particular situation it will be clear which alternative applies. In using the notation $C(U .. V)$ it will always be understood that there are no loops present unless otherwise stated. Even then, the possibility mentioned in 4 above is the only situation where this is likely to be violated.

Whenever it is necessary to distinguish between several different kinds of lists we shall add suitable decorations such as subscripts to the letter C. In this way different collections will be indicated and we know that these are disjoint.

We are now in a position to give a proof of the correctness of the program to add the elements of a linear list L. The initial assertion is basically a statement that L contains no loops, a property we are currently attributing to all our lists unless otherwise stated. The final assertion is that SUM is the total of all the elements in the list, i.e.

$$SUM = \sum_{X=L}^{\textbf{null}} X . ITEM$$

In general, we use the notation

$$\sum_{X=L}^{H} X . ITEM$$

to represent the sum of all the elements in $C(L..H)$. $C(L..\textbf{null})$ is just L itself.

A detailed proof can be based on the following:

$$SUM := 0;$$
$$H := L;$$

$$\textbf{while} \ \text{-} \text{-} \left(SUM = \sum_{X=L}^{H} X . ITEM \right)$$

$$H \ /= \textbf{null loop}$$
$$SUM := SUM + H . ITEM;$$
$$H := H . REST;$$

end loop;

$$\text{-} \text{-} \left(SUM = \sum_{X=L}^{\textbf{null}} X . ITEM \right)$$

In verifying the fact that the loop invariant remains unaltered on successive iterations note that since $H /= \textbf{null}$ we can deduce that

$$H = C(H .. \text{null}) = \langle H . ITEM \rangle \& C(H . REST .. \text{null})$$
$$= \langle H . ITEM \rangle \& H . REST$$

This provides sufficient detail and sufficient notation for a proof of partial correctness. To prove total correctness note that the length of H (which has its obvious meaning) decreases on successive circuits of the loop.

Write a program to count the number of integers in the list.

Assuming initial declarations

$$COUNT : INTEGER := 1;$$
$$H : LIST := L . REST:$$

the required effect can be achieved by

while $H /= L$ **loop**
    $COUNT := COUNT + 1;$
    $H := H . REST;$
end loop;

We shall use the function $SIZE$ to count the number of elements in a set. If initially the list is of the form

$$C(L .. L)$$

which is non-empty, then on completion of the program we require that

$$COUNT = SIZE(C(L .. L))$$

Finding the loop invariant is relatively straightforward. On completion of several executions of the body of the loop we shall have a situation that can be expressed by the following:

$$COUNT = SIZE(C(L .. H))$$

On completion of the loop H will be L and the final result will follow.

Combining lists

We now look at a more complex example. We consider the problem of joining together several lists. We assume all the lists are in an array H declared as

H: **array** $(1 .. N)$ **of** $LIST$;

and suitably initialised. In this example we have both lists and arrays. We shall attempt to prove the correctness of the program given below: L will point to the resulting list and the pointer PT is used to scan through the different lists.

$L := \text{null};$
for I **in** $1 .. N$ **loop**
    $PT := H(I);$
    while $PT /= \text{null}$ **loop**
        $L := \text{new } CELL(PT . ITEM, L);$
        $PT := PT . REST;$
    end loop;
end loop;

In its strict meaning concatenation of lists implies laying the lists end to end. In fact our program does not do this. It actually reverses each list as it attaches it to L. In keeping with our earlier notation for arrays we use the symbol $\sim$ to imply rearrangement.

In the context of lists concatenation can take place in one of two ways, this introducing a certain ambiguity about its meaning. It may involve copying of the lists involved, it may not; in the latter case pointers are merely redirected. Rather than introduce separate notations for the two possibilities we shall proceed on the understanding that the appropriate interpretation will be clear from the context.

The program given earlier can now be rewritten with assertions in the following fashion:

$$L := \mathbf{null};$$
$$\mathbf{for}\ I\ \mathbf{in}\ 1\ ..\ N\ \mathbf{loop}$$
$$PT := H(I);$$

$$\mathbf{while} - - \left\{ L \sim \left(\sum_{J=1}^{I=1} H(J)\ \&\ C(H(I)\ ..\ PT) \right) \right\}$$

$$PT\ /=\ \mathbf{null}\ \mathbf{loop}$$
$$L := \mathbf{new}\ CELL(PT\,.\,ITEM, L);$$
$$PT := PT\,.\,REST;$$

$$\mathbf{end}\ \mathbf{loop};$$

$$- - \left\{ L \sim \sum_{J=1}^{I} H(J) \right\}$$

$$\mathbf{end}\ \mathbf{loop};$$

$$- - \left\{ L \sim \sum_{J=1}^{N} H(J) \right\}$$

All the examples we have given so far have merely involved inspecting a list in some form. No attempt has been made to alter a list. We now look at programs which alter lists and other structures and we investigate techniques for verifying the correctness of such programs.

Inserting an item into a list

Assume that the list L is again of type *LIST* where *LIST* is as in the previous examples. We shall assume that the items in L are arranged in increasing order. The task we shall consider is the problem of inserting into its correct position in L some given integer N. In effect we have to rearrange pointers as shown by the dotted lines in figure 5.2. A program to accomplish this task follows. The given ordered list is L and the integer to be inserted is N.

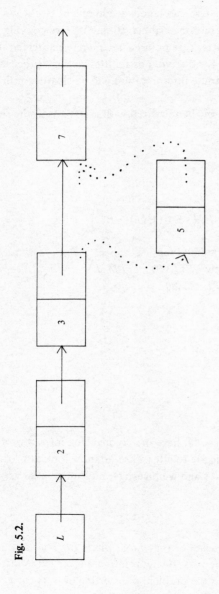

Fig. 5.2.

```
    if (L = null) or else (L .ITEM > N) then
        L := new CELL(N, L);
else
    declare
        H: LIST := L;
    begin
        while H . REST /= null and then H . REST . ITEM < N loop
            H := H . REST;
        end loop;
        H . REST := new CELL(N, H . REST);
    end;
end if;
```

In deciding how to approach the problem of proving the correctness of this program we can again think back to an analogous situation in dealing with arrays. Such consideration readily produces

an initial predicate $\quad (L = L'IN) \wedge ORD(L'IN)$

a final predicate $\quad (L \sim \langle N \rangle \& L) \wedge ORD(L)$

Here $L'IN$ denotes the initial constant list; the term $\langle N \rangle$ denotes a list containing a single element N; and ORD expresses the fact that the list that appears as parameter is ordered in an appropriate manner.

The loop invariant in the else part of the conditional expresses the fact that as H runs down the loop everything remains ordered and all elements are smaller than N. Using the obvious pointwise extension of the relational operator analogous to the situation that arose in discussing arrays, the invariant is

$$(L = L'IN) \wedge LT(C(L .. H . REST), N)$$

or since L remains unaltered

$$LT(C(L .. H . REST), N)$$

A correctness proof can be based on this.

Reversing a list

In this example we consider a situation in which it is necessary to reverse the order of the elements in a list. We imagine a situation in which the required task has to be performed, not by creating a completely new list, but by redirecting the pointers in the original list.

If we assume that the original list is L and is of type $LIST$ then we claim that the program below performs the required task: $TEMP$ and H are temporary variables introduced for the duration of the program; R will be the resulting reversed list.

```
H := L;
R := null;
```

```
      while H /= null loop
            TEMP := H . REST;
            H . REST := R;
            R := H;
            H := TEMP;
      end loop;
```

To prove the correctness of this program we introduce an auxiliary function *rev*, denoting reverse. We hope to achieve a final list R which is the reverse of the original list $L'IN$, i.e. the output predicate should be

$$R = rev(L'IN)$$

A rather detailed version of the program illustrates the direction of the required correctness proof.

```
      - -{L = L'IN}
      H := L;
      R := null;
      while - - {rev(H) & R = rev(L'IN)}
                  H /= null loop
            - -{(H /= null) ∧ (rev(H) & R = rev(L'IN))}
            TEMP := H . REST;
            - -{(TEMP = H . REST) ∧ (rev(H) & R = rev(L'IN))}
            H . REST := R;
            - -{rev(TEMP) & H = rev(L'IN)}
            R := H;
            - -{rev(TEMP) & R = rev(L'IN)}
            H := TEMP;
      end loop;
      - -{R = rev(L'IN)}
```

These examples then complete our investigation into verifying the correctness of programs which use and manipulate lists. As was the case with programs which used and manipulated arrays, we had to invent a certain amount of notation. We make no claim that we have invented enough notation to cover all eventualities. It is possible that in particular situations a programmer/verifier may have to invent his own notation to deal with some particular situation. However it is to be hoped that the general guidelines set out in this section provide sufficient framework for him to be able to tackle such an exercise with confidence.

Perhaps one glaring omission has been the absence of examples involving lists such as in figure 5.3. When we have studied recursive subprograms it will be more natural to deal with examples of this kind and examples involving more general data structures such as trees.

140

Exercises for chapter 5

1. Design a piece of program which will merge together the contents of three ordered arrays.
   Demonstrate the correctness of your final implementation.

2. The bubble sort provides one method of sorting the elements of an array. Successive scans are made of the entire array: each scan consists of interchanging adjacent elements if they are out of order and is guaranteed to put at least one element in its correct place.
   Give a correct implementation of the bubble sort.

3. A modification of the bubble sort entails terminating the series of scans whenever a complete scan fails to result in any interchanges.
   Introduce this modification and prove the correctness of the final piece of program.

4. Given two similarly ordered arrays show how

   (a) they can be merged in such a way that common elements appear only once in the final array,

   (b) an array of the common elements is produced.

   Verify the total correctness of the two separate programs.

5. A lower triangular matrix A has all its elements of the form $A(I, J)$ where $J > I$ set to zero. Suppose it is necessary to introduce such a matrix and make use of only as much space as necessary. Show, by regarding a matrix as a vector of vectors, how access types can be used to achieve a satisfactory effect.
   How are individual elements accessed?

6. A record of a person contains various pieces of information about that person including their age, current wage, and so on. Given an array of such records write a correct program to determine the number of people under 60 who are earning no wage.

7. A rational number P/Q is represented by an object of the type *RATIONAL* where

Fig. 5.3.

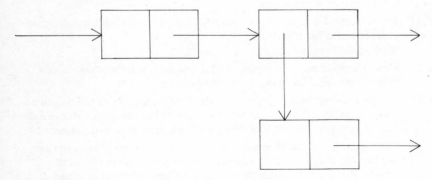

```
type RATIONAL is
    record
        NUM: INTEGER;
        DEN: NATURAL;
    end record;
```

It is desirable (for tests of equality, for example) that the highest common factor of the numerator and the denominator should be unity. In this case we say that the rational is in standard form.

Write correct pieces of program to accomplish the following tasks:

(a) put an arbitrary rational number in standard form,

(b) search an array of rationals and print out all those that are not in standard form,

(c) find the sum of all the rationals in an array of rationals; the result should be in standard form.

8. In considering lists a notation of the form $C(U .. V)$ was introduced. This differs from the corresponding notation for arrays in that the element pointed to by V is excluded.

Discuss the desirability of this – using the alternative convention try to verify some of the programs contained in section 5.3.3.

9. Design a correct piece of program which will merge two sorted lists of integers to produce a third ordered list which contains all the elements in the two original lists.

Compare the program and its correctness proof with the corresponding items which appear in section 5.1.3.

10. Design a correct piece of program which tests whether two separate and similarly ordered lists contain the same set of elements with the same frequency.

11. Write a correct piece of program which takes some linear list L and creates a new list R which is the reverse of the original. The latter remains unaltered.

12. Design correct pieces of program which determine whether a particular item is present in

(a) a linear list of items,

(b) a circular list of items.

13. Design a correct piece of program which removes an integer N from an ordered linear list of integers.

State clearly any assumptions you make.

14. Write a correct piece of program which decides whether there is any item which is repeated in a linear list of items.

15. Design a correct piece of program which concatenates all the lists in an array containing N lists. The lists have not to be copied but all the null pointers except the last have to be replaced by pointers to the next list.

16. Write a correct piece of program to implement the insertion sort: an ordered list R is created by removing items one at a time from the original list L and inserting them into their proper position within R.

17. A mathematical set can be implemented as a (possibly ordered) linear list in which no element is repeated. Using such a representation design pieces of program which simulate the operations of

    (*a*) set union,

    (*b*) set intersection,

    (*c*) finding all the elements in one set but not in another (similar to complement),

    (*d*) testing for set inclusion.

    Prove the correctness of your implementations.

    What other operations should be provided to complete the list?

18. Design a correct piece of program to sort a list of elements by rearranging the pointers.

    State clearly any assumptions you make.

19. Doubly linked lists have two pointers to ensure easy travel in both directions, thus

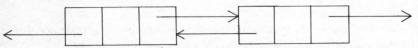

    Design pieces of correct program to add and delete items from an ordered list.

    State clearly any assumptions you make and any pieces of notation you use.

6 FUNCTIONS AND PROCEDURES

Subprograms are a fundamental part of most programming and most programming languages. In Ada they provide a means whereby a programmer can program a particular task and then wrap up the statements etc. as a function, operator or procedure to be used whenever required. Basically functions and operators produce values, the procedures we encounter in this chapter do not. The key advantage of such a facility is that once subprograms have been designed and properly verified the user can forget about the internal workings or the internal mechanism of the procedure. He is then freed from certain considerations and can concentrate solely on using the subprogram properly. Subprograms are therefore a crucial tool in the hierarchical design of programs.

From the verification point of view we of course want to learn how to prove the correctness of the implementation of subprograms. We must also learn how to verify the correctness of other programs which use these subprograms. Since there are overheads in properly designing subprograms and verifying them it becomes sensible to try to write functions and procedures which, though they perform just one single well-defined task and have simple proof rules, are in some sense general. To be more specific a procedure for sorting arrays should sort arrays of arbitrary size and with arbitrary bounds. Moreover, if the procedure works equally well for reals, integers, characters, etc. then the programming language should allow this to be expressed. Thus in Ada there are generic subprograms whereby a kind of type variable can be passed to the subprogram. The correctness proof should then be equally general. In this way the one correctness proof suffices for a large set of similar subprograms. Generic subprograms can, of course, be justified on other grounds such as efficiency both of programmers' time and of compilation time.

6.1 Subprograms in Ada

We begin this chapter by looking at how functions and procedures are defined and used in Ada and by looking at what properties they possess. We then look briefly at generic subprograms. In the later part of the chapter we discuss the correctness of programs which use subprograms, both non-recursive and recursive.

144

6.1.1 Function subprograms

Function subprograms, or functions for short, are used for computing values. Thus functions could be designed to calculate the factorial function, or the square root function, to determine whether an element is in an array, to determine the position of an element in an array, and so on. In all these cases a value of some kind is produced.

To illustrate let us consider the task of finding the maximum value in a non-empty array A of reals. A piece of program to accomplish this task would take the form

> **declare**
> > $MAX: FLOAT := A(A'FIRST)$;
>
> **begin**
> > **for** I **in** $A'FIRST + 1 .. A'LAST$ **loop**
> > > **if** $MAX < A(I)$ **then**
> > > > $MAX := A(J)$;
> > >
> > > **end if**;
> >
> > **end loop**;
> > - - return MAX as result
>
> **end**;

To render this as a suitable function there are only two steps to be taken.

1. A value must be returned; this is done by replacing this comment immediately before the final **end** by
   return MAX;
   since MAX holds the required result.

2. The word **declare** has to be replaced by a heading which gives a name to the function (any appropriate identifier will suffice) and supplies the parameters; different users of the function will in general supply different sizes of arrays of reals and the array will be the only parameter.

These considerations and the fact that the type of a parameter must be expressed as a type or subtype mark lead to a definition which uses

> **type** $FLOAT\_ARRAY$ **is array** $(INTEGER$ **range** $\langle \rangle)$ **of** $FLOAT$;

and is as follows

> **function** $LARGEST$ $(A: FLOAT\_ARRAY)$ **return** $FLOAT$ **is**
> > $MAX: FLOAT := A(A'FIRST)$;
>
> **begin**
> > **for** I **in** $A'FIRST + 1 .. A'LAST$ **loop**
> > > **if** $MAX < A(I)$ **then**
> > > > $MAX := A(I)$;
> > >
> > > **end if**;
> >
> > **end loop**;
> > **return** MAX;
>
> **end** $LARGEST$;

145

The above definition, being essentially a declaration, must occur within a declarative part of a program. Having been properly declared it can be used in the following kind of way. If *SIZES* is a non-empty array of non-negative reals which represent measurements then it is permissible to write in appropriate environments

$$PUT(LARGEST(SIZES));$$
or
$$LONGEST := LARGEST(SIZES)$$

and so on. In other words *LARGEST* is used as if it is a function known to the system; users need only be concerned with what it does, not with how the task is accomplished. *LARGEST(SIZES)* is said to be a *call* of *LARGEST*.

It is desirable to draw a careful distinction between the parameters that are used when a function is being declared and those used when it is being called. Parameters used at declaration time are called *formal parameters*, parameters used at call time are referred to as *actual parameters*. As might be expected it is important that the type of an actual parameter will match the type of the corresponding formal parameter. Thus in the above case *A* is a formal parameter and *SIZES* an actual parameter.

To give another example, a function to calculate the factorial of a non-negative integer can be written in one of two ways. We use the standard type *NATURAL* and the type *NON_NEG_INT* defined as follows:

> **subtype** *NON_NEG_INT* **is** *INTEGER* **range** 0 .. *INTEGER'LAST*;

Then the first version

> **function** *FACT(N: NON_NEG_INT)* **return** *NATURAL* **is**
>   *F: NATURAL* := 1;
> **begin**
>   **for** *I* **in** 1 .. *N* **loop**
>   *F* := *F* * *I*;
>   **end loop**;
>   **return** *F*;
> **end** *FACT*;

is said to be *non-recursive*. This should be compared with the following version which is *recursive*, i.e. within the body of the function there is a call of the function itself,

> **function** *FACT(N: NON_NEG_INT)* **return** *NATURAL* **is**
> **begin**
>   **if** *N* > 1 **then**
>   **return** *N* * *FACT(N* − 1);
>   **else**
>   **return** 1;
>   **end if**;
> **end** *FACT*;

146

This latter version of *FACT* hints at certain properties of return statements:

- (*a*) a return statement can pass across the value of a general expression of the appropriate type;
- (*b*) at least one return statement must be present and there may be several; the **return** causes exit from the function – this must be explicit and will not happen implicitly, on reading the final **end** for example.

The *FACT* function can be used in the expected ways. Thus it is feasible to write in an appropriate environment even such complex expression as

$$BIN\_COEFF := FACT(N)/(FACT(R) * FACT(N-R));$$

with the expected results.

In Ada it is intended that functions should mirror their mathematical counterparts. For this to be realistic care should be taken in their design. Thus programmers should ensure wherever possible that function calls do not alter globally declared variables. The rules of Ada forbid parameters of functions to be altered. In fact we have not yet encountered situations where either of these practices is advisable; consequently we have not illustrated how they can be accomplished. More formally an Ada compiler can choose to evaluate an expression in whatever way it chooses provided it adheres to the rules about precedence etc.; in particular there are no rules about the relative order of evaluation of operands (with the exception of **and then** and **or else**) and the programmer and program verifier should make no such assumptions. Similarly no assumptions should be made about the order of evaluation of actual parameters.

A special kind of function makes it possible for mathematical operators and other kinds of operators to be introduced. The meaning of existing operators (or indeed functions) can be extended in the following way. Suppose we require to introduce addition and multiplication operators to add and find the scalar product, respectively, of vectors with equal bounds. We can proceed as follows:

```
type VECTOR is array (INTEGER range ⟨⟩) of FLOAT;
function "+" (U, V: VECTOR ) return VECTOR is
      W: VECTOR(U'RANGE);
begin
      for I in U'RANGE loop
            W(I) := U(I) + V(I);
      end loop;
      return W;
end "+";
function "*" (U, V: VECTOR ) return FLOAT is
      W: FLOAT := 0 . 0;
begin
      for I in U'RANGE loop
            W := W + U(I) * V(I);
```

end loop;
     return W;
   end $"*"$;

With these definitions it is now possible to write corresponding kinds of statements in programs. Given the declaration

    $A, B, C: VECTOR(1 .. 100)$;
      $A: FLOAT$;

assignments such as

    $X := (A + B) * C$;

can appear.

In this way operators such as $+$ and $*$ can be given new meanings. Not only can they be used for the addition of integers, reals, etc. but now they can be used for adding vectors of reals. The operators are said to be *overloaded* since they have more than one meaning. In any particular situation the meaning that is intended will depend on context, in particular on the types of the operands.

Although operators can be overloaded in the manner described above the precedence of operators cannot be altered. The standard precedence will always hold and so the implied bracketing of expressions remains stable. Given the existence of generic subprograms this is highly desirable!

It is necessary to impose certain natural restrictions on the nature of some operator definitions:

    comparison operators must give results of type *BOOLEAN*,
    unary operators must be overloaded as unary operators and binary
    operators must be overloaded as binary operators,
    the operators $=$ and $/=$ cannot be overloaded explicitly except in
    special cases.

The first two restrictions are imposed to make certain parsing problems that the computer will encounter less difficult.

The latter restriction is imposed since equality and inequality are, by default, defined for all types (other than the **limited restricted** types introduced in chapter 7).

In defining new operators a programmer should ensure that the resulting functions possess the expected mathematical or other properties. The facility to introduce such operators combined with the facility to introduce new type declarations means that the programmer can in some limited sense build his own programming language for his own specific problem. He can design new types and the operators to act on these, e.g. facilities for manipulating vectors, matrices, rational numbers, complex numbers, and so on.

148

6.1.2 Procedures

The procedure subprograms we examine in this section are used for performing tasks which do not produce single results in the sense of functions. We have in mind subprograms for performing tasks such as sorting sets of elements, partitioning sets into subsets, and so on. Also included are subprograms which potentially deliver several results, e.g. finding the sum and average of a set of numbers, finding if an element is present in an array and if so the position it occupies.

Such procedures must communicate with the outside world, with the environment in which they are activated or called. This they can do through their parameters. Parameters can be one of three possible modes:

in   or input parameters we have already seen; these have effectively read only access; the parameters can be used but no attempt to alter them is allowed – they act like local constraints;

out   or output parameters act like local variables; as a result of executing the body of the procedure the final value of the local variable is given to the actual parameter;

in out or input/parameter permits reading from or writing to the actual parameter.

If the mode is omitted **in** is assumed.

We shall now look at some examples which illustrate the possibilities. But first we note that terms such as formal parameter, actual parameter, recursion and call all have meanings analogous to those of the preceding section. Access to and altering of globals is permitted but is usually not to be encouraged.

A procedure $SWAP$ to interchange the values of two integer variables can take the following form:

> **procedure** $SWAP(A, B$: **in out** $INTEGER)$ **is**
> C: **constant** $INTEGER := A$;
> **begin**
> $A := B$;
> $B := C$;
> **end** $SWAP$;

When a procedure call such as

> $SWAP(X, Y)$;

occurs the contents of both X and Y have to be read and altered. Consequently the formal parameters A and B must be of input/output mode.

Note the absence of any return statement in the main body of the procedure. Termination of the procedure call occurs on naturally leaving the end of the procedure.

Let us now take another example. Suppose it is required to design a procedure which searches an array of characters to determine whether or not a particular character is present. If it is, the position it occupies must be determined. A procedure to perform this task is given below.

```
          procedure IS_PRESENT (A: STRING; C: CHARACTER;
                                PRESENT: out BOOLEAN;
                                POSN: out INTEGER) is
begin
     PRESENT := FALSE;
     for I in A'RANGE loop
          if C = A(I) then
               PRESENT := TRUE;
               POSN := I;
               return; - - causes exit from procedure
          end if;
     end loop;
end IS_PRESENT;
```

Note the mode of the various parameters

A is an input parameter since, by default, the mode **in** is assumed;
C likewise is an input parameter;
PRESENT is an output parameter and conveys to the outside world
part of the result produced by the procedure IS_PRESENT;
POSN is likewise an output parameter; it receives a result only if
PRESENT is set to TRUE.

In general the various formal parameters should be given modes which coincide with the expected role of the parameters. Any input parameter could be replaced by a corresponding **in out** parameter. Such a move would cause the compiler to fail to check whether an attempt was made to alter the parameter. The parameter passing mechanism we used for functions forces a programmer to specify input parameters and the default setting of **in** strongly encourages the correct action. The corresponding action for procedures is left to the programmer but a similar philosophy should be adopted.

It is intended that the presentation of both sections 6.1.1 and 6.1.2 should highlight a close relationship between blocks and subprograms, especially procedures. Blocks can be regarded as subprograms with no headings (or vice versa) and they appear *in situ*, where they are required to be used.

In this discussion about subprograms and their calls we have always used a positional notation for parameter passing. In keeping with the spirit of other constructs in Ada an alternative naming notation is possible and then the order in which parameters are presented is irrelevant. To illustrate, a call of the IS_PRESENT procedure can take the following form:

```
     IS_PRESENT(PRESENT => INPUT, POSN => HERE,
                          A => TEXT, C => " ");
```

Note the different order in which the parameters are presented. With suitable choices of formal parameters more readable programs can result.

In an Ada program, formal input parameters can be given default values at declaration time. Thus

procedure *IS_PRESENT*(*A*: *STRING*; *C*: *CHARACTER* := " ";
PRESENT: **out** *BOOLEAN*;
POSN: **out** *INTEGER*) **is**

begin . . . **end** *IS_PRESENT*;

In these circumstances the appropriate input parameters can be omitted when calls are made.

The two parameter passing conventions can be intertwined. However it is necessary to adhere to the following rules (assuming a left to right scan of the text):

> once a named parameter is used all other parameters must be named,
> once an input parameter is omitted all other parameters must be named.

In the remainder of the book we shall tend to adhere to the positional notation for parameter association. This has the advantage of being less bulky and, in terms of other programming languages, a more common way of passing parameters. The reader should find no difficulty in extending the ideas to the alternative methods of parameter association.

6.1.3 Generic subprograms

As mentioned earlier generic subprograms make use of a kind of type parameter which has the effect of making the subprogram more general and applicable to a wider set of values.

Take the case of a function for finding the maximum from a non-empty set of reals represented as an array – see the first example in section 6.1.1. Suppose we wish to find the maximum of a non-empty set of elements of type *SHORT_INTEGER* or *INTEGER*. Surely we do not have to reprogram the entire function merely replacing *FLOAT* by *SHORT_INTEGER* or *INTEGER* as required? We do not. Instead *FLOAT* is replaced by a general mode, *ITEM* say. Now what operations on objects of type *ITEM* are used within the function (other than equality, inequality and the ability to assign values which are generally available)? There is only one, namely the comparison operator ⟨. This must also be passed across with the type *ITEM*. This leads to the idea of a generic subprogram.

The declaration of a generic subprogram consists of two parts. In the first place there is a generic subprogram declaration which basically gives notice of the generic nature of the subprogram. For the above example this would be

generic
        type *ITEM* **is private**;

> **type** *VECTOR* **is array** (*INTEGER* **range** ⟨⟩) **of** *ITEM*;
> **with function** "⟨" (*U, V*: *ITEM*) **return** *BOOLEAN*;
> **function** *LARGEST* (*A*: *VECTOR*) **return** *ITEM*;

Preceding **function** is a generic clause which contains mention of the generalised type and its associated operations. The appearance of **private** implies that the only operation that can be performed by default on objects of type *ITEM* are equality and inequality; assignment may also take place. Any extra operators such as ⟨ must be explicitly mentioned as indicated.

The second part of the declaration of a generic subprogram is the declaration of the generic body. This is akin to a normal function declaration but use is made of the generic parameters. Thus

> **function** *LARGEST*(*A*: *VECTOR*) **return** *ITEM* **is**
>   *MAX* : *ITEM* := *A*(*A'FIRST*);
> **begin**
>   **for** *I* **in** *A'FIRST* + 1 .. *A'LAST* **loop**
>   **if** *MAX* < *A*(*I*) **then**
>   *MAX* := *A*(*I*);
>   **end if**;
>   **end loop**;
>   **return** *MAX*;
> **end** *LARGEST*;

Suppose that having made such a declaration we now want to use the function to find the largest in some sense of a non-empty set of cars, items of type *CAR*. How do we proceed? An instance of a generic subprogram can be obtained by applying a process called *instantiation*. This is typified by the following:

> **function** *LARGEST_CAR* **is new** *LARGEST*(*ITEM* => *CAR*,
>   "<" => *CAR_COMPARE*);

For this to be valid the type *CAR* must have been previously given and the function *CAR_COMPARE* must have been declared.

Let us now take a more realistic example and suppose we wish to find the largest of a set of integers. The comparison operator we will use will be the standard comparison operator derived from the standard environment. In fact, in general if a less-than operator exists in the standard environment we would normally like it to be used. To save trouble generic subprograms can be given generic clauses which are the same as previously described but with a default value for the operator(s):

> **generic**
>   **type** *ITEM* **is private**;
>   **type** *VECTOR* **is array** (*INTEGER* **range** ⟨⟩) **of** *ITEM*;
>   **with function** "⟨" **is** (*U, V*: *ITEM*)**return** *BOOLEAN* **is** ⟨⟩;
> **function** *LARGEST* (*A*: *VECTOR*) **return** *ITEM*;

and so on as before.

152

In these circumstances instantiation is less complex than described. We can now write such statements as

> **function** *LARGEST_INTEGER* **is new** *LARGEST*(*ITEM* =>
> *INTEGER*, *VECTOR* => *INT_ARRAY*);
> **function** *LARGEST_REAL* **is new** *LARGEST*(*FLOAT*, *FLOAT_ARRAY*)

By default the standard operators are selected. Note the similarity to the process of passing actual parameters to functions and procedures.

Generic subprograms can also be used to generalise the usefulness of procedures. The procedure to search a non-empty array to determine whether an element is present and if so what position it occupies (see section 6.1.2) can be dressed up as a generic subprogram in the following way (with default values for operators if required):

> **generic**
>   **type** *ITEM* **is private**;
>   **type** *VECTOR* **is array** (*INTEGER* **range** ⟨⟩) **of** *ITEM*;
> **procedure** *IS_PRESENT*(*A* : *VECTOR*; *C*: *ITEM*; *PRESENT*:
>   **out** *BOOLEAN*; *POSN*: **out** *INTEGER*);

is the generic subprogram specification; the generic body is given by

> **procedure** *IS_PRESENT*(*A* : *VECTOR*; *C*: *ITEM*; *PRESENT*:
>   **out** *BOOLEAN*; *POSN*: **out** *INTEGER*) **is**
> **begin**
>   *PRESENT* := *FALSE*;
>   **for** *I* **in** *A*'*RANGE* **loop**
>   **if** *C* = *A*(*I*) **then**
>   *PRESENT* := *TRUE*;
>   *POSN* := *I*;
>   **return**;
>   **end if**;
>   **end loop**;
> **end** *IS_PRESENT*;

Recall that both equality and inequality are defined on any two objects of the same private type. Instantiation again occurs in the expected way:

> **procedure** *IS_PRESENT_INT* **is new** *IS_PRESENT*(*ITEM* =>
> *INTEGER*, *VECTOR* => *ARRAY*);

The whole concept of generic subprograms is very convenient both from the point of view of writing programs and in proving their correctness. Design, coding and verification have to be undertaken just once and not once per instance. The design of these subprograms will be even more convenient if the number of generic parameters is kept relatively low and if default values are incorporated when possible. Thus it helps if only the greater-than operator can be used rather

153

than a needless rash of other comparison operators. This is a specialised version of a more important consideration.

A very important matter in the design of generic subprograms is their generality. All other matters being equal, subprograms should be written in as general a fashion as possible using only as few specialised properties as possible of any particular type. A nice example which illustrates the point is a procedure for swapping two values. In chapter 2 we gave an example which illustrated how the values of two integer variables might be interchanged. An alternative is to basically perform

$$Z := X; \quad X := Y; \quad Y := Z;$$

Both of these pieces of program could be wrapped up as procedures. From a generic standpoint the latter is much better than the former which relies crucially on the properties of integers and indeed can result in overflow. The latter uses no properties other than the fact that objects can be copied in assignments; the latter is therefore applicable to a much wider class of elements.

As we mentioned above it is preferable that large numbers of parameters do not have to be passed across to a generic subprogram. If such a subprogram wishes to manipulate, say, integers of different sizes it is undesirable to have to pass across as generic parameters all sorts of attributes and operators which can be used on integers. To overcome such difficulties generic types are classified into certain groups and these we illustrate by example:

(i) **type** *INDEX* **is** (⟨ ⟩);
  implies that *INDEX* is any discrete type and consequently attributes associated with discrete types become available.

(ii) **type** *INT* **is range** ⟨ ⟩;
  implies *INT* may refer to any integer type.

(iii) **type** *FLOATING_POINT* **is digits** ⟨ ⟩;
  implies that *FLOATING_POINT* may refer to any floating-point type.

(iv) **type** *FIXED_POINT* **is delta** ⟨ ⟩;
  implies that *FIXED_POINT* may refer to any fixed-point type.

(v) **type** *VECTOR* **is array** (*INDEX*) **of** *ITEM*;
  introducing an array type: *INDEX* is some appropriate indexing type.

(vi) **type** *LIST* **is private**;
  introduces a private type for which only the equality and inequality operators are possible and for which assignment is defined.

(vii) **type** *ITEM* **is limited private**;
  introduces a limited private type for which there are no attributes; even assignment and tests for equality are denied.

(viii) **type** *BUFFER* (*SIZE*: *NATURAL*) **is limited private**;
  introduces a parametrised type.

(ix) **type** *LIST_PTR* **is access** *LIST*;
  introduces an access type.

154

There remains one final possibility, a parameter which can be passed across to a generic subprogram. The generic parameter resembles in many ways the formal parameter of a subprogram. It may be of mode **in** or **in out** (**out** is not an acceptable possibility) and it can be given a default value by using := etc.

6.2   Axiomatics of subprograms

In this section we consider the verification of programs or pieces of program that make use of subprograms of the kind outlined in section 6.1. We shall find that this is merely a very natural extension of the work of the earlier chapters.

The task of verification reduces basically to the consideration of the proof rules for functions and procedures. We shall begin with simple cases and move progressively to the more general and difficult possibilities. The starting point will be proof rules which describe the partial correctness of non-recursive functions and therefore operators. Later we look at more complex cases such as problems involving the total correctness of recursive functions and procedures.

6.2.1   Proof rules for functions

In dealing with the verification of programs which use functions and with the proof rules of function calls the return statement causes a certain amount of difficulty. We shall assume that the statement

return *expression*;

associated with the function F has the effect of assigning the value of the *expression* to a kind of dummy or hidden variable associated with F. This variable will have a type determined by the type of the result produced by the function as set out in the function heading. We denote it by r_F, r as an abbreviation for **return** and F for the function name. r can be given a value only by a return statement associated with F. The return statement actually does more than this for it also causes exit from the function body. Any statement immediately following a return statement can never be executed.

From what has been said above, the meaning of the return statement

return *expression*;

can be likened to the meaning of the pair of statements

r_F := *expression*;
goto *LAB*;

where ⟪*LAB*⟫ is some imaginary label at which the computation of the expression which involved the call of function F continues.

Let us begin then with the declaration of some function. Typically there will be associated with the function some precondition which describes the range of values of and the relationships between the variables. There will also be a postcondition of some kind which describes the result obtained by calling the function.

Non-recursive functions

So that we can be specific let us talk about the non-recursive definition of the factorial function *FACT* given in section 6.1.1. Here the precondition is

$$N >= 0$$

and the postcondition is

$$(\mathbf{r}_{FACT} = N!) \land (N >= 0)$$

It is natural to expect that part of the verification process will involve establishing the truth of

```
--{N >= 0}
        F: NATURAL := 1;
begin
        for I in 1 .. N loop
                F := F * I;
        end loop;
        rFACT := F;
end FACT;
-- {(rFACT = N!) ∧ (N >= 0)}
```

The return statement present in the declaration of the function has been replaced by an appropriate assignment to $\mathbf{r}_{FACT}$. The fact that the return statement appeared at the end obviated the need for any jumps to be inserted in the body of the function. In general, however, jumps will be needed.

To be more general then, let us assume the existence of some function F which takes a single parameter N. We shall look at a skeleton of its declaration. We assume the existence of some precondition $P(N)$ and a postcondition which we write as $Q(N, \mathbf{r}_F)$. It might be imagined that the postcondition will take the form

$$\mathbf{r}_F = \text{some\_expression}$$

e.g. $\mathbf{r}_F = N!$ There are other possibilities. Consider a function designed to calculate the quotient obtained by dividing integer A by the positive integer B. The required postcondition might be written in the form

$$(A = B * \mathbf{r}_F + R) \land (0 <= R < B)$$

This is not of the expected form. Consequently the form $Q(N, \mathbf{r}_F)$ is more general.

We choose to write the precondition and postcondition immediately after the function heading. So we write the skeleton declaration of F as

function $F(N: \ldots)$ **return** ... **is**

156

```
- - pre {P(N)}
- - post { Q(N, r_F)}
  . . .
```

begin

$$S$$

end;

Part of the verification process will involve establishing the truth of

$$\{P(N)\}\ S'; \langle\!\langle END \rangle\!\rangle\ \textbf{null};\{Q(N, r_F)\}$$

where S' is obtained from S by replacing each statement

return *expression*;

by the corresponding statements

$r_F :=$ *expression*;
goto *END*;

It is assumed that the label $\langle\!\langle END \rangle\!\rangle$ and an accompanying null statement are inserted immediately before the final **end**. Moreover, it is assumed that $\langle\!\langle END \rangle\!\rangle$ does not occur elsewhere within S; if it does some other appropriate label can be used.

As it stands this is inadequate as a means of proving properties of programs which contain a call of F. It does not describe what happens when actual parameters are supplied and the function is called. Typical calls of the function F will take the form $F(A)$ where A is some actual parameter. We really require a proof rule whose consequent is just

$$P(N) \supset Q(N, r_F)$$

with the appropriate substitution of formal parameters by actual parameters. More precisely we need a rule whose consequent is

$$P(N)(A/N) \supset Q(N, r_F)(A/N, F(A)/r_F)$$

i.e. in $P(N)$, A replaces N and in $Q(N, r_F)$, A and $F(A)$ replace N and r_F respectively. In the case of the factorial function *FACT* this amounts to a statement of the form

$$(A >= 0) \supset FACT(A) = A\ !$$

This is just what is required. But what of the antecedent? What do we need to establish in order to be able to deduce the truth of the above?

For completeness there are certain comments we can make. We have already established the fact that we need to verify

$$\{P(N)\}\ S'; \langle\!\langle END \rangle\!\rangle\ \textbf{null}; \{Q(N, r_F)\}$$

We must also demonstrate the truth of the following:

1. It must be possible for the truth of P to imply the truth of Q, i.e. P and Q must be consistent in some sense.

2. The actual parameters must be of the proper type and satisfy the proper constraints.
3. The function must be one-valued, i.e. it must be deterministic and define some mathematical function.

There are remarks that we can make about each of these added constraints:

1. We can express 1 above in the following form

   $\exists Z$ such that $(P(N) \supset Q(N, Z))$

   i.e. there exists a Z such that the truth of $P(N)$ can imply the truth of $Q(N, Z)$.
2. The compiler should perform the checks mentioned in 2 above.
3. It is essential that 3 above is true, otherwise it would be possible to declare functions for which $F(A) /= F(A)$. We omit all consideration of such functions and so can omit this from our proof rules.

In a sense the restriction contained in 3 above is unfortunate. It seems to preclude all mention of random number generators. However, proofs of the correctness of programs which use these can still be given. If *RANDOM* is a function which produces real numbers between 0 and 1, possibly including 0 but not 1, then the required postcondition is just

$$0.0 <= r_{RANDOM} < 1.0$$

To summarise what we have described above, the proof rule for a function call $F(A)$ of function F can be expressed as

$$\frac{(\{P(N)\}\ S';\ \langle\!\langle END \rangle\!\rangle\ \mathbf{null};\ \{Q(N, r_F)\}) \wedge (\exists Z \text{ such that } P(N) \supset Q(N, Z))}{P(N)(A/N) \supset Q(N, r_F)(A/N, F(A)/r_F)}$$

The antecedent of this proof rule looks somewhat prohibitive. But it merits close inspection. It contains no mention of actual parameters such as A. It is therefore sufficient to establish the truth of the antecedent once and once only, at the time the function is declared. On each call of the function it suffices to establish the truth of $P(N)(A/N)$. Then the truth of the postcondition follows.

This proof rule shows in a nice way the separation between the tasks of designing a function and using it. If these are performed by different people then the designer establishes the truth of the antecedent. He then passes to users of his function the consequent. The latter is free of all considerations of the internal mechanism used in implementing the function, it is free of all consideration of consistency, and so on. It contains just what is required to use the function.

Example 6.2.1a *Highest common factor*

The function *GCD* is intended to calculate the highest common factor of its two positive integer parameters A and B, i.e. it calculates the largest positive integer dividing both A and B. The *GCD* function makes use of the operator **mod**. M **mod** N has the property that if initially $M, N > 0$ then on completion of the execution of **mod** there are integers Q and $\mathbf{r_{mod}}$ such that

$$M = N * Q + \mathbf{r_{mod}} \quad \text{where } 0 \leqslant \mathbf{r_{mod}} < N$$

To distinguish between the greatest common divisor as calculated by our function and the mathematical notion we use *GCD* for the former and *gcd* for the latter. The relevant mathematical properties of *gcd* can be expressed as follows:

(i) if $M > 0$ then $gcd(M, 0) = gcd(0, M) = M$,

(ii) if $M \geqslant N > 0$ then

$$gcd(M, N) = gcd(N, M) = gcd(N, M - N).$$

By induction it can be shown that as long as $M - N * Q >= 0$ where Q is an integer then

$$gcd(M, N) = gcd(N, M) = gcd(N, M - Q * N).$$

The function *GCD* complete with precondition, postcondition and loop invariant is given below. It makes use of the standard subtype *NATURAL*.

```
function GCD(A, B: NATURAL) return NATURAL is
    -- pre {TRUE}
    -- post {r_GCD = gcd(A, B)}
    U: INTEGER := A;
    V: INTEGER := B;
    W: INTEGER;
begin
    while         -- {(gcd(A, B) = gcd(U, V)) ∧ V >= 0}
                     V > 0 loop
        W := U mod V;
        U := V;
        V := W;
    end loop;
    return U;
end GCD;
```

To establish the loop invariant the required verification condition is

$$(gcd(A, B) = gcd(U, V)) \land V >= 0 \land V > 0$$
$$\supset$$
$$(gcd(A, B) = gcd(V, U \bmod V)) \land (U \bmod V >= 0)$$

Since $V > 0$ we can deduce properties about U **mod** V, i.e. $\mathbf{r_{mod}}$, from the rules for **mod**. Using the mathematical properties of *gcd* the above is readily established. The result follows on noting that on termination of the loop $V = 0$ and then

$$gcd(A, B) = gcd(U, V) = gcd(U, 0) = U = \mathbf{r_{GCD}}.$$

The remarks given above generalise in a very obvious way to functions of a more complex nature, e.g. to functions of several variables. A particular consequence of this extension is that the previous remarks apply to both unary and binary operators, functions of one and two variables respectively. The proof rules which describe the effect of functions and so operators can be used to prove properties of the operators or functions.

Although we have concentrated here on partial correctness it ought to be clear that many of the arguments we have given carry over to total correctness. The extra stipulation of termination requires us to show that the execution of

$$S; \langle\!\langle END \rangle\!\rangle \text{ null};$$

terminates and to insist that the evaluation of the actual parameters also terminate. The former requirement appears in the antecedent, the latter in the consequent.

It remains now to remove the restriction we imposed earlier regarding the recursive or non-recursive nature of functions.

Recursive functions

The remarks of the previous section do not obviously hold when recursive functions are involved. Let us take a recursive definition of some function F with appropriate precondition and postcondition. A skeleton declaration might take the form

> **function** $F(N: \ldots)$ **return** $\ldots$ **is**
>   - - **pre** $\{P(N)\}$
>   - - **post** $\{Q(N, \mathbf{r}_F)\}$
>   . . .
>
> **begin**
> S
> **end** F;

Let us consider the proof rule for the partial correctness of a call of F.

If we use the notation employed on the non-recursive case then at some stage (ideally when the function is declared) we have to establish the truth of

$$\{P(N)\} S'; \langle\!\langle END \rangle\!\rangle \text{ null}; \{Q(N, \mathbf{r}_F)\}$$

Since F is recursive this proof will require knowledge about the effect of a call of F, the function whose correctness we are trying to establish. The antecedent mentioned in the previous section on non-recursive functions contains no such information and so is inadequate.

To cope with recursion it is necessary to add to the antecedent a variant of the consequent. We must add something of the form

$$P(N)(A1/N) \supset Q(N, \mathbf{r}_F)(A1/N, F(A1)/\mathbf{r}_F)$$

This is all that is necessary.

As a mechanism for proving the correctness of recursive functions the antecedent resulting from these remarks is not particularly helpful. The proof rule is in a sense inductive and proofs of properties of recursive program are inductive. But there are better and more appropriate formulations of induction than those given above. The above proof rule is given for completeness but we delay till section 6.3 any consideration of proving properties of recursive programs.

The ideas described here can be extended in an obvious way to cover more complex cases. Functions of several variables can be fitted to the scheme as can mutually recursive functions. Even total correctness can be incorporated. In the latter case it has to be shown that the evaluation of all parameters will terminate and that there is some ordering associated with the values of successive parameters. On successive calls the values of the parameter must belong to a well-founded set and yet decrease.

6.2.2 Proof rules for procedures

Let us begin with some general but non-recursive procedure which does not access global variables; we assume it merely performs some action on the variables supplied as parameters. We shall concentrate for the time being on the partial correctness of this procedure. We shall find that much of the ensuing discussion is similar to the discussion about functions but there are certain important differences.

Associated with the procedure will be a precondition and a postcondition. As might be imagined the precondition describes the expected values of and the relationships between the parameters initially, at the time of a procedure call. The postcondition describes the relationships between the parameters after a call has been successfully executed. We shall therefore write our procedure T in the following kind of fashion, assuming two possible formal parameters M and N:

> **procedure** $T(M: \text{in} \ldots; N: \text{in out} \ldots)$ **is**
>   - - **pre** $\{P(M'IN, N'IN)\}$
>   - - **post** $\{Q(M'IN, N'IN, N'OUT)\}$
>   . . .
>
> **begin**
> S
> **end** T;

Note the presence of $M'IN$, $N'IN$ and $N'OUT$ in the assertions. With the introduction of procedures we introduce also the possibility of parameters changing value as a result of the execution of the procedure. To distinguish between input values and output values – as far as assertions are concerned these are the only values of interest – we adopt this Ada-like notation. $N'IN$ refers to the initial value of N and $N'OUT$ refers to the final value of N. Note that there is mention of $M'IN$ but no mention of $M'OUT$. This is to be expected since M is an input parameter. Conversely for P, an output parameter, $P'OUT$ would be present but not $P'IN$.

So that the notation blends even more naturally with the Ada scene and does not render as obsolete the work of the previous section we shall allow defaults. For input parameters such as M we shall assume that M and $M'IN$ are equivalent.

Let us now return to the discussion about the procedure T. After T has been declared it is natural to expect that it should be possible to prove the truth of

$$\{P(M, N'IN)\}\, S\, \{Q(M, N'IN, N'OUT)\}.$$

In comparison with functions there may be no need to alter S. When return statements are present S should be altered in a suitable way. Such situations are rare and we proceed as if no alteration is required.

The above describes essentially what must be proved at the time when a procedure is declared. It tells us nothing whatsoever about procedure calls. What would we like to be able to deduce on calling a procedure by $T(A, B)$? In keeping with the spirit of the discussion on function calls it might seem that we should have a rule whose consequent is of the form

$$\{P(M, N'IN)(A/M, B'IN/N'IN)\}\, T(A, B)$$
$$\{Q(M, N'IN, N'OUT)(A/M, B'IN/N'IN, B'OUT/N'OUT)\}.$$

But not quite. In general it is unreasonable to suppose that after the call there will be any concept of both $B'IN$ and $B'OUT$. What we deduce after the call is the truth of some predicate R which possesses the property that

$$Q(M, N'IN, N'OUT)(A/M, B'IN/N'IN, B'OUT/N'OUT) \supset R.$$

A more accurate description of the consequent is therefore

$$\{P(M, N'IN)(A/M, B'IN/N'IN) \wedge Q(M, N'IN, N'OUT)$$
$$(A/M, B'IN/N'IN, B'OUT/N'OUT) \supset R\}\, T(A, B)\{R\}.$$

The next question to be answered is: what form should the premise or antecedent take? In other words what must the designer of the procedure prove so that the user of the procedure can employ the above? We have already seen that

$$\{P(M, N'IN)\}\, S\, \{Q(M, N'IN, N'OUT)\}$$

must be verified. Also we must show that the parameters of T satisfy the type conditions and constraints. We can realistically assume that this has been done by a compiler.

The proof rule for the function call T reduces now to

$$\dfrac{\{P(M, N'IN)\}\, S\, \{Q(M, N'IN, N'OUT)\}}{\{P(M, N'IN)(A/M, B'IN/N'IN) \wedge Q(M, N'IN, N'OUT)}$$
$$(A/M, B'IN/N'IN, B'OUT/N'OUT) \supset R\}\, T(A, B)\, \{R\}$$

Again witness the clear distinction between the role of the designer of a procedure and the role of a user. The designer should verify the truth of the premise and this he does just once. The user makes use of the consequent each time he invokes a call of the procedure.

It should be clear how much of the above generalises to take account of several parameters possibly of different modes: for **in out** variables V, $V'IN$ and $V'OUT$ will be present; for input variables V, $V'IN$ (or just V) will be present; and for output variables V, $V'OUT$ will be present.

At this juncture it is essential to introduce some restrictions concerning parameters; otherwise the given proof rule is an inadequate description of the meaning of a procedure call. Problems can arise from aliasing, a process whereby alterations to one variable would apparently influence the value of another variable. For instance, one could envisage a situation whereby different formal parameters could be replaced by the same or a related actual parameter. Such forms of aliasing are to be avoided at all costs. Items which appear to be separate and unrelated at verification time ought to remain so when calls are invoked. For the purposes of this advice access variables should be seen as giving access to the entire associated collection.

Various extensions of these relatively simple situations have to be considered. First there is the possibility of recursion. In keeping with our earlier remarks about recursive functions we can follow essentially the same argument and deduce that proof rules for recursive procedures require an extra clause in their premise namely (using the earlier notation):

$$\{P(M, N'IN)(C/M, D'IN/N'IN) \land Q(M, N'IN, N'OUT)$$
$$(C/M, D'IN/N'IN, D'OUT/N'OUT) \supset R1\} \; T(C, D) \, \{R1\}$$

As remarked earlier this is not particularly useful from the point of view of verifying recursive procedures. There are better methods which will emerge in section 6.3.

Remarks similar to those made for functions can again be made about total correctness. It is important to ensure not just that the body of T terminates but that the evaluation of the parameters also terminate. The successive values of the parameters must also be shown to belong to some well-founded set, etc.

There is one important situation which we have not discussed. Procedures can alter globals. We remarked earlier in section 6.1.2 that although these can appear in general it is not good practice to use them. But there are exceptional cases. Consequently we consider the verification problem, in particular the proof rules, associated with such procedures.

The potential difficulties of using globals are overcome if global variables, etc. are regarded as parameters in the following sense:

> globals accessed for reading purposes only should be treated as **in** parameters;
> globals which are updated directly, or indirectly using another subprogram, should be regarded as **in out** parameters.

These conventions combined with the earlier advice about aliasing indicate that, for example, it is undesirable to equate or confuse parameters and global variables. As far as the proof rules are concerned globals are parameters except in describing the procedure call when they are omitted.

To illustrate let us take some examples. First we look at a procedure to interchange the values of two integer variables

> **procedure** $SWAP(A, B: $ **in out** $INTEGER)$ **is**
>   - - **pre** $\{TRUE\}$
>   - - **post** $\{(A'OUT = B'IN) \wedge (B'OUT = A'IN)\}$
> $C: INTEGER;$
> **begin**
> $C := A;$
> $A := B;$
> $B := C;$
> **end** $SWAP;$

The proof rule for *SWAP* indicates that the implementer of this procedure must establish the truth of

>   - - $\{(A = A'IN) \wedge (B = B'IN)\}$
> $C := A;$
> $A := B;$
> $B := C;$
>   - - $\{(A = B'IN) \wedge (B = A'IN)\}$

This can be done in a straightforward way. Note that the precondition *TRUE* is augmented with the information about the initial values of appropriate parameters together possibly with constraint information derived from the parameter types. The postcondition is also modified in an obvious way.

On the other hand a user of *SWAP* is given the information that

$$\{((A'OUT = B'IN) \wedge (B'OUT = A'IN)) \supset R\}\ SWAP(A, B)\ \{R\}.$$

If the precondition is true prior to the call $SWAP(A, B)$ then R will be true after the call.

As another example consider the problem of looking for an item in an array. A procedure to perform this task was given in section 6.1.2. The heading and accompanying precondition and postcondition can be written (using the pointwise extension notation) as

> **procedure** $IS\_PRESENT(A: STRING; C: CHARACTER;$
> $PRESENT: $ **out** $BOOLEAN; POSN: $ **out** $INTEGER)$ **is**
> - - **pre** $\{A'FIRST <= A'LAST\}$
> - - **post** $\{(PRESENT \wedge C = A(POSN)) \vee$
> - - $(\text{not } PRESENT \wedge NE(C, A))\}$
> **begin** . . . **end** $IS\_PRESENT;$

164

A call of this procedure of the form

$$IS\_PRESENT(INPUT, " ", IS\_SPACE, HERE);$$

indicates the presence or absence of a space. If

$$(IS\_SPACE \wedge " " = A(HERE)) \vee$$
$$(\text{not } IS\_SPACE \wedge NE(" ", A))$$
$$\supset$$
$$R$$

then after this call a user is entitled to assume the truth of R. Prior to this the designer must have checked the correctness of the design.

6.2.3 Proofs involving generic subprograms

As far as generic subprograms are concerned there is really very little to add to the previous discussion. These subprograms will be either functions or procedures. Both these classes of objects have already been studied.

In proving the properties of generic subprograms there will typically be some generic type and perhaps certain operators or whatever which can be legitimately used on these types. Compilers will check that only these operations possibly together with equality, inequality and assignment have been employed.

Associated with generic subprograms will be preconditions and postconditions which describe the task which the subprogram performs. These assertions will themselves be described ultimately in terms of the legitimate operations. We shall illustrate these remarks with some examples.

Let us begin with the *SWAP* procedure for interchanging two values. The procedure supplemented with the preconditions and postconditions will take the form

    generic
        type *ELEM* **is private**;
    procedure *SWAP(U, V*: **in out** *ELEM*);

    procedure *SWAP(U, V*: **in out** *ELEM*) **is**
        -- **pre** {*TRUE*}
        -- **post** {($U'OUT = V'IN$) $\wedge$ ($V'OUT = U'IN$)}
        W: *ELEM*;
    begin ... **end** *SWAP*;

There are no operations involved (other than assignment) and the precondition and postcondition themselves make use only of equality which is defined for all types other than **limited private**. The proof is relatively straightforward, but only if it is assumed that U and V do not interrelate in any sense; thus the actual parameters may not be overlapping arrays, for example.

A more complex example is the case of the generic subprogram to find the largest element in a set. The subprogram heading and accompanying assertions are

generic

    type *ITEM* **is private**;

    type *VECTOR* **is array** (*INTEGER* **range** ⟨⟩) **of** *ITEM*;

    with function "⟨" (*U, V: ITEM*) **return** *BOOLEAN* **is** ⟨⟩;

function *LARGEST*(*A : VECTOR*) **return** *ITEM*;

function *LARGEST*(*A : VECTOR*) **return** *ITEM* **is**

    - - **pre** {$A'LAST <= A'FIRST$, i.e. *A* is non-empty}

    - - **post** {$LE(A, \mathbf{r}_{LARGEST})$ ∧ [there is a

    - -   *J* in *A'RANGE* such that $\mathbf{r}_{LARGEST} = A(J)$]}

    MAX: ITEM;

    begin ... end *LARGEST*;

The postcondition reflects the effect of a function call. It is described only in terms of legitimate operations namely < and equality. Recall that both = and /= are defined for objects of all of the types so far encountered.

Upon instantiation the given types and operators will be particularised and a more definite meaning attributed to the subprogram and assertions.

To conclude we note that functions and procedures can cause exceptions to be raised. In these circumstances the postcondition should include a means of recording such a possibility. Similarly more conventional jumps out of functions and procedures are possible, though usually undesirable; again a means of recording such events is desirable. Postconditions can be written in the form

    {*Q*} or when *EXCEPTION* {*R*}

or

    {*Q*} or at ⟪*LABEL*⟫ {*R*}

(see section 4.2.5), and this provides a means of accommodating these situations.

6.3   The theory of recursive functions

In this section we shall take a close look at properties of recursive subprograms, in particular recursive functions.

A fairly extensive and sophisticated mathematical theory underlies the entire topic of recursion. It is not our intention to provide a rigorous mathematical/ logical treatment of the topic. Instead we review the topic and state important mathematical results without proof. In the process we look at inductive methods which will allow us to prove properties of recursive programs.

In section 6.3.1 we give some background to the mathematics of section 6.3.2. This section is somewhat theoretical and can be omitted by the reader who merely wishes to understand the verification material of section 6.3.3.

Although the following discussion appears to concentrate on recursive functions the ideas can also be applied to subprograms of a more general kind. In fact from a mathematical point of view procedures are special kinds of functions which produce either no result or a single uninteresting result depending on the viewpoint.

6.3.1 Background

Whenever we say that a function f is defined recursively we mean that it is defined in terms of itself in some sense. In the straightforward case, in simple recursion, f is defined in terms of itself explicitly. In this case we say that $f, f_1, f_2, \ldots, f_n$ are mutually recursive.

We shall concentrate on the case of simple recursion and we write

$$f = \tau(f)$$

to express the fact that f is defined in terms of itself. This notation has the effect of hiding the existence of and the number of parameters but it is adequate for our purposes. The function τ will inevitably contain a conditional of some kind otherwise the recursion can never terminate.

There is little loss of generality in taking this apparently restrictive course of action. The mutually recursive case can be expressed in a similar notation. We can regard $F = \{f, f_1, \ldots, f_n\}$ as an array or vector of functions and then write

$$F = \tau(F)$$

so reducing the problem to the simple case though now vector and matrix operations may be present within τ.

For the moment let us resort to simple school algebra. Given an equation of the form (x may now have any integer value)

$$x = \tau(x)$$

there are several possible outcomes:

the equation may possess no solution at all as in the case

$x = x + 1$;

the equation may possess a single unique solution as in

$x = 2x - 1$

where the solution is $x = 1$;

the equation may possess a finite number of solutions (for example

$x = x^2 - 6$

has two solutions namely $x = 3$ and $x = -2$);

the equation may possess an infinite number of solutions, for example

$x = x$.

So now, one, several or an infinite number of solutions are all possibilities.

There are certain similarities between this situation and the case of recursive functions. We use small letters to talk about functions to attract attention to the fact that the definitions below could not appear in Ada programs (return statements would be needed):

Consider the following.

(i) $f(x)$ is defined only for $x = 0$ as follows

    if $x >= 0$ **then** 0 **else** $f(x - 1) + 1$ **end if**;

    This has one solution, namely $f(x) = x$.

(ii) Let $f(x)$ be defined as

    if $x = 0$ **then** 0 **else** $f(x + 1)$ **end if**;

    This has an infinite number of solutions namely $f(0) = 0$ and for $x > 0$
    we have $f(x)$ can be any constant.

These examples are relatively simple. Let us now take a more complex example and define $f(x, y)$ only for non-negative x and y in the following fashion:

    if $x = y$ **then** $x + 1$ **else** $f(f(x + 1, y - 1), y)$ **end if**

This has several possible solutions. Some examples include

    (i) $f_1(x, y) = y + 1$
    (ii) $f_2(x, y) =$ **if** $y >= x$ **then** $y + 1$ **else** $x - 1$ **end if**
    (iii) $f_3(x, y) =$ **if** $(y >= x) \wedge (y - x)$ **mod** $2 = 0$ **then** $y + 1$ **else** *undefined* **end if**

The reader can verify that for each $i = 1, 2, 3$ indeed

$$f_i(x, y) = \text{if } x = y \text{ then } x + 1 \text{ else } f_i(f_i(x + 1, y - 1), y) \text{ end if}$$

i.e. f_i is a solution of the previous recursive equation.

We have seen recursive equations involving functions and these have one, several or an infinite number of solutions. Such a solution we call a *fixed point* of the function τ – applying τ to a solution leaves it unaltered or fixed.

These observations raise an awkward problem. Given a recursive definition of the function f, which function is defined? What will a computer's reaction be to an equation with several possible solutions?

Certain interesting observations can be made about the three solutions f_1, f_2 and f_3 given above. They all agree over certain ranges of values of x and y, namely the values on which f_3 is defined. Moreover, f_3 can be described as the least defined of all the three functions. In fact, in this sense it is the least fixed point of all possible solutions to the equation.

Least fixed points provide the key to understanding recursive functions.

We proceed by trying to formalise the idea of 'being less defined than'. As presented above the idea applies to functions. But we shall have to clarify precisely the functions being discussed. What are their domains and ranges, for example? Does the idea of 'being less defined than' apply to the domain as well as to the functions themselves?

6.3.2 The theory of least fixed points

We now introduce some abstract mathematics. We define an approximation notation on the elements of the set or the domain D. If d_1, d_2 are elements of D we write

$$d_1 \sqsubseteq d_2$$

to mean that d_1 is *less defined than* or *consistent with* d_2. We impose certain properties on the relation $\sqsubseteq$, properties derived from the ideas expressed in section 6.3.1.

Transitive
If $d_1 \sqsubseteq d_2$ and $d_2 \sqsubseteq d_3$ then $d_1 \sqsubseteq d_3$.

Antisymmetric
If $d_1 \sqsubseteq d_2$ and $d_2 \sqsubseteq d_1$ then $d_1 = d_2$.

Reflexive
For all d in D $d \sqsubseteq d$.

Then $\sqsubseteq$ is a *partial order* over the set D (based on the 'less than or equal' operator). It is beneficial to assume that there is in D a least defined element which we denote by $\perp$. Then for all d in D we can state that

$$\perp \sqsubseteq d.$$

$\perp$ is sometimes referred to as the *bottom*, the *undefined* or *inconsistent* element of D or even *chaos*.

In the sequel we shall use $\sqsubseteq$ and $\perp$ in connection with several different sets. In all cases the meaning, i.e. the set to which these are related, should be clear from the context. This saves us the effort of having to devise a rash of confusing notation for different approximation relations and different bottom elements.

Now let us particularise the discussion and talk about a set X of elements like the integers, booleans, characters, and so on. Thus X is now a set of elements on which functions in a programming language may be defined but augmented with the special element $\perp$. We define

$$\perp \sqsubseteq x \quad \text{for all } x \text{ in } X$$

and

$$x \sqsubseteq x \quad \text{for all } x \text{ in } X.$$

Those are the only relationships which are defined. This version of $\sqsubseteq$ is a relation of the kind described above – it is transitive, antisymmetric and reflexive.

In programming languages functions often have several parameters, possibly of different types. An alternative view is that they have a single parameter which is an item taken from the Cartesian product of several sets. Let $X_1, X_2, \ldots, X_n$ be domains on which are defined approximation relations $\sqsubseteq_1, \sqsubseteq_2, \ldots, \sqsubseteq_n$ respectively, the subscripts being used to distinguish the different relations. Then if $\langle x_1, x_2, \ldots, x_n \rangle$ and $\langle y_1, y_2, \ldots, y_n \rangle$ denote n-tuples of elements for which x_i and y_i are in X_i we can define an order $\sqsubseteq$ as follows. We shall say that

$$\langle x_1, x_2, \ldots, x_n \rangle \sqsubseteq \langle y_1, y_2, \ldots, y_n \rangle$$

if and only if

$$x_i \sqsubseteq_i y_i$$

for each $i = 1, 2, \ldots, n$. The relation $\sqsubseteq$ is then an approximation relation on the Cartesian product $X_1 \times X_2 \times \ldots \times X_n$. The minimum element is just

$$\langle \bot_1, \bot_2, \ldots, \bot_n \rangle$$

where $\bot_i$ is the least element of X_i.

Besides Cartesian products it is usually possible in decent programming languages to construct the discriminated union of two domains D_1 and D_2. This we represent by $D_1 + D_2$. An approximation relation $\sqsubseteq$ can be defined on this in a straightforward manner. If x and y are in $D_1 + D_2$ they are related if and only if they both belong to either D_1 or to D_2. Suppose they belong to D_1 then we define

$$x \sqsubseteq y \quad \text{if and only if } x \sqsubseteq_1 y$$

within D_1, where $\sqsubseteq_1$ is the approximation relation defined on D_1.

A final set of objects commonly available in programming languages is the set of lists. The lists of elements from D we write as D^* and then

$$D^* = \mathbf{nil} + D + D^2 + D^3 + \ldots + D^n + \ldots$$

where D^n is just the Cartesian product of D with itself n times.

These remarks then describe the kinds of domains that can be constructed in typical programming languages and they show that natural approximation relations can be defined on them. These are the domains on which functions are defined. We shall now talk about functions and this will lead us to consider the possibility of approximation relations on these.

On these new domains certain functions can be defined. An interesting class of these functions are the monotonic functions. f is said to be *monotonic* if

$$\text{whenever } x \sqsubseteq y \text{ then } f(x) \sqsubseteq f(y)$$

i.e. given a better approximation f produces a better result. An interesting subset of the monotonic functions are the *continuous* functions. Informally as we approach absolute accuracy in an argument of the function we approach absolute accuracy in the result of the function. With continuous functions we have the added benefit that if

$$x_0 \sqsubseteq x_1 \sqsubseteq \ldots \sqsubseteq x_n \sqsubseteq \ldots$$

tends to some limit x then

$$f(x_0) \sqsubseteq f(x_1) \sqsubseteq \ldots \sqsubseteq f(x_n) \sqsubseteq \ldots$$

also tends to some limit and this limit is just $f(x)$.

We have, as yet, not given any meaning to the concept of limit. This we now do. Let

$$y_1 \sqsubseteq y_2 \sqsubseteq \ldots \sqsubseteq y_n \sqsubseteq \ldots$$

We say that the y_i form a chain of successive approximations. We call y the *limit* or the *least upper bound* of this chain,

(i) if $y_i \sqsubseteq y$ for each $i = 1, 2, \ldots$

(ii) if $y_i \sqsubseteq z$ for each $i = 1, 2, \ldots$

then $y \sqsubseteq z$

Thus (i) says that y is an upper bound and (ii) implies that y is a least upper bound. We write

$$y = \lim_{n \to \infty} y_n \quad \text{or} \quad y = \bigsqcup_{n=0}^{\infty} y_n$$

The condition for the continuity of f can then be phrased in the following terms

$$f\left(\bigsqcup_{n=0}^{\infty} x_n\right) = \bigsqcup_{n=0}^{\infty} f(x_n)$$

Fortunately all the functions we can write in programming languages have the properties of monotonicity and continuity. Even if we talk about functions of functions, or functionals as they are often called, then these properties still persist. In particular the functional τ used in the recursive definition of functions is monotonic and continuous. This observation suggests that we impose an approximation relation on functions themselves.

Let f and g be functions which both map the domain D_1 into the domain D_2. We write

$$f \sqsubseteq g$$

if and only if

$$f(d) \sqsubseteq g(d) \quad \text{for all } d \in D_1$$

i.e. if and only if f is less well defined than g throughout the domain D_1.

Given this approximation relation on functions we can now talk about chains of functions. One particular chain is of interest to us. We know that

$$\bot \sqsubseteq \tau(\bot).$$

Since τ is monotonic it follows that

$$\tau(\bot) \sqsubseteq \tau(\tau(\bot))$$

i.e.

$$\tau(\bot) \sqsubseteq \tau^2(\bot).$$

Proceeding in this way we let

$$f_i = \tau^i(\bot) \quad \text{for } i = 1, 2, \ldots$$

and so obtain the chain

$$\bot \sqsubseteq f_1 \sqsubseteq f_2 \sqsubseteq \ldots \sqsubseteq f_n \sqsubseteq \ldots$$

This leads us to an important theorem.

Kleene's theorem
Every recursive equation

$$f = \tau(f)$$

171

has a least fixed point f_τ of the kind described above. This least fixed point is given by

$$f_\tau = \bigsqcup_{n=0}^{\infty} f_n$$

where each $f_i = \tau^i(\bot)$.

Let us illustrate the power of this theorem by taking a close look at a recursive definition of the factorial function:

$$f(n) = \textbf{if } n = 0 \textbf{ then } 1 \textbf{ else } n * f(n-1) \textbf{ end if}$$

Kleene's theorem implies that we look at the successive approximations obtained by replacing f by $\bot$, then $\tau(\bot)$, etc.

$\bot$:   undefined

$\tau(\bot)(n)$:   **if** $n = 0$ **then** 1 **else** $n * \bot\,(n-1)$ **end if**

              i.e. **if** $n < 1$ **then** 1 **else** $\bot$ **end if**

$\tau^2(\bot)(n)$:   **if** $n = 0$ **then** 1 **else** $n * \tau(\bot)(n-1)$ **end if**

              i.e. **if** $n < 2$ **then** 1 **else** $\bot$ **end if**

$\tau^3(\bot)(n)$:   **if** $n = 0$ **then** 1 **else** $n * \tau^2(\bot)(n-1)$ **end if**

              i.e. **if** $n < 3$ **then** $n!$ **else** $\bot$ **end if**

A simple proof by induction yields the fact that

$$\tau^i(\bot)(n) : \textbf{if } n < i \textbf{ then } n! \textbf{ else } \bot \textbf{ end if}$$

Using the earlier interpretation of $f_1, f_2, \ldots$ it follows that the limit of the sequence

$$\bot \sqsubseteq f_1 \sqsubseteq f_2 \sqsubseteq \ldots$$

is just the factorial function, as we would surely have hoped.

When the value of a recursive function has to be computed it will normally happen that a computer is given the task of producing the code for the evaluation of the recursive function and in the process implementing one of the usual parameter calling mechanisms. If a computation sequence, as it is called, produces a value that value will always agree with the value produced by the least fixed point of the recursive equation. In short, a computation sequence produces a value which is less defined than or equal to the least fixed point. Depending on which parameter calling mechanism is used either can occur. In Ada either can occur.

6.3.3   Structural induction

The principle of structural induction can be used to verify properties of recursive programs. It can be stated in the following way:

Principle of structural induction
Let S be some well-founded set with partial ordering $<$. Suppose we want to prove some property θ for all members of S. Let s be any

element in S. If, on the assumption that $\theta(t)$ is true for all $t < s$ and t in S, we can establish the truth of $\theta(s)$ then structural induction allows us to deduce that θ is true for all elements in S.

We shall now give some examples which illustrate the uses of this result. Not all the results are concerned with partial correctness. In one case we prove termination and in another we show that two functions are defined and their values equal for all possible values of their argument. The principle of structural induction is therefore of relatively wide applicability.

Example 6.3.3a Factorial function
Show that if $f(n)$ is defined by

$$f(n) = \textbf{if } n = 0 \textbf{ then } 1 \textbf{ else } n * f(n-1) \textbf{ end if}$$

then for all non-negative integers $n, f(n) = n!$

To prove this result we take the obvious well-founded set consisting of the non-negative integers and the usual 'less than' ordering.

The result is certainly true for $n = 0$. Assume the truth of the result for all non-negative integers k with the property that $k < n$, i.e. for all such k we have $f(k) = k!$ Then

$$f(n) = n * f(n-1)$$

But now $n - 1 < n$ and so $f(n-1) = (n-1)!$ Therefore

$$f(n) = n * (n-1)! = n!$$

and the result follows for n.

By structural induction the result is true for all non-negative integers n.

From this simple example it can be seen that in its simplest form structural induction is very similar to simple induction as found in mathematics. The next two examples are somewhat more ambitious and illustrate more devious applications of the principle.

Example 6.3.3b A 3x + 1 function
Let the function f be defined in the following way:

$$f(x) = \textbf{if } x \textbf{ mod } 2 = 0 \textbf{ then } x/2 \textbf{ else } f(f(3 * x + 1)) \textbf{ end if}$$

Prove that the computation of $f(x)$ terminates in all cases where x is a non-negative integer.

It is clear that the computation of $f(x)$ terminates whenever x is even. We phrase this observation in the following terms. The computation of $f(x)$ terminates for all values of x in which the binary representation of x contains a 0 in the rightmost position. We introduce the following notation:

$P(i)$ denotes the assertion that the computation of $f(x)$ terminates for all values of x for which the binary representation contains a 0 in the ith position from the right but not in the kth position where $k < i$. If

173

necessary place a 0 immediately to the left of the binary representation of x so that 3, for example, appears as 011.

We know that $P(1)$ is true. Assume that $P(k)$ is true for all values of k less than some positive integer i. Any number x whose binary representation contains a 0 in the ith position but not in the kth position where $k < i$ has the form

$$x = 2^{i+1}y + 2^i - 1$$

for some non-negative integer y. Then

$$
\begin{aligned}
3x + 1 &= 2x + x + 1 \\
&= (2^{i+2}y + 2^{i+1} - 2) + (2^{i+1}y + 2^i - 1) + 1 \\
&= 2^{i+2}y + 2^{i+1}(y+1) + 2^i - 2
\end{aligned}
$$

Since x is odd and $3x + 1$ is even we have, from the definition of f,

$$
\begin{aligned}
f(x) &= f(f(3x+1)) \\
&= f(2^{i+1}y + 2^i(y+1) + 2^{i-1} - 1)
\end{aligned}
$$

Now $2^{i+1}y + 2^i(y+1) + 2^{i-1} - 1$ is an integer whose binary representation has a 0 in the $(i-1)$th position but not in the kth position for any $k < i - 1$. By the inductive hypothesis we know that the computation of

$$f(2^{i+1}y + 2^i(y+1) + 2^{i-1} - 1)$$

terminates and so the computation of $f(x)$ terminates.

By the principle of structural induction the required result follows.

Example 6.3.3c   McCarthy's 91-function
Let the functions f and g be defined for all integers x in the following way

$f(x) = $ **if** $x > 100$ **then** $x - 10$ **else** $f(f(x + 11))$ **end if**
$g(x) = $ **if** $x > 100$ **then** $x - 10$ **else** 91 **end if**

We wish to show that, for all values of their argument, these two functions compute the same values, i.e. $f(x) = g(x)$.

To prove this we employ structural induction. Let $(S, <)$ be the well-founded set whose elements are the usual integers and whose ordering $<$ is defined by

$$y \prec x \quad \text{if and only if } x < y <= 101,$$

where $<$ and $<=$ are the usual 'less than' and 'less than or equal to' operators on the integers. That $(S, <)$ is a well-founded set requires some proof but this can be readily provided.

We assume that $f(y) = g(y)$ for all $y \prec x$ and we try to prove that $f(x) = g(x)$. We separate three cases determined by the possible ranges in which x lies.

(i) $100 < x: f(x) = x - 10 = g(x)$
(ii) $90 <= x <= 100:$
      From the definition of f
      $$f(x) = f(f(x + 11)).$$

174

But now $x + 11 >= 101$ and so $f(x + 11) = x + 1$. Therefore

$f(x) = f(x + 1)$.

Now $x < x + 1 <= 101$ and so $x + 1 < x$. Therefore by the inductive hypothesis

$f(x) = f(x + 1) = g(x + 1) = 91 = g(x)$

as required.

(iii) $x < 90$:

From the definition of f, again $f(x) = f(f(x + 11))$. But now

$x < x + 11 <= 101$

and so, by induction and the definition of g

$f(x + 11) = g(x + 11) = 91$.

Therefore

$f(x) = f(91)$
$\quad = g(91)$ from case (ii) above
$\quad = 91$ from the definition of g
$\quad = g(x)$ again from the definition of g.

This completes the consideration of all three cases. The required result follows by structural induction.

Example 6.3.3d   Ackermann's function

Let $A(m, n)$ be defined as follows for non-negative integers m and n.

$A(m, n) = $ **if** $m = 0$ **then** 1
                  elsif $n = 0$ **then** $A(m - 1, 1)$
                  else $A(m - 1, A(m, n - 1))$
                  end if

Prove that $A(m, n)$ is defined for all legal m and n.

The proof is again by induction on the pairs (m, n). We introduce a relation $<$ on such pairs in the following way:

$(m_1, n_1) < (m_2, n_2)$

if and only if

$m_1 < m_2$

or

$m_1 = m_2$ and $n_1 < n_2$.

The proof follows in a straightforward manner using this ordering.

These remarks then complete for the moment our discussion about subprograms and the verification of programs which introduce or use them.

Exercises for chapter 6

1. Design a correct subprogram for calculating the frequency of a particular character within a piece of text.

   Distinguish clearly between the role of the designer and the role of the user in the verification process.

   How would your implementation and its correctness proof alter if you were asked to find

   (*a*) the frequency of all the letters in the text,
   (*b*) the most frequently occurring letter in the text,
   (*c*) the frequency of a particular letter together with the first position at which it occurred?

2. Searching is a process which occurs frequently in practice:

   is a character in a string?
   is a word in a dictionary?
   is an item in a set?

   and so on. Show how a single procedure can be designed to encompass all these possibilities. Verify its correctness.

3. Design a function which, given two arrays, will decide whether or not those arrays contain the same elements possibly occurring with different frequencies. Prove the correctness of your implementation and devise a suitable statement of what your function does in the form of an inductive expression.

4. Devise a generic subprogram which, given a sorted linear list of elements, will determine the largest difference between two adjacent elements. Prove the correctness of your implementation.

5. Implement the binary chop algorithm and verify its correctness.
   Your algorithm has to find whether or not an arbitrary element is present in an ordered array of elements.
   Examine the middle element and determine which half of the array the element is in. Continue this process until either the element is found or it is possible to conclude that the element is absent.

6. Devise a correct function which will determine if the elements in one linear list are a permutation of the elements in a second linear list. Compare and contrast your solution with that of the solution of exercise 3 in this chapter.

7. Consider a tree structure of the form in figure 6.1. This represents an arithmetic expression of the form $2 + 3 * 5$.

   Fig. 6.1.

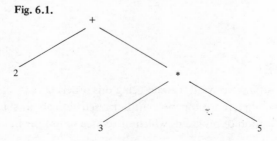

Devise a suitable recursive function which, given such a tree as a parameter, effectively evaluates the expression.

(In the above example the result would be 17.)

8. Devise recursive functions which take a linear list and reverse it

    (*a*) by producing an entirely new list,

    (*b*) by reversing the pointers in the original list.

    Prove the (total) correctness of your implementations.

9. Design a correct subprogram which removes from a linear list all the items with a particular property *P*, say. (*P* is a function which delivers *TRUE* or *FALSE* depending on whether the parameter has this property.)

10. Implement a correct operator for concatenating two arrays.

11. Design a generic subprogram which sorts a one-dimensional array of arbitrary type with respect to some arbitrary ordering.
    Devise appropriate documentation in the form of proof rules for a user. Demonstrate the correctness of your implementation.

12. Design a function which represents the pointwise extension of the usual operator $<=$.
    Prove the correctness of your implementation.
    Does your implementation and accompanying correctness proof extend easily to the other relational operators.

13. It is required to introduce the pointwise extensions of all the usual relational operators.
    Can this be done by means of a generic subprogram?
    If so, show how it can be done and describe the effect on the equality and inequality operators. Verify the correctness of all subprograms.

14. Design a correct subprogram which accepts an array and partitions it in such a way that all the elements at the lower end satisfy some property *P* and all those at the upper end fail to satisfy this property.
    Devise suitable documentation in the form of an inductive expression for a user.

15. Consider the type *L_LIST* is defined in a mutually recursive fashion as follows:

    type *ITEM*; **type** *CELL*;

    type *L_LIST* **is access** *CELL*;

    type *CELL* **is**
        record
            CONTENTS: *ITEM*;
            REST: *L_LIST*;
        end record;

    type *KIND* **is** (*INT, LIST*);

    type *ITEM* (*THING*: *KIND*) **is**
        record
            case *THING* **is**
                when *INT* => *NO*: *INTEGER*;

when $LIST => L: L\_LIST$;
    end case;
  end record;

Here L_LIST and $ITEM$ are mutually dependent on each other. With all such definitions an initial incomplete declaration of one of the types (in this case $ITEM$) must be given before the type is used in the definition of L_LIST; a complete definition is given later, following the definition of L_LIST.

Devise a correct function which will find the sum of all the elements in an object of type L_LIST.

State clearly any reasonable simplifying assumption you make.

16. Devise a correct function which from an object L of mode L_LIST will produce a linear list containing all the elements (with the same frequency) in L.

State clearly any simplifying assumptions you may make.

17. Devise a correct subprogram which, given an item L of mode L_LIST, determines if there is any circularity within L, i.e. is there any sequence of pointers which essentially produces a loop within L?

7 PACKAGES AND ABSTRACT DATA TYPES

In previous chapters we have examined the typical primitive data types in programming languages. These involved scalar types, arrays and records. For simple kinds of programs such facilities are adequate. A programmer who wishes to manipulate integers or reals in a mathematical fashion can readily find the facilities he needs and can proceed accordingly.

We have been able to discuss the properties and operations associated with the basic types in a convenient manner. At no stage have we had to worry at all about matters of implementation. We have not had to concern ourselves with matters of detail which would have been irrelevant for our purpose. The axioms we examined provided just the right amount of detail, the necessary level of abstraction.

For more sophisticated programs these basic facilities are inadequate. Yet the needs of every conceivable user of a programming language will not be met by just increasing the set of standard data types; from a learning point of view and from various other points of view this is also undesirable. It is more sensible for a language designer to provide a facility whereby a programmer can invent his own data types and their accompanying operations.

It would be most convenient if we could again arrange that the necessary separation between implementation details and usage is achieved. This has the desirable consequences of relegating to a lower level details which need not concern the programmer or the program verifier. The axioms provide the necessary interface. However, a new difficulty arises. The implementor must prove that the axioms he supplies are indeed valid; note the analogy with procedures and functions.

Since the various facilities are related an implementor will want to keep his own type declarations and associated operation declarations together in the one piece of program. It is desirable that a programming language should allow this possibility. Fortunately Ada has a package facility for grouping together several related items.

Let us begin by looking at some examples which illustrate typical situations.

7.1 Packages in Ada

We look at several sets of examples which involve in some sense groups of related items of data. With our present knowledge of Ada it is not possible to impose any convenient structuring on such sets of data.

7.1.1 Related information

Consider the problem of supplying for a user a collection of simple but related pieces of information, e.g. a set of commonly used mathematical constants. This can be supplied as an Ada package in the following way:

```
package MATHEMATICAL_CONSTANTS is
        PI: constant := 3.1415_9265;
PI_BY_180: constant := 0.0174_5329;
  LOG_PI: constant := 1.1447_2989;
   PI_INV: constant := 0.3183_0989;
   PI_SQD: constant := 9.8696_0440;
        E: constant := 2.7182_8183;
    E_INV: constant := 0.3678_7944;
    E_SQD: constant := 7.3890_5610;
    GAMMA: constant := 0.5772_1566;
end MATHEMATICAL_CONSTANTS;
```

Such a package will normally be placed in a library file of some kind – the precise details will depend on the particular Ada implementation. To make use of a package of this kind *MATHEMATICAL_CONSTANTS* must have been declared in an outer block and be visible. A programmer can write in his program such selected components, as they are called, as *MATHEMATICAL_CONSTANTS.PI MATHEMATICAL_CONSTANTS.GAMMA*, and so on. Alternatively he may introduce a use clause in his set of declarations, thus:

```
declare
        use MATHEMATICAL_CONSTANTS;
        - - other declarations
begin
        - - statements which can now use
        - - PI, GAMMA, and so on
end;
```

The use clause makes visible all the items present in the package specification. However, it may not render invisible any identifier that would otherwise be visible though it may cause overloading.

Other possibilities can be dealt with in a similar way. Packages can be formed for converting one form of measurement to another, one form of money to another, and so on. Even the following are possible:

```
package SEASONS is
    type YEAR is (JANUARY, FEBRUARY, MARCH, APRIL,
                  MAY, JUNE, JULY, AUGUST, SEPTEMBER,
                  OCTOBER, NOVEMBER, DECEMBER);
    subtype SPRING is YEAR range MARCH .. MAY;
    subtype SUMMER is YEAR range JUNE .. AUGUST;
    subtype AUTUMN is YEAR range SEPTEMBER .. NOVEMBER;
    subtype WINTER is YEAR range DECEMBER .. FEBRUARY;
end SEASONS;
```

or

```
package PDP_11 is
    WORD_SIZE: constant INTEGER := 16;
    BYTE_SIZE: constant INTEGER := 8;
    REGISTERS: constant INTEGER := 8;
    type INSTRUCTION_SET is (CLR, CLRB, ...);
    type CONDITION_CODES is (N, Z, V, C);
end PDP_11;
```

In all these and other similar cases the various items of data are all clearly related and are conveniently gathered together within the one package.

7.1.2 Complex arithmetic

Let us now turn to a different idea which involves the use of some procedures or operations. Suppose we wish to invent some new type COMPLEX, together with certain operations such as

monadic minus −
dyadic addition + and multiplication ∗
functions such as ABS and COMPLEX_CONJUGATE

For convenience we keep the size of this list small but it should be clear how extra facilities could be included.

Recall that we wish to separate the use of a module from the implementation details. From a user's point of view a package might look like the following:

```
package COMPLEX_NUMBERS is
    type COMPLEX is
        record
            RE: FLOAT;
            IM: FLOAT;
        end record;
    function "−" (X: in COMPLEX) return COMPLEX;
    function "+" (X, Y: in COMPLEX) return COMPLEX;
    function "∗" (X, Y: in COMPLEX) return COMPLEX;
```

```
                    function ABS (X: in COMPLEX) return FLOAT;
                    function COMPLEX_CONJUGATE (X: in COMPLEX) return
                                                                    COMPLEX;
            end COMPLEX_NUMBERS;
```

From the user's point of view this specification and some accompanying documentation on meaning is all that is needed. It provides the list of all the facilities made available by the module; it is referred to as the *visible* part of the package. Moreover if the user wishes to compile programs that make use of these facilities then all the necessary information is included in this specification.

From the implementor's point of view much more is of course required. It is necessary to provide the precise definitions of all the various operators, functions, subprograms, etc. that have not yet been defined; no definitions are needed for types, constants or variables since their meaning is already contained in the specification part.

```
            package body COMPLEX_NUMBERS is
                    function "−" (X: in COMPLEX) return COMPLEX is
                        R: COMPLEX := (− X . RE, − X . IM);
                    begin
                        return R;
                    end "−";
                    function "+" (X, Y: in COMPLEX) return COMPLEX is
                        R: COMPLEX := (X . RE + Y . RE, X . IM + Y . IM);
                    begin
                        return R;
                    end "+" ;
                    - - similar declarations of "∗" and
                    - - ABS and COMPLEX_CONJUGATE
                    - - included here
            end COMPLEX_NUMBERS;
```

The body describes how the various features are implemented. From the details it contains, it should be possible for the implementor to prove that the properties a user might expect actually hold.

The two complementary definitions of the package specification and the package body complete the picture. Changes in the body can be made without it being necessary to recompile any other packages or programs which use COMPLEX_NUMBERS.

It should be clear that the ideas conveyed here are of fairly general applicability. Similar facilities for operating on rational numbers, vectors, matrices, etc. can all be supplied in a similar fashion.

There is, however, something slightly unsatisfactory about what we have so far achieved. This uneasiness is aroused by consideration of the following

182

matters:

> Suppose we wish to represent complex numbers as a pair of real numbers of type *LONG_FLOAT*; do we have to reprogram the entire module?
>
> In preparing a module for matrix manipulation, do we need to reprogram for each new type of element?
>
> In preparing a module for rational arithmetic it might seem sensible to ensure that rationals are held in some standardised form, e.g. as a pair of integers (P, Q) where $Q > 0$ and the highest common factor of P and Q is 1. This has the advantage of efficiency and of guarding against unnecessary overflow.
>
> Is it possible to guarantee that a user will not interfere with the proper working by somehow interfering with the standardisation?

In other circumstances these apparently mild criticisms become somewhat substantial. Let us look at such an example.

7.1.3 Stacks

Consider the problem of determining whether or not a sequence of opening and closing round and square brackets match properly. Thus

$$(([()])[()])$$

match but

$$(([()]))$$

do not match – within the square brackets the opening round bracket should have a matching closing bracket.

This problem is only one small part of the much larger task that must be performed by a compiler – it must match the brackets within a program. The usual way of solving this problem is to use a stack. This is a device onto which items can be pushed and from which items can be pulled. Access to elements must always be from the top of the stack.

From an implementation point of view a stack can be represented either as an array *STACK* and a pointer *POINTER* or as a linked list. For simplicity let us use the former representation. Pushing an item X onto the stack then essentially involves executing

> *POINTER* := *POINTER* + 1;
> *STACK* (*POINTER*) := *X*;

Pulling an item from the stack and placing it in *Y* involves performing

> *POINTER* := *POINTER* − 1;
> *Y* := *STACK* (*POINTER* + 1);

With this in mind the bracket matching problem can be solved in the following way:

Step 1. Read a character and place it in the variable *CH*. If it is a terminator go to step 6.

Step 2. If *CH* is an opening bracket, stack it.

Step 3. If *CH* is a closing round bracket look at the topmost element on the stack; if this is an opening round bracket remove it by unstacking; otherwise report brackets mismatch and stop.

Step 4. If *CH* is a closing square bracket look at the topmost element on the stack; if this is an opening square bracket remove it by unstacking; otherwise report brackets mismatch and stop.

Step 5. Go to step 1.

Step 6. If the stack is empty report that the brackets match; if it is not empty report that the brackets do not match. Stop.

Let us now consider the programming of the above. The only fundamental operations that can be executed on the stack are push and pull. But to save contorted programming we add two further operations:

(*a*) to ask if the stack is empty,

(*b*) to read the topmost element of the stack,

together with two exceptions to deal with error situations

(*c*) *STACK_OVERFLOW* and *STACK_UNDERFLOW*.

The items mentioned above are the only facilities that should be made available to any user of the stack. Therefore we introduce a package specification of the following kind:

> **package** *STACK_MANAGER* **is**
>   **procedure** *PUSH*(*C*: **in** *CHARACTER*);
>   **procedure** *PULL*(*D*: **out** *CHARACTER*);
>   **function** *IS_EMPTY* **return** *BOOLEAN*;
>   **function** *TOP* **return** *CHARACTER*;
>   *STACK_OVERFLOW*, *STACK_UNDERFLOW*: **exception**;
> **end** *STACK_MANAGER*;

Note the absence of any mention of either *STACK* or *POINTER*. A user of the package can see and therefore mention explicitly only the facilities mentioned in this specification. Any attempt to access *STACK* or *POINTER* will result in a syntax error. The highly desirable consequence of this is that a user cannot interfere with the proper workings of *STACK_MANAGER*. He must use the facilities provided in a disciplined manner and this discipline is forced on him by the compiler.

The package body can be programmed in the expected way. Thus:

> **package body** *STACK_MANAGER* **is**
>   *STACK*: **array** (1 .. 100) **of** *CHARACTER*;

184

```
    POINTER: INTEGER range 0 .. 100 := 0;
    procedure PUSH(C: in CHARACTER) is
    begin
        if POINTER = 100 then
           raise STACK_OVERFLOW;
        end if;
        POINTER := POINTER + 1;
        STACK (POINTER) := C;
    end PUSH;
    procedure PULL(D: out CHARACTER) is
    begin
        if POINTER = 0 then
           raise STACK_UNDERFLOW;
        end if;
        POINTER := POINTER - 1;
        D := STACK (POINTER + 1);
    end PULL;
    function IS_EMPTY return BOOLEAN is
    begin
        return POINTER = 0;
    end IS_EMPTY;
    function TOP return CHARACTER is
        C: CHARACTER;
    begin
        PULL(C);
        PUSH(C);
        return C;
    end TOP;
  end STACK_MANAGER;
```

The bracket matching problem can now be solved with the aid of
STACK_MANAGER. By writing

```
    use STACK_MANAGER;
```

in the declarative part of a block all the items in the visible part of the stack
package are made available. The following program performs the necessary duty:

```
    declare
    C, D: CHARACTER;
    use STACK_MANAGER;
  begin
    loop
        GET(C);
```

```
                    exit when C = TERMINATOR;
                    if C = '(' or C = '[' then
                            PUSH(C);
                    elsif C = ')' and TOP = '(' then
                            PULL(D);
                    elsif C = ']' and TOP = '[' then
                            PULL(D);
                    end if;
              end loop;
              if IS_EMPTY then
                    PUT ("BRACKETS MATCH");
              else
                    PUT ("BRACKETS MISMATCH");
              end if;
        exception
              when STACK_UNDERFLOW =>
                    PUT ("BRACKETS MISMATCH");
              when STACK_OVERFLOW =>
                    PUT ("STACK OVERFLOW. INCREASE STACK SIZE");
        end;
```

We have gone to some trouble to obtain a satisfactory stack package. If the implementation of a stack as an array and a pointer proves unsatisfactory for whatever reason it is possible to alter the package body by recompiling the body alone. The external attributes of the package as provided in the specification remain the same.

7.1.4   Some generalisations

In some respects the stack module as it has been presented so far is somewhat unsatisfactory. If we require a stack of integers, for example, do we have to alter the entire package (both the specification and the body) by merely replacing *CHARACTER* by *INTEGER*, then recompile, etc.? Fortunately the answer is no. Indeed the observation is reminiscent of a similar observation in connection with procedures and the solution is similar.

In Ada it is possible to introduce parameters which can be passed to the package. We say that the parameters are generic parameters and these form a generic unit which is supplied with the package specification; no change is made to the package body. Recall a similar approach to generic functions and procedures.

In the case of *STACK_MANAGER* it would be perfectly feasible to introduce two parameters, an integer *SIZE* which represents the intended maximum size of the stack and a type *ITEM*. The specification then takes the form

186

```
generic
      type ITEM is private;
      SIZE: NATURAL := 100;
package STACK_MANAGER is
      procedure PUSH(C: in ITEM);
      procedure PULL(D: out ITEM);
      function IS_EMPTY return BOOLEAN;
      function TOP return ITEM;
      STACK_OVERFLOW, STACK_UNDERFLOW: exception;
end STACK_MANAGER;
```

The package body is as before with *SIZE* used for the size of the array and
ITEM used for the type of the individual objects.

By introducing generic units the package becomes a kind of recipe for
manipulating stacks. When a particular kind of stack is needed *instantiation* is
necessary:

```
package STACK_CHARACTERS is
      new STACK_MANAGER (SIZE => 200, ITEM => CHARACTER);
```
or
```
package STACK_INTEGERS is
      new STACK_MANAGER (ITEM => INTEGER);
```

These package declarations are then said to be instances of the generic package.
STACK_CHARACTERS has an internal array of size 200, *STACK_INTEGERS*
has an array of size 100, the default size.

To use both stacks within the one piece of program requires a use clause of
the following kind:

```
use STACK_CHARACTERS, STACK_INTEGERS;
```

As a result *PUSH, PULL*, etc. become overloaded.

It ought to be relatively clear how the idea of a generic package carries across
to other situations. To highlight one of these imagine a package for supplying
matrix manipulation routines. These will likely involve operators +, −, *, etc.
for manipulating individual elements of matrices and these will typically be of
some generic but floating-point type. Recalling the notation introduced in
chapter 6 we obtain

```
generic
      type T is digits ⟨⟩;
package MATRIX_ROUTINES is

      . . .

end MATRIX_ROUTINES;
```

By default the +, − and * will be operators associated with the addition, subtraction and multiplication of two items of type *T*. Instantiation then takes the

form:

> package *FLOAT_MATRIX_ROUTINES* **is**
> **new** *MATRIX_ROUTINES* (*T* => *FLOAT*);

Let us return again to consider the problem of designing a stack package. We make one more criticism of what we have achieved. The stack facilities as they so far exist work satisfactorily if only a single stack of any one kind is required. If several may be required it is desirable to make visible a type called *STACK*. This means of course that the procedures *PUSH*, *PULL*, etc. need an extra parameter, namely the stack to be accessed in a particular case. It is highly desirable that the safeguards we have introduced remain. In Ada it is permissible to write

> **generic**
>   **type** *ITEM* **is private**;
>   *SIZE*: *NATURAL* := 100;
> **package** *STACK_MANAGER* **is**
>   **type** *STACK* **is private**;
>   **procedure** *PUSH*(*S*: **in out** *STACK*; *C*: **in** *ITEM*);
>   **procedure** *PULL*(*S*: **in out** *STACK*; *D*: **out** *ITEM*);
>   **function** *IS_EMPTY*(*S*: **in** *STACK*) **return** *BOOLEAN*;
>   **function** *TOP*(*S*: **in** *STACK*) **return** *ITEM*;
> **private**
>   **type** *STACK* **is**
>   **record**
>   *SPACE*: **array** (1 .. *SIZE*) **of** *ITEM*;
>   *POINTER*: *INTEGER* **range** 0 .. *SIZE* := 0;
>   **end record**;
> **end** *STACK_MANAGER*;

Note that *TOP* cannot now be implemented as, in effect, a call of *PULL* followed by a call of *PUSH*.

The consequence of this new package is that the name of the type *STACK* is made visible but the internal nature of the type is kept private. For private types of any kind only certain operations are allowed:

(*a*) assignment can be made to *STACK* variables,

(*b*) items can be passed as parameters,

(*c*) comparison for equality or inequality can be performed.

Even the right to perform assignment or test for equality can be denied by placing the bold word **limited** in front of **private**. Thus:

> **type** *STACK* **is limited private**;

All that is then possible is to declare variables of type *STACK* and to pass these objects as parameters to the procedures and operators made visible in the specification (or to other procedures which contain calls of this kind). For *STACK* perhaps **limited private** would have been more appropriate than merely **private**.

To make use of the package introduced above instantiation is again required:

> **package** *STACK_CHARACTERS* **is**
> **new** *STACK_MANAGER (SIZE =>* 200, *ITEM => CHARACTER);*

The reader might justifiably think that there is something curious not about the idea of a private data type but about how it appears within a package. The internal details should be of no interest whatever to any user of the module. So why should the private part be contained in the specification part, should it not be relegated to the hidden depths of the package body? To understand the reason for this decision consider the situation of someone who wishes to use the module. He would like to be able to compile his programs using only the information contained in the package specification. If this can be achieved then the body of the package can be repeatedly recompiled without there being any necessity to recompile all programs which use the package. Now part of the duty of a compiler is to arrange that space is allocated whenever variables are declared. Information about how much space is needed must therefore be contained somehow in the package specification. Something like a private part is therefore needed.

The idea of a package supplying a data type and an accompanying set of operations is very important. We say that the package *encapsulates* the data type, usually of a **limited private** type. It can be used by writing

> **declare**
> > **use** *STACK_CHARACTERS;*
> > *S: STACK;*
> > - - other declarations
>
> **begin**
> > - - statements of form *PUSH(S, CH);*
>
> **end**;

Though we have stressed the use of types and operations as generic parameters it is permissible to have arbitrary subprogram specifications. In particular, therefore, package specifications themselves can appear as generic parameters.

7.1.5 The structure of programs

In this section we shall embark on the task of discussing the ways in which packages and other pieces of programs are assembled to provide a complete program. In the course of this discussion we shall examine the flow of information between packages, the structure of programs, and so on.

All implementations of Ada possess a standard environment. This contains the definition of the standard types *BOOLEAN, SHORT_INTEGER, INTEGER, LONG_INTEGER, SHORT_FLOAT, FLOAT, LONG_FLOAT, CHARACTER* and *STRING* together with the usual operators available for their manipulation. Also present are certain standard character constants and a list of standard exceptions. The declaration

> **subtype** *NATURAL* **range** 1 .. *INTEGER'LAST*;

is also present. Noticeably absent is any mention of input and output routines.

The items in the standard environment are all automatically available to all subprograms. There is no need to quote or invoke the standard environment.

Programs themselves will typically be made up of several *compilation units*, as they are called. These can be either package bodies or even subprograms. They will be included in some program library which holds sets of related compilation units.

The pieces of program written in earlier chapters were not programs in the true sense. A simple program will consist of just a single compilation unit. Even the simplest program will usually require use of some input and output routines. Both *GET* and *PUT* are included in a special package entitled *TEXT_IO*. To allow the use of this, the package must be invoked, e.g.

> **with** *TEXT_IO*;
> **procedure** *SIMPLE_PROGRAM* **is**
>   **use** *TEXT_IO*;
>   - - other declarations
> **begin**
>   - - statements of program
>   - -
> **end** *SIMPLE_PROGRAM*;

Precisely how the above, or indeed any compilation unit, is caused to be executed is a matter for the local Ada implementation. The above is our first complete program, albeit a skeleton.

The with clause has the effect of making the mentioned package available to the compilation unit. The use clause means that the identifiers mentioned in the visible part of the package are themselves made visible. Naturally it must appear before the main unit to be compiled. There are other possibilities:

> (*a*) **with** *P, Q, R*;
>   **procedure** *A* **is**
>
>   . . .
>
>   **end** *A*;

has the effect of making packages *P*, *Q* and *R* all available from within *A*.

> (*b*) **with** *P, Q*; **use** *P, Q*;
>   **procedure** *A* **is**
>   - - definition of *A*
>   **end** *A*;

has the effect of making *P* and *Q* and all the objects made visible by *P* and *Q* available within *A*.

(c) **with** P, Q;
   package body A **is**
       - - definition of A
   end A;

causes P and Q to be visible from within A; the with clause need not qualify the package specification; use clauses can again be employed as appropriate.

For completeness we shall describe how the *GET* and *PUT* routines we have been using fit into the general picture. However, we shall not become involved in details.

Files in Ada are ordered sets of elements all of the same type. Thus there are files of integers, files of reals, files of characters, and so on. Associated with each file is a file type and this can be either *IN_FILE* (implying input or read-only access) *OUT_FILE* (implying output or write-only access) or *INOUT_FILE* (implying read and write access).

One can readily imagine the existence of a package which provides a list of procedures which can be used to operate on files. Associated with this package will be some generic type. The package itself is referred to as *INPUT_OUTPUT* and provides facilities for creating files, linking programs to already existing files, reading, writing, and so on; there are also exceptions which can be raised in the event of trouble of some kind. We do not propose to look at the form or details of *INPUT_OUTPUT*.

The most common kind of input and output, and the kind we have used exclusively, is concerned with readable input and output, i.e. character files. A package named *TEXT_IO* provides facilities for operating on such files. Both *GET* and *PUT* can be activated with one or two parameters. If two parameters are used the first will be a file name of the appropriate file type (*IN_FILE* for *GET* and *OUT_FILE* for *PUT*); when only one parameter is used certain standard files *STANDARD_INPUT* or *STANDARD_OUTPUT* are provided automatically by the implementation. The remaining parameter can hold or receive an item of numeric, *BOOLEAN*, *CHARACTER*, *STRING* or even enumeration type. Within the definition of the *GET* and *PUT* procedures are instructions which cause groups of characters to be collected together in the expected ways.

We have given a very brief and sketchy account of the input and output in Ada. The details can be readily found in the definition of Ada or in any work whose main concern is to cover all the details of the language.

7.2 Side-effects

At this juncture it becomes sensible to talk about functions and procedures which have side-effects, but side-effects of a special kind. There is such a thing as a benign side-effect – in other words, it is possible to conceive of functions which produce values yet access and possibly alter global variables in

191

desirable kinds of ways. A consequence of this observation is that the axiomatics of expressions needs to be reconsidered; it is no longer sufficient to appeal to the usual mathematical ideas.

7.2.1 Benign side-effects

In the stack example (see sections 7.1.3 and 7.1.4) one could reasonably imagine the *POP* subprogram being implemented as a function which produces as its value the item removed from the stack. Such a function would have a side-effect, namely the alteration to the stack itself. There are other situations in which such an idea is of interest.

Consider a function designed to produce random integers. This might be programmed in the following fashion:

```
package RAN is
     function RANDOM_INT return INTEGER;
end RAN;
package body RAN is
     VAL: INTEGER := initial value;
     function RANDOM_INT return INTEGER is
     begin
          VAL := alter (VAL);
          return VAL;
     end RANDOM_INT;
end RAN;
```

Some appropriate initial value is inserted together with an appropriate function which produces a sequence of values for *VAL*. The function *RANDOM_INT* accesses the global variable *VAL* and causes an appropriate side-effect. *VAL* retains its value from one call of *RANDOM_INT* to the next and is called an own variable.

These examples are particular cases of a large class of similar subprograms. We can envisage situations where tables, trees, data structures of any kind, and in general some environment has to be introduced. This environment will then have to be accessed or altered in specified ways, described by the set of items made visible in the package specification. Functions and procedures with side-effects have an important role to play in this.

Let us examine yet another example.

Example 7.2.1a   Memo function

Suppose a programmer wishes to perform repeated evaluations of Ackermann's function $A(M, N)$ where, say, $0 <= M, N <= 10$ (see chapter 6). Since a single computation of Ackermann's function can be rather expensive and time-consuming it may be advisable to remember a value of $A(M, N)$ whenever it is calculated. Substantial saving in terms of efficiency can be adopted by the following approach (which makes use of a generic integer type *INDEX* presumably instantiated to $0 .. 10$):

```
generic
      type INDEX is range ⟨⟩;
package ACK_IMPLEMENT is
      function ACK(M, N: INDEX) return INTEGER;
end;
package body ACK_IMPLEMENT is
      STORE: array (INDEX, INDEX) of INTEGER :=
            (INDEX => (INDEX => −1));
      function ACK(M, N: INDEX) return INTEGER is
      begin
            if STORE(M, N) = −1 then
                  if M = 0 then
                        STORE(M, N) := 1;
                  elsif N = 0 then
                        STORE(M, N) := ACK(M − 1, 1);
                  else
                        STORE(M, N) := ACK(M − 1, ACK(M, N − 1));
                  end if;
            end if;
            return STORE(M, N);
      end ACK;
end ACK_IMPLEMENT;
```

The philosophy outlined by this example can be generalised in a very obvious fashion.

It should be relatively clear that the proof rules and proof techniques given for functions and procedures can be easily extended in the required fashion. What we shall now concentrate on is the impact of side-effects on the axiomatics of expressions. Though we concentrate almost solely on expression evaluation it should be realised that the ramifications of having side-effects do not end there. In fact this is potentially but the tip of the iceberg. In calls of functions or procedures where several parameters are present, the evaluation of these parameters can involve side-effects. The evaluation of booleans in conditionals or loops can produce side-effects, the presence of several subscripts in a subscripted variable or in array declarations, etc. can all cause problems.

It is worth drawing attention to the fact that the side-effects we have described tend to be to the variables which are not in scope at the point of call; typically these are own variables associated with some other package.

7.2.2 Axiomatics of side-effects

In Ada the order of evaluation of operands in expressions is not defined; indeed there is a requirement that a programmer should assume nothing whatsoever about the relative order of evaluation of operands.

Let us now undertake the necessary revision of the ideas on axiomatics and proof rules. To introduce the notion of the value of an expression E we invent a dummy variable which we denote by σ (traditionally used for store). After E has been evaluated σ will hold the value of E. In general side-effects may also have occurred. In the course of the evaluation of E other temporary variables may be required. So we adopt the convention that small Greek letters denote variables which can hold values. But always, at the end of the computation, σ will hold the final value. Let us then start with the very simple cases, the simplest expressions.

Constants

A constant C has a value; when the computation ends the value will be in σ. It is as if

$$\sigma := C;$$

had been performed. Consequently

$$\{P(C/\sigma)\}\, C\, \{P\}$$

Variables

As above the effect of encountering a simple variable is to cause

$$\sigma := X;$$

to be performed. The semantics are then

$$\{P(X/\sigma)\}\, X\, \{P\}$$

Operators

If % denotes an arbitrary unary operator then the effect of performing %E can be simulated in

$$\sigma := E; \quad \sigma := \%\sigma;$$

If the postcondition is Q then back substitution over the last assignment gives $Q(\%\sigma/\sigma)$. The proof rule then reduces to

$$\frac{\{P\}\, E\, \{Q(\%\sigma/\sigma)\}}{\{P\}\, \%E\, \{Q\}}$$

Binary operators

If ? denotes an arbitrary binary operator which is not a short-circuit control form then the effect of performing $E\,?\,F$ can be simulated in the following way;

$$\sigma := E; \quad \tau := \sigma; \quad \sigma := F; \quad \sigma := \tau\,?\,\sigma;$$

194

or indeed

$$\sigma := F; \quad \tau := \sigma; \quad \sigma := E; \quad \sigma := \tau ? \sigma;$$

In both cases a particular order of evaluation is defined but these should lead to the same results. If we concentrate on the first of the above alternatives then back substitution over the last assignment leads to

$$\frac{\{P\} E \{Q(\sigma/\tau)\}, \quad \{Q\} F \{R (\tau ? \sigma/\sigma)\}}{\{P\} E ? F \{R\}}$$

It is axiomatic that all proof rules resulting from the selection of different orders of evaluation will produce the same results and the same side-effects.

Function calls

Let $F(A)$ be a function call of some kind. Then A is automatically an **in** parameter and the evaluation takes the form:

$$\sigma := A; \quad \sigma := F(\sigma);$$

In this case an appropriate rule is then

$$\frac{\{P\} A \{Q(F(\sigma)/\sigma)\}}{\{P\} F(A) \{Q\}}$$

If there happen to be several parameters the situation is more complex. Assume F has two actual parameters A and B. Then

$$\sigma := A; \quad \tau := \sigma; \quad \sigma := B; \quad \sigma := F(\tau, \sigma);$$

mirrors a possible evaluation sequence and leads to the rule

$$\frac{\{P\} A \{Q(\sigma/\tau)\}, \quad \{Q\} B \{R(F(\tau, \sigma)/\sigma)\}}{\{P\} F(A, B) \{R\}}$$

Different evaluation sequences will produce the same effect. If more than two parameters are involved a similar process leads to the required proof rule.

Subscripted variables

The rules for these are similar to the rules for function calls.

These remarks take care of most of the possibilities. Now that the semantics of expressions have altered, so also have the semantics of the constructs in which side-effects can appear. We look at the rule for assignment which demonstrates the kind of alteration that is required.

Assignment statements

The assignment $X := E$; can be translated into

$$\sigma := E; \quad X := \sigma;$$

From this observation the rule

$$\frac{\{P\}\,E\,\{Q(\sigma/X)\}}{\{P\}\,X := E\,\{Q\}}$$

follows.

Corresponding rules have to be given for the short-circuit form of binary operators, for conditionals, loops, etc. There are no new concepts required and these tasks are left to the interested reader.

The treatment given above is deficient in the sense that it omits any mention of exceptions. Exceptions can be raised during the evaluation of expressions: overflow, range errors and so on are all possible and these can occur as a result of applying operators or even as a result of assignment itself.

To deal with exceptions it is necessary to extend the ideas of section 4. Thus when an expression is evaluated σ receives a value or an exception takes place, mutually exclusive events. Hence a notation of the form

$$\{P\}\,E\,\{Q\}\ \text{or}\ \textbf{when}\ \textit{NUMERIC\_ERROR}\,\{R\}$$

is appropriate.

7.3   Abstract data types

We have seen how Ada provides facilities for describing objects and the operations that can legitimately be applied to these objects. Moreover the necessary information hiding is permitted and security obtained by ensuring that only the expected operations can be applied.

We looked at stacks of varying kinds. But many of the ideas described here could have been applied equally well to data structures of many kinds:

> queues – items can be added or removed from queues only in certain special ways;
>
> symbol tables – again items can be inserted or removed from symbol tables only in special ways; but also information held in symbol tables can usually be requested in certain particular ways;
>
> random number generators – a simple procedure call is all that should be provided, yet there may be groups of variables or seeds whose values contribute to the internal working of the random number generator.

Let us now view this whole business from a more mathematically rigorous standpoint. Essentially we begin by conceiving of certain data types on which only a certain limited number of legitimate operations are allowed. These we call *abstract data types*. Having conceived of them they must be realised in a programming language. It is then necessary to show that the realisation is a faithful representation of what is expected.

196

7.3.1 The specification of abstract data types

Let us begin by first considering how we might specify the various attributes of our abstract data type. We have already looked at properties of the basic data types such as the integers, reals, characters, booleans, and so on. This provides an obvious method of proceeding. In adopting this approach we are essentially following the route that someone defining a programming language itself might adopt.

Programming languages tend to be defined in essentially two stages. Usually syntactic parts describe the manner in which constructs can be used and these cover such details as use of types, types of parameters and results, and so on. Semantic sections on the other hand describe meaning; we have already seen that meaning can be defined by specifying axioms. As part of the semantics sections, or complementary to them, there are often sections which list restrictions of various kinds. One can immediately cite cases where restrictions are necessary, e.g. to avoid the possibility of division by zero, subscripts out of range.

The problem of describing syntax in an implementation-independent manner is relatively straightforward. The syntactic specification involves

(*a*) naming the individual operations, functions, subprograms, etc. and then

(*b*) defining the number and the types of the parameters and the type of the result, i.e. defining the functionality of the different items.

This can be conveniently mirrored in the mathematical idea of naming some functions and specifying their domain (possibly as a Cartesian product) and their range.

The syntactic specification is, in short, roughly equivalent to what would be inserted in the specification part of an Ada package excluding any private parts. It is clear therefore how this aspect of the description of an abstract data type will be implemented.

What can be said about methods of specifying semantics? There are several properties we should look for in any method:

formality: formal methods tend to be mathematically sound when compared with informal methods, they are suitable for manipulation by computer and for mathematical manipulation; moreover they are desirable from the point of view of the program verifier;

minimality: it should be possible to specify just the properties required and not any subsidiary information such as implementation detail;

applicability: it should be applicable to a wide and interesting range of abstract data types;

simplicity: it ought to be possible to construct specifications relatively simply and naturally assuming familiarity on behalf of the user with the method; it should be possible to keep the size of a specification relative to the complexity of a data type (ideally small).

197

From the above discussion it should be clear that we can dismiss methods such as an informal specification in terms of English, or an implementation in terms of some programming language. Ideally we would also like the details of our abstract data types to be defined in such a way that their properties are independent of any particular method of implementation. This would be in keeping with the philosophy of encapsulating the notion of an abstract data type in a module and keeping implementation details hidden. The procedures and so on which are made visible then share certain resources and certain information related to an implementation and the interpretation to be attributed to variables, etc. Yet to the user of a package the only items of interest are the procedures and their meaning which is independent of implementation.

7.3.2 Specification methods

There are many approaches to the problem of specifying the semantics of abstract data types. The various methods tend to fall into one of two categories. We shall look at one example from each category.

The model approach involves finding some formal mathematical object whose behaviour is likely to reflect that of the abstract data type. Thus if we wish to implement a set we can equate the properties we expect with those of the mathematical concept of a set. Similarly for other constructs such as graphs and so on. In a sense this is nothing more than a generalisation of what we did with the basic data types – integers in a programming language can be likened to their mathematical equivalents with the provision that overflow can occur.

In the definitional approach a user specifies the properties that an abstract data type should possess. There are various ways of doing this – an axiomatic approach will be of particular interest to us.

7.4 The model approach

Let us begin by considering the possibility of introducing an abstract data type *SET*. We assume that this will correspond to the mathematical notion of a set. It is natural to use set theory to provide the model on which we shall base our notion of the abstract data type. Let all the elements of our set be of some type *ELEM*.

7.4.1 The abstract data type *SET*

We define several basic operations on a set. If we use the traditional mathematical operations of set union $\cup$, set intersection $\cap$ and set complement — these can be described as follows:

EMPTY_SET	creates an empty set
INSERT(S, I)	inserts element I into S; the effect is thus to produce $S \cup \{I\}$

REMOVE(*S*, *I*)	deletes element *I* from *S*; the effect is to produce $S \cap \neg \{I\}$
MEMBER(*S*, *I*)	asks if *I* belongs to *S*
NULL(*S*)	asks if $S = \emptyset$, the empty set
CHOOSE(*S*)	selects an arbitrary element from the non-null set *S*.

We choose also to allow assignment involving sets and tests for equality and inequality. (In fact *NULL*(*S*) is unnecessary but more efficient than the test $S = EMPTY\_SET$.) The specification of a package to implement these in Ada might then be as shown below – items are assumed to be of some generic type *ELEM* and *EMPTY* is raised when an attempt is made to select from an empty set.

```
generic
      type ELEM is private;
package SET_MANAGER is
      type SET is private;
      function EMPTY_SET return SET;
      function INSERT(S: in SET; I in ELEM) return SET;
      function REMOVE(S: in SET; I in ELEM) return SET;
      function MEMBER(S: in SET; I in ELEM) return BOOLEAN;
      function NULL(S: in SET) return BOOLEAN;
      function CHOOSE(S: in SET) return ELEM;
      exception EMPTY;
private
      type SET is access CELL;
      type CELL is
            record
                  ITEM : ELEM;
                  REST : SET;
            end record;
end;
```

Note that a set is represented as a linked list. We shall make the stipulation – also present in normal mathematical usage – that each element is present at most once.

A corresponding package body is given below. We have deliberately made use of recursive procedures where this simplifies the programming. We make no apology for this – at a later stage (see section 7.5.2) we shall embark on proofs which are greatly simplified by this decision.

```
package body SET_MANAGER is

      function COPY(S: in SET) return SET is
      - - expected function for copying a linear list

      EMPTYSET: constant SET := null;
```

```
function EMPTY_SET return SET is
begin
      return EMPTYSET;
end EMPTY_SET;

function INSERT(S: in SET; I: in ELEM) return SET is
      TT, T: SET := COPY(S);
begin
      while T /= EMPTYSET loop
            if T . ITEM = I then
                  return TT;
            end if;
            T := T . REST;
      end loop;
      return new CELL (ITEM => I, REST => TT);
end INSERT;

function REMOVE(S: in SET; I in ELEM) return SET is
      IDASH : ELEM;
      T: SET := COPY(S);
begin
      if T = EMPTYSET then
            return EMPTYSET;
      else
            IDASH := T . ITEM;
            T := T . REST;
            if IDASH = I then
                  return T;
            else
                  return INSERT (REMOVE(T, I), IDASH);
            end if;
      end if;
end REMOVE;

function MEMBER(S: in SET; I in ELEM) return BOOLEAN is
      FOUND : BOOLEAN := FALSE;
begin
      if S /= EMPTYSET then
            FOUND := (I = S . ITEM) or MEMBER(S . REST, I);
      end if;
      return FOUND;
end MEMBER;

function NULL(S: in SET) return BOOLEAN is
begin
```

```
                return (S = EMPTYSET);
        end NULL;

        function CHOOSE (S: in SET) return ELEM is
        begin
                if S = EMPTYSET then
                        raise EMPTY;
                end if;
                return S . ITEM;
        end CHOOSE;
    end SET_MANAGER;
```

7.4.2   Correctness of implementation

We now look more closely at precisely what we have achieved. We have
a definition of an abstract data type and supposedly an implementation which
realises this. Corresponding to the abstract operation *REMOVE* we have a procedure *REMOVE*, corresponding to the abstract operation *MEMBER* we have
a function *MEMBER*, and so on. Corresponding to the abstract data type *SET*
we have a corresponding Ada type *SET* which is private. Basically we have
established a mapping or correspondence between the abstract data type and
the items made available by the Ada module *SET_MANAGER*. This mapping
we call, for obvious reasons, the *representation mapping* and we denote it by χ.
For each abstract operation we therefore produce an appropriate piece of
program. Thus χ maps

> the abstract operation *INSERT* into the procedure *INSERT*
> the abstract operation *REMOVE* into the procedure *REMOVE*

and so on.

To prove that the implementation we have provided is correct or faithful
something more is required. We have to show essentially that the pieces of Ada
program perform the tasks they are intended to perform. In keeping with our
previous attitude this demonstration should take the form of a rigorous mathematical proof.

Consider again the abstract operations for *INSERT* and *REMOVE*, for
example. The definitions of these can be expressed axiomatically in the form:
the result of

$$INSERT(S, I) \text{ is } S \cup \{I\}$$

and of

$$REMOVE(S, I) \text{ is } S \cap \neg \{I\}.$$

We now want to deduce corresponding proof rules which have to be verified for
the more concrete Ada subprogram. Essentially we apply χ to each aspect of the
proof rules given above. But there is an important complication.

We remarked earlier that we would represent a set as a linked list of items in which each item could appear at most once. It is imperative that this situation is maintained since otherwise the operations may malfunction. Associated with the implementation therefore is an invariant called the *representation invariant*. If we denote it by R then $R(S)$ is merely a statement that no item in the linked list S is repeated.

In general R might be more complex. For efficiency purposes it might be thought advisable to represent a set as a list whose items are ordered, e.g. to save searching the entire list. In this case R would contain information that all the elements were distinct and ordered in some appropriate manner. Other possibilities also exist.

Having introduced the idea of a representation invariant R it is important to ensure that R is always true. More accurately R must be true initially and the application of any legitimate operation to a set must leave R true. This we must verify.

We have certain rules to establish for our Ada procedures. To avoid repeated use of χ we shall (conveniently) misuse notation to some considerable extent and use S, for example, to denote either a set or a linked list depending on whether S is used within a predicate or within a piece of program; similarly for items of the set. The designer of *INSERT* and *REMOVE* must then show that (see section 6.2.1):

$$\{R(S)\} \text{ modified text of } INSERT(S, I) \{R(\mathbf{r}_{INSERT}) \land \mathbf{r}_{INSERT} = S \cup \{I\}\}$$

and similarly

$$\{R(S)\} \text{ modified text of } REMOVE(S, I) \{R(\mathbf{r}_{REMOVE}) \land \mathbf{r}_{REMOVE} = S \cap \neg \{I\}\}$$

The proof of correctness of these and the other subprograms can be established in the usual way. To illustrate take the *INSERT* function:

```
function INSERT(S: in SET; I in ELEM) return SET is
        TT, T: SET := COPY(S);
begin
    while - -{R(T) ∧ R(TT) ∧ I ∉ (TT ∩ ¬ T)}
                    T /= EMPTYSET loop
        if T. ITEM = I then
                return TT;
        end if;
        T := T. REST;
    end loop;
    return new CELL (ITEM => I, REST => TT);
end INSERT;
```

7.4.3 Discussion of the model approach

In many respects the definition of a set given above was satisfactory. It was possible to prove that the implementation was correct. The method of

202

representation, as given by the representation invariant, was local to the package and was hidden from the user. The resulting abstract data type could be used, programs of a meaningful nature could be written and proofs of their correctness given. A piece of program to perform set union is given in figure 7.1. Invariants are included and it is clear that no aspect of implementation need concern the user.

There are however drawbacks, some rather severe. An abstract data type such as *SET* does have a convenient mathematical equivalent. But sets are of limited applicability. It is not always possible to find such a convenient equivalent. Take for instance the idea of a stack. No mathematical equivalent readily comes to mind. Admittedly it is possible to invent a suitable concept but it is unrealistic to have to do this every time a new abstract data type is required.

Another substantial danger exists with the model approach. Often a user will not want to make use of all the mathematical properties of a set. A user is liable to conclude the existence of properties which are not allowed. The model therefore overspecifies. It is too general and violates the desire for minimality. Moreover proofs are made more complex since proofs must deal with relevant details but also with irrelevant details.

The methods given in the next section are designed to overcome the deficiencies outlined above.

7.5   Algebraic axiomatics

We now look at the possibility of specifying the axiomatics of an abstract data type in a highly abstract manner. We list a set of algebraic equations which the operations of the data type must satisfy.

7.5.1   The abstract data type *SET* revisited

If we return to the idea of a set then figure 7.2 claims to capture the essence of the semantics of a set. An obvious notation is used. Advocates of this

Fig. 7.1.

```
- - {(A = A' IN) ∧ (B = B' IN)}
declare
     C: SET := EMPTY_SET;
     I: ELEM;
begin
     while - - {C ∪ A = A' IN}
               not NULL (A) loop
          I := CHOOSE (A);
          A := REMOVE (A, I);
          C := INSERT (C, I);
     end loop;
     - - {C = A' IN}
     while - - {C ∪ B = A' IN ∪ B' IN}
               not NULL (B) loop
          I := CHOOSE (B);
          B := REMOVE (B, I);
          C := INSERT (C, I);
     end loop;
     - - {C = A'IN ∪ B'IN}
end;
```

203

approach claim that just the necessary detail is provided in a simple and compact fashion.

The specification consists of a syntactic part and a semantic part as before. The semantic part however contains a sequence of axioms in the form of algebraic equations and these describe the properties that a user is permitted to assume.

Special mention should be made of the definition of *REMOVE*. Note that if $I' = I$ then $REMOVE(INSERT(S, I'), I)$ is defined to be $REMOVE(S, I)$. At first sight one might expect this to be defined to be S. Such a statement would be wrong. The algebraic specification is given without any reference to how a set might be represented in a particular implementation. It would be possible, for example, to make use of a linear list as before. *INSERT* might merely add an item without bothering to check whether or not the item was already present in the list. So multiple copies could exist; *REMOVE* must remove them all.

7.5.2 Correctness of implementation

Let us assume the implementation of *SET* given in section 7.4.1. We therefore represent a set as a linear list of elements all of which are distinct. Associated with the implementation is the same representation invariant R as before. Again it is necessary to show that R is true for *EMPTY_SET* and that each operation that can be applied to a set leaves it true. In proofs that follow the truth of R can be assumed.

Fig. 7.2. Algebraic axiomatics for *SET*.

SYNTAX

$$
\begin{array}{lll}
EMPTY\_SET: & & \to SET \\
INSERT: & SET \times ELEM & \to SET \\
REMOVE: & SET \times ELEM & \to SET \\
MEMBER: & SET \times ELEM & \to BOOLEAN \\
NULL: & SET & \to BOOLEAN \\
CHOOSE: & SET & \to ELEM
\end{array}
$$

exception   *EMPTY*

SEMANTICS

(a) Let S be an arbitrary item of type *SET* and let I, I' be items of type *ELEM*

$REMOVE\ (EMPTY\_SET, I) = EMPTY\_SET$
$REMOVE\ (INSERT\ (S, I'), I) =$ **if** $I' = I$ **then** $REMOVE\ (S, I)$ **else**
                              $INSERT\ (REMOVE\ (S, I), I')$ **end if**

$MEMBER\ (EMPTY\_SET, I) = FALSE$
$MEMBER\ (INSERT\ (S, I'), I) =$ **if** $I' = I$ **then** $TRUE$ **else**
                              $MEMBER\ (S, I)$ **end if**

$NULL\ (EMPTY\_SET) = TRUE$
$NULL\ (INSERT\ (S, I)) = FALSE$

$CHOOSE(S) = $ any I with the property that $INSERT\ (REMOVE\ (S, I), I) = S$

(b) $CHOOSE\ (EMPTY\_SET)$ raises the exception *EMPTY*

To establish the correctness of this implementation with respect to the algebraic axioms for *SET* we must basically substitute the procedures for the operations and verify that the results are as required. Many of the axioms can be dealt with simply. Let us take one of the more substantial cases, e.g.

$$REMOVE(INSERT(S, I'), I) = \text{if } I' = I \text{ then } REMOVE(S, I) \text{ else}$$
$$INSERT(REMOVE(S, I), I') \text{ end if}$$

If we look at the Ada declaration of the procedure *REMOVE* we see that the body of the procedure begins

if $S \mathrel{/=} EMPTYSET$ **then**

. . .

In the case where the parameter is of the form $INSERT(S, I')$ the condition is certainly true and so the **then** part is executed. Tracing the remainder of the procedure in this way (i.e. performing symbolic execution) and making use of R where necessary shows that indeed the required algebraic equation is true. A similar kind of exercise will result in all the axioms being verified; to justify the correct implementation of *CHOOSE* it is only necessary to show that the particular element I selected satisfies the property that

$$INSERT(REMOVE(S, I), I) = S$$

The proofs given so far have established only partial correctness. We have not shown that the various operations are totally correct, i.e. that they terminate. However, in all cases this can be achieved with little extra difficulty.

The reader should note that the recursive nature of the procedures in the implementation produces certain very pronounced advantages. Had these not been recursive, proofs that the algebraic equations are satisfied would have been much more complicated. Anyone concerned about the presence of recursion should reserve judgement till after chapter 10.

7.5.3   Another example – stacks

We again look at the stack example and show how the type *STACK* can be specified in an algebraic fashion. We assume for the sake of generality that the elements of the stack belong to some general type *ELEM*, in Ada a generic type.

The algebraic specification of *STACK* must give only the relevant details yet it must cover all legitimate possibilities. Situations such as attempting to remove an item from an empty stack, or attempting to read the top element of an empty stack are not meaningful and restrictions must be included to take these into account. These restrictions will form part of the semantic specification and are included as predicates which must be satisfied before attempts can be made to remove items from a stack or read items on top of a stack.

The complete algebraic specification of *STACK* is given in figure 7.3.

An implementation of *STACK* can take the form of a linear list of elements together with suitable procedures given as an Ada module. Proof of the correctness of the representation proceeds as for the abstract data type *SET* – no new ideas are involved.

7.5.4 Properties of axioms

Like any set of mathematical axioms it is important that the axioms associated with an abstract data type should satisfy certain desirable properties. It is important, for example, that the axioms should be

(*a*) consistent – i.e. it should not be possible to deduce a contradiction from the axioms;

(*b*) complete in the sense that the axioms should describe all the properties of the data type and should not leave some aspect of their use undefined.

Ideally the axioms should also be

(*c*) independent – i.e. no axiom can be deduced from the remaining axioms or rules; such a property, though not absolutely essential, encourages economy of effort on the part of all concerned.

We do not propose to go into these matters in detail. Such an exercise would take us into the deep caverns of mathematical logic and we refrain from this. But there are certain general pieces of advice that can be given in a short discussion.

Experience shows that while inconsistency can admittedly be a problem, difficulties of this nature tend to arise only with designers who are unfamiliar with the particular data type. Those who are familiar with the type tend to be aware of the properties and of the pitfalls.

In practice the designer of an abstract data type should take special care to ensure that the completeness criterion is satisfied. It is very easy to overlook special cases, such as attempting to remove an item from an empty stack. If such

Fig. 7.3. Algebraic specification of the abstract data type *STACK*.

SYNTAX

CREATE:		→ *STACK*
PUSH:	*STACK* × *ELEM*	→ *STACK*
POP:	*STACK*	→ *ELEM*
TOP:	*STACK*	→ *ELEM*
EMPTY:	*STACK*	→ *BOOLEAN*

SEMANTICS

(*a*) Let S be an arbitrary element of type *STACK* and I an item of type *ELEM*

$$
\begin{aligned}
POP\,(PUSH\,(S, I)) &= S \\
TOP\,(PUSH\,(S, I)) &= I \\
EMPTY\,(CREATE) &= TRUE \\
EMPTY\,(PUSH\,(S, I)) &= FALSE
\end{aligned}
$$

(*b*) The following restrictions apply:

POP (*EMPTY*)	raises exception	*STACK_UNDERFLOW*
TOP (*EMPTY*)	raises exception	*STACK_EMPTY*

206

situations are ignored a package which faithfully implements the incomplete axioms is liable to behave quite unpredictably. Most violations of the completeness criterion stem from a disregard of the special cases.

All of the problems described above can usually be lessened if care is taken to keep the number of axioms to a minimum. A reasonable number is around four or five. One exception to this rule occurs when there are large sets of constants as in the case of the characters where each of $'A' < 'B'$, $'B' < 'C'$, etc. may have to be listed. If the number of axioms is kept to a minimum inconsistencies tend to be easy to establish and incompleteness of any kind becomes more apparent.

7.6   Conditional correctness

It is often convenient to provide implementations of certain abstract data types such as sets, stacks, etc. in terms of arrays. In principle, however, sets and stacks can contain an arbitrarily large number of elements. Yet in most programming languages it is not possible to introduce arrays which expand indefinitely. In these circumstances a given implementation or representation will remain valid provided any user of the abstract data type is prepared to work only with items of a limited size. Consequently it is convenient to introduce the notion of conditional correctness.

Definition

An implementation of an abstract data type is said to be *conditionally correct* provided that a user or calling program obeys certain rules.

Let us return again to discussion of an abstract data type for sets. Assume that use is to be made of an array of size N and a pointer PTR. It may be appropriate to introduce a declaration of the form:

type *SET* **is**
> **record**
>> *SPACE*: **array** $(1 .. N)$ **of** *ELEM*;
>> *PTR*: *INTEGER* **range** $0 .. N := 0$;
> **end record**;

For a given object S of type *SET* we denote by $\mathscr{S}(S, PTR)$ the set of elements held in $S.SPACE(1 .. S.PTR)$. The number of elements in this set we denote by $size(\mathscr{S}(S, PTR))$.

Consider now the insertion routine. This might take the form

function *INSERT*(S: **in** *SET*; I: **in** *ELEM*) **return** *SET* **is**
> T: *SET* := S;

begin
> **for** J **in** $1 .. T.PTR$ **loop**
>> **if** $T.SPACE(J) = I$ **then**
>>> **return** T;

207

```
                    end if;
                end loop;
                T . PTR := T . PTR + 1;
                T . SPACE(T . PTR) := I;
                return T;
            end INSERT;
```

It is necessary to insist, prior to calling the insertion routine, that its execution will not cause the bounds of the array to be violated. The precondition C can be stated in the form

$$size(\mathcal{S}(S, PTR) \cup \{I\}) = S . PTR + 1 <= N$$

Any use of *INSERT* must be preceded by a check to ensure that this precondition is satisfied. Note that no other of the set operations is liable to cause violation of the bounds and consequently these others require no special precondition; their success is unqualified.

The representation invariant R can also be adjusted to take this limitation into account. The new representation invariant R' is

$$(0 <= S . PTR <= N) \wedge (size(\mathcal{S}(S, PTR)) = S . PTR <= N)$$

The proof of correctness of the insertion function can be outlined in the following way:

```
        --{C ∧ R' ∧𝒮(S, PTR) = TT}
        function INSERT(S: in SET; I: in ELEM) return SET is
            T: SET := S;
        begin
            for J in 1 .. T . PTR loop
                if T . SPACE(J) = I then
                    return T;
                end if;
                --{C ∧ R' ∧ (𝒮(T, PTR) = TT ∧ (I ∉𝒮(T, J))}
            end loop;
            T . PTR := T . PTR + 1;
            T . SPACE(T . PTR) := I;
            return T;
        end INSERT;
        --{R' ∧𝒮(S, PTR) = TT ∪{I}}
```

Although we have introduced the idea of conditional correctness it should be noted that we could have treated the possibility of array subscripts going out of range by introducing exceptions and suitable exception handlers. However it is important to be aware of the fact that conditional correctness is caused by a deficiency of some kind in the *implementation* of an abstract data type. It is important not to confuse exception situations caused by implementation

208

deficiencies with those which are an essential part of the semantics of the abstract data type. For this reason we chose not to introduce exceptions.

7.7   Recursive abstract data types

Although we have looked at the problem of representing abstract data types in terms of a particular programming language the ideas we have discussed generalise in a natural way to the problems of representing one abstract data type in terms of another abstract data type. To take one example the symbol table could be implemented in terms of stacks. The stack axioms alone – and not any aspect of their implementation – would be used in proving the correctness of the symbol table operations and implementation. The ideas we have discussed are therefore very general and widely applicable. But there is one sense in which they are incomplete.

We have discussed the problem of implementing one kind of abstract data type in terms of other (presumably simpler) abstract data types. There is, of course, the possibility of some form of recursion whereby one type can be defined in terms of itself. As often happens in these situations induction comes to the rescue. *Data type induction* or *generator induction* is analogous to the usual principle of induction over the integers. We look at this briefly.

Let T be some abstract data type with basic operators $f_1, f_2, \ldots, f_n$. Suppose it is necessary to show that all objects X of type T have some property P. Data type induction then involves showing that, for all $i = 1, 2, \ldots, n$

> if the parameters of f_i which are of type T satisfy P then any output from f_i of type T also satisfy P.

If this is indeed so then it can be deduced that all the elements of type T satisfy P.

Exercises for chapter 7

1. Consider the possibility of sets which themselves have sets as elements. Then Russell's paradox takes the following form:

   let S be the set of all sets T which have the property that T is not a member of T;

   then S belongs to S if and only if S does not belong to itself.

   The latter statement is a clear contradiction. Can this idea be formulated in Ada?

2. Write the complete version of a program which reads a positive integer N and prints out $N!$

3. A set of N people have to cast votes which have then to be counted. Three routines are required:

   (a) *POLLS_OPEN* has the effect of allowing people to cast their votes;

   (b) *CAST_VOTE(NAME, OPINION)* causes a vote to be cast, assuming a vote has not previously been cast; in the event of repeated votes no vote shall count;

(*c*) *POLLS_CLOSE* ends voting and initiates the production of statistics about the result of the poll.

Show how such a scheme might be implemented as an Ada package. State clearly any assumptions you make.

4. Devise axioms which describe

  (*a*) the short-circuit form of binary operators,
  (*b*) conditional and loop statements whose condition may result in side-effects when evaluated.

5. Devise a package to permit the manipulation of rational numbers. Verify the correctness of the implementation.
   Use a representation invariant which ensures that rationals are held in such a way that the denominators are positive and the highest common factor of the numerator and denominator is one.

6. Discuss the impact of side-effects on the axiomatics of expressions and assignments which might involve subscripted variables.

7. Give an example which illustrates the possible advantage of having a package specification as a generic parameter.

8. A programmer has a need to make repeated calls of the factorial function $F(N)$ where N lies in the range $0 \ .. \ 10$. To prevent repeated calculations of values he decides to form an array which will hold values already calculated. This function F then takes the form of a memo function, i.e. a function which will inspect the array before undertaking the calculation of any particular value.
   Design a package which is an implementation of the above idea.
   Prove the correctness of the implementation.

9. Symmetric matrices are square matrices with the property that
   $$A(I, J) = A(J, I)$$
   for all I and J within the bounds of A. In general, therefore, it is necessary to hold both $A(I, J)$ and $A(J, I)$ when $I \ /= J$.
   Devise a package which produces the outward appearance of being an implementation of a matrix but which actually holds only one of $A(I, J)$ and $A(J, I)$.

10. Provide a correct implementation of an abstract data type *SEQUENCE*. It should be possible to

   concatenate sequences,
   remove the first element of a sequence (leftmost end),
   add an element to the end of a sequence (rightmost end),
   test if a sequence is empty.

11. Complete the proof of the fact that the implementation of the abstract data type *SET* does indeed satisfy the algebraic axioms given in section 7.5.1.

12. Give a complete implementation of the abstract data type *STACK* whose algebraic specification is given in section 7.5.3.
   Prove the correctness of the implementation.

13. A queue can be defined as a kind of a list with a head and a tail. Items

can be added to the queue only at the tail and they can be removed only at the head.

Show how this abstract data type might be suitably encapsulated in the concept of an Ada package.

Verify the correctness of the implementation.

14. Design and implement a package for performing multiple precision integer arithmetic.

Include such operations as unary and binary addition and subtraction together with multiplication, division and **mod**; it should be possible to perform arithmetic to arbitrarily high precision.

Verify the correctness of your implementation.

Show how you would use your package to find the first prime number in excess of 10^{50}; verify the correctness of this program.

15. In a particular application it is frequently necessary to find all the elements in some set which possess some property P (both the act and the property may vary from instance to instance).

Would you add an appropriate operation to the list of basic operations already available for sets or would you make do with those in existence? Give sound reasons for your answer.

16. A bag is defined to be a collection of objects, similar to a set except that elements can occur with arbitrary frequency.

Introduce an abstract data type BAG and a suitable set of axioms similar to those for sets: inserting an item increases the frequency of the item by one and removal of an item decreases the frequency of the item by one.

Provide an implementation of BAG and prove its correctness.

17. Consider

type $T(LENGTH: INTEGER$ **range** $0 .. INTEGER'LAST)$
record
    $CONTENT$: **array** $(1 .. LENGTH)$ **of** $ITEM$;
end record;

Is it possible to devise an Ada subprogram which will extend by some amount N the discriminant and the size of the accompanying array without apparently losing its contents?

If so devise a correct subprogram to accomplish this task.

18. In writing a text editor a programmer will require to perform only a limited set of operations on lines of text. Devise a package of routines for this purpose.

State clearly and formally the effect of each routine and verify the correctness of your implementation.

8   PARALLEL PROCESSING

The programs that we have investigated in previous chapters have all been sequential in nature. During the execution of such a program it can be imagined that operations are performed one at a time and each operation takes a finite amount of time. Statements are performed in a strict orderly fashion one after the other. There are certain crucial observations that can be made as a result, assuming that there are no real-time constraints: the effect of executing a program is independent of the speed of execution of the various operations; the results delivered by a program are the same each time the program is executed.

Parallel processing adds a new dimension to programming. It permits the possibility of the execution of two or more parts of a program to be overlapped in time. For convenience we refer to these parts of programs as processes and denote them by $P1, P2, \ldots$. The idea of parallel processing can be taken to encompass both of the following situations:

(a) Only one operation is being performed at any one time but the various sets of instructions which constitute the different processes are interleaved in time; thus part of $P1$ may be executed, then part of $P2$, then another part of $P1$, and so on.

(b) The various sets of instructions $P1, P2, \ldots$ are being executed simultaneously.

Indeed a mixture of both (a) and (b) is possible.

There are various reasons for parallelism being desirable. Perhaps the most obvious reason is one of efficiency. If several operations can be performed simultaneously the time taken to execute a particular program will be reduced. The processes $P1, P2, \ldots$ which are executed simultaneously might not interrelate in any way – typically no variable accessed by $P1$ will be accessed by $P2$ or any of the other processes. We then say that $P1$ and $P2$ are *disjoint* or noninteracting. The effect of executing these in parallel is, ignoring the time discrepancy, equivalent to the effect of executing the individual processes one after the other. The proofs of correctness and termination present no new problems.

212

There are other cases where the situation is not so simple and where new proof techniques are needed. In these situations processes share common variables. Now, sharing alone is not sufficient to cause trouble – for example, all the processes may merely read or use the value of a variable. The problem arises when one process is reading the value of a variable and another process is liable to alter that value. Then there are certain disturbing areas of uncertainty. The effect of programs may vary on successive runs since the order in which instructions are executed can vary and might depend on various outside influences such as what is happening in the rest of the computer or in another computer at the time. It might not therefore be a simple matter to reproduce a particular situation or a particular combination of events. This gives rise to the notion of time-dependent errors and these are a major source of trouble with parallel programs; testing becomes even less reliable than normal. Errors can now appear and then disappear only to reappear at a later stage when a particular sequence of events occurs.

Another reason can be given for favouring the idea of parallelism, and it is not unrelated to those already mentioned. There are elements or aspects of the real world which are naturally modelled as a set of parallel tasks. In keeping with good programming practices, and with the ideas of Jackson mentioned in section 9.1.4 of the next chapter, we note that the structure of a program should reflect the structure of the objects it models; transformations may be used to increase efficiency.

We begin by looking at the facilities in Ada for expressing parallel processing. We do this by looking at some examples and showing how these might be programmed. We then consider what role verification can play in increasing the degree of reliability that can be placed on the parallel programs we write. The need for proofs of correctness of parallel programs is more pronounced than for sequential programs.

8.1   Some examples
8.1.1   Producers and consumers – simple case

We begin with an extremely simple example. Let us suppose that there is a set of processes called producers and another set called consumers. The producers place information in a variable V; consumers take information from V. For simplicity we assume V is a variable of type $INTEGER$.

A task $PASS\_1$ will be used to describe the operations that can be performed on V. Basically there are two such operations:

> $INPUT$ places information in V
> $OUTPUT$ removes information from V.

The task specification therefore takes the form

> **task** $PASS\_1$ **is**
> > **entry** $INPUT(I:$ **in** $INTEGER)$;

213

```
        entry OUTPUT(I: out INTEGER);
end;
```

An entry is a special kind of procedure or subprogram. Only one entry can be in the process of execution at any one time.

The task body is more complex:

```
task body PASS_1 is
    V : INTEGER;
begin
    loop
        accept INPUT(I: in INTEGER);
            V := I;
        end;
        accept OUTPUT(I: out INTEGER);
            I := V;
        end;
    end loop;
end PASS_1;
```

The task body consists of a loop which processes two accept statements. These accept statements serve two distinct purposes:

(a) They give the definition of entries INPUT and OUTPUT.

(b) They specify the order in which INPUT and OUTPUT must be performed; since these are the only statements within the loop then essentially the following must happen

```
loop
    call of INPUT;
    call of OUTPUT;
end loop;
```

The consequence of these remarks can now be considered. If a call of INPUT is invoked by some task which uses PASS_1 this can be granted (i.e. execution of the entry will be performed) only if PASS_1 has reached the **accept** INPUT statement. In this case a *rendezvous* is said to have occurred. If the request for ˙execution is not accepted immediately the calling task will be suspended and the request will be remembered until such time as PASS_1 is prepared to service it.

Immediate execution of an entry may not occur either because another call of INPUT or a call of OUTPUT may already be in the process of being executed. But associated with each entry will be a queue of requests for executions of this entry. These queues may be empty and in such cases the PASS_1 task is suspended until such time as a call to the appropriate entry occurs. Notice the two-way effect of synchronisation:

the task issuing an entry call is suspended if the appropriate accept

214

statement has not been reached;

the task managing the shared resource is suspended if an appropriate entry call is not forthcoming.

This problem discussed above is typical of a class of problems usually referred to as the mutual exclusion or lock-out problems. These are characterised by the fact that only one process should have access to the shared resource at any one time. Moreover the following stipulations are usually added: a process should complete its operations on shared variables in a finite time; a process will be able to gain access to shared variables within a finite time if it so wishes. If the latter condition is not met then a condition known as deadlock occurs; this is sometimes also called a deadly embrace.

The problem of sharing the resource V has been performed by the designer of the task $PASS\_1$. The user need not concern himself at all with the details of ensuring mutual exclusion, managing the resource V, and so on. That is as it should be.

The example given above illustrates various ideas such as the role of entries and accept statements in performing mutual exclusion, the idea of the rendezvous, and so on. But there are certain gaps in what we have discussed. How, for example, would the $PASS\_1$ task be used, how would it be initialised or started up, how would the infinite loop be terminated? Is it necessary to perform abnormal terminations by issuing the instruction

abort $PASS\_1$;

and so on? We shall attempt to answer these and other questions when looking at the next example.

8.1.2 Gathering statistics

Let us now turn to a simple problem involving statistics. Integer values of some kind are calculated and added to a variable V. Periodically the value in V can be printed and then reset to zero. We assume that several processes may be involved in collecting statistics and several may be involved in the printing of results.

How can this simple statistical problem be programmed? We approach this by asking the same kind of questions that we asked in the previous case and when designing packages. What are the legitimate operations which can be performed on V? The answer is that there are two such operations:

ADD accumulates information in the variable V;

$PRINT$ outputs information and sets V to zero.

But we add a third operation:

$STOP$ ends the process of collecting information.

The specification of the statistical package is therefore

```
        task STATISTICS is
            entry ADD(S: in INTEGER);
            entry PRINT;
            entry STOP;
        end;
```

A package could be designed for the above purpose. However, the various processes may want to make contributions in the form of statistics and may try to access the shared variable simultaneously. Some form of synchronisation is needed.

The task body may take the form:

```
        task body STATISTICS is
            V : INTEGER := 0;
        begin
            STATS:
                loop
                    select
                        accept ADD(I: in INTEGER) do
                            V := V + I:
                        end;
                    or
                        accept PRINT;
                        PUT(V);
                        V := 0;
                    or
                        accept STOP;
                        if V /= 0 then
                            PUT(V);
                        end if;
                        exit STATS;
                    end select;
                end loop;
        end STATISTICS;
```

The new feature of this task body is the select statement. In this case any of the alternative accept statements may be chosen for execution. In general, alternatives of a select statement take the form of an initial accept statement followed by a (possibly null) sequence of other statements. A select statement may also have an else part but this must not include an accept statement.

Task declarations of the kind we have been examining are really simple instances of task type declarations. A task type STATISTICS would be declared in the following way:

```
task type STATISTICS is
        - - specification part
end;
task body STATISTICS is
        - - task body
end;
```

Objects of this new type are like limited private types – no assignment is permitted, no test for equality or inequality is allowed and task types can be passed only as input parameters.

If we assume that this type has been declared in the same or some outer declarative part then objects of a task type are declared in the usual way:

$P, Q, R: STATISTICS;$

Activation of the three tasks P, Q and R occurs in some unspecified order on encountering the first statement following the **begin** (that follows the declarative part). There are then four different tasks in execution: P, Q, R and the main initiating task itself.

Termination of P, Q and R must occur before the main task can be regarded as terminated. The main task will remain suspended until this state of affairs is reached. We now note that a possible alternative in a select statement is just the bold word **terminate**, thus:

```
select
        - - one or more select alternatives;
or
        terminate;
end select;
```

When this is used the main initiating task will, on reaching its final **end**, attempt to cause termination of all subordinate tasks by (automatically) issuing an instruction which selects this terminate alternative and thereby terminates the subordinate task, assuming of course that nothing remains to be done by the task.

When the bold word **type** is omitted from a task declaration a special case arises. Something of the form

```
task S is
        - - specification and body
end;
```

is equivalent to

```
task type ANONYMOUS is
        - - specification and body
end;
S: ANONYMOUS;
```

where ANONYMOUS is not used elsewhere.

In all cases entries can be accessed by using the dot notation, thus:
P. ADD(S); or *Q. STOP*; Especially in the case where only a single task is in evidence this can be offputting but the deficiency can be overcome by renaming in the following way

        procedure *ADD(I: INTEGER)* **renames** *S. ADD*;

and so on.

In what follows we shall concentrate on task types. Other possibilities can then be regarded as special cases.

8.1.3   Producers and consumers revisited

      The first example we gave involved passing messages between processes. But the eventual result was of rather limited use and applicability. Processes had to access *V* in the order producer, consumer, producer, consumer, and so on. Let us now consider a more useful facility which employs a message buffer capable of holding several messages simultaneously. Messages will be deposited and read on a first in, first out basis. We therefore use an array with two pointers: a front pointer *F* and a back pointer *B*. Figure 8.1 illustrates the general idea.

We design the message passing task as a type which makes use of a global type *MESSAGE* and an integer type *SIZE*. We also employ a terminate alternative. The task specification might be

```
task MESSAGE_PASSING is
        entry INPUT(M: in MESSAGE);
        entry OUTPUT(M: out MESSAGE);
end;
```

The task body might take the form:

```
task body MESSAGE_PASSING is
        BUFFER: array (1 .. SIZE) of MESSAGE;
        COUNT: INTEGER range 0 .. SIZE := 0;
        B, F: INTEGER range 1 .. SIZE := 1;
begin
        loop
            select
                when COUNT < SIZE =>
                        accept INPUT(M: in MESSAGE) do
                            BUFFER(F) := M;
                        end;
                        F := F mod SIZE + 1;
                        COUNT := COUNT + 1;
            or
                when COUNT > 0 =>
                        accept OUTPUT(M: out MESSAGE) do
```

218

$$M := BUFFER(B);$$

end;

$$B := B \bmod SIZE + 1;$$
$$COUNT := COUNT - 1;$$

or

terminate;
end select;
end loop;
end *MESSAGE_PASSING*;

In the task body the **accept** *INPUT* statement is said to have a guard, namely the boolean expression $COUNT < SIZE$; the *INPUT* entry can be executed only when the guard is *TRUE*. Similarly the *OUTPUT* accept statement has a guard $COUNT > 0$. Execution of the select statement proceeds as follows: the various guards are evaluated in order; if no guard is present a guard of *TRUE* is assumed. From the guards which yield *TRUE* and for which a rendezvous is possible an accept statement is selected for execution. If no alternatives can be immediately accepted the else part of the select statement, if it is present, is executed; otherwise the task waits until an alternative can be selected. The given task *MESSAGE_PASSING* therefore does as is required.

It is worth passing a remark about the entries *INPUT* and *OUTPUT*. Note that in *INPUT* the statements

$$F := F \bmod SIZE + 1;$$
$$COUNT := COUNT + 1;$$

are excluded from the entry. This has the desirable effect of allowing any calling tasks to proceed as soon as possible. From their point of view the necessary action has been taken; the remaining instructions can be classed as housekeeping which is the sole concern of the task *MESSAGE_PASSING*.

8.2 Verification

We shall now investigate certain aspects of the problem of verifying the correctness of programs which involve parallelism.

Fig. 8.1. Message buffer.

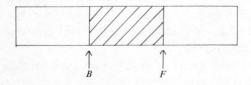

Shaded section holds messages.
Blank sections are such that either messages have not been deposited or messages have been removed.
B, *F* point to the back, front, respectively of the messages.
COUNT is the number of messages in the buffer.

It should be relatively clear that many of the problems involved are similar to those we have already met. Entries themselves are like subprograms and we know how to verify the correctness of these. In both conception and design tasks usually resemble packages. In the cases we consider, there is usually some resource associated with the task and there are entries or procedures which provide the only ways of accessing or altering the resource. There are differences in the sense that the entry and procedure calls generally have to be synchronised in some special way. However, in chapter 7 we dealt with many facets of packages and their correctness; this will be of considerable relevance in the discussion that follows.

What are the new difficulties we shall encounter? There is the question of synchronisation. Not unrelated to this is the problem of drawing a clear distinction between the role of the implementor of a task and the role of the user. Who proves what? Another problem is that of ensuring mutual exclusion. Let us explain.

Whenever several processes are acting in parallel there is always the possibility that two or more of them may attempt to access a variable or resource simultaneously. To overcome difficulties such as the above shared resources must be accessed in mutual exclusion, i.e. access by one kind of process precludes access by another kind.

8.2.1 Mutual exclusion

In its most primitive form mutual exclusion can be expressed in terms of the following requirements:

(i) At most a single process has access to shared resources at any one time.
(ii) A process shall always complete its operation on shared resources within a finite time.
(iii) A process will be able to access a common variable within a finite time if it so wishes.

If the latter condition is not satisfied then the condition known as *deadlock* occurs. This can also be called a *deadly embrace* and results from errors of synchronisation. We consider this in the next section.

Of the above, (ii) is concerned with termination and (iii) with synchronisation. In this section we shall concentrate on requirement (i). We have already implied that in some sense this requirement is unnecessarily restrictive – several readers may read information simultaneously.

The task of ensuring the correct degree of mutual exclusion is basically the sole responsibility of the designer of the task which manages the resource. It is no concern whatsoever of the user of the task. All the information necessary to establish mutual exclusion is contained in the text of the task body.

By means of sympathetic language design the designers of Ada have arranged that the job of proving that mutual exclusion occurs is minimised. This they have done by introducing the notion of an entry and by forbidding variables, etc., to occur in the visible part of a task.

To establish mutual exclusion it is first necessary to identify the shared resource together with any auxiliary variables necessary to monitor access to it. If, following initialisation, all access to these is through the use of entries there is no problem whatsoever. Both the calling and the called task are suspended while an entry is executed and so mutual exclusion is immediately guaranteed.

The remarks made above remain true in a slightly more general case. When the shared resource is accessed either in the accept statement or in the sequence of statements that may follow in a branch of a select statement the remarks are still valid.

Now let us consider the more difficult case which occurs when procedures may be used to access and alter a shared resource. By their very nature procedures are capable of being executed by several processes simultaneously.

Any attempt at access must be preceded by instructions which set a condition used to suspend any attempt to write to or alter the resource. The condition itself will typically take the form of a test on the value of a boolean or integer variable. Since this is used to monitor progress it must be regarded as part of the shared resource. Setting conditions and unsetting them must be performed under mutual exclusion and so should involve the use of entries (usually local entries).

To illustrate these remarks consider the example in figure 8.2. Since procedures are being supplied to the user a package is used to introduce the necessary mechanism. Internal to this is a local task called *INTERNAL* which maintains the necessary degree of synchronisation.

How do we show mutual exclusion? The shared resource is V. The variable *READERS* is used to monitor access to V. Besides their appearance in declarations, in guards and their appearance in entries (or in the statements immediately following) the only appearance of either variable is in the procedure *OUTPUT* where the statement

$$V := I;$$

appears. Immediately before this there is a call to the entry *INTERNAL . START*. The statement in this part of the select statement in *INTERNAL* ensures that *READERS* is set to a positive value and this prohibits any possible attempt to alter V by the *INPUT* entry or procedure. Thus mutual exclusion is guaranteed.

Note that the use of procedures as opposed to entries is basically a form of optimisation. To the user of a task the interface is essentially the same in both cases. The use of procedures permits a greater degree of sharing and an increase in efficiency. Compare the task *PASS_2* and the task *PASS_1* in section 8.1.1.

8.2.2 Synchronisation

We now turn to the more difficult question of synchronisation bearing in mind such devastating possibilities as deadlocks. Who should be concerned with the avoidance of deadlocks (the implementor of a task or the user) and how should this be done?

Synchronisation usually takes place at two different levels. Problems can occur at both.

The designer of a task will usually have some preconceived idea about how some resource has to be accessed. There may be some well-defined order in which accesses should occur. Alternatively there may be some less rigid method of performing access. However, it is natural that the designer should implement his

Fig. 8.2.

```
package PASS_2 is
    procedure INPUT (I: in INTEGER);
    procedure OUTPUT (I: out INTEGER);
end;

package body PASS_2 is
    V: INTEGER;

    task INTERNAL is
        entry START, STOP;
        entry INPUT (I: in INTEGER);
    end INTERNAL;

    task body INTERNAL is
        READERS: INTEGER := 0;
    begin
        accept INPUT (I: in INTEGER) do
            V := I;
        end;
        loop
            select
                accept START;
                READERS := READERS + 1;
            or
                accept STOP;
                READERS := READERS - 1;
            or  when READERS = 0
                accept INPUT (I: in INTEGER) do
                    V := I;
                end;
            or
                terminate;
            end select;
        end loop;
    end INTERNAL;

    procedure INPUT (I: in INTEGER) is
    begin
        INTERNAL . INPUT (I);
    end;

    procedure OUTPUT (I: out INTEGER) is
    begin
        INTERNAL . START;
        I := V;
        INTERNAL . STOP;
    end;

end PASS_2;
```

222

task by ordering the accept statements or using the select statements in as appropriate a manner as possible.

The designer will inform the user of the correct order in which accesses should take place. If the user or users do not act accordingly and obey the given instructions then synchronisation errors may well occur.

Let us consider the role of the designer of a task body. In a very simple situation the task body may take the form:

> initialisation sequence;
> **accept** A ... **do**
>   - - statements defining A
> **end**;
> sequence of statements following A;
> **accept** B ... **do**
>   - - statements defining B
> **end**;
> sequence of statements following B;

A and B are entries (or procedures) and these will have associated assertions. A precondition associated with entry A will describe the state of the shared resource, etc. prior to the execution of the accept statement A. A postcondition again associated with A will describe the state of the shared resource, etc. after the execution of A. Similar sets of assertions will be associated with each entry.

From the verification point of view we can now highlight various matters that should be verified:

> After the initialisation sequence the precondition associated with A should be established.
> It has to be shown that the entry does as expected and indeed is totally correct.
> The execution of the sequence of statements following the accept statement A must result in the precondition associated with B being true.
> B must be shown to be totally correct.

And so on. All of this is relatively straightforward in the sense that it uses material and techniques we have already studied and discussed.

Consider now a task body of the form:

> initialisation sequence;
> **loop**
>   **accept** A ... **do**
>   - - statements defining A
>   **end** A;
>   sequence of statements following A;
>   **accept** B ... **do**

```
        - - statements defining B
        end B;
        sequence of statements following B;
    end loop;
```

In this case the situation is similar to that described earlier. However there is an extra degree of complexity in that all the assertions must be shown to be essentially loop invariants. Again, we know from the earlier chapters how to cope with this.

Let us now look at a task body which contains a select statement and let us consider the following piece of program to which we have added assertions:

```
    initialisation sequence;
    loop
        select
                --{A1}
                accept A ... do
                - - statements defining A
                end A;
                --{A2}
                sequence of statements following A;
                --{A3}
        or
                --{B1}
                accept B ... do
                - - statements defining B
                end B;
                --{B2}
                sequence of statement following B;
                - - {B3}
        or
                when condition =>
                    - - {C1}
                    accept C ... do
                    - - statements defining C
                    end C;
                    - - {C2}
                    sequence of statements following C;
                    - - {C3}
        end select;
    end loop;
```

Note that the condition will probably be incorporated within $C1$.

224

Again in this case we have to prove the truth of certain conditions associated with the various assertions:

(i) After the initialisation sequences either $A1$ or $B1$ or $C1$ must be true.

(ii) On the assumption that $A1$ is true the execution of A must leave $A2$ true; after the execution of the sequence of statements following A then $A3$ must be shown to be true.

(iii) Remarks similar to (ii) above apply for B and C.

(iv) It must be shown that

$$A3 \lor B3 \lor C3 \supset A1 \lor B1 \lor C1.$$

Note that (iv) can be rephrased in another way: the predicate $A1 \lor B1 \lor C1$ is a loop invariant.

The specific cases given above are representative of the kinds of task bodies that are likely to be required. Essentially no new ideas are required for other possibilities.

The discussion so far has centred around proofs of partial correctness of task bodies. To establish total correctness it is only necessary to show that loops terminate and that accept statements terminate. The latter is usually straightforward – the same techniques that were used earlier apply. Termination of a loop will usually result from receipt of a suitable entry or from selection of a terminate alternative; consequently it is often not possible to give a proof of total correctness based on a task body alone.

Until now we have dodged the question of what the assertions associated with tasks look like. It is to be hoped that implementation details will be absent, that local variables introduced to ensure mutual exclusion, etc., will not be present, and so on. In the next section we take some examples and illustrate the possibilities.

8.3 Verification of some tasks

We shall now look at some examples which illustrate the design of simple tasks. One of the first problems we encounter is that of conveying to a user the precise effect that a task performs. Ideally this specification should not be concerned with details that are purely a matter of implementation. In keeping with the earlier discussion on packages and so on, axioms and rules should be free of implementation considerations, they should be concise, etc. We proceed by looking at some examples.

8.3.1 Simple semaphores

The history of parallel processing is decorated with the concept of a semaphore. This can be described by a task called *SEMAPHORE* whose specification is

```
                task type SEMAPHORE is
                        entry P;
                        entry V;
                end;
```
Its body may be implemented as
```
                task body SEMAPHORE is
                begin
                        loop
                                accept P;
                                accept V;
                        end loop;
                end SEMAPHORE;
```

As procedures, P and V are particularly uninteresting. They have no effect whatsoever. But they do provide synchronisation. We know that the P and V operations must be performed in the order $P, V, P, V, \ldots$. We describe this by saying that for the task *SEMAPHORE* the *calling sequence* or *path expression* is

$$(P \circ V)^*$$

The small circle $\circ$ indicates that P will be followed by V and the user can regard these operations as happening in mutual exclusion. The star indicates an arbitrary number (even zero) of occurrences of P followed by V.

The entire specification of the task *SEMAPHORE* therefore takes this form:
```
                task type SEMAPHORE is
                        entry P;
                        entry V;
                end;
```
effect of P:	$\{Q\} P \{Q\}$
effect of V:	$\{Q\} V \{Q\}$
calling sequence:	$\{P \circ V\ ^*\}$

Note that in the first two proof rules P and V are regarded as procedures. (Rather than use *SEMAPHORE* . P etc. outside the task *SEMAPHORE* we abuse notation and employ the obvious abbreviation.) We must show that the given implementation is a correct and faithful representation.

Several aspects of the implementation must be verified. Although all of them are straightforward in this case, we itemise the various matters to be checked:

(i) There is mutual exclusion between P and V.

(ii) P does as expected.

(iii) Q does as expected.

(iv) The stated calling sequence or path expression is an accurate reflection of the order in which P and V can be performed.

226

To verify the latter we note that a call of *P* can be followed only by a call of *V* and vice versa.

8.3.2   Signals

Another common method of performing synchronisation (in the old days) was using signals. A specification of *SIGNAL* might be:

> **task type** *SIGNAL* **is**
>   **entry** *SEND*;
>   **entry** *WAIT*;
> **end** *SIGNAL*;

The task body could be implemented as

> **task body** *SIGNAL* **is**
>   *RECEIVED* : *BOOLEAN* := *FALSE*;
> **begin**
>   **loop**
>   **select**
>   **accept** *SEND*;
>   *RECEIVED* := *TRUE*;
>   **or**   **when** *RECEIVED* =>
>   **accept** *WAIT*;
>   *RECEIVED* := *FALSE*;
>   **end select**;
>   **end loop**;
> **end** *SIGNAL*;

The meaning or effect of using a *SIGNAL* can be described as follows:

> effect of *SEND*: $\{Q\}\, SEND\, \{Q\}$
> effect of *WAIT*: $\{Q\}\, WAIT\, \{Q\}$
> calling sequence: $(SEND^+ \circ WAIT)^*$

The plus sign $+$ indicates that at least one call of *SEND* must occur: $SEND^+$ is equivalent to $SEND \circ (SEND)^*$. As procedures, therefore, *SEND* and *WAIT* have no effect. They merely perform a synchronisation role.

To prove the correctness of the implementation the only item worthy of some discussion is the consideration of whether the implementation accurately reflects the stated calling sequence. From the specification of *SIGNAL* and in particular the calling sequence it should be clear that we have to verify the following:

> *SEND* must be executed initially.
> A call of *SEND* may be followed by either another call of *SEND* or by a call of *WAIT*.
> Any call of *WAIT* must be followed by a call of *SEND*.

These are easily shown to be true since

> When *RECEIVED* is false only a call of *SEND* can occur.
> When *RECEIVED* is true either a call of *SEND* or a call of *WAIT* can take place.

8.3.3 Integer semaphores

We now consider the case of a semaphore which is more general than that discussed in section 8.3.1. We consider a semaphore where specification in Ada makes use of the global N of type *NATURAL*; it is

> **task** *SEMA* **is**
>   **entry** P;
>   **entry** V;
> **end** *SEMA*;

and has a task body of the form

> **task body** *SEMA* **is**
> M: *INTEGER* := 0;
> **begin**
>   **loop**
>   **select when** $M < N$
>   **accept** P;
> $M := M + 1$:
>   **or**   **when** $M > 0$
>   **accept** V;
> $M := M - 1$;
>   **end select**;
>   **end loop**
> **end** *SEMA*;

Note that an integer variable has been used instead of the boolean variable in task *SEMAPHORE*. A user of the task is permitted to perform N calls of the P operation before the first call of V. In the case when $N = 1$ this degenerates into the simple kind of semaphore.

To specify precisely the meaning of this new generalised semaphore we can proceed as follows. The effects of P and V when considered as procedures are trivial and merit no further discussion. The calling sequence is more complex:

> When $N = 1$ it is just $P, V, \ldots$
> When $N = 2$ examples of calling sequences are
> $P, V, P, V, P, V, \ldots$
> $P, P, V, V, P, P, \ldots$
> $P, P, V, P, V, P, \ldots$

The calling sequence can be described as C_N where

$$C_1 = (P \circ V)*$$

and

$$C_N = (P \circ C_{N-1} \circ V)* \quad \text{for all } N >= 2$$

More accurately any permitted calling sequence will be some initial subsequence of C_N. Let us justify the definition of C_N.

Basically C_N must be the set of all sequences of Ps and Vs in which the number of occurrences of P and V – we denote these by $n(P)$ and $n(V)$ – always satisfies

$$0 <= n(P) - n(V) <= N$$

Eventually we shall require that $n(P) = n(V)$.

To prove that we have a proper definition of C_N we note the following. Any sequence from C_N must be null or begin with P. Between such an occurrence of P and the next call of V which results in $n(P) = n(V)$ there will be a sequence of occurrences of P and V and this will belong to C_{N-1}. The definition

$$C_N = (P \circ C_{N-1} \circ V)*$$

is therefore justified.

To prove that our implementation is correct we shall rewrite our definition of the task body and in the process introduce the dummy variables $n(P)$ and $n(V)$. The key to the proof of a correct implementation lies in the loop invariant which is also specified.

```
task body SEMA is
    M: INTEGER := 0;
    - - n(P), n(V): INTEGER := 0;
begin
    loop - - {0 <= M = n(P) - n(V) <= N}
        select when M < N
            accept P; - - n(P) := n(P) + 1;
                M := M + 1;
        or    when M > 0
            accept V; - - n(V) := n(V) + 1;
                M := M - 1;
        end select;
    end loop:
end SEMA;
```

Thus the loop produces an arbitrary sequence of calls to P and V, the only restriction being that

$$0 <= n(P) - n(V) <= N$$

which is as required.

8.3.4 Readers and writers

We now consider the task $PASS\_2$ described in section 8.2.1. Viewed as procedures $INPUT$ and $OUTPUT$ satisfy

$$\{TRUE\}\,INPUT(I)\,\{MESSAGE = I\}$$
$$\{TRUE\}\,OUTPUT(I)\,\{I = MESSAGE\}$$

These rules make use of an auxiliary variable called $MESSAGE$ which holds the values deposited. The calling sequence associated with the task is

$$INPUT \circ (OUTPUT \mid INPUT) *$$

Thus $INPUT$ and $OUTPUT$ deposit and copy messages which are held in $MESSAGE$. The vertical bar indicates 'or'; then any sequence of either $OUTPUT$ or $INPUT$ is permitted after the initial $INPUT$.

It is possible to dispense with the use of the dummy variable $MESSAGE$. One can note that the calling sequence can be written alternatively as

$$(INPUT \circ OUTPUT*)^+$$

and we can note that the effect of

$$INPUT(E) \circ OUTPUT(I) *$$

is to place in each different I the value E.

The package body $PASS\_2$ is more naturally viewed as a generic package with the message type $INTEGER$ replaced by a generic type $ELEM$. Accordingly we present a modified package body $PASS\_3$ together with some accompanying assertions.

```
package body PASS_3 is
      MESSAGE: ELEM;
      task INTERNAL is
            entry START, STOP;
            entry INPUT(I: in ELEM);
      end INTERNAL;
      task body INTERNAL is
            READERS: INTEGER := 0;
      begin - -{READERS = 0}
            accept INPUT(I: ELEM) do
                  MESSAGE := I;
            - -{MESSAGE = I ∧ READERS = 0}
            end;
            loop - -{READERS >= 0}
                  select - -{READERS = R'}
                        accept START;
                        READERS := READERS + 1;
                        - -{READERS = R' + 1}
```

230

```
or     - - {READERS = R' ∧ R' > 0}
       accept STOP;
       READERS := READERS − 1;
       - -{READERS = R' − 1 ∧ R' > 0}
or     when READERS = 0 =>
       - -{READERS = 0}
       accept INPUT(I: in ELEM) do
            MESSAGE := I;
       - -{MESSAGE = I ∧ READERS = 0}
       end;

or
       terminate;
     end select;
   end loop;
end INTERNAL;
procedure INPUT(I: in ELEM) is
- - pre {TRUE}
- - post {MESSAGE = I}
begin
     INTERNAL . INPUT(I);
end;
procedure OUTPUT(I: out ELEM) is
- - pre {TRUE}
- - post {I = MESSAGE}
begin
     INTERNAL . START;
     I := MESSAGE;
     INTERNAL . STOP;
end;
end PASS_3;
```

We itemise the various matters that have to be checked:

(i) *INPUT* and *OUTPUT* are performed under mutual exclusion.

(ii) Both *INPUT* and *OUTPUT* perform the desired tasks, *MESSAGE* being just the repository of messages unseen by the user of the task.

(iii) The calling sequence is an accurate description of the way in which *INPUT* and *OUTPUT* can be called.

Following the discussion earlier about mutual exclusion and about procedure calls only (iii) above wants further attention. This necessitates proof that

A single *OUTPUT* can be followed by either an *INPUT* or an *OUTPUT*.
A single *INPUT* can also be followed by either an *INPUT* or an *OUTPUT*.

231

Both of these can be shown to be true, and this completes the proof.

Note the marked absence of implementation details in the specification of the *PASS_3* package. There is no mention of anything related to mutual exclusion, local entries, the existence of *READERS*, and so on. We now have a notation reasonably close to what we had for abstract data types. For further reading see Campbell & Habermann (1974).

At this stage we draw the discussion to a halt. The treatment of tasks has been a somewhat simplified version of what may be necessary in practical situations. Ada tasks can include timing constraints and they abort for curious reasons – the discussion of such matters is beyond the scope of this text.

Exercises for chapter 8

1. Compare and contrast the methods of specifying the properties of abstract data types and tasks in Ada.

2. Discuss the separation of concerns between a user of a task and an implementor of a task with regard to verification.

3. What aspects of the design of tasks have been influenced by verification conditions?

4. Consider the readers and writers problem discussed in section 8.3.4. Show how the ideas described here can be extended by introducing an array capable of holding several messages simultaneously.

5. Design appropriate specifications for the tasks implemented in section 8.1. Verify the correctness of the implementations.

6. In all our implementations of semaphores the difference between the number of calls of a *P* operation and the number of calls of a *V* operation has always been bounded.
   Implement a semaphore where this difference may be unbounded; the only constraint is that the number of calls of *P* always exceeds the number of calls of *V*.
   Provide suitable documentation for your semaphore and verify the correctness of your implementation.

7. A mail box is a structure which allows messages to be left at particular addresses. The only legitimate operations on the structure are the act of placing a message at a location in the mail box and the act of reading a message from a location. Consider two situations:

   (*a*) The reading operation is not destructive and leaves the message intact.
   (*b*) The reading operation is destructive and destroys the message.

   Design suitable documentation for your implementations of these concepts and verify that the implementations are correct.

8. It is possible to implement a readers and writers task which in effect has a buffer of infinite size by using a list of messages.
   Demonstrate how such a task might be implemented and the correctness of its implementation established.

9. Comment on the possibility or otherwise of

   (*a*) recursive entries,
   (*b*) accept statements containing other accept statements,
   (*c*) an entry containing calls of other entries

   in Ada.

10. The abstract data type *QUEUE* (see exercise 13 in chapter 7) could be implemented either as a module or as a task.
    Compare and contrast these two implementations and the problem of establishing their correctness.

11. Show how one might proceed with the correct and proper design of a task which would permit the allocation and deallocation of space in a parallel environment.

Until now we have been looking for the most part at the task of verifying the correctness of pieces of program. The manner in which these pieces of program have been conceived, designed and coded has not been of any concern. As a result we have encountered certain somewhat unnatural problems such as finding loop invariants.

In this chapter we take an important step forward and discuss the possibility of viewing verification and program design as complementary and not separate processes. The task of verifying the correctness of short, well-written programs is much simpler than the task of verifying the correctness of long, badly written programs. It is natural to expect therefore that much of the ensuing discussion will revolve around methods of properly designing, structuring and writing programs.

In one single chapter it is not possible to do justice to proper methods of programming. We can only hope to outline the proper practices and illustrate these with some examples.

9.1   Elementary considerations

In this section we review some elementary considerations about programming. We begin by discussing the proper use of programming languages, in particular Ada. We then proceed to look at two programming techniques or methodologies. In some respects the order of presentation is somewhat misleading. It perhaps suggests that design is a secondary issue. Nothing could be further from the truth. The chances of obtaining the proper structure for programs will be greatly enhanced by undertaking design before coding is even contemplated. It can be argued with good reason that the programming language itself is almost irrelevant from the point of view of proper design and structure.

The overriding considerations in all our programming will be simplicity and clarity. If programs are designed in this way the chances of misunderstandings of any kind are greatly reduced and correctness is more likely. In much of the ensuing discussion we shall talk about writing simple, relatively short, pieces of program. Of course, large tasks do have to be undertaken. But if these are properly contemplated they can usually be split into a set of smaller tasks which are then much simpler to program. At no stage should a programmer ever be involved in programming and verifying the correctness of a large complex module.

Before undertaking any programming task it is important to obtain a clear and accurate statement of the task to be performed. Obtaining this may involve a great deal of work. At one extreme it might require several man-years of work on behalf of a team of system analysts. We do not propose to consider such matters any further ; we merely note the possibility. We shall assume that a clear description of the task has been obtained.

9.1.1 The proper use of programming languages

A statement of a particular task will often be phrased in terms which might include the use of words such as integers, a set of numbers, a piece of text, an account number, a record of a person, a stack, a family tree, and so on. One of the first tasks a programmer has to perform can best be described as *abstraction*: he must decide which aspects of the objects in the problem statement are relevant for the purposes of programming. Having done this he should try to select from the basic set of data types available in his language the data type whose allowable operations best mirror those of the objects in the problem specification. At this juncture several possibilities arise.

The matter may be very simple to resolve: integers can be represented by items of type *INTEGER* in Ada for example; pieces of text may be represented by arrays of characters; and so on.

There may be no suitable data type in the language. Consider for example the case of a stack. Languages such as Ada will allow the programmer to devise his own abstract data type and to encapsulate this concept in a sensible and meaningful manner in a package. The design of these we consider at a later stage.

The decision may not fall into either of these two categories. Take an account number. Should this be represented by an *INTEGER* (or perhaps *LONG_INTEGER*) or by an array of characters? The matter can and should be resolved by considering the set of operations that can be performed on these two alternative data types. The set of operations permitted on character arrays is more in keeping with the type of operation one would normally associate with account numbers. After all, one would not normally think of adding, multiplying or dividing account numbers and any attempt to do so would be regarded as an error.

Choosing a data type is only the first step in finding a programming equivalent of an object in the problem statement. The second step is to impose whatever constraints can be imposed: if an integer always lies in the range 1 to 100 the appropriate declaration within the program should reflect this; if arrays are at most 20 in size again the declaration should reflect this. Note that the attitude which states that 'a constraint should not be imposed since it may lead to an error' is particularly unhelpful and wrong. If a constraint does lead to a breakdown of the program it is a symptom of something more serious – there has been an error in the program itself or an error in the programmer's conception of what should happen. The real error should be removed, not the symptom.

Analogous to the matter of constraints is the matter of deciding whether an item is constant or variable. Again a programmer who expects an item to be constant in a certain part of a program should arrange his declarations accordingly. Violation of this is a symptom of a more fundamental error or misunderstanding which should be removed.

Besides data types, identifiers have to be selected. In so doing a programmer has the ability to provide names which describe in some sense the role that the identifiers will play in the program. This he should do since it will tend to make programs more readable and understandable. A proper balance must be found between

> choosing names that are too long and hopefully very clear, but awkward to use in formulae, in correctness proofs and inhibiting in terms of ease of achieving a balance between speed of thought and speed of writing programs;
> choosing names that are short and less clear, but easy to manipulate.

This matter is often relatively easy to resolve because it is bad practice for a programmer to have at his disposal at any one time large numbers of variables. The number of variables needed at any one time in the performing of any task should always be relatively small. An Ada programmer can use the scope rules of Ada and the package facilities to achieve these ends. Remember however that in general programs are written once but read often.

A programming language should provide a set of well thought out constructs and facilities for allowing a programmer to express his intentions in a clear and concise manner. The constructs applicable in a particular situation will generally be those with the most appropriate and simplest proof rule. There are two special cases which deserve mention.

In Ada the **for** version of a loop statement should be used in preference to other versions wherever possible: not only is the proof rule likely to be more appropriate and safer but the programmer is saved the trouble of declaring the control variable explicitly, of performing the increment (or decrement) and test to ensure proper termination of the loop; moreover compiler checks ensure that no attempt is made to alter the control variable within the loop or to access the variable outside the loop.

The second remark concerns the much maligned goto statement. The use of the jump often betrays a sad lack of understanding of the proper structure of

236

a program or of the constructs in the programming language and hence has the reputation of being harmful. Some people argue without sufficient reason that avoidance of **goto** will lead to well-structured programs. There are however situations where the **goto** can be used correctly: in these cases the jump is *not* used to create a loop but instead causes a discontinuity of some kind such as terminating a loop or ending a procedure or program – it is more natural to do this than introduce a boolean, set it to *FALSE* and then test it in a while statement to cause termination.

The usual scope rules associated with block-structured programming languages are very suitable and appropriate from the point of view of the programmer and the program verifier. They imply that a programmer can introduce auxiliary or temporary variables for the purposes of performing a particular task. When that task is completed the auxiliary items will no longer be in scope if the scope rules are used correctly; the auxiliary variable cannot therefore interfere with what follows.

As a general rule a programmer should arrange that the use of variables and their declarations are bound as closely together as possible. The use of items is therefore concentrated in particular sections of programs and not scattered in a haphazard fashion over the length and breadth of large programs. This argument is basically a plea for not using the global variable if at all possible. It must be recognised, however, that it is not always possible to proceed in such a desirable fashion. In these circumstances it will often be the case that either

> the globals will be constant over a large section of the program and then appropriate constant declarations are desirable, or
> there will be service routines which manage the changes which occur to the global variable and then a suitable package can be constructed.

Procedures, in all their shapes and forms, should be used to perform tasks which are conceptually simple in the effect they produce. Being simple their effect should be expressible in terms of a simple proof rule. These remarks tend to advise against the use of global variables and against the use of large numbers of parameters; where appropriate, the types of parameters should be constant and contain constraints. Similar advice can be given about the design of packages and the number of declarations in the visible part, the number of parameters, etc. Further discussion of package design we leave till later.

The remarks contained in this section have been about the use of a programming language, not about designing programs. We now set the record straight and discuss some aspects of the very important topic of program design and construction.

9.1.2 Divide-and-conquer

For certain kinds of problems, often of a mathematical or numerical nature, divide-and-conquer can be used to readily obtain solutions to seemingly awkward or intractable problems.

Divide-and-conquer can be likened to mathematical induction. If a programmer is given a problem of size N, say, where N is some non-negative integer he proceeds as follows:

First show how the problem can be solved for special values of N, e.g. $N = 0$ or $N = 1$.

Then assume that problems of size K where $K < N$ can be solved and use these results to show that problems of size N can be solved.

As might be expected the resulting solutions are usually recursive in nature. Let us illustrate the technique by looking briefly at some examples.

Sorting

Suppose that it is required to sort the elements of some set S which can be represented by an array. One way of accomplishing this is to split S into two subsets or subarrays $S1$ and $S2$. These can be sorted and the resulting subarrays merged. In the trivial case where a set happens to contain zero or one element there is no need to perform any action. These observations lead to the merge sort. Given the existence of a suitable procedure *MERGE* the required process can be programmed in the following fashion:

```
procedure SORT(S: in out SET) is
        - - declaration of S1 and S2
begin
        if S'LENGTH > 1 then
                S1 := - - some non-empty proper subset of S;
                S2 := - - rest of S, again a non-empty set;
                S := MERGE (SORT(S1), SORT(S2));
        end if;
end SORT;
```

In this illustration the problem of size N is the task of sorting the elements of an array or set of size N. Divide-and-conquer has taken the form of splitting this into smaller problems, these being the tasks of sorting the smaller sets $S1$ and $S2$.

Finding the largest and second largest of a set

In some ways this is similar to the previous example. However there are enough differences to make the separate consideration of this worthwhile. The largest and second largest elements of a set can be obtained by first sorting the set and then merely picking off the top and the second top elements. This involves much more time and effort than a direct approach. We produce below a skeleton procedure to accomplish the task in hand. Since the required procedure has to produce a pair as its result we introduce an appropriate type declaration:

```
type TOP_TWO is
        record
```

$ONE, TWO : ITEM;$
　　　　end record;

The ONE component indicates the largest of the set, the TWO component indicates the second largest.

　　The following process is adopted. If the set is small no action is entailed. Otherwise split the set into two subsets, find the largest and second largest of these subsets and from the information obtained in this way find the required largest and second largest of the entire set. More precisely the following illustrates the actions required (MAX selects the larger of its two parameters):

function $PAIR(S: SET)$ **return** TOP_TWO **is**
begin
　　　　case $S'LENGTH$ **is**
　　　　　　when $1 =>$ **return** $(S(S'FIRST), S(S'FIRST));$
　　　　　　when $2 =>$ **if** $S(S'FIRST) > S(S'LAST)$ **then**
　　　　　　　　　　　return $(S(S'FIRST), S(S'LAST));$
　　　　　　　　else
　　　　　　　　　　　return $(S(S'LAST), S(S'FIRST));$
　　　　　　　　end if;
　　　　　　when others $=>$
　　　　　　　　$S1 :=$ - - some non-empty proper subset of $S;$
　　　　　　　　$S2 :=$ - - rest of S, again a non-empty set;
　　　　　　　　declare
　　　　　　　　　　$R1: TOP\_TWO := PAIR(S1);$
　　　　　　　　　　$R2: TOP\_TWO := PAIR(S2);$
　　　　　　　　begin
　　　　　　　　　　if $R1 . ONE > R2 . ONE$ **then**
　　　　　　　　　　　　return $(R1 . ONE, MAX(R1 . TWO, R2 . ONE));$
　　　　　　　　　　else
　　　　　　　　　　　　return $(R2 . ONE, MAX(R2 . TWO, R1 . ONE));$
　　　　　　　　　　end if;
　　　　　　　　end;
　　　　end case;
end $PAIR;$

Solving a certain kind of Diophantine equation
Consider the equation

$$A_1 X_1^2 + A_2 X_2^2 + \ldots + A_N X_N^2 = B$$

where both B and each A_i $(1 \leqslant i \leqslant N)$ are some positive integers. It is required to determine whether or not this equation has a solution in integers, i.e. do there exist integers $X_1, X_2, \ldots, X_N$ with the property that

$$A_1 X_1^2 + A_2 X_2^2 + \ldots + A_N X_N^2 = B?$$

If not so indicate; if there are, then again indicate and produce in $X_1, X_2, \ldots, X_N$ an appropriate set of values.

To illustrate the possibilities note that

$$4X^2 + Y^2 = 17$$

does have a solution, namely $X = 2, Y = 1$. On the other hand

$$4X^2 + Y^2 = 6$$

has no solution; there are no integers X and Y with the property that
$4X^2 + Y^2 = 6$.

A rather crude approach merely entails looking at all possible combinations of $X_1, X_2, \ldots, X_N$. A set of nested loops would be appropriate. Unfortunately the value of N is unknown and so the set of for loops cannot be programmed directly. We therefore adopt the following approach.

If the above equation does have a solution then so also does the equation

$$A_1 X_1^2 + A_2 X_2^2 + \ldots + A_{N-1} X_{N-1}^2 = B - A_N X_N^2$$

and vice versa. Let X_N scan through all possible values, namely 0 up to the largest integer less than or equal to $\sqrt{(B/A_N)}$ and determine whether this equation has a solution. We now give a procedure which achieves the desired effect.

type *VECTOR* **is array** (*NATURAL* **range** ⟨⟩) **of** *INTEGER*;
function *CANSOLVE* (*A: VECTOR*; *B: NATURAL*; *X* **out** *VECTOR*)

return *BOOLEAN* **is**

  RESULT: *BOOLEAN*; *N*: **constant** *INTEGER* := *A'LAST*;
begin - - both arrays *A* and *X* should have same upper bound
  - - and lower bounds should both be 1
  if $N = 0$ **then**
    RESULT := $B = 0$;
  else
    for *I* **in** 0 .. *ROUND* (*SQRT*(*B*)/*A*(*N*)) **loop**
      X(*N*) := *I*;
      RESULT := *CANSOLVE* (*A*(1 .. *N* − 1),
             B − *A*(*N*) ∗ *X*(*N*) ∗∗ 2, *X*(1 .. *N* − 1));
      exit when *RESULT*;
    end loop;
  end if;
  return *RESULT*;
end *CANSOLVE*;

Before ending this section on divide-and-conquer we note that the technique is often accompanied by a process called *balancing*. Whenever a subdivision of a problem is performed balancing dictates that subproblems of roughly equal size should be produced if possible. If this happens the resulting algorithms tend

240

to be efficient. Thus in the sorting procedure and in the procedure to find the top two elements of a set the subdivisions entailed should produce subsets of approximately the same size, namely $N/2$; in the Diophantine equation problem a similar arrangement could occur.

All the examples we have given constitute special cases of the general principle of divide-and-conquer which can be phrased in the following terms:

To solve a problem of N points in k-dimensional space first recursively solve two problems of $N/2$ points in $(k-1)$-dimensional space and then recursively solve one problem of N points in $(k-1)$-dimensional space.

We have dealt with the $k=1$ case only! Some of the examples at the end of the chapter illustrate the more general cases.

9.1.3 Backtracking

An interesting class of programming problems is amenable to a process called *backtracking*. In such cases it is usually necessary to search through a large number of possible situations to determine whether a particular pattern holds or to determine how many such patterns hold. Let us take an example.

A famous problem, the eight queens problem, is concerned with the question of whether it is possible to position eight queens on a conventional chessboard in such a way that no queen can take any other queen given the normal rules of chess. In fact ninety-two possible solutions exist; one of these is depicted in figure 9.1. Let us imagine we want to find all solutions.

An initial but very crude approach to this problem involves looking at every possible way of placing the eight queens on the board and for each such possibility asking whether or not the queens can take each other. For all practical purposes this is unsatisfactory; it is too slow and too uneconomical.

Before discussing the details of a more elegant solution we shall introduce some notation which is made possible by the observation that each queen must

Fig. 9.1.

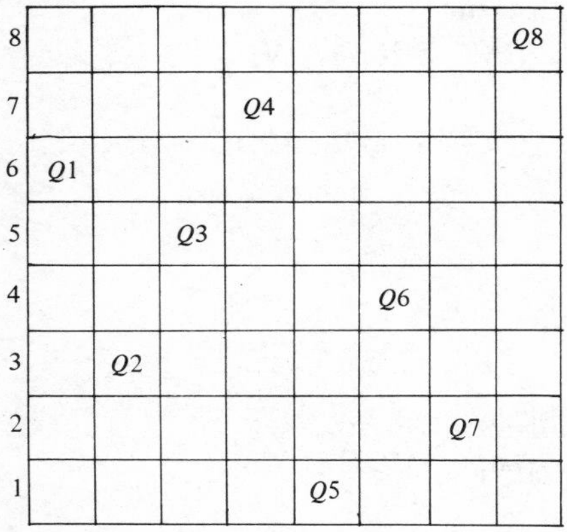

occupy a distinct row and a distinct column. We shall, for instance, write
$(6, 3, 5, 7, 1, 4, 2, 8)$ to denote the position depicted in figure 9.1. In other
words, the first coordinate denotes the position (i.e. row) occupied by the
first queen $Q1$, the second coordinate denotes the position occupied by the
second queen $Q2$, and so on.

Suppose we now look at how the queens might be positioned. We might
legitimately proceed as follows:

> Position $Q1$ in position 1, i.e. row 1.
>
> Position $Q2$ in the first valid position in column 2; rows 1 and 2 are
> invalid since $Q1$ could take $Q2$; so row 3 is the required position.
>
> Position $Q3$ in the first valid position in column 3, namely row 5.
> Similarly position $Q4$ in row 2 and $Q5$ in row 4.

See figure 9.2.

Now try to position $Q6$. This task turns out to be impossible; no legitimate
position exists for $Q6$. So we backtrack. $Q5$ is moved to its next legitimate
position, namely row 8. Having obtained a legitimate position for $Q5$ we now
try to find suitable positions for $Q6$, $Q7$ and $Q8$. In this way progress is made
until all possibilities have been examined and either discarded or taken into
account.

How is the above process programmed? A skeleton solution can be obtained
in the following way. Suppose we talk about some *BOARD*, perhaps implemented
as a boolean array. We can talk about positions on this board, we can ask if they
are legitimate, and so on. A procedure for placing a queen at a suitable position
in the *C*th column would be (in skeleton form):

```
procedure PROCESS_COLUMN (C: INTEGER range 1 . . 8) is
begin
        for R in 1 . . 8 loop
            PLACE_A_QUEEN_ON (POSITION(C, R));
            if MOVE_IS_LEGAL then
                if C = 8 then
                    PRINT_SOLUTION;
                else
                    PROCESS_COLUMN(C + 1);
                end if;
            end if;
        end loop;
    end PROCESS_COLUMN;
```

All that remains to be done is

```
SET_UP_INITIAL_BOARD;
CALL PROCESS_COLUMN(1);
```

242

The entire backtracking process is hidden within the recursion in the procedure. Other problems requiring backtracking can be programmed in a similar way.

9.1.4   Jackson's methodology

Experienced programmers will no doubt be aware of the fact that in certain circumstances the design and the structure of programs are dictated by the design and structure of the data they process. There are three very common examples of this

(a) recursive data structures (or elements of recursive types in Ada) are often processed by correspondingly recursive procedures;

(b) the design of compilers is often based on a grammar that describes the structure or syntax of the language processed by the compiler;

(c) similar to (b) above is the process of describing semantics, cf. abstract data types.

Though widely used in the applications cited above the same practice is not generally applied to other forms of program. M. A. Jackson has applied them to data processing applications where the programs are heavily input/output oriented and their structure can be appropriately determined. In this section we briefly examine Jackson's methods.

To start with we need some means of describing the structure of data. In compiling techniques this would normally be performed by some appropriate grammar. In the meantime we shall keep the discussion relatively simple and use the structure diagrams invented by Jackson. Note that these are very definitely not flowcharts. They do *not* express flow of control. They express the structure of data. They will eventually be used to express the structure of programs, again *not* the flow of control.

Fig. 9.2.

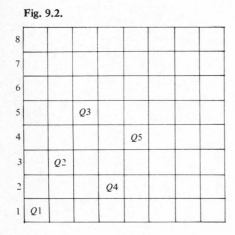

In data processing applications data usually take the form of records or files which are made up of possibly different components. The various kinds of structure diagrams reflect the various possibilities. Let us look at these in turn and at the same time consider how these might be processed.

Structures or records

A record A with three components B, C and D can be represented by figure 9.3. The action of processing A then takes the form (using an Ada-like notation):

$$\langle\!\langle process\_A \rangle\!\rangle$$
$$process\_B;$$
$$process\_C;$$
$$process\_D;$$

In fact we can write as in figure 9.4. The statements required to process each record can be placed in the appropriate box. The structure of the required piece of program will then materialise.

Fig. 9.3.

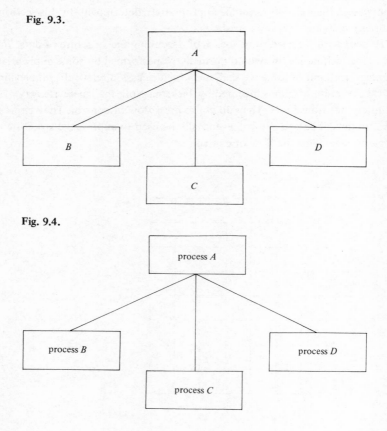

Fig. 9.4.

Sequences or iterations

A file or part of it may consist of a sequence of zero or more records of a simpler kind. If *A* is a sequence or iteration of occurrences of *B* we can write as in figure 9.5. Processing *A* can be performed by repeatedly processing the various instances of *B*. Thus

《*process_A*》
        while *there is a record B* **loop**
            process this record;
            move to next item;
        end loop;

In programming it frequently happens that a sequence contains one or more instances of a record of some kind. This situation can be depicted as in figure 9.6. We have basically produced a structure with two components: *B* followed · by *B**. The first record has been highlighted since frequently it requires special

Fig. 9.5.

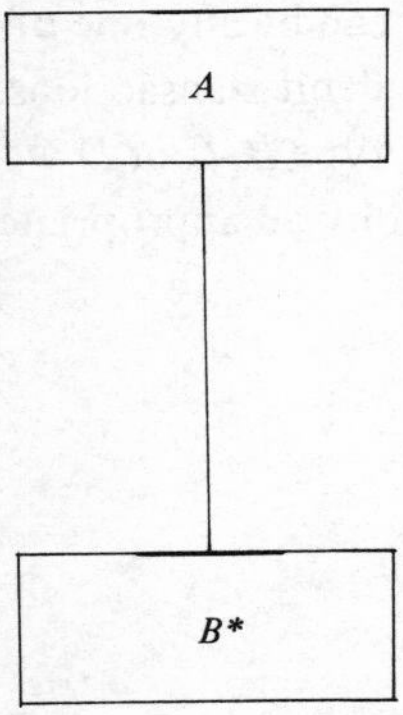

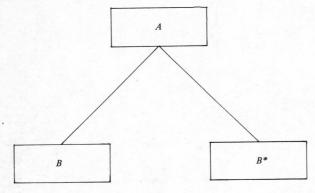

Fig. 9.6.

245

processing. The above can be programmed as

```
《process_A》
        process the first B;
        move to the next item;
        while more records B exist loop
                process this record;
                move to next item;
        end loop;
```

The same effect could be achieved by the following

```
《process_A》
        loop
                process this record B;
                move to next item;
                exit when no more records B exist;
        end loop;
```

Choice or alternative

In many situations records, or parts thereof, can be any one of several possible kinds. Thus it is possible to imagine credit or debit transactions, records for males or females, and so on. If record *A* can be of type *B, C* or *D* we indicate this as in figure 9.7. Processing can then be performed by an appropriate if statement or case statement. Thus either

```
《process_A》
        if record is of type B then
                process as a B record;
        elsif record is of type C then
                process as a C record;
        elsif record is of type D then
                process as a D record;
        end if;
```

Fig. 9.7.

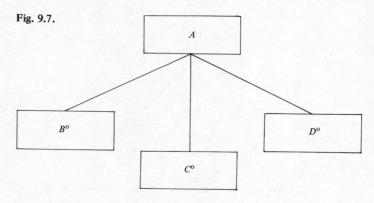

or

$\langle\langle process\_A \rangle\rangle$

    case *A* **is**

        when *B type* $=>$ *process as a B record*;
        when *C type* $=>$ *process as a C record*;
        when *D type* $=>$ *process as a D record*;

    end case;

There are several important aspects to what we have just accomplished. We have drawn a parallel between data structures and control structures; so it is natural to expect that the structure imposed on data will provide a corresponding structure for the eventual program. Another very important observation is to witness the concentration or localisation of considerations. In processing any particular record we require to know only about the structure of that record, not about what follows. Thus in programming an iteration or sequence we write

    while *more records exist* **loop**

      . . .

    end loop;

and not

    while *terminator not reached* **loop**

      . . .

    end loop;

This is a simple but important extension of the ideas we have already outlined in discussing modules for encapsulating abstract data types. Separate the concerns, localise and concentrate on one thing at a time.

Processing pension records

    The data for a program consists of a set of records followed by a terminator. The records are of males and females and contain information about names, ages, and so on. For the purposes of obtaining a pension

    males qualify when they attain the age of 65 or over,
    females qualify when they attain the age of 60 or over.

Any program which processes this data for the purposes of doing calculations involving pensions will have a structure based broadly on the structure diagram of figure 9.8. Thus to calculate the number of old age pensioners essentially place certain instructions in the appropriate boxes as given by the table:

Markings of box	Instruction
DATA	$OAP: INTEGER := 0$;
65 *OR OVER*	$OAP := OAP + 1$;
60 *OR OVER*	$OAP := OAP + 1$;
TERMINATOR	$PUT(OAP)$;

The general format of any program based on the above structure diagram is:

```
loop
        read record;
        exit when not male or female;
        if male record then
                . . .
                if less than 65 then
                        . . .
                elsif 65 or over then
                        . . .
                end if;
                . . .
        elsif female record then
                . . .
                if less than 60 then
                        . . .
```

Fig. 9.8.

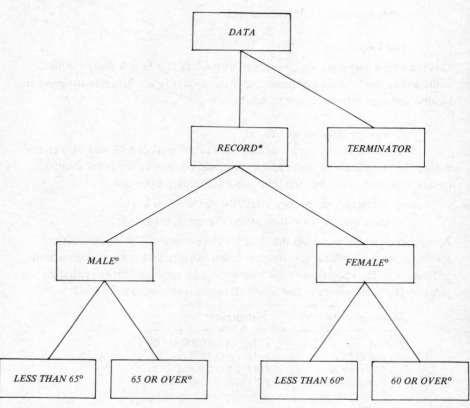

```
                elsif 60 or over then
                    . . .
                end if;
        end if;
    end loop;
    . . .
process terminator;
```

Looking for palindromes

We only sketch the solution to this problem. However, enough of the detail is included for the reader to construct his own complete solution.

Consider the task of scanning through a piece of text looking for words which are palindromes, i.e. read the same forwards as backwards. Examples are *MADAM*, *DEED* and *DAD*. We assume the data consists of a non-empty sequence of words separated by spaces and terminated by a period. We assume that the maximum size of any word is 20 characters.

The structure diagram representing the data is figure 9.9. Note that we have stopped short of expressing words in terms of non-empty sequences of characters. The reason for this is that the problem itself was expressed originally in terms of words, not individual characters. The above is therefore very natural.

The piece of program which will eventually process words can be designed in a straightforward way. If we represent a word as a string of characters the function which decides if a word is a palindrome will take the form

```
function PALIN(W: STRING) return BOOLEAN is
    PAL : BOOLEAN := TRUE;
begin
    for I in O .. (W'LAST − W'FIRST)/2 loop
        PAL := W(W'FIRST + I) = W(W'LAST − I);
        exit when not PAL;
    end loop;
    return PAL;
end;
```

From the structure diagram given earlier the eventual structure of the program can be deduced. This is illustrated by figure 9.10. The required program can now be produced in a natural fashion.

It may seem that the structure diagram above has highlighted the initial word in an unnatural way. But the first word must be processed in a different way; in all cases except the first the initial character of the word will have been read.

Processing transactions

Here we shall be concerned with the common process of taking a master file, in this instance of bank accounts, and updating these using a set of daily

249

transactions – credits to or withdrawals from the individual accounts. We assume that there is for each customer an initial record which contains such details as his name, account number and the current amount of his account. Following this is a set of transaction records which contain details of the credits to or withdrawals from the account that day. The input data can therefore be represented by figure 9.11. In fact the initial records could have formed one file and the transactions another file. This may have been more natural but conceptually is no more difficult.

The corresponding output takes the form of figure 9.12.

Fig. 9.9.

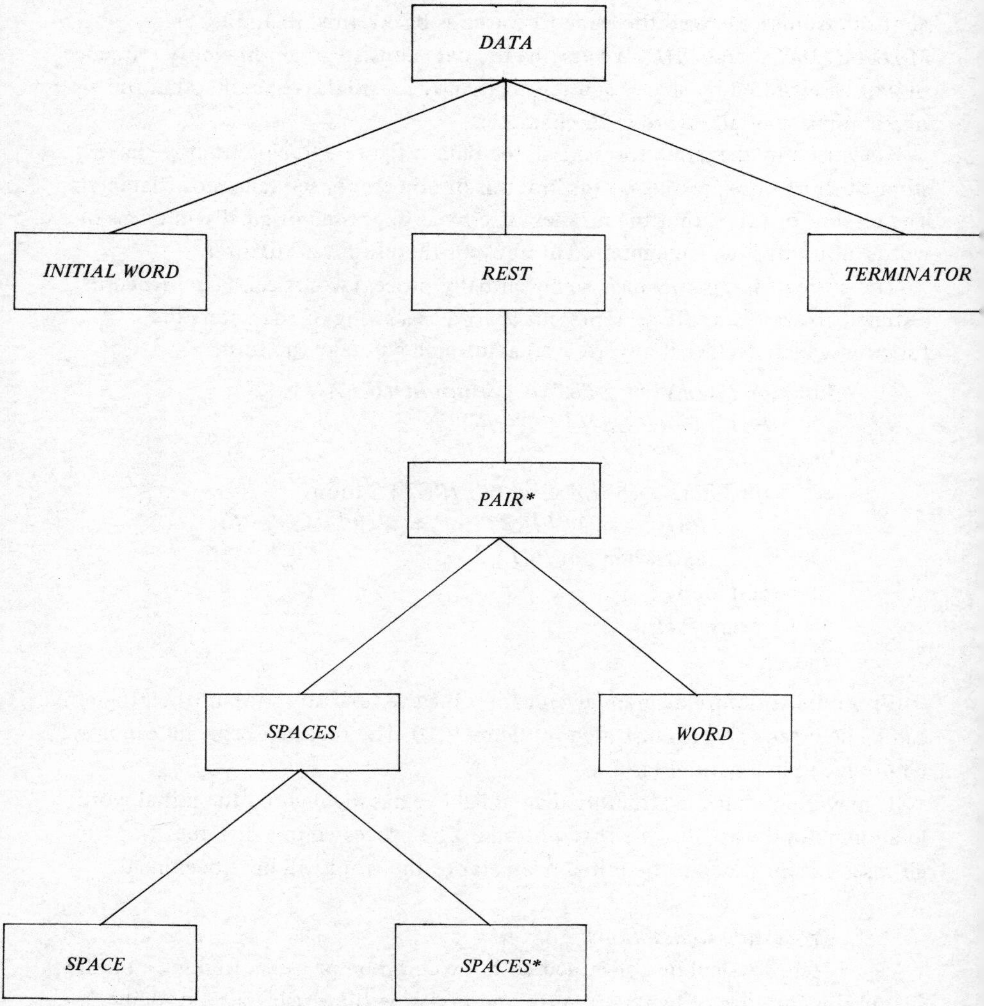

The task the program has to accomplish is to map one structure diagram in a convenient way to the other. There is a clear correspondence between the different parts of the structures. These are marked in figure 9.13. The program itself should reflect this relationship. This is achieved very naturally as follows:

> *process header*
> > *output header*;
>
> *process contents*
> > **while** *records exist* **loop**
> > > *read initial record*;
> > > *initialise SUM appropriately*;
> > > **while** *transactions exist* **loop**
> > > > **if** *credit* **then**
> > > > > *add to SUM*;
> > > >
> > > > **elsif** *debit* **then**
> > > > > *subtract from SUM*;
> > > >
> > > > **end if**;

Fig. 9.10.

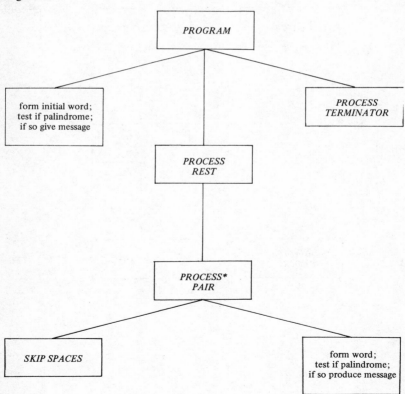

251

```
      end loop;
          output new record to other file;
          read terminator;
      end loop;
  process eof
      output end of file;
```

We have given only a very simple and very brief introduction to Jackson's
methodology. The techniques are appropriate for certain kinds of problems.
When used properly the methods indicate the correct structure of the required

Fig. 9.11.

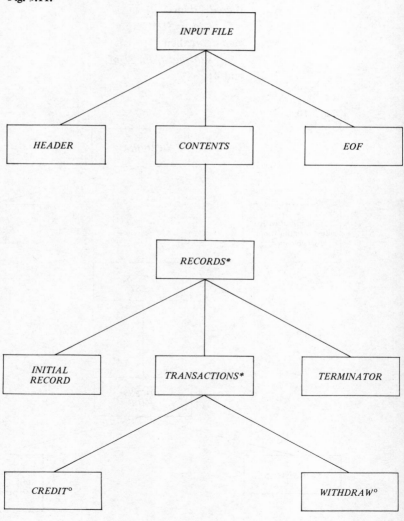

program. Such programs are likely to be correct and hopefully proofs of corrections will be relatively straightforward.

Jackson's basic method will break down in certain circumstances. There are situations where the structure of the input and the structure of the output are so ill-matched that it is just not possible to produce a simple program which converts from one to the other. In these situations *structure clashes* are said to have occurred. Some common examples serve as illustration:

(*a*) Transpose a matrix.

(*b*) Perform some task which requires elements to be sorted.

Another situation where difficulties can occur is where there are two different structures imposed upon the data and the input routines naturally make the wrong choice:

(*c*) Consider some input made up of a sequence of lines of data. This same data can be interpreted as sets of messages, each message being terminated by a full stop.

This example can be reformulated in terms of sequences of blocks of data, e.g. on magnetic tape, holding messages.

In cases such as these it is necessary to break the programming task into several different programs. Earlier programs then remove some of the structure clashes, iron out difficulties or irregularities in such a way that all the programs can be properly designed:

In the case of transposing a matrix essentially the entire array must be read in before the operation can be performed.

Fig. 9.12.

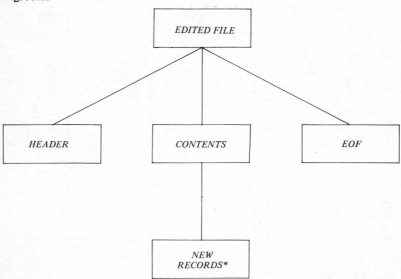

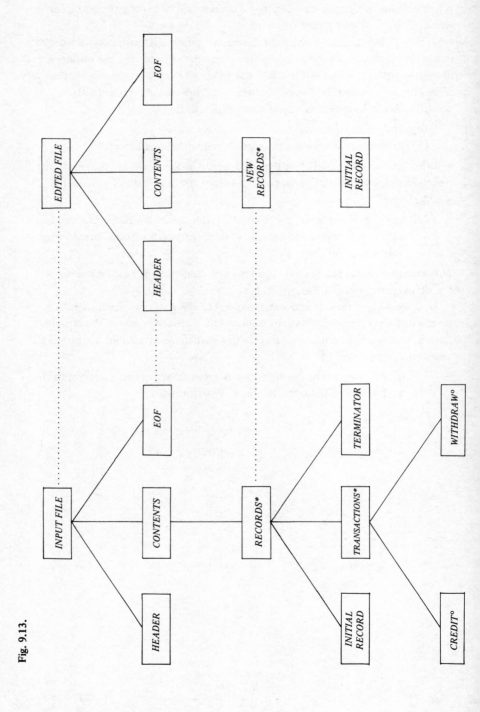

Fig. 9.13.

In the example which requires sorting again all the elements have to be read in and sorted before further processing can occur.

In case (c) above the first program produces a stream of characters on which only a single structure can be imposed, namely a sequence of messages.

We have provided only a brief description of Jackson's methodology. For further reading see Jackson (1972). It should also be mentioned that Jackson's ideas have something in common with other techniques developed by Yourdon, Constantine and Warnier. See references.

9.2 Structured programming

Let us begin by considering the very nature of the programming process. Given a large programming task the structured programming or stepwise refinement approach suggests that the task should be divided into several subtasks which can then be programmed separately. These subtasks themselves may require further refining into other subtasks and so on. In this way, then, a large task is broken into much simpler tasks; ideally the programming of each of these subtasks is manageable. This view gives rise to a tree structure. See figure 9.14.

The requirement for such a breakdown of a complex task is based partly on the high degree of complexity of large programs or programming systems. This is not peculiar to programming. The design and construction of large engineering structures such as large engines, bridges, buildings, motorways, towns and even computers themselves provide similar difficulties. It is just not possible for human beings to sensibly contemplate and approach the problem of designing

Fig. 9.14. Tree structure of programs as a result of stepwise refinement.

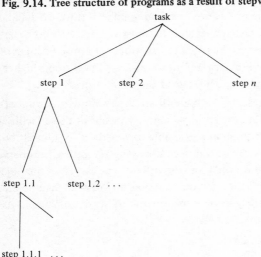

255

and building large complex systems (of whatever kind) which have to be reliable and easily maintained unless a definite attempt is made to simplify the task by isolating separate subtasks to be performed.

If the process of stepwise refinement is performed in a sensible manner then at each stage of the programming process all the tasks that have to be performed are of a reasonable and manageable size. In particular the programming of these can be performed and proofs of correctness provided.

While expressing an important basic idea the description of the programming process that we have just given is somewhat naive and oversimplified. In particular it pays no attention whatsoever to the problem of how the division into subtasks might be performed. Nor does it take into account the quite definite possibility that separate subtasks may require similar routines, e.g. to perform stack manipulation or pattern matching. Consequently the earlier ideas have to be modified to take these criticisms into account.

We look now at further developments of the idea of abstraction, a concept which paves the way for the introduction of hierarchies of abstract machines and abstract programs. These will replace the idea of stepwise refinement and provide more of an insight into the programming process.

9.2.1 Abstraction

Abstraction is one of the most important means of dealing with complexity. It entails the separation of the relevant and the irrelevant aspects of an object in a particular situation. Most programmers are familiar with this. They frequently write procedures or subprograms to perform certain well-defined tasks which should possess simple proof rules (and a sensible number of parameters). Having programmed these they no longer worry about the (then irrelevant) details of the internal mechanism used to obtain the desired effect. They proceed to use the procedure or subprogram as if it were a standard object supplied by the implementation. In this way the irrelevant details are ignored. The programmer is thus able to construct for himself a higher level of language in which to program. By means of nested constructs higher and higher levels of languages can be designed and produced.

The use of procedures alone is rather limiting. Even the provision of functions and operators leaves room for improvement. By means of these facilities together with type declarations a programmer is able to construct for himself objects of increasing complexity with suitable accompanying attributes, i.e. operators, functions, etc. We use the word 'complexity' in a special sense; the objects may be complex in design but they should be simple and easy to manipulate. For instance a programmer may be able to construct rational numbers in Ada by means of a type declaration such as

       type *RATIONAL* **is**
          record

$$NUMERATOR : INTEGER;$$
$$DENOMINATOR : NATURAL;$$
end record;

A suitable set of operators and functions can be defined for manipulating rationals. In a similar sort of way a type *POLYNOMIAL* could be defined together with an accompanying set of operators and functions.

In these and other cases it helps if the programmer can be freed from the worry of accidentally or deliberately performing some illegal operation which might interfere with the proper working of his program. This is where the language designer has a significant role to play. Thus in Ada the concept of a package permits the necessary degree of abstraction. The objects appearing in the visible part of the module, usually functions and operators, then provide the only means of accessing or manipulating the objects and this is checked by the compiler.

The programmer should ensure that the operations made available by a package exhibit the expected properties. In the case of rationals or polynomials with integer coefficients for example one would expect addition and multiplication to be both commutative and associative and to possess the other expected mathematical properties. Even in the case of polynomials with real coefficients one would hope that the properties exhibited by the operators would be as close as possible to their expected mathematical ideals. The closer an implementation comes to possessing the properties of the object it pertains to reflect the easier the verification process is likely to be. The programmer and the program verifier must be freed from remembering peculiar and unexpected differences.

We have already witnessed another use of packages namely the provision of abstract data types. In designing an abstract data type a programmer will typically ask:

What data structure most suitably represents the object I wish to process or manipulate?

What are the fundamental operations that can be performed on such an object?

What properties should these operations possess?

When these questions are answered only the relevant information is made available to a user of a package which claims to implement such an abstract data object. In particular, details of implementation are again hidden from the user, certain identifiers may not be made available, and so on. The implementor is freed from any consideration of how a module is to be used. An important separation of concerns occurs and an appropriate degree of abstraction is performed. Proofs must be given to ensure that the implementation is a faithful representation of what is required or expected. The provision of a facility for generic types introduces considerable savings – proofs do not have to be repeated for similar objects.

257

In summary then, abstraction in programming languages is designed to allow a user to specify his own objects and his own operations which in turn possess particular properties. These operations are then the only permitted basic operations; all others must be built from them. This is checked in Ada by the compiler. In this way the programmer has a small number of ideas to concentrate upon and so the complexity of the situation at any one time is reduced.

The process of abstraction can be viewed from another angle. It is the means provided within a programming language of supplying axioms for objects of varying degrees of sophistication.

9.2.2   Language and machine hierarchies

The programming process as described above is just the process of stepwise refinement modified in certain ways. It can best be viewed as a process of constructing hierarchies of abstract machines $M_0, M_1, M_2, \ldots, M_n$ and corresponding abstract programs $P_0, P_1, P_2, \ldots, P_n$. The abstract machine M_0 is the most primitive, for instance the machine code of an actual computer. $M_1, M_2, \ldots, M_n$ are successively higher levels of machines. Each of the programs $P_0, P_1, \ldots, P_n$ realises the task to be performed. Program P_0 is the machine code program whereas at the other extreme P_n is the required program written in terms of the primitive operations supplied by the high level abstract machine M_n.

The task of verifying the correctness of each of $P_0, P_1, \ldots, P_n$ can itself be subdivided. This can be done in the following way:

(a) verify the correctness of the abstract program P_n;

(b) then verify that the primitive operations of each machine M_i are faithfully implemented in terms of the primitive operations of machine M_{i-1}, i.e. show that each abstract machine M_i is correctly implemented on a more primitive machine.

At no stage then is it necessary to verify directly the correctness of program P_0. The proof is, however, performed indirectly in the manner described above.

Now we have already discussed how to perform each of these tasks. We know about verifying the properties of programs written in high level languages such as Ada; we know also about verifying the properties of programs which make use of abstract data types. These together cover topic (a) above. As far as (b) is concerned we have also demonstrated methods of coping with this since we have shown how to verify the correct implementation of abstract data types, and so on. (A strict progression would actually require us to prove the correctness of the compiler and even the underlying hardware).

All that remains then is to answer the question: how should abstract machines be designed and how should abstract programs be composed? At this stage there is something to be said for making a remark along the following lines. If we could provide a complete set of rules for the design and construction of these items then programming would be a terribly mechanical and uninteresting task. No such rules exist nor is it reasonable to expect them to exist. However, it is possible to offer some guidelines which help in the construction of abstract machines and abstract programs.

9.2.3   The design of packages or modules

The idea of decomposition, the basis of stepwise refinement, is crucial to all the ensuing discussion. More generally it is crucial to all forms of building, construction and engineering – our particular concern happens to be the construction of programs. In passing it is worth mentioning that the divide-and-conquer technique and the techniques of Jackson are themselves different forms of decomposition into tasks which are in some sense smaller.

In performing the division into subtasks we note that each separate subtask, whether it is a function, operator, procedure, package or whatever, should perform some coherent unit of work. Tasks which are independent should be separated, tasks which are somehow related should have this relationship reflected in the structure of the program. The effect of a subtask should be capable of being described in terms of suitable assertions. One consequence of this is that the interface between successive subtasks should be simple and easily described. Thus procedures, functions, etc. should have relatively few parameters, they should perform the natural or expected operations and should have simple proof rules; modules should make visible only a few items with the expected properties, proof rules, etc. To demonstrate an analogy with other forms of construction note that a television or car has a relatively complex internal mechanism required to make it function. However there are usually only a few controls required by a user. Each of these performs some relatively simple well-defined task. Even the internal mechanisms themselves are built in terms of units which perform relatively simple and well-defined tasks.

The whole idea of decomposition does require some justification. Splitting into subtasks introduces the necessity of deciding where interfaces should occur and of deciding what the interface specifications should be. Given that this can be achieved it is in general easier to program smaller tasks than larger tasks; different programmers can be employed to program these different tasks. The economics of programming in all shapes and forms tends to suggest that cost as a function of size is more than linear especially when the potential size of a program becomes large.

The very mention of specifications and interfaces introduces the problem of deciding how these specifications should be described. Specifications must, of course, be absolutely clear and unambiguous. This immediately excludes English and other natural languages and causes a move towards the more formal methods outlined earlier in chapter 7.

Another aspect of program construction and the economics thereof concerns the interrelationship between separate parts of programs and in particular separate modules. In order to discuss this sensibly let us begin from a rather remote standpoint and talk about modules in general and their interactions, i.e. the flow of information between them.

There are two factors which tend to have a very strong influence on the design of modular programs and their cost. These are usually referred to as *coupling* and *cohesion*.

> Coupling relates to the interconnections between modules: *highly coupled* modules have a strong interconnection and so rely heavily on each other,
> *loosely coupled* modules have a weak interconnection,
> *decoupled* or *uncoupled* modules have no interconnection whatsoever.

Thus the higher the coupling between modules the greater the flow of information between them.

Highly coupled modules are somewhat undesirable – there is a high probability that if a programmer has to alter one module he will also have to alter the other. Uncoupled modules are in some sense ideal, in another sense they are rather uninteresting. It is possible to design, write, verify, etc. one module without any reference whatsoever to the other; they can be designed independently by different people.

From our point of view the most interesting modules are loosely coupled. Modules such as those encapsulating data types and so on tend to fall into this category. Modification of one module can occur without causing the modification of another. This then makes it possible for a programmer to construct a module without paying any attention to how it will be used and with little or no knowledge of any other module. In fact the module may be used in several different ways by possibly different people. If the programmer is isolated from considerations of use he can concentrate on the task in hand and produce a correct implementation. Conversely the user of a module is isolated from implementation considerations and can concentrate solely on using the module in the proper way. This separation of concerns is itself a version of divide-and-conquer!

The other factor which influences the design of programs is cohesion. This relates to the strength of the bonds which bind together the various items in the module. Ideally, related items should be grouped together. The bonds which bind can take various forms: similar functions and procedures which are used for some mathematical topic, items which share a common environment, items sharing knowledge about the implementation (e.g. of a stack), error routines, routines required to start up a system (e.g. by opening files), routines for handling communication, and so on. All these are possible examples of the proper cohesion of modules.

260

These simple guidelines then indicate the kind of modules that it is desirable to construct. Modules which implement stacks, which encapsulate data types and which contain entire programs will, if properly designed, pass the specified tests. Let us now look more closely at the specification and the design of appropriate modules.

Let us begin with the design of the specification part of a module. Suppose we have to supply a set of operations for allowing access to a data structure; for convenience we shall refer to the resulting module as a service module and distinguish it from a user module (which makes use of the service module). There is a strong argument for the service module designer deciding to supply a minimal set of operations which will allow a user to perform the kind of tasks he is required to perform. The argument can be justified on the grounds that the fewer the operations, the fewer the correctness proofs associated with the design of the module, the simpler the interface, and so on. This attitude also tends to endorse the view that user modules should be constructed with as little knowledge as possible of the service module. The fewer the operations the less information a user is likely to have of the workings of the service module and the greater the freedom the service module designer has in selecting a suitable method of implementation. However the basic philosophy must be tempered with a certain amount of common sense.

Consider the designer of a service module for allowing the manipulation of a stack. Basic operations include pushing an item onto the stack and removing an item from the stack. A service module could be constructed with only these operations available. A user of the service module wishing to read the topmost element of the stack can do so by removing an item, noting it and then returning it to the stack; it is cumbersome but possible. It is even possible for a user to ask whether or not a stack is empty; to accomplish this it is necessary to take the precaution of putting on the stack initially some value which will not be used for any other purpose. Again the operation is possible but cumbersome.

For various reasons it is sensible for a designer of the service module to supply more than just the basic operations; in the case of a stack module there should be special operations to read the topmost element and to test if the stack is empty. These special operations are likely to be more efficient than the alternatives. More important, however, is the observation that both the construction of programs and their correctness proofs within the user module are vastly simplified. A little extra effort on the behalf of the designer of the service module is more than justified by savings in the efforts of anyone using this module (and there may be many!)

From these observations it should be clear that the designer of a service module should not be attempting to minimise the set of operations. Rather he should minimise what might be called the kinds of access that a user has to the (hidden) data structure. The design of the individual operations are then governed by various factors which might include ease of use, ease with which correctness proofs both within the service module and within user modules can be constructed, limiting the kinds of access, hiding information and aspects of an implementation which are not the concern of a user.

The operations which are typically provided for abstract data types tend to fall into three categories:

> primitive constructors – used to create objects of the abstract data type; typical of these are operations to create stacks, queues, sets, and so on;
> combinational constructors – used to join together in some sense objects of the abstract data types; typical of these are set union and set intersection, etc.,
> access operations – used for accessing data structure with a view to inserting or retrieving information of some kind, e.g. putting an item on a stack, enquiring if a stack is empty.

If any or all of these operations on abstract data types are intended to mirror some mathematical entity the designer should arrange that the implementation is as genuine as possible.

There is another difficulty. Consider the design of a package for manipulating rational numbers. Following the guidelines described above various operations will be supplied including $+$, $-$, $*$, $/$ and the comparison operators. Of these let us concentrate on dyadic $+$. Should a designer introduce only addition between two rationals or should he supply addition of integers and rationals, rationals and integers, and finally rationals and rationals? At this stage there is a great deal to be said in favour of providing a *natural extension* of the base language. Consider Ada. What is permitted with regard to real arithmetic involving objects of type *FLOAT*? Only addition between two reals is allowed. If a user wishes to add an integer and a real he must first convert the integer into a corresponding real. Accordingly the natural step to take with regard to rational arithmetic is to supply only addition between two rationals. For other forms of addition use type conversion.

In the cases mentioned the crucial observation is that there is some data structure or some resource which is in a sense owned by the module. The various routines which are made visible by the module share some environment and knowledge about the implementation. The more detail that module can keep hidden the better.

Now let us turn to the task of constructing an abstract program or a subprogram. At this stage we can appeal to some of the techniques described at the start of the chapter. The methods of Jackson are appropriate for certain kinds of programs. But they do indicate a more general philosophy. Ideally the structure of a program should reflect (some view of) the structure of the problem. If this

262

can be achieved – it is not always apparent what this structure should be – then it is likely that the designer will be able to prove correctness, etc. in a relatively simple way.

For mathematical kinds of problems divide-and-conquer techniques have a role to play. For such problems another technique is often appropriate. It is possible to construct programs by looking first for invariants and using these to provide a guide to a sensible situation. We shall look at this task later in section 9.3.

The design of complete programs then involves both the construction of abstract data types and the design of abstract programs. The two interrelate to a considerable extent. There are two common approaches to overall program design and construction; these are usually referred to as top-down and bottom-up.

In bottom-up design a programmer will proceed by producing the lower level abstract data types first. Having produced these, verified and tested them he will then move to the next higher level, and so on. There are certain advantages in this approach. Testing which should accompany verification (the reader will recall) is usually done in a bottom-up fashion – modules are easily isolated and test data easily provided. Bottom-up design has the advantage that separate modules can be prepared by separate programmers. Moreover time-critical modules which require high levels of efficiency are often best programmed in this way. In general, bottom-up techniques ensure that modules have been correctly implemented. The disadvantages of these methods are reflected in the corresponding virtues of top-down methods, and vice versa.

In the top-down approach a programmer will proceed by assuming the existence of certain other modules, namely the modules which implement the various levels of abstract machines. To be more precise these module specifications will exist but not the module bodies. Such an approach has certain advantages: the top levels of module specifications are checked and proofs of correctness can be provided; moreover it is generally the case that a skeleton program can be obtained relatively quickly. Stubs or dummy modules can be incorporated – these can be designed to work for special cases, to allow programmers to interact and supply intermediate results, to work inefficiently, and so on.

In general, programs will be eventually produced by a combination of various techniques. As we confessed earlier there are no rules for deciding how programs should be designed and constructed just as there are no rules for designing and constructing proofs in mathematics. There we let the matter rest.

9.3 Programming using invariants

To conclude the chapter we look at some relatively simple examples and show how consideration of the correctness proof can suggest the proper structure of a program. This technique has come to be known as a semi-formal method of program derivation. Thus program construction and program verification go hand-in-hand and so lead to a much higher degree of confidence in the resulting program. In the process problems such as finding loop invariants all but disappear.

It is only reasonable to remark that much of the work in this area is still in its infancy. At the time of writing it would be unreasonable to think of developing all programs in this way. But it does seem a fruitful direction of progress.

Example 9.3a   The factorial

Suppose that we have to produce an iterative program which, given the non-negative integer N, produces in the integer variable Z the quantity $N!$

Let us assume that at some stage a partial result has been calculated and that

$$Z = (R - 1)!$$

for some $1 <= R <= N$. We then ask: what has to be done to ensure that

$$Z = R!$$

Clearly the instruction

$$Z := Z * R$$

has to be performed. For

$$--\{Z = (R - 1)!\}$$
$$Z := Z * R;$$
$$--\{Z = R!\}$$

This should strongly suggest the use of the **for** version of the loop statement. Thus

> **for** R **in** $1 .. N$ **loop**
> $\quad--\{Z = (R - 1)!\}$
> $\qquad Z := Z * R;$
> $\quad--\{Z = R!\}$
> **end loop**;

This program certainly produces in Z the desired result. It remains only to ask: what should we do initially to ensure that the invariant

$$Z = (R - 1)!$$

is true on first entering the loop. Clearly Z must be initialised to 1. Thus we obtain the final correct program

> $Z := 1;$
> **for** R **in** $1 .. N$ **loop**
> $\quad Z := Z * R;$
> **end loop**;

Example 9.3b   Highest common factor

Consider an iterative program to find the highest common factor of two positive integers M, N. The program should make use of the mathematical results regarding the highest common factor of $n, m (n \geqslant m)$ namely $hcf(n, m)$:

(a) if $m = 0$ then $hcf(n, m) = n$

(b) $hcf(m, n) = hcf(n, m)$

(c) $hcf(m, n) = hcf(n, m \bmod n)$

The clue to the construction of the program lies in observing the nature of relationship (c) above. We shall introduce two integer variables X and Y and observe that

$$hcf(M, N) = hcf(X, Y)$$

for some suitable X and Y. In each circuit of the loop X and Y can be altered in such a way that the above relationship remains true and yet they decrease towards zero. This leads to the following skeleton program

    while - -$\{hcf(M, N) = hcf(X, Y)\}$
                $Y \mathrel{/}= 0$ **loop**

    . . .

    end loop;

The answers to two questions lead to a complete correct program:

(i) How should we initialise X and Y to ensure that the invariant is true initially?

(ii) What instructions have to be inserted in the loop to ensure that the values of X and Y change in accord with rule (c) given above?

The following (correct) program emerges.

    declare
           X, Y, Z: *INTEGER*;
    begin
        if $M > N$ **then**
            $X := M$;
            $Y := N$;
        else
            $X := N$;
            $Y := M$;
        end if;
        while - -$\{hcf(M, N) = hcf(X, Y)\}$
                    $Y \mathrel{/}= 0$ **loop**
            $Z := X$;
            $X := Y$;
            $Y := Z \bmod Y$;

end loop;
      - - X holds the required highest common factor
end;

Example 9.3c   Iterative problem (due to Dijkstra)
Let the function f be defined on the natural numbers as follows:

$f(1) = 1$
$f(2n) = f(n)$
$f(2n + 1) = f(n) + f(n + 1)$

Write an iterative program which produces in Z the value of $f(N)$ where N is some positive integer supplied as data.

    Let us look closely at the definition of f. In both the odd and even cases the definition expresses $f(N)$ as a linear combination of the values of $f(n)$ and $f(n + 1)$ for some suitable n. We can therefore write

$$f(N) = Af(K) + Bf(K + 1)$$

for some A, B, K whose precise values for the moment we leave unspecified.

    The definition of f then suggests that we (roughly) divide K by 2 to give K' say and so express $f(N)$ in terms of a (different) linear combination of the values of $f(K')$ and $f(K' + 1)$. If, during the loop, we make appropriate changes to the values of A, B and K, then again we shall have

$$f(N) = Af(K) + Bf(K + 1)$$

This strongly suggests that the required loop invariant is just of the form

$$f(N) = Af(K) + Bf(K + 1)$$

    The basic structure of the program can now be expressed as

while - -$\{f(N) = Af(K) + Bf(K + 1)\}$
          $K \mathrel{/}= 0$ **loop**

      . . .

end loop;

There are three matters to be considered.

  (i) What initial values should A, B, K receive to ensure the invariant is initially true?

 (ii) What changes should be made within the loop body to the values of A, B, K?

(iii) When the loop terminates $K = 0$. It appears there is a value for $f(0)$. Yet this is undefined. What value should $f(0)$ be given to ensure consistency with the remainder of the definition? (Put $n = 0$ to give $f(0) = 0$.)

Consider question (ii). Assume that K is even, that $K = 2K'$ say. Then

$$f(N) = Af(K) + Bf(K + 1)$$

266

$$= Af(2K') + Bf(2K' + 1)$$
$$= Af(K') + B(f(K') + f(K' + 1))$$
$$= (A + B)f(K') + Bf(K' + 1)$$

It follows therefore that on one circuit of the loop during which K is even the values of A, B, K have to be altered to $A + B, B, K/2$ respectively. A similar analysis produces the corresponding changes on a circuit of the loop during which K is odd.

The above remarks then lead to a program of the following kind:

$K := N; A := 1; B := 0;$
while $- - \{f(N) = Af(K) + Bf(K + 1)\}$
        $K \mathrel{/=} 0$ **loop**
    if $K \bmod 2 = 0$ **then**
        $A := A + B; K := K/2;$
    else
        $B := A + B; K := (K - 1)/2;$
    end if;
  end loop;

Note that an obvious simplification results in a single assignment to K outside the conditional.

Example 9.3d   Finding the mode

Given an ordered set of integers $A(1 .. N)$ find the integer which occurs most often in this set, i.e. find the mode, $mode(A, N)$, of the set $A(1 .. N)$. If there are several such integers any solution will suffice.

Assume that at some intermediate stage of the calculation the first I elements of A have been processed. Assume that

X occurs most frequently in $A(1 .. I)$.
X occurs P times in $A(1 .. I)$.
C is the number of occurrences of $A(I)$ in $A(1 .. I)$.

We write this in the form

$$X = mode(A(1 .. I)) \wedge P = freq(X, A(1 .. I)) \wedge$$
$$C = freq(A(I), A(1 .. I))$$

We now regard this as a loop invariant and ask again

(i) What instructions must be performed to ensure that this invariant is initially true?
(ii) What must be done to ensure that it remains true when I is increased by 1?

The answers to these questions lead to the following (correct) program:

$X := A(1); P := 1; C := 1;$

```
for I in 1 .. N − 1 loop
    if A(I) = A(I + 1) then
        C := C + 1;
        if C > P then
            P := C; X := A(I);
        end if;
    else
        C := 1;
    end if;
end loop
```

On completion of the program we then have

$$X = mode(A(1 .. N)) \wedge P = freq(X, A(1 .. N)) \wedge$$
$$C = freq(A(N), A(1 .. N))$$

and the required effect has been obtained.

Sorting a set of elements

We look now at the task of programming a method of sorting into ascending order the elements of an array $A(1 .. N)$. For definiteness we assume that the elements of the array are of type *ELEM* and that the array is indexed by integers. The method we look at is called Quicksort.

Quicksort was invented by C. A. R. Hoare and is based on the observation that in sorting by exchanging elements of an array it seems better to perform exchanges over longer distances rather than over shorter distances. Thus we do not exchange adjacent elements but we try to exchange elements which are much further apart.

Choose an arbitrary element S of the array $A(1 .. N)$. Now scan up through $A(1), A(2), \ldots$ until we find an element which is greater than S – call it $A(I)$. Similarly scan down through $A(N), A(N-1), \ldots$ until we find an element $A(J)$ which is less than S. Then, assuming that $I < J$, interchange $A(I)$ and $A(J)$. Again proceed to scan up starting from the new $A(I)$ looking for another element which is greater than S and scan down from the new $A(J)$ looking for an element which is less than S. Again perform the necessary interchange and repeat the process until I is greater than J. On completing the scan over the elements of A we know that all the elements between $A(J)$ and $A(I)$ are in their correct position and in fact are all equal.

Let us assume that the above scan through the elements of the array is performed by a procedure which is called *PARTITION*. The relevant call of the procedure is just $PARTITION(A, I, J)$.

The final phase of the Quicksort process then involves applying precisely the same technique to the smaller arrays $A(1 .. J)$ and $A(I .. N)$. A suitable recursive procedure does as is required.

This description then conveys the idea of what must be done. But how do we design a program to achieve the necessary effect? Consider first the procedure *PARTITION*. Let us select an element S in the following way:

$S := A(N/2);$

In stating invariants associated with the Quicksort methods we ought to include the assertion that the set of elements in the array A remains unaltered. The only operation which interferes in any way with the elements is the swapping operation which interchanges the values of two variables; this clearly does not alter the set of elements. Consequently we omit mention of this from the assertions but recognise that it ought to be present. (Note also that swapping may cause $S = A(N/2)$ to become false.)

After each individual process of scanning the array A to find a suitable I and J it should be clear that the following invariant ought to hold true (note the use of pointwise extensions):

$$LE(A(1 \ldots I-1), S) \wedge LE(S, A(J+1, N))$$

Again we ask

(i) What must be done to ensure that this is true initially?
(ii) What must be done to keep this invariant true and yet obtain a new I and J?

The answers to these questions lead to the following piece of program:

```
S := A(N/2);
I := 1; J := N;
loop
        while A(I) < S loop
            I := I + 1;
        end loop;
        while S < A(J) loop
            J := J - 1;
        end loop;
        exit when I >= J;
        SWAP(A(I), A(J)); I := I + 1; J := J - 1;
    end loop;
```

On completion of the above we can assume that, using the pointwise extension notation,

$$(I >= J) \wedge LE(A(1 \ldots I-1), A(J+1 \ldots N))$$

(Indeed is $EQ(A(J \ldots I), S)$ true?)

The entire Quicksort method can now be programmed as in figure 9.15.

A detailed proof of correctness of the final routine can be given in the usual way.

Solving an equation

Consider the problem of finding a solution in integers of an equation of the form

$$AX^2 + BY^2 = R,$$

where each of A, B and R are themselves positive integers. We would like to determine whether there exists a pair of non-negative integers P and Q with the property that

$$AP^2 + BQ^2 = R.$$

This is a simpler version of a problem we encountered earlier. But we attempt a different solution.

We can phrase the input and output predicates in the following manner:

input predicate:

$$A > 0 \land B > 0 \land R > 0$$

output predicate:

$$(SOLN = TRUE \land AX^2 + BY^2 = R)$$

$$\lor$$

$$(SOLN = FALSE \land \text{there is no } X, Y \text{ such that } AX^2 + BY^2 = R)$$

Fig. 9.15. Quicksort routine.

```
generic
     type ELEM is private;
     type VECTOR is array (INTEGER range <>) of ELEM;
     with function "<" (A, B: ELEM) return BOOLEAN is <>;
procedure QUICKSORT (A: in out VECTOR);

procedure QUICKSORT (A: in out VECTOR) is
     I, J: INTEGER;
     procedure PARTITION (A: in out VECTOR; I, J: out INTEGER) is
          procedure SWAP (X, Y: in out ELEM) is
               Z: ELEM;
          begin
               Z := X; X := Y; Y := Z;
          end SWAP;
          S: ELEM := A ((A' FIRST + A' LAST)/2);
     begin I := A' FIRST; J := A' LAST;
          loop
               while A(I) < S loop
                    I := I + 1;
               end loop;
               while S < A(J) loop
                    J := J - 1;
               end loop;
               exit when I >= J;
               SWAP (A(I), A(J)); I := I + 1; J := J - 1;
          end loop;
     end PARTITION;
begin if A' LENGTH > 1 then
          PARTITION (A, I, J);
          QUICKSORT (A(A' FIRST .. J));
          QUICKSORT (A(I .. A' LAST));
     end if;
end QUICKSORT;
```

The method of solution we adopt is illustrated in figure 9.16. Without loss of generality we look for a solution (X, Y) with the property that $X >= 0 \wedge Y >= 0$. We then start at grid point P_0 on the X-axis (either at or just beyond where the ellipse crosses the X-axis). We then successively decrease X until we move inside the ellipse, then increase Y till we are on or outside the ellipse again, and so on. We continue to zigzag round the perimeter of the ellipse in this way; whenever we reach a grid point P_i we ask if this is a solution of the equation.

From this description of the process we can make the following deductions.

(i) P_0 is $(X, 0)$ where $A(X-1)^2 < R <= AX^2$.

(ii) Each P_i $(i = 1, 2, \ldots,)$ is a point (X, Y) at which

$$AX^2 + B(Y-1)^2 < R <= AX^2 + BY^2.$$

Note that each P_i is characterised by the fact that a decrease of 1 in Y alone causes a move from outside or on the ellipse to the inside.

(iii) Each Q_i $(i = 1, 2, \ldots,)$ is a point (X, Y) at which

$$AX^2 + BY^2 < R <= A(X+1)^2 + BY^2.$$

Again note that each Q_i is characterised by the fact that an increase of 1 in X causes a move from the inside to the ellipse itself or beyond.

To help in describing certain invariants it is convenient to introduce some notation. Note that we are searching for solutions of the equation in the order of increasing magnitude of Y; we look for solutions with $Y = 0$, then $Y = 1$, and so on. Consequently we let $P(Y)$ denote the following predicate:

$SOLN = FALSE \wedge$ there is no solution of $AP^2 + BQ^2 = R$ with $Q < Y$.

These remarks now provide the framework on which to hang the program and its corresponding correctness proof.

Fig. 9.16.

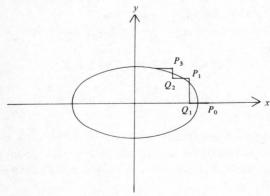

$P_0, P_1, \ldots$ are on or outside the ellipse.
$Q_1, Q_2, \ldots$ are inside the ellipse.

271

```
- -{A > 0 ∧ B > 0 ∧ R > 0}
- - perform initialisation of X, Y and SOLN
        X := 0;
        Y := 0;
        SOLN := FALSE;
- - now seek P_0
        while A * X ** 2 < R loop
            X := X + 1;
            - -{A * (X − 1) ** 2 < R ∧ SOLN = FALSE}
        end loop;
- -{(A * (X − 1) ** 2 < R <= A * X ** 2) ∧ P(0) ∧ (Y = 0)}
- - check if P_0 represents a solution
        SOLN := A * X ** 2 = R;
- - seek other solutions
        while (X >= 0) ∧ (not SOLN) loop
            - - move horizontally back to Q_i, if it exists
                while (A * X ** 2 + B * Y ** 2 >= R) ∧ (X > 0) loop
                    X := X − 1;
                end loop;
            - -{(X >= 0) ∧ (A * X ** 2 + B * Y ** 2 < R <=
            - - (A * (X + 1) ** 2 + B * Y ** 2) ∧ P(Y)) ∨
            - - (X = 0 ∧ B * Y ** 2 >= R ∧ P(Y))}
            - - now move vertically looking for next P_i
                while A * X ** 2 + B * Y ** 2 < R loop
                    Y := Y + 1;
                end loop;
            - -{(X >= 0) ∧ (A * X ** 2 + B * (Y − 1) ** 2 < R <=
            - - (A * X ** 2 + B * Y ** 2) ∧ P(Y)) ∨
            - - (X = 0 ∧ B * Y ** 2 >= R ∧ P(Y))}
            - - check whether P_i is a solution
                SOLN := A * X ** 2 + B * Y ** 2 = R;
        end loop;
- -{SOLN = TRUE ∧ A * X ** 2 + B * Y ** 2 = R
- - ∨
- - SOLN = FALSE and there is no X, Y such that
- - A * X ** 2 + B * Y ** 2 = R}
```

The program given here is grossly inefficient in the sense that there are certain calculations which could profitably be moved from inner to outer loops. This topic we leave until chapter 10. For the moment we note that we have produced a correct program.

In all the examples of this section we began by selecting an invariant. We then considered what instructions had to be performed to leave the invariant unaltered.

In this way programs were developed.

Note that by attacking a programming problem in this way the tasks of constructing the program and verifying its essential correctness are tackled hand-in-hand. One of the consequences of this is that there is then no problem associated with choosing assertions. Proofs are more easily provided and greater reliability results.

The reader might like to consider how the earlier problems of this section might have been solved recursively, and perhaps with more ease. At least two observations can be made: note the strong relationship between the recursive programs and the invariants associated with the loops of the iterative programs; though they are less efficient recursive programs are often simpler to write and verify.

Exercises for chapter 9

1. Discuss the idea that the actual programming language used in any programming task is of little consequence; the important considerations are the techniques used to design the programs.

2. How does the design of Ada encourage (and discourage) the proper structure of programs?

3. Some authors advocate the practice of 'firewalling' (i.e. always including within subprograms checks on the validity of parameters).
   Discuss the merits or otherwise of such practices.

4. Prove the total correctness of the divide-and-conquer problems of section 9.1.2.

5. Prove that the Quicksort routine given in section 9.3 terminates. Generalise the Quicksort procedure in such a way that an arbitrary discrete type can be used to index the array; verify the correctness of the resulting procedure.

6. Generalise the technique used for solving $AX^2 + BY^2 = R$ in section 9.3 so that it deals with equations of the form
   $$A_1 X_1^2 + A_2 X_2^2 + \ldots + A_N X_N^2 = R$$
   where each A_i and R are all positive.
   Verify the total correctness of your program.

7. Design a suite of procedures, etc. to solve the eight queens problem. Verify the total correctness of the final result.

8. Consider again the problem of finding integral solutions of
   $$A_1 X_1^2 + A_2 X_2^2 + \ldots + A_N X_N^2 = R.$$
   Show how this might be solved using

   (*a*) divide-and-conquer techniques with balancing,
   (*b*) backtracking techniques.

9. A set of N discs all of different sizes and with a hole in the middle are given, together with three rods. The N discs are placed on a rod in such a way that no disc is placed above a smaller disc.

Show how these discs can all be moved to another rod. The only legitimate move consists of taking a disc from one rod and placing it on another rod ensuring that no disc is ever placed over a smaller disc. Demonstrate the correctness of your solution.

10. Consider an $N \times N$ squared board. On $N^2 - 1$ of the squares are blocks numbered $1, 2, \ldots, N^2 - 1$; zero can be represented by the vacant square.
    Determine whether it is possible to move from one initial configuration of the board to a final configuration and if so how. All moves must take the form of sliding blocks from square to square within the confines of the board.

11. Using any three characters, e.g. $+, -, *$ generate a sequence of N characters with the property that no two immediately adjacent subsequences are equal.
    Verify the correctness of the resulting program.
    Show how your program and its correctness proof might be modified to find all sequences of length N with no two immediately adjacent subsequences.

12. Write a program to determine whether a knight, when started at an arbitrary position on a conventional chessboard, can be made to visit each and every other square once and once only; a move consists of moving two squares horizontally and one vertically or two vertically and one horizontally.
    Verify the correctness of your program.

13. Consider the following approach to sorting an array of elements into ascending order:

    scan the array looking for the smallest element;
    on finding it move it into the bottom position within the array;
    now look for the next smallest element and move it into the second lowest position;
    continue in this way until all elements are examined.

    By considering invariants show how a program for the above process might be developed.

14. Attempt to develop a solution to the eight queens problem by concentrating on the invariants.

15. Consider a set S of points in k-dimensional space. Let $A = (a_1, a_2, \ldots, a_k)$ and $B = (b_1, b_2, \ldots, b_k)$ be two points in S. We say that A dominates B if and only if

    $$a_i > b_i \quad \text{for all } i = 1, 2, \ldots, k.$$

    The rank of A is then the number of points in S which A dominates. Design a *correct* Ada subprogram to find the rank of each point in a set S where S is supplied as a parameter; use a divide-and-conquer technique.

10 PROGRAM TRANSFORMATIONS

In chapter 9 we remarked that program design, construction and proof should pay little or no attention to considerations of efficiency. The philosophy we expounded was that programs should be simple and easy to verify. Yet programs do have to be executed, and frequently some measure of efficiency is important.

In this chapter we look at the topic of program transformations. We look at methods whereby, from a given source program, a better (usually this means more efficient) program can be produced. The resulting program will again be expressible in the source language and its effect will be the same as that of the original program. Typical of the kind of alteration that can occur is the replacement of certain kinds of recursion by iteration.

The methods we look at can, for the most part, be performed automatically by some programming system. Particular syntactic patterns can be sought and then replaced by alternative pieces of program. Often such transformations systems operate interactively – they look for prompts from the programmer to act as a guide towards the most sensible sequence of transformations.

Though we have stressed the use of transformations as a mechanism for producing efficient programs (which are, almost incidentally, correct) from correct programs there are other uses of these transformations. It is also possible to transform a program which is difficult to verify into another equivalent program which is easier to verify. Later we give an example of such a situation.

Program transformations fall into several categories depending on whether they are applied at the statement, procedure or module level. We look at these in turn. Note that we omit from consideration transformations involving the manipulation of tasks and exceptions.

10.1 Basic transformations

We shall begin this investigation into transformations by looking at some very simple and obvious cases. The reader may think that much of this material is terribly obvious and would never be applicable to any reasonable program. In one sense this is true. But there are cases where the transformations are useful. In later parts of this chapter we look at more complex transformations which might involve relatively large pieces of programs. At that stage the transformations will be described in a very general form. Much of the benefit that can result from these might be lost unless some of the simple transformations are then applied.

10.1.1 Some simple cases

Transformations frequently applied to programs concern the replacing of some calculation which is unnecessarily performed several times by a single calculation. There are various instances of this:

If a subexpression Z is common to several expressions then Z can be calculated only once, its value held in some temporary variable T, say, and T can thereafter be used in place of Z; T is such that it is not used for any other purpose within that piece of program.

If an expression is repeatedly calculated within a loop and yet is essentially a constant this calculation can be moved to a point just before the beginning of the loop.

Statements which occur within a loop and produce the same effect on each circuit can often be moved out of the loop.

We now look at another set of transformations and we take a more formal view of these. Symbols such as S, T are used to denote statements or sequences of statements. The reader should impose the obvious interpretation in the particular circumstances. Note in particular that we often assume there are no labels in S and T to which a jump can be made from another part of the program. The following transformations are typical.

Let X and Y denote distinct variables and let $EXP1$ and $EXP2$ be arbitrary expressions which do not produce side-effects.

Interchanging assignments
If X is not present in $EXP1$ and Y is not present in $EXP2$

$X := EXP1;$ $Y := EXP2;$

can be replaced by

$Y := EXP2;$ $X := EXP1;$

Combining assignments

$X := EXP1;$ $X := EXP2;$

can be replaced by the single assignment

$X := EXP2\ (EXP1/X);$

Removing assignments
If X and Y have the same value the assignment

$$X := Y;$$

can be replaced by **null** and this can often be removed entirely.

Tests

If the evaluation of B involves no side-effects then

(*a*) If B is always true,

   if B **then** S **else** T **end if**;

   is equivalent to S.

(*b*) If B is always false,

   if B **then** S **else** T **end if**;

   is equivalent to T.

(*c*) If B is always well-defined,

   if B **then** S **else** S **end if**;

   is equivalent to S.

(*d*) If the evaluation of conditionals involves no side-effects,

   if $B1$ **or** $B2$ **then** S **else** T **end if**;

   is equivalent to

   if $B1$ **then** S **else if** $B2$ **then** S **else** T **end if**; **end if**;

   and similarly,

   if $B1$ **and** $B2$ **then** S **else** T **end if**;

   is equivalent to

   if $B1$ **then if** $B2$ **then** S **else** T **end if**; **else** T **end if**;

(*e*) $X := EXP1;$

   if B **then** S **else** T **end if**;

   is equivalent to

   if $B(EXP1/X)$ **then** $X := EXP1;$ S **else** $X := EXP1;$ T **end if**;

   provided $EXP1$ is evaluated just once.

Although the terms absorption and expansion (see page 278) are usually applied to control structures we note that they also have relevance to declarations. Thus it is possible to talk about transformations which involve

   moving local declarations to an outer level to save repeated generation of space;

   moving declarations out of subprograms, changing parameters and local variables into global variables, etc.;

   converting procedure declarations to labels and procedure calls to jumps, appropriate action being taken to cause the correct return.

It is important to be aware of certain difficulties in such an exercise:

certain naming conflicts caused, e.g. by two declarations of the same identifier, must be resolved;

declarations of such items as dynamic arrays cannot be moved.

The ideas expounded here might seem contrary to much of what we have been preaching. However, we note that programs should be constructed and verified in a proper manner. We have been discussing transformations that are applied to a correct working program with the aim of achieving greater efficiency.

10.1.2   More complex cases

We now look at transformations which are of a slightly more ambitious nature. To begin with we note that procedure or function calls can often be removed and effectively replaced by the procedure or function body. Two simple cases are worthy of special mention:

With simple, frequently executed operators the overheads involved in the calls often exceed the cost of evaluating the body; considerable savings can often be made in these cases.

If a procedure contains no parameters and if there is only one call then that call can be replaced by a jump to the start of the procedure body provided an appropriate jump is incorporated at the end of the procedure body.

We now look at other transformations.

Absorption and expansion

As a general rule absorption involves taking constructs from outside to within a construct. To illustrate

if B **then** S **else** T **end if**; U

is equivalent to

if B **then** S; U **else** T; U **end if** ;

There are many other similar situations involving other kinds of conditionals including case statements. Absorption can also be applied to loops of various kinds. Thus

loop S;   **exit when** B; T **end loop**; U;

is equivalent to

loop S;   **if** B **then** U;   **exit**;   **end if**; T;   **end loop**;

Other similar examples can be given.

The converse of absorption is sometimes referred to as expansion. The transformations are similar to those above, though applied in reverse.

Transformations involving loops

A variety of transformations can be applied to loops of various kinds. These are illustrated by what follows.

278

False iteration

loop S; **exit when** *TRUE*; T **end loop**

is equivalent to S. There are other versions of this for the different kinds of loops.

Removing double iteration

loop loop S **end loop**; **end loop**

is equivalent to

loop S **end loop**

provided that any exit statements within S are suitably modified.

Loop inversion

loop S; T **end loop**

is equivalent to

loop S; **loop** T; S **end loop**; **end loop**

provided the exit statements are suitably modified, i.e. exit statements inside the inner loop must be replaced by other exit statements which cause a jump completely out of the double loop.

Test inversion

loop if B **then** S; **exit**; **else** T **end if**; **end loop**

is equivalent to

if B **then** S **else loop** T; **exit when** B; **end loop**; **end if**

Repetition

loop S **end loop**

is equivalent to

loop S; S **end loop**

or even

loop S; S; S **end loop**

etc. These are particular cases of a transformation which states that

loop S **end loop** is equivalent to **loop** T **end loop**

if and only if

loop S **end loop** is equivalent to **loop** T; S **end loop**

Loop expansion

Assuming that each possible exit from F ends with a sequence of statements G then

279

loop F **end loop**;

is equivalent to

loop loop F' **end loop**; G **end loop**;

where F' is obtained from F by replacing all occurrences of G by **exit** and suitably adjusting the other exit statements.

10.1.3 An example

We look now at an example which illustrates the use of several of the transformations we have mentioned. The example involves a discussion about

while not B **loop if** T **then** U **else** V **and if**;   **end loop**;

For convenience we rewrite this as

loop
     if B **then exit**; **end if**;
     if T **then** U **else** V **end if**;
end loop

and abbreviate this to

loop G **end loop**

where G is shorthand for

if B **then exit**; · **end if**;
if T **then** U **else** V **end if**;

We require to show that the above loop is equivalent to

while not B **loop if** T **then** U; G **else** V **end if**;   **end loop**;

By the repetition rule we know that

loop G **end loop**;

is equivalent to

loop
     if B **then exit**; **end if**;
     if T **then** U **else** V **end if**;
     G
end loop;

Absorbing G into both branches of the preceding conditional produces

loop
     if B **then exit**; **end if**;
     if T **then** U; G **else** V; G **end if**;
end loop;

Now loop expansion can be employed to move one of the occurrences of G out of the loop, thus giving:

280

L : **loop**

    loop

        if B **then exit** L; **end if**;

        if T **then** U; H **else** V; **exit**; **end if**;

    end loop;

    G

    end loop;

where H is now an abbreviation for

    if B **then exit** L;   **end if**;

    if T **then** U **else** V **end if**;

We have now established the fact that the original loop

    loop G **end loop**;

is equivalent to a loop of the form

    loop loop K **end loop**; G **end loop**;

for some appropriate K. Application of the repetition rule now implies that the original loop is equivalent to

    loop loop K **end loop**;   **end loop**;

Removing double iteration this is equivalent to

    loop K' **end loop**

where K' is obtained from K by suitably adjusting or removing the exit statements. If we now note that when the exit statements are adjusted then H become equivalent to G, we obtain the result that the original loop is equivalent to

    loop

        if B **then exit**; **end if**;

        if T **then** U; G **else** V **end if**;

    end loop;

This gives the required result.

Let us now look at a particular use of this example. The following illustrates how transformations can be used to change a program which is difficult to handle from a verification point of view into an equivalent program which is easier to handle. In particular consider the problem of establishing the fact that the following terminates:

    while $N >= 2$ **loop**

        if $ODD(N)$ **then**

            $N := N + 1$;

        else

            $N := N/2$;

        end if;

    end loop;

Here N is an integer variable and *ODD* tests for odd integers.

Employing the rule we have just established gives the equivalent program

> **while** $N >= 2$ **loop**
> > **if** *ODD*(N) **then**
> > > $N := N + 1$;
> > > **if** $N < 2$ **then exit; end if**;
> > > **if** *ODD*(N) **then** $N := N + 1$; **else** $N := N/2$; **end if**;
> >
> > **else**
> > > $N := N/2$;
> >
> > **end if**;
>
> **end loop**;

Consider the body of the loop in the case where $N >= 2$ and N is odd. Incrementing N by 1 makes N even and certainly greater than 2. Thus if redundant tests are removed the above is equivalent to

> **while** $N >= 2$ **loop**
> > **if** *ODD*(N) **then**
> > > $N := N + 1$;
> > > $N := N/2$;
> >
> > **else**
> > > $N := N/2$;
> >
> > **end if**;
>
> **end loop**;

It is relatively simple to establish that the above terminates. The value of N decreases on each circuit of the loop yet it is never made negative by the loop. Termination can be readily guaranteed.

10.2   Removal of recursion

Of all the program transformations that appear in the literature this is undoubtedly the most common.

In earlier chapters we saw that recursive procedures tend to be simpler and easier to verify than their iterative counterparts. Apart from this

> recursive solutions are often apparent whereas corresponding iterative solutions are less obvious;
>
> programming techniques such as divide-and-conquer tend to encourage recursion;
>
> recursive data structures tend to suggest recursive procedures.

We mention another very important aspect of recursion. In specifying axioms for abstract data types we saw that algebraic axiomatics provided one very convenient approach. To prove that a given implementation was faithful we had to establish that calls of Ada procedures, etc., satisfied the algebraic axioms. The difficulty of this task was greatly reduced by making use of recursive procedures.

282

On occasion it is possible to introduce recursion into a program only to remove it by some of the transformations given below and so obtain a gain in efficiency. This may seem strange and unnatural. However it sometimes happens in programs that make use of stacks. Placing an item on the stack may be interpreted as an obligation to perform an operation on that item. It is often possible to interpret this as a recursive call. If the recursion can be removed without recourse to a stack gains in efficiency may be anticipated. In looking at the transformations below the reader should look at them with these ideas in mind.

Some of the transformations we give can be interpreted as transformations which give a better structure to programs. There is a strong similarity between labels and parameterless procedures. The occurrence of a label L can be regarded as constituting the definition of a procedure L. Jumps to L can be interpreted as procedure calls; these may effectively be recursive.

To appreciate the advantages of removing recursion let us begin with a simplified view of how a compiler might implement recursion. This will have the added advantage of hinting at possible methods of replacing recursion.

10.2.1 Implementing recursion

In block-structured programming languages the storage that is allocated for the use of variables and so on is often taken from a kind of stack. Below we discuss one possible (simplified) view of what can happen at execution or run time. In fact much of what follows must also be performed in a modified way at compile time in order to calculate appropriate addresses and so on.

We shall represent a stack as an (unbounded) array and a pointer. As items are added to the stack the pointer is incremented, as items are removed the pointer is decremented.

Consider the program fragment:

```
declare
        A, B: INTEGER;
        - - other declarations
begin
        - - statements
        declare
                B, C: CHARACTER;
                - - other declarations
        begin
                - - statements
        end;
        - - statements
end;
```

Initially the stack can be thought of as being empty. As execution progresses it can be imagined that the following happens. On entering the outer block space is allocated for A and B, as in figure 10.1. On entry to the next block a new stack frame is introduced – the current value of the pointer is placed on the stack, the pointer is moved to point to the topmost element on the stack and space is allocated for the new variables (see figure 10.2). The act of placing the current pointer on the stack can be viewed as a process of remembering the previous state of affairs. Indeed, on leaving a block the stack pointer is restored to its former value by just recovering it from the stack.

It can easily be seen that the idea generalises to programs which have blocks nested to an arbitrary depth, and to programs which make use of dynamic arrays. The entire mechanism works satisfactorily.

Within the object code (usually machine code) program variables are represented by offsets from the current or some previous value of the stack pointer. Thus in the inner block above B will be represented by the current value of the pointer offset by 1; A will be represented by the previous value offset by 1. This is very suitable from the point of view of recursion.

Procedure calls can be processed in much the same manner as entry to blocks. When a call occurs

> a new stack frame is introduced;
> the current stack pointer is remembered by placing it on the stack as before;
> parameters are placed on top of the stack (and represented as offsets from the current pointer).

Fig. 10.1.

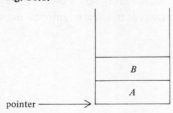

Fig. 10.2.

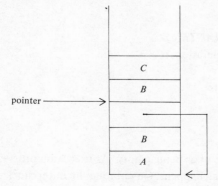

284

The instructions that form the procedure body can then be executed and this may involve further allocation of space on the stack. When the execution of the procedure body ends, the stack pointer is reset to the value it held immediately before the call occurred. All the necessary information is on the stack. Note that also a return address must be kept somewhere, either on the same or on another stack; when the procedure call ends the next instruction to be executed is obtained by interpreting the return address in an appropriate manner.

With recursive calls this same mechanism still works. On successive calls successive sets of pointers, parameters and return addresses are stacked, only to be removed as the recursion unwinds. If some of these overheads can be removed by eliminating recursion substantial increases in efficiency can be obtained.

We have given only a very brief résumé of what might be involved in implementing recursion. A more complete picture would include:

> introduction of other pointers to deal with certain features of programming languages;
> discussion of how the above process might be simplified to avoid excessive use of pointers and to 'compactify' the stack.

However, the brief description given above will suffice for the ensuing discussion on program transformations designed to remove recursion.

10.2.2 Removal of recursion from procedures

We divide the topic of recursion removal into two and talk first about the removal of recursion from procedures. Section 10.2.4 will be concerned with the removal of recursion from functions.

In what follows we wish to make the description of the transformation as general as possible. Accordingly we shall use P for predicate, ST for a statement or sequence of statements, and so on. In this way each transformation that is described is applicable to a large family of programs.

Recursive procedure I

procedure *FF* **is**
begin
       if *P* **then**
           ST;
           FF;
       end if;
end *FF*;

Equivalent iterative procedure I

procedure *FF* **is**
begin

```
            while P loop
                  ST;
            end loop;
      end FF;
```

Recursive procedure II

```
procedure FF(X: in T) is
begin
      if P(X) then
            ST(X);
            FF(G(X));
      end if;
end FF;
```

Equivalent iterative procedure II

```
procedure FF(X: in T) is
      Y : T := X;
begin
      while P(Y) loop
            ST(Y);
            Y := G(Y);
      end loop;
end FF;
```

Notes

(a) Y is a suitable auxiliary variable not used for any other purpose. If there is conflict with another variable some different identifier should be employed.

(b) If there are several input parameters, several variables have to be introduced and the corresponding initialisations performed.

Recursive procedure III

```
procedure FF(X: in T) is
begin
      if P(X) then
            F(X);
      else
            ST(X);
            FF(G1(X));
            FF(G2(X));
      end if;
end FF;
```

Equivalent iterative procedure III

The iterative procedures given below make use of an auxiliary variable Y which, it is assumed, is used for no other purpose. Should this not be so some other suitable variable can be used.

A stack S is also introduced. We assume that there is available an abstract data type *STACK* with the properties outlined in chapter 7. In particular, declaration of an item of type *STACK* automatically produces an empty stack. The elements of *STACK* are assumed to be of type T, similar to the type of the parameter. Should several parameters of possibly differing types be required it may be necessary to have several stacks. The principles involved are similar.

Equivalent iterative procedure III(i)

procedure $FF(X: \text{ in } T)$ **is**
    $Y: T := X;$
    $S: STACK;$ - - initialises S to empty stack; elements of type T
begin
    $PUSH(S, Y);$
    loop
        $PULL(S, Y);$
        if $P(Y)$ **then**
          $F(Y);$
        else
          $ST(Y);$
          $PUSH(S, G2(Y));$
          $PUSH(S, G1(Y));$
        end if;
        exit when $NULL(S);$
    end loop;
end $FF;$

An improvement to the above can be obtained by noting that $PUSH(S, G1(Y))$ is essentially followed by $PULL(S, Y)$. This pair of instructions can be replaced by an assignment

    $Y := G1(Y);$

The result is as follows:

Equivalent iterative procedure III(ii)

procedure $FF(X: \text{ in } T)$ **is**
    $Y: T := X;$
    $S: STACK;$ - - initialises S to empty stack; items of type T
begin
    $PUSH(S, Y);$

```
            loop
                    PULL(S, Y);
                    while not P(Y) loop
                            ST(Y);
                            PUSH(S, G2(Y));
                            Y := G1(Y);
                    end loop;
                    F(Y);
                    exit when NULL(S);
            end loop;
      end FF;
```

Recursive procedure IV

```
procedure FF(X: in T) is
begin
      if P(X) then
        F(X);
      else
        FF(G1(X));
        FF(G2(X));
        ST(X);
      end if;
end FF;
```

Equivalent iterative procedure IV(i)

We again make use of a stack S which holds pairs of quantities, a function and its argument. Since only a limited number of functions are involved a code can be introduced for each function (e.g. a distinct integer). These codes are assumed to be of some type *CODE*. The code for *FF* is represented by *FF_CODE* and the code for *ST* by *ST_CODE*.

The operations *PUSH* and *PULL* operate by placing two items on the stack or removing two items from the stack on each call.

Equivalent iterative procedure IV(ii)

```
procedure FF(X: in T) is
      Y: T := X;
      FN_CODE : CODE;
      S: STACK; - - initially empty stack
begin
      PUSH(S, FF_CODE, Y);
      loop
```

```
            PULL(S, FN_CODE, Y);
            if FN_CODE = ST_CODE then
                ST(Y);
            else
                if P(Y) then
                   F(Y);
                else
                   PUSH(S, ST_CODE, Y);
                   PUSH(S, FF_CODE, G2(Y));
                   PUSH(S, FF_CODE, G1(YY));
                end if;
            end if;
            exit when NULL(S);
        end loop;
    end FF;
```

As in the case of procedure III improvements can be made on noting that the call

```
        PUSH(S, FF_CODE, G1(YY))
```

is essentially followed by

```
        PULL(S, FN_CODE, Y)
```

This leads to:

Equivalent iterative procedure IV(iii)

```
procedure FF(X: in T)is
        Y: T := X;
        FN_CODE : CODE;
        S: STACK; - - initially empty stack
begin
        PUSH(S, FF_CODE, Y);
        loop
            PULL(S, FN_CODE, Y);
            if FN_CODE = ST_CODE then
                ST(Y);
            else
                while not P(Y) loop
                    PUSH(S, ST_CODE, Y);
                    PUSH(S, FF_CODE, G2(X));
                    Y := G1(Y);
                end loop;
                F(Y);
```

```
                    end if;
                exit when NULL(S);
            end loop;
        end FF;
```

10.2.3 Justifying the transformations

Close examination of the method of implementing recursion will lead to the conclusion that the following rule holds:

> If the last action of a procedure A before returning is to call procedure B then merely reset any parameters that are used and jump to the start of procedure B.

This rule holds even when A and B are the same procedure.

To understand the transformation applied to recursive procedure III we take a special view of the stack. Putting an item Z on the stack can be regarded as an obligation to perform the calculation $FF(Z)$. Thus:

> the procedure begins by putting X on the stack;
> each circuit of the loop begins by removing the next item from the stack;
> the recursive calls $FF(G1(X))$ and $FF(G2(X))$ merely cause appropriate items to be placed on the stack;
> the computation ends when the stack is empty.

In performing transformation IV the stack is viewed in a more complex manner. It records obligations to evaluate either $FF(Y)$ or $ST(Y)$ for some appropriate Y. The stack must therefore be more complex than before and it must hold both functions and arguments. Since there are only two alternative functions FF and ST it is convenient to code these in some obvious fashion, e.g. FF may be represented by the integer 0 and ST by the integer 1. The iterative solution IV(i) follows from these observations.

10.2.4 Removing recursion from functions

We now examine the problem of showing how recursion can be removed from functions. It is convenient to give iterative equivalents of certain recursive definitions. To provide some measure of generality we again make use of schemas – which use arbitrary functions such as P, F, K, H, etc.

For the recursive schemas I–VI below we give certain equivalences. In each of the iterative versions: the variable Z is used as the location in which the result is to be placed; the type VAR is used as a suitable type of any auxiliary variables; it is assumed that there is no confusion or interference caused by the introduction of auxiliary variables.

The schemas given are of a very general nature. Take for example recursive schema VI. This can be interpreted in various ways:

(i) Let X be of type *INTEGER*; then if

$P(X)$	is	$X = 0$,
$F(X)$	is	1,
$G1(X)$	is	X,
$G2(X)$	is	$X - 1$,
$H(X, Y)$	is	$X * Y$,

then *FF* calculates the factorial function.

(ii) Let X be a list of elements; then if

$P(X)$	is	$NULL(X)$,
$F(X)$	is	**null**,
$G1(X)$	is	$HEAD(X)$,
$G2(X)$	is	$TAIL(X)$,
$H(X, Y)$	is	$APPEND(Y, X)$ and adds X to the end of list Y,

then *FF* reverses the list X.

We now look at the transformations. In the recursive schemas obvious abbreviations are used for describing the recursive functions; the Ada equivalents can readily be produced. In all cases it is tacitly assumed that *FF* is well-defined, i.e. that the recursion actually terminates; frequently the function H can be interpreted as an operator of some kind; note that in Ada parameters of functions must be input parameters, so removing a source of difficulty. Proofs of the equivalences will be given in section 10.2.5.

Recursive schema I

$FF(X)$: **if** $P(X)$ **then return** $F(X)$; **else return** $FF(G(X))$; **end if**;

Equivalent iterative schema I

declare
      $Y: VAR := X$;
begin
      while not $P(Y)$ **loop**
          $Y := G(Y)$;
      end loop;
      $Z := F(Y)$;
end;

Recursive schema II

$FF(X)$: **if** $P(X)$ **then return** $F(X)$; **else return** $H(K(X)$,
$$FF(G(X)))\ \textbf{end if};$$

291

Equivalent iterative schema II

After execution of the following Z has the value $FF(X)$.

```
if P(X) then
    Z := F(X);
else
        declare
                Y: VAR := X;
        begin
                Z := K(Y);
                loop
                        Y := G(Y);
                        exit when P(Y);
                        Z := H(Z, K(Y));
                end loop;
                Z := H(Z, F(Y));
        end;
end if;
```

Assumption

This equivalence is dependent on the fact that H is associative, i.e. for arbitrary α, β and γ

$$H(\alpha, H(\beta, \gamma)) = H(H(\alpha, \beta), \gamma)$$

Recursive schema III

$FF(X, Y)$: **if** $P(X, Y)$ **then return** $F(X, Y)$; **else return** $FF(G1(X, Y),$
$$G2(X, Y)); \text{end if};$$

Equivalent iterative schema III

```
while not P(X, Y) loop
        declare
                T: VAR := G1(X, Y);
        begin
                Y := G2(X, Y);
                X := T;
        end;
end loop;
Z := F(X, Y);
```

Recursive schema IV

$FF(X)$: **if** $P(X)$ **then return** $F(X)$; **else return** $H(FF(G1(X)),$
$$FF(G2(X))); \text{end if};$$

Equivalent iterative schema IV

declare
$\quad\quad$ $Y1, Y2: VAR := F(X);$
begin
$\quad\quad$ $Z := F(X);$
$\quad\quad$ **while not** $P(X)$ **loop**
$\quad\quad\quad\quad$ $Z := H(Y1, Y2);$
$\quad\quad\quad\quad$ $Y1 := Y2;$
$\quad\quad\quad\quad$ $Y2 := Z;$
$\quad\quad\quad\quad$ $X := G1(X);$
$\quad\quad$ **end loop**;

Restrictions:

(*a*) H possesses the property that for all α, β and γ

$$H(\alpha, H(\beta, \gamma)) = H(\beta, H(\alpha, \gamma))$$

(*b*) $G1$ is obtained from $G2$ by replacing all occurrences of X by $G2$

Recursive schema V

$FF(X, Y)$: **if** $P(X, Y)$ **then return** $F(X, Y)$; **else return** $H(K(X, Y),$
$\quad\quad\quad\quad\quad\quad\quad\quad\quad\quad\quad\quad\quad\quad$ $FF(G1(X, Y), G2(X, Y)))$; **end if**;

Equivalent iterative schema V

$Z := F(X, Y);$
while not $P(X, Y)$ **loop**
$\quad\quad$ $Z := H(K(X, Y), Z);$
$\quad\quad$ **declare**
$\quad\quad\quad\quad$ $T: VAR := G1(X, Y);$
$\quad\quad$ **begin**
$\quad\quad\quad\quad$ $Y := G2(X, Y);$
$\quad\quad\quad\quad$ $X := T;$
$\quad\quad$ **end**;
end loop;

Restrictions

H satisfies the rule that for all α, β and γ

$$H(\alpha, H(\beta, \gamma)) = H(\beta, H(a, \gamma))$$

Recursive schema VI

$FF(X)$: **if** $P(X)$ **then return** $F(X)$; **else return** $H(G1(X),$
$\quad\quad\quad\quad\quad\quad\quad\quad\quad\quad\quad\quad\quad\quad$ $FF(G2(X)))$; **end if**;

Equivalent iterative schema VI

if $P(X)$ **then**
>$Z := F(X)$;

else
>$Z := G1(X)$;
>
>**loop**
>>$X := G2(X)$;
>>**exit when** $P(X)$;
>>$Z := H(Z, G1(X))$;
>
>**end loop**;
>$Z := H(Z, F(X))$;

end if;

Restriction

H is associative, i.e. for all α, β and γ

$$H(\alpha, H(\beta, \gamma)) = H(H(\alpha, \beta), \gamma)$$

Example of use

Let us give one illustration of the use of these transformations. In chapter 7 we examined certain abstract data types including *SET*. One of the operations which could be performed on an item of type *SET* was *MEMBER* which asked whether or not an element was a member of a set. The appropriate Ada routine was:

function *MEMBER* (*S*: **in** *SET*; *I* **in** *ELEM*) **return** *BOOLEAN* **is**
>$FOUND : BOOLEAN := FALSE$;

begin
>**if** $S /= EMPTYSET$ **then**
>>$FOUND := (I = S . ITEM)$ **or** $MEMBER(S . REST, I)$;
>
>**end if**;
>**return** *FOUND*;

end *MEMBER*;

Note that a corresponding iterative version can be obtained in a straightforward manner, essentially by applying transformation V with

$P(X, Y)$	is	$X = EMPTYSET$,
$F(X, Y)$	is	$FALSE$,
$G1(X, Y)$	is	$X . REST$,
$G2(X, Y)$	is	Y,
$K(X, Y)$	is	$Y = X . ITEM$,
$H(X, Y)$	is	X **or** Y.

An appropriate iterative solution can then be obtained. The standard transformation gives one version but some very obvious improvements (simpler transformations) can be given to produce the much better version:

```
function MEMBER(S: in SET; I in ELEM) return BOOLEAN is
        FOUND : BOOLEAN := FALSE;
        T: SET := S;
begin
        while (T /= EMPTY_SET) and (not FOUND) loop
                FOUND := I = T . ITEM;
                T := T . REST;
        end loop;
        return FOUND;
end MEMBER;
```

The transformations given so far are all relatively straightforward in that nothing corresponding to a stack is present – it is not required. However there are transformations where the concept of a stack does appear and is necessary.

Consider again recursive schema IV but without the restriction on the relationships between $G1$ and $G2$. The transformation given below does what is required.

Recursive schema VII

$FF(X)$: **if** $P(X)$ **then return** $F(X)$; **else return** $H(FF(G1(X))$,
$$FF(G2(X)))\text{: }\textbf{end if;}$$

Equivalent iterative schema VII

```
declare
        S: STACK;
        Z: VAR := UNIT;
        T: VAR;
begin
        PUSH(S, X);
        while not IS_EMPTY(S) loop
                PULL(S, T);
                if P(T) then
                        Z := H(Z, F(T));
                else
                        PUSH(S, G2(T));
                        PUSH(S, G1(T));
                end if;
        end;
```

Restrictions and notes

(a) H is associative as in schema IV.

(b) *UNIT* has the property that for all α

$H(UNIT, \alpha) = \alpha$.

(c) *VAR* is the type of the result delivered by *FF*.

10.2.5 Proofs of equivalence

A statement that there are equivalences between recursive schemes and corresponding iterative schemas is not good enough. These equivalences require justification in the form of mathematical proofs. In this section we examine how such proofs might be obtained.

Recursive schema I

Let us begin with recursive schema I. A proof of the (partial) correctness of the transformation can be obtained from the following:

declare
> $Y: VAR := X$;

begin
> **while not** $P(Y)$ - - $\{FF(Y) = FF(X)\}$
>> **loop**
>>> $Y := G(Y)$;
>> **end loop**;
>> $Z := F(Y)$;

end;
- - $\{Z = FF(X)\}$

To establish that the above iteration terminates define a relation $>$ as follows:

> if **not** $P(Y)$ then $Y > G(Y)$

Since we assume that *FF* is well-defined the sequence must be well-founded and termination can be guaranteed.

Recursive schema II

A proof of equivalence can be used on the following:

if $P(X)$ **then**
> $Z := F(X)$;

else
> **declare**
>> $Y: VAR := X$;

> **begin**
>> $Z := K(Y)$;
>> **loop**
>>> $Y := G(Y)$;
>>> - - $\{H(X, FF(Y)) = FF(X)\}$

296

$$\textbf{exit when } P(Y);$$
$$Z := H(Z, K(Y));$$
$$\textbf{end loop};$$
$$Z := H(Z, F(Y));$$
$$\textbf{end};$$
$$\textbf{end if};$$
$$- -\{Z = FF(X)\}$$

The essence of the proof is the loop invariant. This can be established in the usual way, by back substitution using the associativity of H. The verification condition is

$$[H(Z, FF(Y)) = FF(X)] \wedge \textbf{not } P(Y)$$
$$\supset$$
$$[H(H(Z, K(Y)), FF(G1(Y))) = FF(X)]$$

$$H(H(Z, K(Y)), FF(G1(Y)))$$
$$= H(Z, H(K(Y), FF(G1(Y)))) \quad \text{by associativity of } H,$$
$$= H(Z, FF(Y)) \quad \text{from definition of } FF \text{ since } \textbf{not } P(Y),$$
$$= FF(X) \quad \text{as required.}$$

To establish the initial truth of the invariant note that on first reaching the cutpoint

$$Y = G(X) \quad \text{and} \quad Z = K(X).$$

So

$$H(Z, FF(Y)) = H(K(X), FF(G(X)))$$
$$= FF(X) \text{ since } \textbf{not } P(X).$$

Now suppose that the loop terminates. Then

$$H(Z, FF(Y)) = FF(X)$$

and also $P(Y)$ is false. The latter implies that $FF(Y) = F(Y)$ and the required partial correctness is readily established. Total correctness depends on the fact that $FF(\dot{X})$ is well-defined: define a relation $>$ as follows

$$\text{if } \textbf{not } P(Y) \text{ then } Y > G(Y)$$

The sequence $X > G(X) > G(G(X))$ is well-founded since FF is well-defined.

This completes the proof of equivalence between the iterative and the recursive schemas.

Recursive schema VII

The proof associated with this will, naturally, make use of a stock. We denote by $S|X$ a stack whose topmost element is X; removing an item from this stack then leaves S.

We introduce a relation $>$ defined as follows:

$$\text{if } FF(X) \text{ is well-defined then}$$

297

$$\text{if } \mathbf{not}\ P(X) \text{ then } X > G1(X) \text{ and } X > G2(X)$$

This produces a sequence which can have no infinite decreasing subsequences – otherwise the recursion would never end and $FF(X)$ would not be well-defined.

We now introduce another relation $>$ derived from the iterative schema VII. Basically this describes how one circuit of the loop alters the pair consisting of the stack and the value held in Z:

$$\text{if } P(T) \text{ then } (S|T;Z) > (S;H(X,F(T)))$$
$$\text{if } \mathbf{not}\ P(T) \text{ then } (S|T;Z) > (S|G2(T)|G1(T);Z)$$

We now show that for any stack S and any value X for which $FF(X)$ is well-defined there is a positive integer t with the property that t applications of $>$ leave S unaltered and the value $H(Z, FF(X))$ in Z. In mathematical terms

$$(S|X;Z) >^t (S;H(Z,FF(X)))$$

We give a proof by induction based on the relation $>$ defined earlier. There are two cases to consider:

1. Suppose $P(X)$ is true; then

$$(S|X;Z) > (S;H(Z,F(X))) = (S;H(Z,FF(X)))$$

as required.

2. Suppose $P(X)$ is not true; then

$$(S|X;Z)$$
$$>(S|G2(X)|G1(X);Z).$$

Now we can apply the inductive hypothesis since we have a stack with $G1(X)$ on top and $X > G1(X)$. At a later stage we can again use induction since $X > G2(X)$. Thus

$$(S|X;Z)$$
$$> (S|G2(X)|G1(X);X)$$
$$>^{t1} (S|G2(X);H(Z,FF(G1(X)))) \quad \text{by induction,}$$
$$>^{t2} (S;H(H(Z,FF(G1(X))),FF(G2(X)))) \quad \text{by induction,}$$
$$= (S;H(Z,H(FF(G1(X)),FF(G2(X))))) \quad \text{by associativity of } H,$$
$$= (S;H(Z,FF(X))) \quad \text{by definition of } FF.$$

We have therefore shown that

$$(S|X;Z)$$
$$>^t (S;H(Z,FF(X)))$$

for $t = t1 + t2 + 1$.

The required result now follows by induction on $>$.

We have proved the equivalences of certain transformations. The remainder will be left as exercises for the reader. From the proofs an important observation can be made. We note that the original recursive function plays an important role in the loop invariant of the iterative version. Conversely it can be argued that finding invariants of loops is aided by finding the underlying recursive function.

298

10.2.6 Folding and unfolding

The transformations we have given for removing recursion appear to cover a wide variety of situations. Indeed they do. But suppose we have a function which evaluates the scalar product of two vectors A and B of size N - vectors are essentially arrays of real numbers:

function $SCALAR\_PRODUCT(A, B: VECTOR\ N: INTEGER)$
$$\text{\textbf{return} } FLOAT \text{ \textbf{is}}$$

$\quad\quad SUM: FLOAT;$

begin

$\quad\quad$ **if** $N = 0$ **then**

$\quad\quad\quad\quad SUM := 0.0;$

$\quad\quad$ **else**

$\quad\quad\quad\quad SUM := A(N) * B(N) + SCALAR\_PRODUCT(A, B, N - 1);$

$\quad\quad$ **end if**;

$\quad\quad$ **return** $SUM;$

$\quad\quad$ **end** $SCALAR\_PRODUCT;$

The function given above could be used in the following way:

$$SCALAR\_PRODUCT(A, B, N) + SCALAR\_PRODUCT(C, D, N)$$

None of the transformations we have discussed obviously applies to this situation. Yet if we could arrange that the two recursive calls were in some way combined to form a single recursive call then at least the overheads of recursion could be halved. In fact it may be possible to remove them completely since it may be the case that one of the earlier transformations can be applied to the resulting function.

Suppose we introduce the function $F(A, B, C, D, N)$ defined so that

$$F(A, B, C, D, N) = SCALAR\_PRODUCT(A, B, N) +$$
$$SCALAR\_PRODUCT(C, D, N).$$

We can also write, on the assumption that $N \geqslant 0$,

$$SCALAR\_PRODUCT(A, B, C, D, N + 1) =$$
$$A(N + 1) * B(N + 1) + SCALAR\_PRODUCT(A, B, C, D, N).$$

We now apply a process called *unfolding*; unfolding with this definition of $SCALAR\_PRODUCT(A, B, C, D, N + 1)$ takes

$$F(A, B, C, D, N + 1) = SCALAR\_PRODUCT(A, B, N + 1) +$$
$$SCALAR\_PRODUCT(C, D, N + 1)$$

to

$$F(A, B, C, D, N + 1) = A(N + 1) * B(N + 1) + SCALAR\_PRODUCT(A, B, N) +$$
$$C(N + 1) * D(N + 1) + SCALAR\_PRODUCT(C, D, N)$$

At this stage we apply folding to give

$$F(A, B, C, D, N + 1) = A(N + 1) * B(N + 1) + C(N + 1) * D(N + 1) +$$
$$F(A, B, C, D, N)$$

299

A suitable recursive definition of F can be produced as a result.

We have used the terms unfolding and folding above. We now give formal definitions of these

Definition of unfolding

If $E = E'$ and $F = F'$ are equations and if some instance of E appears in F' then unfolding involves replacing that instance by the corresponding instance of E' and F''. Then the equation $F = F''$ can be assumed.

Definition of folding

If $E = E'$ and $F = F'$ are equations and if some instance of E' appears in F' then folding involves replacing that instance by the corresponding instance of E to obtain F''. Then the equation $F = F''$ can be assumed.

In the examples given previously unfolding was equated with expanding by applying a definition in the same way; folding took the form of contracting, again using a definition. By means of these we managed to replace two recursive definitions by one. Equivalently it could be used to replace two iterations by one. Various other situations which do not necessarily involve recursion can be viewed as instances of folding and unfolding, e.g. replacing a procedure call by the corresponding procedure body with appropriate substitution for parameters.

10.3   Module level transformations

In this section we look at transformations which involve potentially large sections of programs, in particular complete modules. Before proceeding to look carefully at some specific transformations, we list some other transformations which should be mentioned but which we shall not study in any great detail.

In view of what we said earlier regarding procedures we note that it is possible to essentially remove module and procedure boundaries and in effect transfer pieces of code from one module to another. This is desirable especially when the flow of information between modules would otherwise be very high.

We also note that in certain circumstances there are advantages to be gained by introducing transformations which would permit

parts of programs to be overlaid, so providing economies in terms of savings in store;

the introduction of parallelism which did not previously exist.

Having noted the possibility of these we choose to avoid further discussion of them and proceed to look at other transformations involving modules.

10.3.1   Implementing abstract data types

In looking at the problems of specifying and implementing abstract data types we witnessed a division between what the user of an abstract data

300

type would see and what the implementor would see; only the relevant operations and a description of their effect would be available to the user whereas the implementor had to have access to every single aspect of the implementation.

From the point of view of transformations these observations mean that a module can be replaced by another module which supplies the same facilities – to the user and the program verifier the same operations must be provided and their effect must be the same. In the event of an implementation of an abstract data type being inefficient in some sense it may be possible to provide an alternative implementation which is more efficient in given circumstances.

Example 10.3.1a   Stacks and queues

Data structures such as stacks and queues can be implemented using linked storage. Such implementations can involve large amounts of allocating and deallocating space and can be costly. Alternative implementations of

(a) a stack may use an array (possibly of fixed size) and a pointer for the top of the stack;

(b) a queue may use an array and two pointers, one for the front and the other for the back of the queue. On reaching the top of the array, items can then be added in at empty positions at the foot of the array.

The ideas mentioned above can be generalised to some considerable extent. Essentially the transformation that is being performed results from an alternative and more appropriate kind of data structure or from an alternative or more appropriate algorithm.

10.3.2   Program inversion

The view that all programs should be simple and perform simple tasks can result in the proliferation at the design stage of small programs each of which performs simple tasks. This becomes all the more likely when, in dealing with data processing examples, structure clashes occur and are resolved by the introduction of intermediate files. It is often desirable to optimise and if possible remove such files, not at the design stage but when the system has been implemented. A transformation process known as *program inversion* can be used to accomplish this. Let us illustrate program inversion by describing a common application of the process.

Compilers generally consist of several distinct phases. In a simplified scheme the structure of a compiler may be described in the following terms:

Lexical analysis phase: the source code is read and the individual characters are grouped together in the natural way; in the process irrelevant spaces and comments are removed; the output is generally a coded representation of the input text and some associated symbol tables.

Syntax analysis phase: the input to this phase is the coded version of the source program produced by the lexical analysis phase; during syntax analysis the structure of the input is determined and represented as a tree structure which then forms the output.

Code generation phase: the tree from the syntax analysis phase and the symbol tables from the lexical analysis phase are used by the code generator which produces code for the original source program.

In the above description we used the word phase and we were careful to do so. These separate phases could be implemented as three distinct (and possibly more) programs. Alternatively the phases could be implemented as a single program.

When implemented as separate programs it is necessary to have intermediate files to hold the output from one phase which then acts as input to the next phase. The large amount of input and output entailed is a source of inefficiency which can be removed in the following way. The lexical analyser can be wrapped up as a procedure which is called by the syntax analyser when the next item is required; read statements within the syntax analyser are replaced by procedure calls. We say that the lexical analyser is inverted with respect to the intermediate file which thereby disappears. Alternatively the syntax analyser could be inverted with respect to the intermediate file: in this case write instructions within the lexical analyser are replaced by calls to the syntax analyser which is wrapped up as a subroutine which returns control to the lexical analyser.

In cases of program inversion it should be noted that the resulting programs are much larger. Essentially two programs have been combined into one program. In the process few instructions have been disposed of, the two sets of instructions have merely been carefully combined. Whatever instructions are saved occur in the input and output of information and possibly its packing and coding.

We have described one use of program inversion. There are many other ways in which it can be used in (such apparently diverse areas as) compiling techniques, in data processing and in many other areas.

10.3.3 Basic block reorganisation

We now look at a transformation technique for performing some potentially massive reorganisation and restructuring of programs. The transformations can be performed at several possible levels: at the level of individual statements, at the level of modules, or at an intermediate level which uses the concept of a basic block.

Definition By a *basic block* we shall mean a sequence of consecutive statements which have precisely one entry point, namely the first statement of the block.

The term basic block has its origins in the definition of Fortran 1966. The Fortran designers were originally preoccupied with considerations of efficiency

and basic blocks were seen as a means whereby a compiler could reorganise
a given program to produce something much more efficient.

We now note that a compiler can determine all the basic blocks within a given
program together with the interconnections between them. We shall not be
concerned with precisely how the various basic blocks are interconnected –
adjacent parts may be in separate modules, they may be connected by labels and
jumps by procedure calls, etc. We are only concerned with identifying the basic
blocks and their interconnections.

The basic structure of a program can be represented by a diagram which shows
basic blocks and the connections between them. If we represent basic blocks by
(capital or small) letters we can have a flow of control of the kind given in
figure 10.3. The start and end we denote by ∇ and Δ respectively.

The example shows the two possibilities, a forward jump and a backward
jump which is effectively a loop. Capital letters represent basic blocks with
multiple exits and small letters represent basic blocks with single exits. Between
each basic block there is no noticeable action performed, not even a test or the
like; the complete flow of control is represented in the diagram.

We now introduce some definitions which we shall need in the sequel.

Definitions

Let B_1 and B_2 be basic blocks. Then

(*a*) B_2 is said to be a *post-dominator* of B_1 if each path from B_1 to the end Δ
 contains B_2.

(*b*) B_2 is an *immediate post-dominator* of B_2 if B_2 is a post-dominator of B_1
 and if B_2 is the first post-dominator to occur in each path from B_1 to Δ.

On the assumption that a program is correct and therefore terminates, the
immediate post-dominator of each basic block can be given.

Example 10.3.3a

Consider the program structure of figure 10.1. The immediate post-
dominators are as follows:

Basic block: a b c d e f g A B C ∇ Δ
Immediate post-dominator: A B C e f Δ b e e e a none

Having reached this stage we can now demonstrate a strong similarity between
the above and a grammar. The flow of control within a program can be written

Fig. 10.3. Example of flow of control using basic blocks.

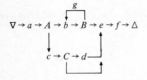

303

in the form of each basic block followed by its immediate post-dominator:

$$\nabla \to a \to A \to e \to f \to \triangle$$

or, omitting arrows,

$$\nabla \, a \, A \, e \, f \, \triangle$$

Now, however, A must be presented in a similar notation as either

$$b \, B \quad \text{or} \quad c \, C.$$

C and D have now to be defined in a similar way. In short the entire structure can be represented as the following (using vertical bars for 'or' and : := for 'is defined to be')

$$
\begin{aligned}
program: &:= \nabla \quad a \quad A \quad e \quad f \quad \triangle \\
A: &:= b \quad B \quad | \quad c \quad C \\
B: &:= g \quad b \quad B \quad | \quad \emptyset \\
C: &:= d \quad | \quad \emptyset
\end{aligned}
$$

The symbol $\emptyset$ denotes the empty symbol or null block.

This description of the flow of control through the program can now be used for restructuring purposes. Let us illustrate the possibilities:

Basic block A
This can be replaced by

A;
if *condition*_1 **then**
    $b; B$;
else
    $c; C$;
end if;

Here *condition*_1 decides whether $b; B$ or $c; C$ is selected.

Basic block B
Since B is effectively defined recursively the basic block B may be replaced by

loop
    B;
    exit when *condition*_2;
    $g; b$;
end loop;

Here *condition*_2 determines whether $g; b; B$ or the null block will be performed.

Basic block C
This is replaced by

```
      C;
      if condition_3 then
            d;
      end if;
```

where *condition_3* determines which exit to select.

Suppose we now attempt to put all these pieces together to form the complete program:

```
      ∇; a; A;
      if condition_1 then
            b;
            loop
                  B;
                  exit when condition_2;
                  g; b;
            end loop;
      else
            c; C;
            if condition_3 then
                  d;
            end if;
      end if;
      e; f; Δ;
```

In the manner described above we can impose a sensible structure on programs; note the lack of labels and so on. In this discussion the various items represented by the letters a, b, c, A, B, C, etc., represented larger pieces of program such as procedures or modules. The same techniques could be applied to restructuring a combination of these or even the procedures or modules themselves.

By such methods a program originally written in terms of modules, procedures, and so on, and shown to be correct can be restructured to produce an equivalent but efficient program.

10.4   Further illustrations

Before ending this chapter let us give two examples which further extol the virtues of transformations. There are two simple examples – the first is due to Wirth, the second to Griffiths – and they show how transformations can help in the development of very neat and efficient programs.

Integer multiplication

Consider the task of multiplying together two non-negative integers A and B using only repeated addition, doubling and halving. The latter two operations can be executed efficiently on modern computers since they are implemented by shifting.

This example is very simple, in one sense. It is also somewhat unnatural in that most computers will effectively perform the operation in one machine instruction. However, we can assume that our computer does not have such an instruction.

The 'obvious' simple program is, if X, Y and R are suitable predeclared integer variables

```
X := A;
Y := B;
R := 0;
while Y /= 0 loop
      --{Y > 0 ∧ A * B = X * Y + R}
      R := R + A;
      Y := Y - 1;
end loop;
```

This version is particularly inefficient. Note, however, that the following piece of program will leave the invariant unaltered.

```
while Y mod 2 = 0 loop
      Y := Y/2;
      X := X * 2;
end loop;
```

This can now be inserted into the original program to produce a much more efficient version, namely

```
X := A;
Y := B;
R := 0
while Y /= 0 loop
      --{Y > 0 ∧ A * B = X * Y + R}
      while Y mod 2 = 0 loop
            Y := Y/2;
            X := X * 2;
      end loop;
      R := R + A;
      Y := Y - 1;
end loop;
```

What we have done in this example is to improve the program by considering the invariant. A correctness proof was obtained using a very simple-minded approach. The loop invariant and proof were left unaltered but the program was improved to produce a more efficient final version. The basic idea and the technique generalise in an interesting fashion.

Finding the mode

Let us now turn to an example we encountered earlier (see example 9.3*d*). This is the problem of finding the mode of a set of integers given as an array of elements in ascending order. Previously we saw a program produced by appealing to invariants. We now take a different approach.

Let $MODE(A, N)$ be a two-valued function which produces a pair consisting of the value of the mode and the number of times that mode appears in the array. Then we can state that

> if $N = 1$ then $MODE(A, N) = (A(1), 1)$
> if $N > 1$ then let $(P, Q) = MODE(A, N - 1)$;
>   now if $A(N) = A(N - Q)$ then $MODE(A, N) = (A(N), Q + 1)$
>   otherwise $MODE(A, N) = (P, Q)$

This (informal) definition of $MODE(A, N)$ is basically a definition of a recursive function. Transforming this into an iterative equivalent gives the neat and efficient program:

```
declare
        VALUE : INTEGER := A(1);
        NUMBER : INTEGER := 1;
begin
        for I in 2 .. N loop
                if A(I) = A(I − NUMBER) then
                    VALUE := A(I);
                    NUMBER := NUMBER + 1;
                end if;
        end loop;
        - - print results or whatever
end;
```

Exercises for chapter 10

1. Discuss how transformations may be used to transform

```
if P <= N then
        for I in M .. N loop
                if J < P then
                    X;
                else
                    Y;
                end if;
        end loop;
end if;
```

into

```
for J in M .. P loop
    X;
end loop;
```

for J **in** $P + 1 .. N$ **loop**
    Y;
end loop;

where the given variables have an appropriate meaning. Is it necessary to impose any restrictions on the form of P, N, X, etc.?

2. Consider the recursive program given in section 10.4 for finding the mode of a set of integers. What transformations are needed to produce an equivalent iterative program?

3. Demonstrate how recursive versions of the

   (*a*) factorial,
   (*b*) highest common factor

functions may be transformed into iterative functions.

4. What aspects of the design of Ada simplify the matter of applying transformations to Ada programs?
Are there any features of the design which tend to complicate it?

5. By considering some simple examples discuss how transformations affect the *proof* of correctness of a program.

6. To what extent are the transformations given in this chapter affected by the issue of side-effects resulting from Ada subprogram evaluation?
If there are difficulties how might these be overcome?

7. Give proofs of the correctness of the transformations II, IV, V, VI for removing recursion from function definitions.

8. Consider the sequence of recursive functions whose first two elements are:

   (*a*) $FF(X)$: **if** $X > 100$ **then return** $(X - 10)$;
       else return $FF(FF(X + 11))$; **end if**;
   (*b*) $GG(X)$: **if** $X > 100$ **then return** $(X - 10)$;
       else return $GG(GG(GG(X + 21)))$; **end if**;

Transform these into equivalent iterative versions. The fixed point is, in both cases, McCarthy's 91-function, namely $MC(X)$ where

$MC(X)$: **if** $X > 100$ **then return** $(X - 10)$; **else return** 91; **end if**;

9. Take two functions, e.g. the factorial and the highest common factor, which have commonly used iterative and recursive formulations. Show how the recursive version and an appropriate transformation help in determining the loop invariant of the iterative version.

10. From a recursive definition of the Fibonacci numbers derive by a sequence of transformations an equivalent efficient iterative version.

11. It is required to design a piece of program which takes a sequence of opening and closing brackets and decides whether or not the brackets match, i.e. the number of closing brackets equals the number of opening brackets and in a left to right scan never exceeds the number of opening brackets.
In forming his program a programmer decides to use a stack onto which opening brackets are placed. An occurrence of a closing bracket causes inspection of the stack and removal of the topmost opening bracket or a 'mismatch' message should this not exist.

By viewing the act of placing an open bracket on the stack as a recursive call show how recursion can be introduced into the program.

Now show how the recursion can be removed to produce a program more efficient than the original.

How would the above process have been affected if both round and square brackets could have appeared in the data?

12. Tree traversals usually take one of three forms: preorder, postorder or inorder. Demonstrate how the corresponding recursive procedures can be transformed into iterative counterparts.

13. Justify the claim that

procedure *FF* **is**;
begin

    if *P* **then**

      *ST*1; *FF*; *ST*2;

    else

      GG;

    end if;

end;

can be replaced by

procedure *FF* **is**

    I: *INTEGER* := 0;

begin

    while *P* **loop** *ST*1; $I := I + 1$; **end loop**;

    GG;

    while $I > 0$ **loop** *ST*2; $I := I - 1$; **end loop**;

end;

State clearly any limitations that must be imposed on the nature of *ST*1, *ST*2, *GG*.

Can these ideas be extended to procedures with parameters?

14. Show that

procedure *FF* **is**
begin

    if *P* **then**

      *ST*1; *FF*; *ST*2; *FF*;

    else

      GG;

    end if;

end;

can be replaced by

procedure *FF* **is**

    I: *INTEGER* := 0;

begin

    loop

      while *P* **loop** *ST*1; $I := I + 1$; **end loop**;

      GG;

      exit when $I = 0$;

      *ST*2;

$$I := I - 1;$$
  end loop;
end;

State any restrictions involving $ST1$, $ST2$, etc.
Extend the transformation to procedures which use parameters.

15. Extend the ideas of examples 13 and 14 to cover procedures of the following kind.

procedure *FF* **is**
begin
  if *P* **then**
   $ST1; FF; ST2; FF; \ldots; FF, STn;$
  else
   $GG;$
  end if;
end;

16. Consider a function of the following kind.

function $FF(X, Y:$ **in** $T1)$ **return** $T2$ **is**
begin
  if $P(X, Y)$ **then**
    return $FF(FF(F(X, Y), Y), Y);$
  else
    return $G(X, Y);$
  end if;
end;

Rewrite this in the form

function $FF(X, Y:$ **in** $T1)$ **return** $T2$ **is**
  $RESULT: T2;$
begin
  procedure *FFF* **is**
  begin
    if $P(X, Y)$ **then**
    $X := F(X, Y); FFF; X := RESULT; FFF;$
    else
     $RESULT := G(X, Y);$
    end if;
  end;
  FFF;
  return $RESULT;$
end;

Use the transformations of example 14 to show how recursion can be removed from a function.
Is this method applicable to recursive functions already examined?

17. Devise an iterative schema equivalent to

$FF(X):$ **if** $P(X)$ **then return** $F(X);$ **else return** $H(F(G(X)));$ **end if;**

Give a proof of the correctness of the transformation.

310

18. Show how transformations can be used to transform a recursive version of Ackermann's function into an equivalent iterative version.

19. Discuss the possibility of transformations for replacing iteration by recursion. What advantages might this have in relation to program verification (see section 7.4.2, etc.)?

11 AUTOMATIC METHODS

In examining and studying the various aspects and techniques involved in program verification the reader will no doubt have jumped to the conclusion that many of these techniques may well be candidates for automation. It might be imagined that it is possible to write programs which themselves find loop invariants, prove partial or total corrections, prove consistency of axioms, even construct parts or all of a program, and so on.

This chapter is concerned with putting the matter in perspective. We shall begin by looking at some slightly disturbing theoretical results. We then look at what can be salvaged.

11.1 Decidability

There are various mathematical results which should be mentioned in connection with the different aspects of program verification. These are concerned with the subject of decidability.

Definition

A particular question is said to be *decidable* if it is possible to design an algorithm which (always terminates and) answers the question giving the reply *yes* or *no*. A question is *undecidable* if it is not possible to device an algorithm of the kind described above.

The matter of decidability should not be regarded as any kind of slight on the ability of programmers. Decidability is not a statement about competence or a statement of the fact that a good enough programmer has not yet been born. If a question is undecidable then it has been shown mathematically that it is not possible (and never will be possible) to devise a suitable algorithm.

11.1.1 Some relevant theoretical results

Having introduced the idea of decidability we can now look at some results. Whenever we talk about programs it will be assumed that these are written in a language of the expressive power of Ada, say.

The halting problem theorem
The question of whether an arbitrary program terminates is undecidable.

In particular cases it is certainly possible to decide that a program terminates: a program which is free of all forms of loops including jumps and recursion must always terminate. But in general it is not possible to devise an algorithm to answer this question.

From the above result it naturally follows that we can deduce the following theorem.

Total correctness theorem
The question of whether an arbitrary program is totally correct is undecidable.

So far we have mentioned results which relate to total correctness but not partial correctness. In the context of the latter the following is appropriate.

Identity problem theorem
There is no algorithm for deciding whether or not two arbitrary arithmetic expressions are equivalent, i.e., yield the same result for all values of their parameters.

Suppose now that it were possible to decide whether or not an arbitrary program was partially correct. Then the decision procedure could be applied to programs of the following general form

$\quad$-- declarations and initialisation of $X1, X2, \ldots, XN$ and Z
$\quad\quad Z := F(X1, X2, \ldots, XN);$
$\quad$--$\{Z = G(X1, X2, \ldots, XN)\}$

Here F and G are arbitrary expressions involving $X1, X2, \ldots, XN$. The existence of a decision procedure to determine partial correctness would imply the existence of a decision procedure for determining the equivalence of arithmetic expressions. We know that the latter is not possible. Therefore we have the following.

Partial correctness theorem
There is no algorithm for determining whether or not an arbitrary program is partially correct.

One glaring omission from our discussion so far has been any mention of the question of whether automatic methods can help in determining loop invariants. In chapter 3 we noted certain heuristics which could be brought to bear on this task. Although we give no firm theoretical results it certainly appears that human inspiration in some form is needed to accomplish this task in general.

11.1.2 Abstract data types

In studying axioms for abstract data types we encountered the problems of deciding whether a given set of axioms did in fact define the semantics of the data type. There were problems in deciding whether the axioms were complete and whether they were inconsistent.

So that a clear distinction can be drawn between the meaning of the word completeness as used in mathematical logic and its meaning in abstract data types the term *sufficiently complete* has been coined to describe the latter. Briefly it means that the axioms provide semantics or meaning.

The problem of deciding whether a set of axioms is sufficiently complete is undecidable. However, by placing certain limitations on the axioms and on the language used to describe the axioms it is possible to provide an interesting enough set of axioms for which the question of sufficient completeness can be answered. Automatic methods therefore have a role to play. See Guttag and Horning (1978) for further reading.

The question of the consistency of a set of axioms is also undecidable. But in this case there are certain techniques that can be exploited and which are sufficient to demonstrate consistency. If it can be proved that an implementation of an abstract data type is correct then this is sufficient to guarantee consistency. It is to be hoped that such correctness proofs will always be provided and so consistency will be guaranteed.

11.2 Aids to program verification

Over the years programs have been designed to accomplish several of the tasks involved in program verification. We shall not attempt to list the details of them all. Instead we shall give a brief account of a few selected and significant examples.

11.2.1 The Boyer–Moore theorem prover

One of the first successful systems for mechanical program verification was designed by R. Boyer and S. Moore for operating on Lisp programs.

The Boyer-Moore theorem prover takes programs written in pure Lisp Properties of these programs are also stated as expressions which themselves are expressed in Lisp. The theorem prover then attempts to show that the program possesses the desired properties. It does this by applying simple heuristics and also structural induction – Lisp programs tend to be heavily recursive.

To illustrate the use of the system consider the case of a function called *REVERSE* for reversing the order of the elements in a list. To test the correctness of this function a programmer could input a Lisp expression such as

$$(EQUAL(REVERSE(REVERSE\ A))A)$$

This asks if the reverse of a reversed list gives the original list. If *REVERSE* has been properly programmed the above will be true. Unfortunately it can still be true if *REVERSE* has not been properly programmed, e.g. if *REVERSE* just leaves the list unaltered.

Boyer and Moore were acutely aware of the limitations of their system. They recognised that it could be used as a verification tool to establish properties of programs about as complex as a sorting procedure but not much more. However, they did recognise the worth and the promise that their approach held.

11.2.2 Synthesisers of inductive assertions

Given a program together with its input and output assertions a mechanical verifier might be expected to deduce whether or not the program meets its specifications as described by the assertions. One of the major obstacles to achieving this aim is the problem of deriving loop invariants.

At the Palo Alto Research Center in California S. M. German and B. Wegbriet have been working on this problem. Their system called VISTA provides assistance to a programmer in producing correct inductive assertions:

> In many cases it can produce the loop invariants, etc., substantially using the kinds of techniques we outlined earlier at the end of chapter 3.

> In a larger set of cases it can produce accurate invariants from incompletely specified assertions.

> There are modules which apply individual techniques and these can be invoked by the programmer who can interact with the verifier and request that particular modules or techniques be applied.

11.2.3 Program verifiers
The Stanford Pascal verifier

The Stanford Pascal verifier, SPV for short, is a program which basically checks the correctness of the proof of a Pascal program. It is written in a version of the programming language Lisp for use on the PDP 10 range of computers. It checks the correctness of programs written in Pascal Plus, a version of Pascal extended to include module facilities and concurrency.

One of two inputs to the verifier is a Pascal program supplemented with appropriate assertions. Of course this must possess an input assertion and an output assertion. There must also be assertions accompanying each repetitive statement (essentially loop invariants) and there must be pre- and post-conditions accompanying each procedure.

The SPV basically attempts to automate the inductive assertions method. The first action of the verifier is to generate sets of verification conditions which have to be satisfied. In general these will be relatively complex. Unless some precautions are taken the system would eventually run into the problem of being unable to decide on the equivalence of two equivalent arithmetic expressions. The second phase of the verifier employs a theorem prover which takes as input the verification conditions which have to be established and also a set of rules which can be used by the theorem prover. These rules can take various forms. Suppose we wish to make use of a term $MAXOF$ where $MAXOF(X, A, L, R)$ indicates that X is the maximum value of the set $A(I): L \leqslant I \leqslant R$. In logical terms writing $MAXOF(X, A, L, R)$ is equivalent to writing

$$(\forall I)(L \leqslant I \leqslant R \supset A(I) \leqslant X) \wedge$$
$$(\exists J)(L \leqslant J \leqslant R \supset A(J) = X)$$

From these remarks it follows that

$$MAXOF(A(L), A, L, L);$$
$$MAXOF(X, A, L, R) \wedge A(R + 1) \leqslant X \supset MAXOF(X, A, L, R + 1)$$
$$MAXOF(X, A, L, R) \wedge A(R + 1) > X \supset MAXOF(A(R + 1), A, L, R + 1)$$

These rules could be presented to the theorem prover in the following kind of way:

$$INFER\ MAXOF(A(L), A, 1, 1);$$
$$INFER\ MAXOF(X, A, 1, R)\ FROM\ R \geqslant 2$$
$$\wedge A(I) \leqslant X \wedge MAXOF(X, A, 1, R - 1);$$
$$INFER\ MAXOF(A(1), A, 1, R)\ FROM\ R \geqslant 2$$
$$\wedge A(I) > X \wedge MAXOF(X, A, 1, R - 1);$$

These are examples of what are called backward rules. They take the form

$$INFER\ A\ FROM\ B.$$

Forward rules convey similar information but take the form

$$FROM\ B\ INFER\ A.$$

Replacement rules appear as

$$REPLACE\ A\ BY\ B.$$

The theorem prover interprets these and other similar rules and applies them in different ways according to the type of rule. These rules give the theorem prover the information needed to check the verification conditions.

The SPV system is basically interactive. If the verification conditions can be established then the system will indicate that the program meets its specification and is correct. If the system is not able to verify the program then one of two conclusions is possible. Either the program is erroneous or for some reason the SPV has not been able to prove correctness.

The latter can occur because assertions have been imprecisely described or because rules which the theorem prover requires are missing. In either event the system will print out the verification conditions that it has been unable to prove. The user should react accordingly, modify the program, its documentation or the rules, and try again. In this way progress is made.

The CIP Project at Munich

At the Technical University in Munich a team of researchers under the leadership of F. L. Bauer have been looking into the development of what they call a wide spectrum language designed to support program specification and program development. The project is referred to as the CIP project (computer-aided, intuition-guided programming).

These researchers envisage a situation whereby a programmer will begin with some accurate specification of the task he wishes to accomplish. The program to perform this task is then developed interactively by a dialogue between the computer and the programmer. The computer applies correctness preserving trans-formations which result in an executable program which is correct and efficient. The development process involves replacing specifications by algorithms (i.e. what is to be done by how it is to be done), recursion by iteration, and so on

The eventual system then supports the top-down development of programs. The wide spectrum language is intended to be of sufficient generality to encom-pass the original specification of the problem and all the intermediate levels. The alternative to a series or hierarchy of intermediate languages was found to be too inflexible from the point of view of transformations.

To give some feeling for the different possibilities we consider a procedure for finding the quotient and remainder on dividing the non-negative integer a by the positive integer (or natural number) b. We begin by introducing two useful mode declarations

mode nonneg $\equiv$ (**int** $x : x \geqslant 0$), **nat** $\equiv$ (**nonneg** $x : x > 0$)

Then the specification of the *div* function can be given in the form

funct $div = ($**nonneg** $a,$ **nat** $b)$ (**nonneg, nonneg**):
    that (**nonneg** $q,$ **nonneg** r): $a = b \times q + r \wedge r < b$

The result produced by *div* is a pair (q, r) with the property that

$a = b \times q + r \wedge r < b$

This function is then transformed in the following ways:

(*a*) into a recursive formulation

if $a \geqslant b$ **then** div $(a - b, b) + (1, 0)$ **else** $(0, a)$ **fi**

(*b*) into a non-recursive version which uses variables

(**var nonneg** $vq,$ **var nonneg** vr) := $(0, a)$:
while $vq \geqslant b$ **do** $(vq, vr) := (vq + 1, vr - b)$ **od**;
(vq, vr)

(*c*) into a form where multiple assignments are replaced by single assign-ments, where multiple declarations like the above declaration of vq and vr are replaced by single declarations, where loops are replaced by conditionals and jumps, and so on;

(*d*) into a machine language formulation.

Edinburgh LCF

Edinburgh LCF ('Logic for Computable Functions') is a system which aids users in proving properties of programs. Its origins lie in the earlier and less sophisticated Stanford LCF. Both systems have been developed by R. Milner and his collaborators.

Underlying the Edinburgh system is a formal deductive logic called PPλ ('Polymorphic Predicate λ-calculus'). This is a development of the fundamental work of Dana Scott on LCF, a logic for expressing and proving properties of recursively defined functions; this is not unrelated to the fixed point theory, etc. introduced in section 6.3.1. In such a system proofs are very formal, very long and very intricate, and beyond the comprehension of most programmers.

In a sense the particular formal logic system that underlies the Edinburgh LCF system is irrelevant. It happens to be PPλ but it could have been some other deductive logic. The more important aspect of the system is ML, an interactive metalanguage which sits on top of PPλ.

ML is basically a functional general-purpose programming language specially designed for program verification. It has a type discipline which provides security against false proofs, it has declarations including type declarations, the usual sorts of expressions, lambda expressions, assignments, conditionals, loops of certain kinds, functions, and so on.

With such a system it is possible to experiment with strategies for finding proofs about the correctness of programs. Much of the work that has been done by Milner and his group has been concerned with this.

The University of Southern California verifier

At the University of Southern California D. I. Good, R. L. London and W. W. Bledsoe have developed a system which is similar to the Stanford Pascal Verifier. Like the last mentioned system it attempts to check that a Pascal Program actually meets its specification. Again at the first stage verification conditions are generated. At the second stage these have to be checked.

Checking of verification conditions is done in two steps. Initially an algebraic manipulation system called Reduce is brought to bear on the problem. Should this fail an interactive theorem prover initiates a dialogue with the programmer aimed at resolving the situation. This kind of interaction is not present in the Stanford verifier.

11.2.4 Program transformations

Automatic program improvement

At the University of Edinburgh R. M. Burstall and J. Darlington have produced an automatic program improvement system based on the programming language POP-2. The system takes programs which are easy to understand and easy to verify and converts these into much more efficient but equivalent programs. The initial programs tend to be recursive in nature.

The system is interactive. A user can request that any one of the following processes be performed.

318

Certain forms of recursion can be removed.

Redundant computations of particular kinds can be removed – eliminating common subexpressions and combining loops.

Procedure calls can be replaced by their bodies.

List processing can be improved so as to re-use space.

The system is based on transformations. These make use of a set of program schemes and this can be augmented if necessary.

With such a system available a programmer should then write his programs in such a way that they can be easily verified. The systems guided by the user will then translate each program into an equivalent but efficient version.

It is worth remarking that of course an optimising compiler can be expected to perform some kind of optimisation without having to enlist the help of the user. In general, however, it is unlikely that enough information can always be gleaned from the source program to make this a realistic possibility. It is more likely that interactive systems will evolve where cooperation between the user and the system will ensure correct and sensible improvements.

11.3 Concluding remarks

This concludes our discussion about automatic methods as they apply to various aspects of program verification. Many of the ideas discussed are at a relatively early stage of evolution. Much work on these and on program verification in general remains to be done.

Appendix

LANGUAGE DESIGN AND PROGRAM VERIFICATION

The task of verifying the correctness of a program can be significantly affected by the programming language used to express programs. At one extreme assembly language programs for Fortran 66 programs are far harder to verify than the equivalent programs expressed in more modern programming languages.

In this appendix we consider the relationship between programming language design and verification. These two topics influence each other to some considerable extent:

(i) as mentioned above, choice of programming language influences ease of verification;

(ii) ideas from program verification, in particular the complexity of proof rules, influence the design of programming languages.

From the point of view of verification (and this is the main consideration in this book) the more important influence is (i) above.

We do not consider the influence of the more general topic of reliability on language design. Consideration of the latter would entail a discussion of other issues which would include a detailed discussion of the roles of declarations, type checking, sensible redundancy, syntactic punctuation, and so on. It would also be necessary to compare classes of languages such as statement-oriented and expression-oriented languages. Other features of languages which dealt with error situations would also have to be discussed in more detail, e.g. recovery blocks, exception handling, event routines.

We shall look at the aspects of languages which tend to simplify verification and at aspects which tend to hinder the process. Of necessity we shall make remarks about programming languages in general. But, in keeping with the spirit of the rest of this book, we shall tend to slant our remarks towards Ada.

A.1   General remarks

The most important aspect of a programming language which has been used for expressing programs which have to be verified appears to be simplicity.

If a programming language has many concepts which are not woven into a coherent unit the language is generally difficult to learn and even more difficult to master. On the other hand if a language is simple and if its more powerful features have an obvious effect which is easily described then programmers are more likely to be able to master the language and therefore write programs in which they have confidence. The notion of simplicity in a programming language must of course be tempered with the understanding that the language should be capable of expressing the kinds of algorithms which programmers wish to write. If a programmer has to consistently produce correct, or nearly correct, programs, he must be able to master his programming language. Simplicity and a small language will make this a realistic possibility for a large class of programmers.

With these introductory remarks it follows that there are certain fundamental properties that should be possessed by a language to be used for writing programs which have to be verified. Peculiar, unnatural and unexpected rules of all kinds are certainly undesirable. Irregularities, especially those associated with meaning, should be absent at all costs. These could lead to obscure programs and they tend to provoke errors in proofs of correctness.

Ideally a language should be defined *orthogonally*, i.e. it should possess only a few well-chosen concepts but it should be possible to use these in a manner which, as the Algol 68 Report says in discussing orthogonality, 'maximises the expressive power of the language'. A language defined in this way is likely to be simple to learn, simple to use and simple to implement properly.

At this juncture we note that facilities such as operations on arrays and assignments involving arrays can be beneficial. They simplify both the programming process and the verification process.

As we have seen the problems arising from real arithmetic can provide a headache. The provision of both floating-point and fixed-point numbers in Ada, together with a thorough understanding of how these are manipulated, goes some way towards providing a manageable environment.

Strongly typed languages with a sensible approach to automatic mode or type changes are desirable since large classes of errors can be trapped at compile time. Ada, Algol 68 and Pascal were designed with this in mind. All constants, variables, etc. are associated with one specific type or mode at the time they are declared. This then governs the way in which the object can be used or manipulated within the program. Some very simple and natural mode changes will happen automatically. But in general any contravention of the somewhat strict rules results in an error which is then reported to the programmer. A PL/I compiler on the other hand will adopt a different and, from our point of view, less helpful attitude. It will attempt to produce, eventually, a machine code program to be executed. In so doing it will force unnatural and devious mode or type changes to achieve its objective. It can happen that these changes were not intended by the programmer and this tends to lead to obscurity.

A sensible approach to type checking in itself does little to ensure the correctness of programs. What it does do is to relieve the programmer from the onerous task of ensuring that he has not performed some illegal operation either accidentally or deliberately, perhaps in the interests of efficiency. In this way the programmer is free to concentrate on the problem of verification.

Associated with the idea of a type is the idea of a constraint. If it is known that a particular variable will hold only a limited set of values then it is convenient if the programming language permits the expression of such a situation by means of range constraints. Ranges can occur in ordinary arithmetic but they are more likely to arise in indexing arrays, and so on. Of course, Ada permits range constraints and violation of such a constraint raises the exception *CONSTRAINT_ERROR*.

Throughout this discussion the overriding consideration has been simplicity and lack of error-proneness. Thus long programs, procedure calls with long parameter lists and so on are all undesirable. Indeed a programming language designer can take positive steps to discourage these. Thus in Ada there are packages to encourage structuring, there are default options in parameters and parameters can be passed by both position or by name.

In a similar way individual constructs should exhibit these same properties of simplicity and lack of error-proneness. Thus it can be argued that certain kinds of side-effects are undesirable, case statements where the selection is done by position are undesirable, and so on. Again positive measures rather than merely negative steps can be taken. Thus in the Ada case statement the various choices must collectively cover all possible values of the expression used in making the selection.

In the proof rules given in chapters 4 and 5 the reader may have noticed the restrictions which tended to decorate each proof rule; these usually took the form of restrictions excluding side-effects of some kind. This situation can be viewed in two ways. One view is that the proof rule is an inadequate mechanism for describing meaning. The other more interesting view is that the proof rule is the correct mechanism and the programming language itself is deficient. Languages such as Euclid and to some extent Ada, have been designed from the latter point of view.

To conclude this section we make some, perhaps obvious, remarks concerning programs and their proofs. It is highly desirable that certain properties of programs exist, basically to remove the amount of effort required in providing correctness proofs:

(a) the meaning of a piece of program (and therefore its correctness proof) should be independent of the context in which that piece of program is used;

(b) if a piece of program such as a sort routine can be used to successfully manipulate objects of possibly several different types then a single subprogram and accompanying correctness proof should suffice.

Note that (*b*) above implies the desirability of generic subprograms. Taken together (*a*) and (*b*) imply that correctness should be a property of a program and be independent in some sense of locality, context, implementation, method of use and, in the case of generic subprograms, type. To achieve all this is far from straightforward.

A.2   Correctness as an invariant property

To ensure that the correctness of a piece of program does not depend on implementation certain important decisions that can affect the meaning of programs must not be left to the whim or whatever of an implementor. All important aspects of a programming language must be carefully defined – the formal definition must be complete. Thus one might expect to find in the definition of Ada clear statements about the order of evaluation of operands, indices, parameters, items in aggregates, left and right hand side of assignment statements, and so on. Unfortunately the situation is not so straightforward.

All this discussion about the order of evaluation of operands, etc. is irrelevant if one excludes the possible inclusion of user-defined functions which allow side-effects, either directly or indirectly through the use of subprogram parameters. (In Ada, function parameters must be of input type.) For then there is no possibility of the evaluation of one operand affecting another. There is then the highly desirable state of affairs whereby subexpressions appearing several times can be evaluated only once, rearrangement of expressions is permitted subject to the rearranged expression giving the same value as the original, and so on.

What happens when functions with side-effects are introduced? Should they be allowed at all? In preliminary Ada the answer was 'no'. A new kind of procedure, the value-returning procedure, was introduced to cater for the cases where functions with benevolent side-effects (e.g. popping an item from a stack) could appear. These new objects could appear only in a limited number of syntactic positions within programs; it became necessary to define exactly the order of evaluation of operands, to possibly repeat the evaluation of common subexpressions and so on. To illustrate, value-returning procedures would be forbidden in *expr* in

      if *expr* **then**

           sequence_of_statements,

      end if;

so that if *expr* delivered *FALSE* this was equivalent to **null**, surely desirable. Unfortunately there was a snag.

A special kind of side-effect arose from space allocation. Operations for multi-length arithmetic should be allowed to allocate space and it should be possible for these operations to appear in the expected positions. This combined with the desire to allow rearrangement, to optimise and to simplify the whole concept lead to the following: nothing should be assumed about the relative order of evaluation of operands, etc. – any program which relies on a specific order is undefined.

In a sense this is unfortunate from the point of view of the program verifier. It leaves a potential gap between what the program verifier would regard as ideal and what a compiler ought to do. If a function does have an undesirable side-effect it would be nice if the compiler should note the fact and draw it to the attention of the programmer. Note, however, that this discussion does not preclude such a possibility. A compiler can produce a warning of an appropriate kind.

We have looked only at one single aspect of having program correctness as an invariant property of a program. There are other sides to this question usually associated with portability. It is possible to cite remarks about the accuracy of arithmetic, about character sets, and generally about the environment in which a program runs. Considerations of this nature do affect the design of Ada – hence accuracy constraints, model numbers, definite character set, and so on. (We do not propose to discuss the problems of proving the correctness of real-time programs.)

Another aspect of design concerns generic subprograms. Consider for instance

$$A := C;$$
$$B := C;$$

It would be natural to conclude that $A = B$, no matter the common type of A, B and C. Of course there are difficulties if instantiation causes the common type to be *FLOAT*. But there is another sort of difficulty. Consider

$$A := C(1 .. 3);$$
$$C(2 .. 4) := C(1 .. 3);$$

If overlapping slices such as $C(1 .. 3)$ and $C(2 .. 4)$ are permitted in assignments then a deduction of the above kind would be erroneous. Such unfortunate occurrences can happen in Ada – actual generic parameters can interrelate in undesirable ways. Even the simple interchange program of section 2.2 will fail if $I1$ and $I2$ are overlapping slices.

For completeness we mention a particular property of operators. It is very desirable that, if correctness is to be independent of environment, it should not be possible to give a peculiar or unexpected priority to operators. Ada forbids changes to these priorities.

The topic of side-effects has already occupied much of our attention in this section. We have discussed perhaps the most common kind of side-effect, where a subprogram alters the value of some non-local variable. There are other kinds of side-effects which merit some attention and discussion. Many of these are related to the global variable.

The dangers associated with globals arise from considerations of the following nature. In Algol-like languages the effect of the scope rules is to arrange that the identifiers and variables available to the programmer tend to increase with the depth of nesting; in many applications the lowest level concepts have to be declared at the outermost level. When large name spaces are made to exist in this way it is quite possible for a programmer to inadvertently forget to declare a variable and yet this error will not be caught at compile time due to the existence of a more global declaration of the same identifier. Conversely, access to a global variable can be accidentally lost by interposing an additional declaration at some intermediate level either explicitly or implicitly through the use of a formal parameter, for example.

Consideration about globals and their associated problems leads to restrictions about the variables that can be used within any one programming unit and indeed about the nature of those programming units themselves. Thus in Ada the package limits the scope of global variables and the flow of names between units. This modular structure is superimposed upon an Algol-like block structure scheme. By careful screening the effect of a piece of program is then independent of how and where it is invoked (assuming the absence of machine code segments, etc. – see later).

In many programming languages there is a facility called *aliasing* whereby a particular variable or object can be referenced in several ways. Let us give several examples of this:

(*a*) The programming language Fortran allows *COMMON* and *EQUIVALENCE.*

(*b*) In languages which permit the unrestricted use of pointers, e.g. Algol 68, variables can be altered in obscure and unintended ways.

(*c*) Most programming languages have a procedure calling mechanism which allows actual parameters to be the same, to overlap or to interrelate in some manner.

(*d*) Call by reference can provide a form of aliasing.

Whenever aliasing is allowed, and this may not be at all obvious, then obscurities and uncertainty can occur in programs. Take case (*c*) above. A proof of correctness of a procedure might assume quite naturally that all the formal parameters are different. Yet when the procedure is called with parameters which interrelate or overlap in awkward ways the results can be unexpected. Take, for example, the Algol 60 procedure

procedure *swap* (x, y); **integer** x, y;
begin integer d; $d := x$; $x := y$; $y := d$ **end**

What is the effect of

swap $(a[i], i)$ or *swap* $(i, a[i])$ or even *swap* $(a[i], a[a[i]])$?

Similar questions can be asked about subprograms which have actual parameters which overlap (e.g. a and $a[i]$) or actual parameters which coincide with globals which are explicitly accessed from within the subprogram.

These remarks have had several bearings on the design of Ada. As far as subprograms are concerned we note that if we consider just parameters of a scalar or access type:

> for input or input/output parameters the value of each actual parameter is copied into the corresponding formal parameter prior to execution of the subprogram body;
> on returning, the value of each input/output or output parameter is copied back into the corresponding actual parameter.

For parameters of array, record or private types the copying might happen as above. Alternatively the formal parameter may merely give access directly to the corresponding actual parameter. Any program or proof which relies on the method of implementation is erroneous. Note again the possible benefit of compiler warning messages.

To return now to the problem of globals we note the desirable effect of the idea of a collection. Access types are pointers into collections; they cannot be used to point to identifiers or whatever that have been introduced in object declarations. There is therefore no possibility of using an access type variable to achieve aliasing.

Many programming languages allow the inclusion of machine code segments or modules. These are usually provided so that aspects of operating systems can be programmed properly or to allow extreme efficiency when it is required. When they are permitted, great care should be taken to limit the possible harm which can result from their use.

As we illustrated in chapter 2 it is certainly possible to prove the correctness of programs written in machine code or assembly code. Consequently properties of machine code segments can be proved in the expected way. But often these machine code segments are used, typically by systems programmers, to place information in particular locations, to override type-checking and so on. The machine code segments are therefore interfering with the sections of program written in the high level programming language and their correctness proofs. Any proof of correctness therefore requires an intimate knowledge of the workings of a local compiler including a guarantee of its correctness. The intimate knowledge required would include information about the locations and registers the compiler uses, the purposes for which these are used, and so on. There are enormous dangers associated with this kind of activity. Obscure errors are very likely to occur; for example, optimisation often dictates that some particular value is held in two places, in a location in store and in a register and care has to be taken to ensure these keep in step. Moreover changes in the compiler or use of a different

326

compiler mean that any programs using machine code segments have to be verified.

Finally we mention briefly an interesting class of languages called applicative languages. These possess no concept of assignment and so the very idea of a side-effect is absent. The best known of these languages is Lisp but the development of this class as a whole is, at the time of writing, in a relatively primitive state.

A.3 Structuring facilities

In chapter 9 we remarked that well-structured programs were easier to deal with from a program verification point of view than badly structured programs. Consequently a programmer wishing to write correct programs should look for a language which supplies a sufficient range of facilities capable of permitting the proper expression and encouragement of structured programs. Thus loop constructs, case and conditional constructs, procedure declarations, function declarations, operator declarations are all highly desirable as is a complementary set of data structuring facilities which includes type or mode declarations. The meaning and effect of all such constructs must be simple and clear. Structure can be made more apparent if implementations provide automatic paragraphing of programs.

The facilities mentioned above should, of course, not be misused. Programmers should not make use of low level constructs when suitable high-level constructs exist. When operators are declared the resulting operations should possess properties which are as close as can reasonably be expected to the expected mathematical properties, and so on. In Ada this is partially enforced by allowing the operators in the language to be redefined (using function declarations) for arbitrary operands; the expected implied bracketing occurs.

In providing structuring facilities there is one further step that can be taken. The concept of type can be generalised. In chapters 4 and 5 we looked at axiomatics. Ideally a means should be provided whereby a programmer can introduce his own data types together with a suitable complementary set of operations. We describe this by saying that a user should have a means of supplying his own abstract data types. This can be viewed from a different standpoint.

Structured programming by itself, of course, pays no attention to the fact that, as a consequence of refining a programming task in a particular way, certain operations have to be performed in separate parts of a program. Typically stacks may have to be manipulated, trees may have to be created, destroyed, modified, etc. Thus the original concept of stepwise refinement should be modified to permit the provision of packages which perform certain well-defined tasks.

The concept used in Ada to supply the desired effect is the package. This is similar to the module concept of the Algol 68 group and to the form used by the Alphard designers. We have already witnessed its use in chapter 7. The

327

package specification describes the items made available to users of the package; the package body defines the way in which the available libraries, abstract data objects, etc. are realised. The whole concept is made more useful by the related concepts of private types, generic types and instantiation.

Ada permits the package body and the package specification to be compiled separately, thus reflecting the separation of concerns involved. Note the inherent advantages, assuming the existence of a package to implement a stack, for instance.

(a) The method of implementing the stack and other inessential details need not concern the user. Typically this will take the form of an array and a pointer or perhaps a linked list of some kind. Subject to the inclusion of a private part the method of implementation can be altered without affecting either the programs which use the package or their correctness.

(b) The user has the discipline of using only the routines provided, and no others imposed on him. Thus he must use the stack in the proper way. The user cannot interfere, inadvertently or otherwise, with the proper functioning of the stack. (Note that this is a kind of type checking.)

(c) The preparation of the stack routines and the use of them are conveniently separated into different tasks.

(d) The concept of a generic subprogram and in particular a generic package introduces a desirable amount of generality.

Finally, note that the facilities provided perform very simple tasks which are easily described without reference to the method of implementation. The provision of such facilities eases the task of proving the correctness of programs which use them.

These observations have certain far-reaching consequences. Take point (b) mentioned above. This leads to the concept of information hiding. For if the stack is implemented as an array and a pointer then both these must remain in existence while the stack package is being used. Yet the array and its pointer must be invisible to any user of the package, i.e. it must not be possible to access the array or the pointer directly. It therefore becomes necessary to have a means of hiding the identifiers for the array and pointer and yet releasing for public use the identifiers associated with the routines which access these in a disciplined manner, i.e. the create, push, pop, etc. routines. Most of the common programming languages such as Fortran, Algol 60, Algol 68, Pascal, PL/I, etc. do not provide such a facility. In these circumstances it is necessary to make global declarations of variables which have to exist throughout the course of a program. All sorts of risks, dangers and difficulties follow.

There is one further consequence of the modular approach or abstract data type approach to programming. We mentioned earlier that the method used for

328

implementing the abstract data type may be altered. If such an alteration does occur then it would be very undesirable to have to alter any pieces of program (perhaps other packages or modules) which make use of these abstract data types. In Ada such a situation has been taken into account although of necessity modified by the realisation that private parts may exist within package specifications.

Consider another related matter. In normal circumstances a function can be represented as a subprogram, but in other circumstances where efficiency is of importance and the values of the function can be remembered a function might be implemented as an array. Ideally the array subscripting and the function call should take the same syntactic form, for example $F(I)$. This idea of *uniform referents* tends to encourage useful modifications to programs and a more healthy attitude to abstract data types.

Module-like facilities and separate compilation facilities can be justified on other grounds. Their existence tends to place desirable limits on scopes and in the process tends to encourage the structuring of programs and in particular their refinement into smaller and more manageable fragments. One particular form of this is the provision of private libraries of subprograms. Another is the segmenting of programs into pieces of code which can be compiled separately and later linked together. From the point of view of program verification the size of program fragments should be kept within reasonable and manageable bounds. It must be possible to verify the individual program fragments and so size must be limited and the number of concepts (related to the number of identifiers visible) must be severely limited.

Finally, we note that to allow freedom in the hierarchical design of programs no unnatural limitations should be placed on the way in which modules and other forms of subprograms can be combined.

A.4   Assert statements

Of all the statements which typically occur in programming languages it might be imagined that the assert statement is the most useful from the point of view of verification. But the truth of this is rather limited. (Ada possesses no assert statement.)

Assert statements typically take the form of the bold word **assert** followed by a boolean expression which represents a predicate which ought to be true at a particular point in a program. At execution time a test is typically performed and if it is false an error or exception occurs. This is what happened in the preliminary version of Ada. There are certain clear advantages in such a facility. For tests can then be made to ensure that what pertains to be a correctness proof indeed seems to be valid.

Ultimately one would of course like to see the assert statement being used by a compiler to check the correctness of a program. This would involve a compiler in performing some symbolic manipulation to check that the precondition and postcondition and the statements of the program were consistent. However the days when such events become everyday occurrences are as yet some way off.

The success of typical assert statements must be qualified in a variety of ways:

> being statements they can appear in only a limited number of syntactic positions within programs;
>
> orthogonality considerations suggest that assert statements are a prime candidate for axing since much of their effort can be achieved by a conditional;
>
> the notation used for expressing assertions is usually somewhat limited; in particular it is often not possible to use such mathematical notation as the factorial symbol nor the array notation of the kind mentioned in chapter 5;
>
> auxiliary variables cannot normally be used; we saw in chapter 3 that such variables are often desirable;
>
> typically no compile time checks are made to ensure that the assertions are sensible.

This last remark requires some further elaboration. We devote most of the rest of this section to discussing it.

We have already noted that program verification requires the existence of preconditions and postconditions. Now, structured programming demands that programming tasks should be subdivided into subtasks which will themselves have associated preconditions and postconditions and their own correctness proofs. Preconditions and postconditions will be expressed in terms of certain variables. It is natural to expect that these will not contain mention of any auxiliary variable needed for performing that task. Indeed such variables should not even be in scope. But all the variables appearing in the precondition and the postcondition must be in scope. It would appear therefore that the block structure of Algol-like languages (including Ada) is ideally suited to the needs of the program verifier.

Yet there is evidence to the contrary. We have written about the hazards of the global variable and remarked on the dangers which spring from the fact that in inner blocks any global variable at all can be accessed and usually altered. Consequently designers of programming languages have tried to place limits on the variables which can be accessed from an inner block; for instance, a user might be forced to list in some way the more global variables he proposes to access in his inner block.

The problem can be solved in another way by giving the assert statement a new role to play. Assert statements (when they are used as preconditions and postconditions) contain the necessary information about what variables can be altered in the performing of a particular task. If a variable is to be altered in a piece of program then the postcondition must mention this, otherwise it is incomplete. On the other hand, if the postcondition is incomplete in that it fails to mention some alteration to a global then a seemingly illegal assignment will occur. It can be arranged that a compiler enforces the two-way protection afforded by this idea.

Although we have focused most attention on the role of the assert statement in specifying preconditions and postconditions a similar discussion could be carried out concerning the role of the assert statement as a loop invariant. In both cases there is a considerable link between assertions and the ability to alter a variable.

A.5   The for statement

Let us consider the history of the design of the for statement in programming languages. This will be instructive from the point of view of noting the sequence of events which began with a construct which was a nightmare for the program verifier and ended with a construct which was much neater and simpler to use. The development happened not from the desire to simplify the verification process but for efficiency reasons. Often, however, it is the case that verification considerations blend well with other considerations in the design of programming languages.

In Algol 60 the for statement existed in the form

for $cv := init$ **step** $incr$ **until** $final$ **do** $statement\ S$

Furthermore the Algol 60 Report stated that the effect of such a statement was equivalent to the effect of

$$cv := init;$$
$$L1: \textbf{if } (cv - final) \times sign\ (incr) > 0$$
$$\textbf{then goto } Element\ exhausted;$$
$$statement\ S;$$
$$cv := cv + incr;$$
$$\textbf{goto } L1;$$

where *Element exhausted* referred to the next statement to be executed.

This leads to a wide variety of problems. Consider the possibility of

> *cv* and perhaps other variables being subscripted variables whose subscript could be altered, e.g. by the *statement S*;
>
> *incr* being a procedure call which caused certain other variables to be altered; on each circuit of the loop *incr* would have to be called twice at least;
>
> interfering with the value of *cv* within the *statement S*;
>
> jumps into loops;

and so on.

331

It can be argued with good reason that constructs in high level programming languages should be designed to be abstractions of certain frequently occurring situations. They should simplify the task of programming and should allow an implementor to cause such statements to be executed efficiently. Reliable programming will also be encouraged if the construct is simple and has a simple and compact proof rule. For then the meaning and effect of the construct can be simply described and peculiar situations causing obscure errors are less likely to occur.

With these ideas in mind let us look again at the for statement. Considerable efficiency can be obtained by arranging that the quantities *init*, *incr* and *final* are evaluated once only. This also results in greater clarity and simplicity with regard to the meaning of the construct. Accordingly in languages such as Ada and Algol 68 this is indeed the case, the evaluation occurring immediately before the iteration commences. In Ada and Algol 68 also, the control variable *cv* is declared as a result of its appearing after a **for**; furthermore it is assumed to be a constant within the body of the loop. Consequently jumps into loops are forbidden as a natural consequence of the scope rules. The value of the control variable is then also undefined on leaving the loop, so allowing the implementor some freedom in choosing how best to compile the for statement so that it is executed efficiently on his machine; incrementing *cv* can be done before the execution of the *statement S* or after its execution.

All these alterations to the design of the for statement can be regarded as simplifications. Historically they occurred to allow implementors the freedom to provide efficient implementations. But these same alterations can also be viewed from another angle. They certainly cause the proof rule for the for statement to be simplified enormously. For instance termination is no longer a problem provided that the increment is non-zero; note that this necessitates

no assignment to *cv* within the *statement S*;

only a single evaluation of each of *incr* and *final* (and, of course, *init*);

no looping caused by the evaluation of these various quantities or of *S* itself.

Before discussing the proof rule for the for statement we introduce some notation for intervals. Assume that p, q, k are integer constants and that t is a positive integer. Then we let

$$[p \mathrel{..} q]_t = \{i : i = p + kt \text{ for some } k \geq 0 \text{ and } p \leq i \leq q\},$$
$$[p \mathrel{..} q)_t = \{i : i = p + kt \text{ for some } k \geq 0 \text{ and } p \leq i < q\},$$
$$(p \mathrel{..} q]_t = \{i : i = p + kt \text{ for some } k > 0 \text{ and } p < i \leq q\},$$
$$(p \mathrel{..} q)_t = \{i : i = p + kt \text{ for some } k > 0 \text{ and } p < i < q\},$$
$$[\ ]_t = \text{the empty set.}$$

The interval $[p \mathrel{..} q]_t$ is often called a closed interval, $[p \mathrel{..} q)_t$ is said to be *open* at the top, $(p \mathrel{..} q]_t$ is *open* at the bottom and $(p \mathrel{..} q)_t$ is an *open* interval.

Now consider a version of the Algol 60 for statement

for $x := a$ **step** t **until** b **do** S

Let $I(r)$ be some assertion about the interval r. We shall assume that, if $I([a .. a + kt))$ is true for some $k >= 0$ prior to the execution of the body S of the loop, then $I([a .. a + kt])$ will be true after execution; in other words I is the loop invariant.

If it is assumed that the step length $t > 0$ it might be hoped that the proof rule for the for statement can now be expressed as

$$\frac{a <= x = a + kt <= b \wedge \{I([a .. x)_t)\}\ S\{I([a .. x]_t)\}}{\{I[\ ]\}\ \textbf{for } x := a \textbf{ step } t \textbf{ until } b \textbf{ do } S\{I([a .. b]_t)\}}$$

This proof rule is relatively simple and its truth depends on the kind of restrictions we have already discussed. But it also highlights others:

    none of a, b and t must be altered within S;
    I should contain no mention of x.

The rule as stated above also suggests a generalisation of the for statement. It suggests a similar construction involving not integers but items of other modes, e.g. other discrete types. To illustrate, let a, a_1 and a_2 denote sequences of some kind and let & denote concatenation of sequences. Then the following proof rule is suggested

$$\frac{a = a_1 \& x \& a_2 \wedge \{I(a_1)\}\ S\{I(a_1 \& x)\}}{\{I([\ ])\}\ \textbf{for } x \textbf{ in } a \textbf{ do } S\{I(a)\}}$$

The progression from here to the Ada for statement is minimal.

Although the original motivation for making alterations to the Algol 60 for statement arose from considerations of efficiency another reason for introducing these same alterations (and some others) has now been unearthed – program verification is simplified. In fact the latter is by far the more important consideration. If programs can be written in such a way that they can easily be verified then far greater reliability can be expected.

Much simplicity has been gained from looking at the for statement from the program verification point of view. But something has been lost. The for statement cannot now perform some – typically very few – of the tasks it could perform previously. However these tasks can still be performed, in a more appropriate manner, using while statements, if statements, etc.

A.6   Exception handling

Anyone who attempts to write robust and accurate programs faces all kinds of difficulties concerned with the checking of possible error situations. The various checks and tests that have to be performed are often enormous and increase substantially the complexity and understandability of a program. They also tend to detract from the overall structure of a program and reduce the ease with which verification can be accomplished. Another important consideration is the fact that it can often be extremely awkward for a programmer to perform certain checks, e.g. checks for overflow. If a programming language possesses features which reduce or remove the difficulties mentioned above much can be gained. Note also that suitable facilities of this kind also provide a means of (partially) overcoming some of the difficulties mentioned in chapter 1 regarding the whole topic of program verification.

In Ada exception handlers are used to cope with error situations or situations which are unexpected or likely to lead to abnormal termination of a program. In the design of exceptions the Ada designers took the needs of the program verifier into account to some extent. In general, however, the application of transformations such as recursion removal can play havoc – occurrences of exceptions can be introduced, removed or altered. This is somewhat unfortunate given the intended uses of Ada.

In chapter 4 we mentioned certain standard exceptions such as *CONSTRAINT_ ERROR* and *NUMERIC_ERROR*. A complete list of the standard Ada exceptions is given in figure A.1.

A.7 Conclusion

In this appendix we have discussed the very important relationship between program verification and language design. It should be apparent that practically every aspect of the design of a programming language can affect the ease with which correctness can be proved.

At the beginning of this book (in chapter 1) we attempted to put the topic of program verification in some kind of focus. We mentioned certain difficulties associated with the process and made certain criticisms of it. Perhaps we are now in a better position to put the entire topic in perspective. For certain kinds of program written in typical programming languages, perhaps correctness modulo the raising of appropriate kinds of exceptions is a realistic and achievable goal. With sympathetic language design, even exceptions can be handled.

Fig. A.1. List of standard exceptions.

exceptions	circumstances
CONSTRAINT_ERROR	when a range constraint, index constraint or discriminant constraint is violated
NUMERIC_ERROR	the range of a predefined numeric operation does not lie within required range
SELECT_ERROR	when none of the possible alternatives in a select can be executed
STORAGE_ERROR	when the available storage becomes exhausted
TASKING_ERROR	when intertask communication cannot be properly completed

334

REFERENCES

Alagić, S. & Arbib, M. A. (1978). *The design of well-structured and correct programs.* New York: Springer-Verlag.

Anderson, R. B. (1979). *Proving programs correct.* New York: John Wiley and Sons, Inc.

Arbib, M. A. & Alagić, S. (1979). 'Proof rules for gotos.' *Acta Informatica,* **11,** 139–48.

Arsac, J. J. (1977). *La construction de programmes structurés.* Paris: Dunod.

Arsac, J. J. (1979). 'Syntactic source to source transforms and program manipulation.' *Communications of ACM,* **22,** 1, 43–53.

Ashcroft, E. A., Clint, M. & Hoare, C. A. R. (1976). 'Remarks on "Program proving: jumps and functions" by M. Clint and C. A. R. Hoare.' *Acta Informatica,* **6,** 317–18.

Auslander, M. A. & Strong, H. R. (1978). 'Systematic recursion removal.' *Communications of ACM,* **21,** 2, 127–34.

Barnes, J. G. P. (1980). 'An overview of Ada.' *Software – Practice and Experience,* **10,** 11, 851–87.

Bauer, F. L. (1976). 'Programming as an evolutionary process' in *Language Hierarchies and Interfaces,* Lecture Notes in Computer Science (46), ed. F. L. Bauer & K. Samelson, pp. 153–82. Berlin: Springer-Verlag.

Bentley, J. L. (1980). 'Multidimensional divide-and-conquer.' *Communications of ACM,* **23,** 4, 214–29.

Bird, R. S. (1975). 'Speeding up programs.' *The Computer Journal,* **17,** 4, 337–9.

Bird, R. S. (1977). 'Notes on recursion elimination.' *Communications of ACM,* **20,** 6, 434–9.

Bird, R. S. (1977). 'Improving programs by the introduction of recursion.' *Communications of ACM,* **20,** 11, 856–63.

Boyer, R. & Moore, J. S. (1975). 'Proving theorems about LISP functions.' *Journal of ACM,* **22,** 1, 129–44.

Broy, M. & Krieg-Bruckner, B. (1980). 'Derivation of invariant assertions during program development by transformation.' *ACM Transactions on Programming Languages and Systems,* **2,** 3, 321–37.

Burstall, R. M. (1969). 'Proving properties of programs by structural induction.' *The Computer Journal,* **12,** 1, 41–8.

Burstall, R. M. (1972). 'Some techniques for proving correctness of programs which alter data structures.' *Machine Intelligence,* **7,** 23–50.

Burstall, R. M. & Darlington, J. (1977). 'A transformation system for developing recursive programs.' *Journal of ACM,* **24,** 1, 44–67.

Campbell, R. H. & Habermann, A. N. (1974). 'The specification of process synchronisation by path expressions' in *Operating systems,* Lecture Notes in Computer Science (16), ed. E. Gelenbe & C. Kaiser, pp. 89–102. Berlin: Springer-Verlag.

Clint, M. (1973). 'Program proving: coroutines.' *Acta Informatica,* **2,** 50–63.

Clint, M. & Hoare, C. A. R. (1972). 'Program proving: jumps and functions.' *Acta Informatica,* **1,** 3, 214–24.

335

Cooper, D. C. (1966). 'The equivalence of certain computations.' *The Computer Journal,* **9,** 45–52.

Correll, C. H. (1978). 'Proving programs correct through refinement.' *Acta Informatica,* **9,** 121–32.

Darlington, J. & Burstall, R. M. (1972). 'A system which automatically improves programs.' *Acta Informatica,* **6,** 41–60.

De Millo, R. A., Lipton, R. J. & Perlis, A. J. (1979). 'Special processes and proofs of theorems and programs.' *Communications of ACM,* **22,** 5, 271–80.

Dijkstra, E. W. (1968). 'Goto statement considered harmful.' *Communications of ACM,* **11,** 3, 147–8.

Dijkstra, E. W. (1968). 'The structure of "THE" multiprogramming system.' *Communications of ACM,* **11,** 5, 341–6.

Dijkstra, E. W. (1968). 'A constructive approach to the problem of program correctness.' *BIT,* **8,** 174–86.

Dijkstra, E. W. (1972). 'The humble programmer.' *Communications of ACM,* **15,** 10, 859–66.

Dijkstra, E. W. (1972). 'Hierarchical ordering of sequential processes' in *Operating systems techniques,* ed. C. A. R. Hoare & R. H. Perrott, pp. 72–93. London: Academic Press.

Dijkstra, E. W. (1972). 'Notes on structured programming' in *Structured programming,* ed. O. Dahl, E. W. Dijkstra & C. A. R. Hoare. New York: Academic Press.

Dijkstra, E. W. (1976). 'On-the-fly garbage collection: an exercise in cooperation' in *Language hierarchies and interfaces,* Lecture Notes in Computer Science (46), ed. F. L. Bauer & K. Samelson, pp. 43–56. Berlin: Springer-Verlag.

Dijkstra, E. W. (1976). *A discipline of programming.* Englewood Cliffs, New Jersey: Prentice Hall, Inc.

Dijkstra, E. W., Lamport, L., Martin, A. J., Scholten, C. S. & Steffens, E. F. M. (1978). 'On-the-fly garbage collection – an exercise in cooperation.' *Communications of ACM,* **21,** 11, 966–75.

Elpas, B., Levitt, K. N., Waldinger, R. J. & Waksman, A. (1972). 'An assessment of techniques for proving program correctness.' *ACM Computing Surveys,* **4,** 2, 97–147.

Floyd, R. W. (1967). 'Assigning meanings to programs' in *Mathematical aspects of computer science,* 19, American Mathematical Society, Providence, Rhode Island, 19–32.

German, S. M. & Wegbriet, B. (1975). 'A synthesizer of inductive assertions.' *IEEE Transactions on Software Engineering,* **SE-1,** 1, 68–75.

Good, D. I. & London, R. L. (1970). 'Computer interval arithmetic: definition and proof of correct implementation.' *Journal of ACM,* **17,** 4, 603–12.

Good, D. I., London, R. L. & Bledsoe, W. W. (1975). 'An interactive program verification system.' *IEEE Transactions on Software Engineering,* **SE-1,** 1, 59–67.

Goodenough, J. B. & Gerhart, S. L. (1977). 'Towards a theory of testing' in *Current trends in programming methodology,* vol. 2, ed. R. T. Yeh, pp. 44–79. Englewood Cliffs, New Jersey: Prentice-Hall, Inc.

Gordon, M. J., Milner, A. J. & Wadsworth, C. P. (1979). *Edinburgh LCF.* Lecture Notes in Computer Science (78). Berlin: Springer-Verlag.

Gries, D. (1977). 'An exercise in proving parallel programs correct.' *Communications of ACM,* **20,** 12, 921–30.

Gries, D. & Gehani, N. (1977). 'Some ideas on data types in high-level languages.' *Communications of ACM,* **20,** 6, 414–20.

Griffiths, M. (1976). 'Program production by successive transformations' in *Language hierarchies and interfaces,* Lecture Notes in Computer Science (46), ed. F. L. Bauer & K. Samelson, pp. 125–52. Berlin: Springer-Verlag.

Guttag, J. V. (1977). 'Abstract data types and the development of data structures.' *Communications of ACM,* **20,** 6, 396–404.

Guttag, J. V. & Horning, J. J. (1978). 'The algebraic specification of abstract data types.' *Acta Informatica,* **10,** 1, 27–52.

Guttag, J. V., Horowitz, E. & Musser, D. R. (1978). 'Abstract data types and software validation.' *Communications of ACM,* **21,** 12, 1048–64.

Hantler, S. L. & King, J. C. (1976). 'An introduction to proving the correctness of programs.' *ACM Computing Surveys,* **8,** 3, 331–53.

Hoare, C. A. R. (1969). 'An axiomatic basis for computer programming.' *Communications of ACM,* **12,** 10, 576–80, 583.

Hoare, C. A. R. (1971). 'Procedures and parameters: an axiomatic approach' in *Symposium on Semantics of Algorithmic Languages,* ed. E. Engeler, pp. 102–16. New York: Springer-Verlag.

Hoare, C. A. R. (1972). 'Proof of correctness of data representations.' *Acta Informatica,* **1,** 4, 271–81.

Hoare, C. A. R. (1972). 'Proof of a structured program: "the sieve of Eratosthenes".' *The Computer Journal,* **15,** 4, 321–5.

Hoare, C. A. R. (1972). 'A note on the for statement.' *BIT,* **12,** 334–41.

Hoare, C. A. R. (1972). 'Towards a theory of parallel programming' in *Operating systems techniques,* ed. C. A. R. Hoare & R. H. Perrott, pp. 61–77. London: Academic Press.

Hoare, C. A. R. (1974). 'Proof of a program: FIND.' *Communications of ACM,* **14,** 1, 39–45.

Hoare, C. A. R. (1974). 'Monitors: an operating system structuring concept.' *Communication of ACM,* **17,** 10, 549–57. Corrigendum in *Communications of ACM,* **18,** 2, 95.

Hoare, C. A. R. (1975). 'Recursive data structures.' *International Journal of Computer and Information Sciences,* **4,** 2, 105–32.

Hoare, C. A. R. (1975). 'Data reliability' in *Proceedings of International Conference on Reliable Software, SIGPLAN Notices,* **10,** 6, 528–33.

Hoare, C. A. R. (1976). 'Parallel programming: an axiomatic approach' in *Language hierarchies and interfaces,* Lecture Notes in Computer Science (46), ed. F. L. Bauer & K. Samelson, pp. 11–42. Berlin: Springer-Verlag.

Hoare, C. A. R. & Wirth, N. (1973). 'An axiomatic definition of the programming language PASCAL.' *Acta Informatica,* **2,** 335–55.

Howard, J. H. (1976). 'Proving monitors.' *Communications of ACM,* **19,** 5, 273–9.

Huet, G. & Lang, B. (1978). 'Proving and applying program transformations expressed with second-order patterns.' *Acta Informatica,* **11,** 31–55.

Ichbiah, J. D., Barnes, J. G. P., Heliard, J. C., Krieg-Brueckner, B., Roubine, O. & Wichmann, B. A. (1979). *Preliminary Ada reference manual* and *Rationale for the design of the Ada programming language.* In *SIGPLAN Notices,* **14,** 6.

Igarashi, S., London, R. L. & Luckham, D. C. (1975). 'Automatic program verification I: a logical basis and its implementation.' *Acta Informatica,* **4,** 1, 145–82.

Jackson, M. A. (1975). *Principles of program design.* London: Academic Press.

Katz, S. M. & Manna, Z. (1973). 'A heuristic approach to program verification' in *Proceedings of Third International Conferences on Artificial Intelligence,* pp. 500–12.

Katz, S. M. & Manna, Z. (1975). 'A closer look at termination.' *Acta Informatica,* **5,** 333–52.

Katz, S. M. & Manna, Z. (1975). 'Towards automatic debugging of programs' in *Proceedings of International Conference on Reliable Software, SIGPLAN Notices,* **10,** 6, 143–55.

Katz, S. M. & Manna, Z. (1976). 'The logical analysis of programs.' *Communications of ACM,* **19,** 4, 188–206.

King, J. C. (1971). 'Proving programs to be correct.' *IEEE Transactions on Computers,* **C-20,** 11, 1331–6.

King, J. C. (1976). 'Symbolic execution and program testing.' *Communications of ACM,* **19,** 7, 385–94.

King, J. C. (1976). *On generating verification conditions for correctness proofs.* Report RC5808 (No. 25187), IBM Thomas J. Watson Research Center, Yorktown Heights, New York.

Knuth, D. E. (1974). 'Structured programming with go to statements.' *ACM Computing Surveys,* **6,** 4, 261–301.

Kowaltowski, T. (1977). 'Axiomatic approach to side effects and general jumps.' *Acta Informatica,* **7**, 357–60.

Lamport, L. (1979). 'Proving the correctness of multiprocess programs.' *IEEE Transactions on Software Engineering,* **SE-3**, 2, 125–43.

Lamport, L. (1979). 'On the proof of correctness of a calendar program.' *Communications of ACM,* **22**, 10, 554–6.

Lampson, B. W., Horning, J. J., London, R. L., Mitchell, J. G. & Popek, G. L. (1977). 'Report on the programming language Euclid.' *ACM SIGPLAN Notices,* **12**, 2.

Ledgard, H. F. & Taylor, R. W. (1977). 'Two views of data abstraction.' *Communications of ACM,* **20**, 6, 382–4.

Lipton, R. J. (1975). 'Reduction: a method of proving properties of parallel programs.' *Communications of ACM,* **18**, 12, 717–21.

London, R. L. (1970). 'Proving programs correct: some techniques and examples.' *BIT,* **10**, 2, 168–82.

London, R. L. (1970). 'Bibliography on proving the correctness of computer programs.' *Machine Intelligence,* **5**, 569–80.

London, R. L. (1972). 'Correctness of a compiler for a LISP subset' in Proceedings of ACM Conference on Proving Assertions about Programs. *ACM SIGPLAN Notices,* **7**, 1, 121–7.

London, R. L. (1975). 'A view of program verification' in *Proceedings of International Conference on Reliable Software,* Los Angeles, California, pp. 534–45.

London, R. L. (1977). 'Perspectives on program verification' in *Current trends in programming methodology,* vol. 2, ed. R. T. Yeh, pp. 151–72. Englewood Cliffs, New Jersey: Prentice-Hall, Inc.

London, R. L., Guttag, J. V., Horning, J. J., Lampson, B. W., Mitchell, J. G. & Popek, G. J. (1978). 'Proof rules for the programming language Euclid.' *Acta Informatica,* **10**, 1, 1–26.

Luckham, D. C. & Polak, W. (1980). 'Ada exception handling: an axiomatic approach.' *ACM Transactions on Programming Languages and Systems,* **2**, 2, 225–33.

Luckham, D. C., German, S. M., van Henke, F. W., Karp, R. A., Milne, P. W., Oppen, D. C., Polak, W. & Scherlis, W. L. (1979). *Stanford Pascal Verifier User Manual,* Stanford Verification Group Report No. 11, Computer Science Department, Stanford, California.

McCarthy, J. & Painter, J. (1967). 'Correctness of a compiler for arithmetic expressions' in *Proc. Symp. in Applied Mathematics,* 19, American Mathematical Society, Providence, Rhode Island, pp. 33–41.

McGettrick, A. D. (1980). *The definition of programming languages.* Cambridge: Cambridge University Press.

Manna, Z. (1974). *Mathematical theory of computation.* New York: McGraw-Hill.

Manna, Z., Ness, S. & Vuillemin, J. (1973). 'Inductive method for proving properties of programs.' *Communications of ACM,* **16**, 8, 491–502.

Manna Z. & Pneuli, A. (1970). 'Formalization of properties of functional programs.' *Journal of ACM,* **17**, 3, 555–69.

Manna, Z. & Pneuli, A. (1974). 'Axiomatic approach to total correctness.' *Acta Informatica,* **3**, 243–63.

Manna, Z. & Vuillemin, J. (1972). 'Fixpoint approach to the theory of computation.' *Communications of ACM,* **15**, 7, 528–36.

Manna, Z. & Waldinger, R. J. (1971). 'Towards automatic program synthesis.' *Communications of ACM,* **14**, 3, 151–65.

Manna, Z. & Waldinger, R. J. (1977). *Studies in automatic programming logic.* New York: Elsevier North-Holland, Inc.

Manna, Z. & Waldinger, R. J. (1978). 'Is "sometimes" better than "always"?' *Communications of ACM,* **21**, 2, 159–72.

Moore, J. S. (1975). 'Introducing iteration into the pure LISP theorem prover.' *IEEE Transactions on Software Engineering,* **SE-1**, 3, 328–38.

Myers, G. J. (1975). *Reliable software through composite design.* New York: Petrocelli/Charter.

Myers, G. J. (1978). 'A controlled experiment in program testing and code walkthroughs/ inspections.' *Communications of ACM*, **21**, 9, 760–8.

Owicki, S. (1975). 'Axiomatic proof techniques for parallel programs.' Ph.D. thesis, Cornell University, Ithaca, New York.

Owicki, S. & Gries, D. (1976). 'Verifying properties of parallel programs: an axiomatic approach.' *Communications of ACM*, **19**, 5, 279–85.

Parnas, D. L. (1972). 'A technique for software module specification with examples.' *Communications of ACM*, **15**, 5, 330–6.

Pepper, P. (1979). 'A study on transformational semantics' in *Program construction*, Lecture Notes in Computer Science (69), ed. F. L. Bauer and M. Broy, pp. 322–405. Berlin: Springer-Verlag.

Pyle, I. C. (1980). 'Axioms for user-defined operators.' *Software – Practice and Experience*, **10**, 307–18.

Reynolds, J. C. (1979). 'Reasoning about arrays.' *Communications of ACM*, **22**, 5, 290–9.

Robinson, L. & Levitt, K. N. (1975). *Proof techniques for hierarchically structured programs*. Stanford Research Institute report, Stanford, California.

Tanenbaum, A. S. (1976). 'In defense of program testing or correctness proofs considered harmful.' *SIGPLAN Notices*, **11**, 5, 64–8.

Turski, W. M. (1978). *Computer programming methodology*. London: Heyden.

Wegbriet, B. (1974). 'The synthesis of loop predicates.' *Communications of ACM*, **17**, 2, 102–12.

Wegbriet, B. (1975). 'Property extraction in well-founded property sets.' *IEEE Transactions on Software Engineering*, **SE-1**, 3, 270–85.

Wegbriet, B. (1975). 'Mechanical program analysis.' *Communications of ACM*, **18**, 9, 528–39.

Wegbriet, B. (1977). 'Constructive methods in program verification.' *IEEE Transactions on Software Engineering*, **SE-3**, 3, 193–209.

Webriet, B. & Spitsen, J. M. (1976). 'Proving properties of complex data structures.' *Journal of ACM*, **23**, 2, 389–96.

Wegner, P. (1980). *Programming with Ada: introduction by means of graduated examples*. Englewood Cliffs, New Jersey: Prentice-Hall, Inc.

Wirth, N. (1971). 'The programming language Pascal.' *Acta Informatica*, **1**, 35–63.

Wirth, N. (1971). 'Program development by stepwise refinement.' *Communications of ACM*, **14**, 4, 221–7.

Wirth, N. (1973). *Systematic programming: an introduction*. Englewood Cliffs, New Jersey: Prentice-Hall, Inc.

Wirth, N. (1974). 'On the composition of well-structured programs.' *ACM Computing Surveys*, **6**, 4, 247–59.

Wulf, W. A. (1977). 'Languages and structured programs' in *Current trends in software methodology*, vol. 1, ed. R. T. Yeh, pp. 33–60. Englewood Cliffs, New Jersey: Prentice-Hall.

Wulf, W. A. & Shaw, M. (1973). 'Global variables considered harmful.' *SIGPLAN Notices*, **8**, 2, 28–34.

Yeh, R. T. (ed.) (1977). *Current trends in programming methodology, vol. 1, Software specification and design*. Englewood Cliffs, New Jersey: Prentice-Hall, Inc.

Yeh, R. T. (ed.) (1977). *Current trends in programming methodology, vol. 2, Program validation*. Englewood Cliffs, New Jersey: Prentice-Hall, Inc.

Yourdon, E. (1975). *Techniques of program structure and design*. Englewood Cliffs, New Jersey: Prentice-Hall, Inc.

INDEX

pointwise extension 139
Polak, W. 338
Popek, G. L. 338
POS 67
positional notation 150
postcondition 11, 86, 96–8, 156, 223
post-dominator 303–5
postulates 3, 4
precedence 23
precondition 86, 96–8, 156, 223
PRED 67, 134
predicate 33, 62–5
premise 86
primitive constructor 262
private type 151–5
procedure 10, 13, 144, 149–50, 152, 237,
    256, 285–290
producers and consumers 213–14, 218–19
program inversion 301–2
proof 3, 4
proof rule 85–92, 96–9, 155–65, 194–6, 322
Pyle, I. 339

qualifier 66
Quicksort 269

range 23
range 64
range constraint 64–5
readers and writers 230–1
rearrangement 114–15
records 118–40, 244
recursion 13, 48, 146–7, 160–1, 166–75,
    209, 282–98
recursion removal 282–90
relational operator 23
recursive schema 290–8
Reduce 318
reliability 1–2, 5, 21
rem 22–3, 69
rendezvous 214
repetition 279
representative mapping 201
reserved word 25
result variables 11–13
return 146–8, 153–7
reverse 32, 64, 90
Reynolds, J. C. 339
robustness 5
Roubine, O. 337
rule of inference 85–7

Samelson, K. 336
scalar type 22, 63–8, 87
schema 290–7
Scherlis, W. L. 338
Scholten, C. S. 336
Scott, D. 318
SELECT_ERROR 334
select statement 216–19

semantics 100, 197–8
semaphore 225–30
service module 261
set 198–208
Shaw, M. 339
side-effects 191–6, 277, 322–7
SMALL 68, 71
software crisis 1, 8
software engineering 1
sort 117–18, 238, 268–70
specification 197–208, 226–31, 259–61
Spitsen, J. M. 339
square root 39–40
stack 183–9, 205–7, 283–90, 301, 328
Stanford Pascal verifier 315–16, 318
statement 24–7, 30–3
Steffens, E. F. M. 336
stepwise refinement 2, 255–6
STORAGE_ERROR 131, 334
strings 23, 31, 105–6
Strong, H. R. 335
strong typing 321
structural induction 172–6, 314
structure *see* record
structure clash 253–5
structure diagram 244–55
structured programming 255, 328
structuring facilities 327–9
stub 263
subprogram 144–75
subscripted variable 102, 195
subtype 64–6, 87, 130
SUCC 23, 67
swapping 109, 164
switchon 18
symbolic execution 16–18, 28, 37–8
symbolic execution tree 19, 29
synchronisation 221–4
synthesisers 315

Tanenbaum, A. S. 339
task 213–19
task type 216–17
TASKING_ERROR 334
Taylor, R. M. 338
terminate 217
termination 30–4, 48–61, 83, 215–17, 237
termination condition 52–3
test inversion 279
testing 1, 7, 8, 19
text processing 41–3
top down 263
total correctness 33–4, 48–61, 98, 313
trace 35
transformation 275–307
tree 126–30
Turski, W. M. A. 339
type 21–7, 62–7, 320–3
type conversion 66
type declaration 64–6, 88, 103–5, 118–37

344